Object-Oriented Programming for Artificial Intelligence

A Guide to Tools and System Design

Object-Oriented Programming for Artificial Intelligence

A Guide to Tools and System Design

Ernest R. Tello

Addison-Wesley Publishing Company, Inc.

Reading, Massachusetts • Menlo Park, California • New York
Don Mills, Ontario • Wokingham, England • Amsterdam • Bonn
Sydney • Singapore • Tokyo • Madrid • San Juan

Many of the designations used by manufacturers and sellers to distinguish their products are claimed as trademarks. Where those designations appear in this book and Addison-Wesley was aware of a trademark claim, the designations have been printed in initial capital letters.

Library of Congress Cataloging-in-Publication Data

Tello, Ernest R.
　　Object-oriented programming for artificial intelligence : a guide
　to tools and system design / Ernest R. Tello.
　　　　p.　　cm.
　　Bibliography: p.
　　Includes index.
　　ISBN 0-201-09228-X
　　1. Artificial intelligence.　2. Object-oriented programming
　(Computer science)　I. Title.
　　Q336.T44　　1989
　　006.3 -- dc19　　　　　　　　　　　　　　　　　　　　　　89-147
　　　　　　　　　　　　　　　　　　　　　　　　　　　　　　CIP

Sponsoring Editor: Carole Alden
Cover design by Liz Alpert
Text design by Ken Wilson
Set in 10-point Janson by Compset, Inc.

ABCDEFGHIJ-AL-89
First printing, July 1989

This book is dedicated to the programmers and researchers who are busy at work creating the next generation of software technology.

Table of Contents

Chapter 9 *Concurrent Object-Oriented Systems*

Acknowledgments

First of all I would like to thank the people at Addison-Wesley who worked on this book with me, starting with Carole Alden, Aquisitions Editor; Rachel Guichard, Assistant Editor; Joanne Clapp, Developmental Editor; the Production Supervisor, Perry McIntosh; and numerous other people in various departments and roles too numerous to mention.

I would also especially like to thank Alan Kay for his visionary role in the development of object-oriented programming and the thousands of programmers worldwide who have helped develop this important new software technology.

The following people, whose names are listed alphabetically, also contributed to the writing of this book: Jim Anderson, Jerry Barber, Dan Bobrow, Alan Borning, George Bosworth, Ron Clark, Will Clinger, Brad Cox, Linda DeMichiel, Chuck Duff, Richard Gabriel, Les Gasser, Adele Goldberg, Carl Hewitt, Danny Hillis, Dan Ingalls, Chris James, Ken Kahn, Sonya Keene, Gregor Kiczales, Doug Lenat, Marvin Minsky, David Moon, Amos Oshrin, Kamran Parsaye, Patrick Perez, Alain Rappaport, Kurt Schmucker, Doug Shaker, Randy Smith, Mark Stefik, Bjarne Stroustrup, Michael Teng, Terry Winograd.

Preface

It is a very exciting time to be involved in advanced software systems for machines that are rapidly becoming such a familiar presence in businesses, schools, and homes. It's not every day that irreversible advances are made in a field like computing. New languages are added to the list of those in widespread use relatively rarely. New models for programming are rarer still. But with object-oriented programming we are faced with one of those advances that changes the way computers are programmed in such a significant way that in the near future most people will not resort to previous methods, except for special reasons.

The evolution of software technology can be compared to the growth of a tree. Athough it is an organic process that takes place continually, after all is said and done, there are definite "rings" or layers that can be seen that represent both its current structure and the distinct phases through which it has passed. The place where the analogy breaks down is that in software systems, in some cases, the layers continue to be functional, whereas in the case of trees, it is apparently only the uppermost layer at the surface that is alive at any given time.

The various layers of today's computers' software were built up one by one over the last forty years or so. On the very first layer we have the ubiquitous ones and zeros, the binary code on which all else is built. Then, on the next layer, we have the bit patterns that are encoded as primary instructions for the current generation of processing hardware. As everyone in computing knows, at one time these were the only layers that existed. Programmers had the thankless task of writing codes composed of just these ones and zeros as elements. But, before long, a new layer had to be developed—that of assemblies of binary instructions according to mnemonic symbols. Never again will programmers be required to program in the impoverished vocabulary of binary digits. As software technology advanced, new layers were added to the original ones when it became clear that the next tier of the programmer's interface to machines had been discovered.

Alan Kay, one of the developers of the object-oriented paradigm, has said that "hardware is crystallized software." We have experienced the truth of this in a number of different ways. If it is true as applied to the object-oriented paradigm itself, we can see that it is here that our metaphor based on the rings of a tree trunk breaks down. Not only is the object-oriented paradigm the latest external software layer surrounding a hardware core. This paradigm is pregnant with implications for the architecture of the core itself. The message-passing metaphor of object-oriented languages is of the utmost relevance because it mirrors one of the most influential parallel hardware designs. But here we arrive the other part of our theme in this book because the human brain is clearly a parallel processing system on a vast scale.

Artificial intelligence is involved with attempting to fulfill the dream probably first envisioned by a marketing executive who described the computer as an "electronic brain." A discernible degree of success in this endeavor has resulted in increasing commercial use of AI techniques and tools, particularly in the field of expert systems. However, taking the field of AI beyond this rather modest level of accomplishment and on a road that can bring it closer to its ambitious goal has proven far more difficult than many had suspected. This has led to larger and larger AI programs, and the trend continues. The object-oriented paradigm fits in well with this trend because all of its practitioners agree that this programming paradigm is particularly well suited to the development of very large applications.

This book has been designed to serve readers in both academic and commercial settings. It is especially well suited for use with one of the various object-oriented programming tools that are currently available for low-cost computers. The emphasis is on choosing the right tool for the right job and on cultivating the new skill called object-oriented design and applying it to some of the current problems of AI, in both of its main spheres of activity, that is, commercial AI and AI research.

Chapter 1 is intended as a simple introduction to object-oriented programming concepts for those who are entirely new to them. Chapter 2 briefly introduces some of the main problems addressed in the field of artificial intelligence and gives reasons for regarding the object-oriented paradigm as particularly suitable for well-crafted attempts at their solution. This is hardly a new discovery, but rather the stating of a conclusion categorically that many people have already arrived at through practical experience.

Chapter 3 surveys of some of the most interesting AI applications to date that have implications for how object-oriented systems may most effectively be used in AI. Chapter 4 takes the reader on a tour of all the major object-oriented programming languages and tools that are commercially available. Chapter 5 focuses on object-oriented extensions to the LISP language. Here, the high point is a thorough overview of CLOS, the new object-oriented extension to CommonLISP that is being proposed as a temporary pragmatic standard until a more permanent one can be devised with the virtue of some invaluable hindsight.

Chapter 6 moves to a vital topic in commercial AI, that of evaluating object-oriented expert systems tools. Chapter 7 demonstrates some state-of-the-art techniques in expert systems technology, using a tool called Nexpert Object, and demonstrates using object-oriented programming to build inference engines. Chapter 8 is devoted to exploring the importance of object-oriented techniques for representing and modeling the world. The topics of discrete and continuous simulation, rule-based simulation, content-addressable memory, and neural modeling are introduced. Finally, Chapter 9 explores the topic of concurrent object systems. It is here that the message-passing paradigm is truly fulfilled.

One of the more important ideas presented in this book is that of active data. At this point in time, this is as much a prescriptive concept as it is a descriptive one. That is, it is something that is just beginning to appear in practice, but it is a most important goal for those involved in practical applications development today as well as those who are hard at work researching those techniques that will become the staples of tomorrow's programming experts.

Although the era of active data machines is just beginning, it is still important to ask what it will mean for the future of computing and AI. So many of the algorithms that have provided the backbone of our current era of computing assume a duality of active processes and passive data. We need to ask how many of these solutions can still be applied in the new architectures that are now emerging. To what extent can the active data model make a difference on current hardware still based on the Von Neumann model? These are some of the important questions that will be raised in this book, though they are of such magnitude that the full answer awaits us only in the decisive years of the next decade.

Object-Oriented Programming for Artificial Intelligence

A Guide to Tools and System Design

Chapter 1

Object-Oriented Programming Defined

Although this book is about artificial intelligence from the point of view of object-oriented programming, it is important to look at object-oriented programming in its own right first, before considering its relation to AI. The result should be a more balanced perspective—one that will provide a somewhat more objective background for what follows. This chapter assumes that the reader has had no previous exposure to object-oriented systems, but does have some general programming background.

Object-oriented programming is the most recent stage in the development of programming. It represents a significant technological advance, just as the structured programming of Algol and Pascal was an improvement over the earlier block-structured programming of FORTRAN. As with most technological advances, it is not difficult to see that there is something very "correct" about object-oriented programming, which is why it is here to stay.

1.1 Programming Paradigms

A *programming paradigm* is a basic model for approaching the way programs are written. To some, it may come as a surprise that different programming paradigms even exist. Most programmers are familiar with just one paradigm, that of procedural programming. But there are now many others. The object-oriented paradigm, which is what we are concerned with here, is one, but there are also the rule-based programming, logic programming, parallel programming, visual programming, constraint-based, data flow, and rehearsal paradigms.

Why are there so many paradigms? The answer is partly because programming computers is still a relatively new discipline and partly because people still want to be able to do many different things with computers. Also, the current type of digital computer is just one type of machine architecture among many. Developers are currently experimenting with alternative machine architectures that are considered to be improvements in one respect or another. Many of them either require or expect an alternative programming paradigm.

1.2 The Object-Oriented Paradigm

If you ask someone what object-oriented programming is, you should be prepared for somewhat different answers, depending on the person you ask. People are apt to use the latest "buzz words" to describe their projects, but they often do this with surprisingly little justification. When it is a question of object-oriented programming methodology rather than products and tools, the emphasis tends to be on what the programmer finds most interesting or useful about an object-oriented system. Object-oriented programming, then, can be different things to different people.

Before proceeding any further, we need to eliminate any confusion in terminology, for there is at least one other use of the term "object-oriented" besides the one that will be used in this book. Certain graphics application programs are referred to as object-oriented programs. Generally speaking, this is a way of contrasting such applications with pixel-based or screen-oriented graphics programs. The main idea is that the object-oriented type of graphics program stores images in such a way that the objects that make up a complete picture retain their individual identity. This means that we can always perform various changes on an object-by-object basis with such a program. More often, computer graphics images are stored on a pixel-by-pixel basis, simply as screen information.

As it is used in this book, the term "object-oriented" has an entirely different meaning. In the sense that we are using it, "object-oriented" does not refer merely to specific graphics application programs, but rather to a style of programming or programming tool. It is true that the type of graphics program in question is particularly easy to write with object-oriented programming techniques. However, it is also true that such applications can be written without the type of programming we will be discussing, and also that pixel- or screen-oriented graphics programs can be written with object-oriented tools and methods. In this book, the only sense in which we will refer to application programs as being "object-oriented" is when they have been written in the object-oriented manner.

The preliminary definition of object-oriented programming that we adopt here should allow the reader to follow the current introduction, but it will be expanded upon at a later point. The initial definition we will adopt for now is as follows:

> Object-oriented programming is a type of programming that provides a way of modularizing programs by establishing partitioned memory areas for both data and procedures that can be used as templates for spawning copies of such modules on demand.

According to this definition, an object is considered to be a partitioned area of computer memory. Many people take the phrase "object-oriented" literally to mean that this type of programming is concerned with objects in the world, as opposed to being the state of the computer being programmed. There is some truth to this, but it is not the essence of object-oriented programming.

Essentially, object-oriented programming's method of partitioning a computer's memory allows each module or object to function relatively independently of one another. There are various consequences of this, most of which are advantageous to the programmer. However, most programmers tend to emphasize primarily those advantages that they find most interesting, or with which they are most impressed.

What exactly do we mean by partitioning the memory of the computer? This means to provide a system of dividing the computer's memory into areas that have a certain functional independence. The memory partitions are independent in the sense that they may be used in a variety of different programs without modification and with complete assurance that none of the memory locations will be overwritten or in any unanticipated way function differently because of their presence in a different environment.

The definition states that the partitioned areas of memory are not just those that store data, but also those that store code in the form of executable procedures. This is essential to keeping the object protected. Any procedure that was allowed access to the memory locations of an object could alter or even corrupt the data stored in the object. This would clearly interfere with its functionality. For this reason, the active processes of an object-oriented system are defined as local functions or procedures that alone may have access to the object's data. In this way, the object protects itself from having its data and functionality corrupted by unknown events external to it. Thus, a functioning element of a program that has been written correctly and completely debugged cannot be changed by subsequent additions or modifications to any of the programs in which it is used.

Finally, the definition states that the partitioned memory structure can be used as a template for spawning further copies of the object. For example, once a window object has been defined, as many of these objects can be created as memory allows, without writing additional code to ensure against interference between different instances. In stating that additional copies are made, we are referring only to the behavior of the objects. Everything behaves as though complete multiple copies are in operation. Note, however, that we are not suggesting how the objects should actually be implemented.

1.3 Object-Oriented Programming Metaphors

Each programming paradigm has its own metaphors that contribute to the ways in which programmers think about program design. Computer science itself is full of metaphors that have become the jargon of the field. Two excellent examples of this are the terms "memory" and "windows." If you really think about it, these metaphors are actually rather remote. Memory and windows in computing have little resemblance to those we encounter in the everyday world. Nevertheless the terms have stuck and we use them indiscriminately, apparently without any great difficulty.

The metaphors used in describing programming models present a somewhat different situation in that to be of service, they must reflect a genuine model whose features actually have practical implications. The more accurate these metaphorical models, therefore, the better. What are some of the metaphors of object-oriented programming? As soon as we ask the question, we can see that many of the basic concepts such as message passing and inheritance have a metaphorical significance. However, at least in the case of these two metaphors, the analogy can be taken quite far with good results.

Some of the metaphors adopted to explain object-oriented systems, however, can be more remote and, therefore, less useful. In his book *Object-Oriented Programming*, Brad Cox uses the metaphors of software ICs and factories to try to explain the concepts of object-oriented systems. As we will argue later in more detail, although these metaphors have pedagogical value, they are not adequate to serve as more lasting metaphorical models of the components of object-oriented systems. Object-oriented systems have features that actually make them significantly more powerful technologically than ICs or factories. This is largely due to their extreme modularity. We cannot use off-the-shelf ICs to build other ICs, and the end products of factories generally do not resemble the factories that make them. However, it is an everyday matter in object-oriented programming to use existing objects to make still newer ones that inherit all the properties of their ancestors.

1.4 Active Data

One very useful way to understand objects is to think of them as an attempt at providing a form of *active data*. It would be true to say that an object represents active data if the paradigm for performing operations in an object-oriented system were to send messages to objects telling them what we wish them to do. So, for example, if we wish to print a string on the screen, we send the string a message telling it to print itself. An object that is a string is not just a passive piece of textual data. It is an active entity that knows how to perform various operations on itself correctly.

One of the most basic distinctions in programming is that between data and procedures. To some degree, this reflects the hardware difference between memory chips and processors. The basic model of a program according to this design of computers is that data is stored in memory chips and the instructions of processors are used to manipulate the data. In this model, therefore, data is essentially passive and instructions are the active elements that operate on the passive element. Object-oriented programming is part of a movement to define the programming model somewhat differently. An object is both code and data. It is a form of active data.

1.5 Message Passing

One of the main models in object-oriented programming for allowing object modules to interact is the *message-passing* model. Objects are seen as communicating by passing messages that they can either accept or reject. Generally an object accepts messages it recognizes and rejects those it does not. In this way, the types of interactions between objects are carefully controlled. Because all interactions follow this protocol, code external to an object has no opportunity to interfere in any way with the object's functioning in unpredictable and undesirable ways.

At the very minimum, sending a message involves specifying the name of an object and the name of the message to be sent to that object. Often, arguments will also have to be specified. The arguments may be the names of variables known only to the type of object that recognizes the message, or they may be global variables known to all objects. They may not be variables known privately by another unrelated type of object.

As mentioned earlier, message passing produces the appearance of active data. You can send a message to an object to write itself to disk, display itself on the monitor, delete itself, and so on. Is this only an appearance, or is there more substance to the connection between active data and message passing? This is a difficult question that requires more background than we have provided so far to answer adequately. Let us just say for the moment that message passing has the effect of making objects behave as active data from outside them, but not from inside. From within an object we have the same dichotomy between passive data and active procedures that is found in conventional programming.

What differences does it make whether or not a system uses message passing? Again, a final answer to this question is not possible here. However, the general answer is that message passing allows for advanced programming techniques that can exploit the partitioned functionality of objects that respond to messages. Although there are ways to achieve many of the same results without message passing, it is generally more difficult to do and requires greater knowledge and skill on the part of the programmer.

On the whole, objects in message-passing systems have a very special kind of autonomy that is unique in programming. In a certain sense, each object behaves like a little specialized computer communicating with other specialized computers. Although this is, of course, another metaphor, it is a fruitful metaphor that is worth pursuing. As we will see later, using the message-passing model can suggest many interesting and powerful algorithms that might not otherwise have occurred to programmers and software designers.

1.6 Classes, Instantiation, and Inheritance

One of the most basic concepts in object-oriented programming is that of *class*. As it is understood in this context, a class is a template for creating actual functioning objects of a given type. In many object-oriented systems, a class is an object in its own right, but one with very limited capabilities. We might say that whereas a class provides the blueprint or genetic code for creating cows, it is the actual cow instance, not the cow class, that gives milk.

We say that a class is *instantiated* when it has actually been used to stamp out one or more objects of its type. Appropriately, the objects that have been created from a given class are called *instances* of that class. What really gives practical justification to the class structure is the facility for *inheritance*, which provides the ability to create classes that will automatically model themselves on other classes. When a class B has been defined so as to model itself on class A, B is called a subclass of A. Reciprocally, we can also say that A is a superclass of B, or, in other words, B inherits all of A's behavior.

Having one class inherit the behavior of another would be pointless if that were all that was involved. The point of creating a subclass is to add some additional behavior besides whatever is inherited. Usually the subclass is outfitted with behavior that allows it to act as a more specialized version of its superclass. Some object-oriented systems also have *multiple inheritance*, which means that they may have more than one superclass. In such systems, sometimes we create a new class so that it can inherit from two or more superclasses. Other times we provide the additional behavior by hand coding. In either case, the result is a class that can stamp out objects with a somewhat different behavior.

Through this process of defining subclasses, an object-oriented system comes to have a *class hierarchy*. This is a tree or network of classes that starts with the most general as the

most branches and descends to the bottom leaves which are the most specific. The
r of an object-oriented environment is principally defined by the class hierarchy and
pabilities. Programmers extend an object-oriented language by expanding its class
hierarchy and the vocabulary of messages that can be exchanged by various objects.

The active element of objects, the messages, are also known as *methods* and are similar
to functions that are local to a particular object. The names of these methods are often
called *selectors*. They have this designation because, when they are called by name, they
allow the system to select which code is to be executed.

One of the great advantages of object-oriented systems is that the protocol for
handling various objects stays essentially the same as the language becomes extended.
Thus, large systems that are developed by more than one programmer can be managed
efficiently because minimal communication and documentation of new features are
required between programmers.

One practice that facilitates this is often called *overloading*. Overloading is the
convention of giving the exact same selector name to methods that do the same thing for
different classes of objects. Most strictly typed languages require that functions that
perform the same operation but for different datatypes be given different names. So, for
example, we might have two distinct functions named divideInteger and divideReal that
perform the operation of division for integers and real numbers, respectively. Systems
with many classes could become very difficult to use because the programmer must
continually look up function names. With overloading, the method is simply called
"divide" for all classes of numbers, even though the code that implements the divide
method may vary from class to class. This way, the programmer or user has a uniform
protocol for classes in a large range of operations, which makes the system much easier to
use. The programmer does not have to look at the code written by other programmers to
know how to use that code in writing new routines.

1.7 Types of Object-Oriented Systems

The various types of object-oriented systems can be distinguished in several different
ways. The most basic distinction is between pure and hybrid systems.

A *pure* object-oriented system is one in which everything is an object. An example of
this is Smalltalk. In this type of system, even classes are objects that are instances of a
class. At first this may appear confusing, but there is nothing at all paradoxical about it.
It is in fact a direct result of the desire for total consistency in the system. Just as objects
are created from a class that serves as their model or template, classes themselves are
objects that are created according to the blueprint laid out in a specific class. Usually this
blueprint is called the *metaclass*.

The more inquisitive and logically minded reader will undoubtedly have sensed a
familiar conceptual pattern here. The question may have come to mind that if classes
always have to be instances of another class, how does the original class come into being.
The answer is that we are not dealing just with concepts here. An object-oriented system

is a practical system that is designed to meet certain tangible ends, not to create a logical but illusory structure. The designers of pure object-oriented systems decided to make each class an instance of another class because this was the most coherent and consistent way for such a system to operate. However, if the metaclass that serves as the template for all other classes is not itself an instance of a class, this is not a flaw in the system. What we have is a working system that has been able to carry the object-oriented paradigm as far as possible.

A *hybrid* system is one in which objects coexist within a conventional programming language. Examples of this include the various object-oriented extensions to C and LISP, which will be considered in some detail in a later chapter. Because they must coexist with already existing programming languages, the elements in hybrid systems obviously cannot all be objects. Whether or not encapsulation or memory protection can exist in a hybrid system depends on the design and implementation of the host language. Usually there will be ways that the protection can be broken.

Another way to classify object-oriented systems is by type of inheritance scheme. The two main types are single and multiple inheritance. As was mentioned earlier, multiple inheritance systems are those that allow a class to inherit from more than one superclass. Multiple inheritance is still a relatively new feature of object-oriented systems, and many implementations still do not have this feature.

The main issue that prevents multiple inheritance from becoming as straightforward as one might wish is the possibility of conflicts between the names of variables and names in the different classes that are to be inherited. Although this is a rare situation, it is one that has to be handled in a rigorous manner. As yet there is no agreement on a standard method for handling this issue.

A final distinction between different types of object systems is between those that have actual concurrent processing and those that do not. In a concurrent message-passing system, for example, the messages that are exchanged between objects can occur in parallel rather than waiting for their turn as in sequential processing systems.

1.8 How Object-Oriented Systems Work

For some applications, the programmer need not consider how the object-oriented system is implemented nor how it really works. In fact, it is true that one of the goals of object-oriented systems is to allow programmers to use code without knowing the details of its implementation. However, for many artificial intelligence applications, this is a luxury we cannot afford. Moreover, many goals of AI are pushing the capabilities of a programming system beyond its limits. For this reason, we will end this chapter with a general discussion of the basic mechanisms used to provide most object-oriented systems with their characteristic behavior.

What actually happens when a message is sent to an object? In most object-oriented systems, objects generally have both a shared part and a private part. There is no need to copy the parts of an object that are always the same. This would be a waste of memory.

Generally, the parts of an object that are the same for all objects of this type are stored at the class level. This often turns out to consist of all the code for methods as well as the data for *class variables*, which comprises the shared part of objects. When a message is sent, therefore, it is handled by a routine that attempts to look up the shared part in the area of memory owned by the class.

The *instance variables* and their values are private, however. Each object actually stores its own instance variables. The class provides the information concerning which instance variables to create, but their actual storage is done by the instance itself. If the data or code being sought is inherited from another class, it is only stored once, at the highest level. Routines that access it are redirected up the hierarchy until they reach the class from which all others have been inherited.

1.9 Using an Object-Oriented System

Largely due to the design of Smalltalk, the first full-fledged object-oriented language, systems of this type are known for their special user interface facilities that assist programmers. The multiwindow mouse-oriented environment that has become popular for all types of user applications on today's personal workstations was originally closely associated with the first object-oriented systems. Some of the unique features and requirements of object-oriented programming are enhanced by the use of tools that make programs highly visible to the programmer. So, for example, one of the tools that has come to be associated with object-oriented systems is the *browser*. As the name suggests, a browser is a facility that allows the programmer to peruse at will some aspect of the programming environment. For example, in Smalltalk, there is the System Browser, which allows the programmer first to get an overview of the class hierarchy of the current system and then to move down into some aspect of the hierarchy to inspect or edit its contents.

Object-oriented systems provide many desirable capabilities, but they do so only if the programmer knows how to use them. A number of programmer responsibilities are unique to object-oriented systems. First, the programmer has to know how the basic operations such as defining classes, creating objects, and performing operations are performed. In addition, the programmer has to know what methods are available to what classes of objects. Although many useful classes and methods often exist in an object-oriented system, programmers will not benefit from them unless they know what exists and how it may be used.

1.10 Why Object-Oriented Programming?

Programmers find the object-oriented approach important for a variety of reasons. To one programmer, it might be the possibility of eliminating redundant code that is most appealing. To another, it might be the protection that objects have from being invaded by code in other parts of the program. To still another, it might be the time savings involved

in being able to build programs out of standard working parts that commur,
another, rather than having to start writing code from scratch. Finally, to so,
the most appealing feature is the ability to have as many instances of an obje;
like copresent without any interference.

Most object-oriented systems provide the facilities for allowing programs to
these features. Which of them is the most important depends on the requireme;
project as well as on the preferences of those who undertake it. As your knowle; ; ; and
experience with object-oriented systems increases, you might find that your preference
shifts from one of these features to another. But this is not of very great importance,
since, in theory at least, it is possible for programs to reap all these advantages without
any compromises.

When programmers stopped using just ones and zeros to program computers and
began to use assemblers that could recognize mnemonic symbols that stood for the actual
binary machine instructions executed, there was little chance that the old method would
survive. Advances in programming technology have become increasingly more subtle
since that time, and thus important breakthroughs are not always immediately recognized
by all. The development of compiled high-level languages led to just as wide an adoption
as the assemblers before them. However, compilers did not replace assemblers. It would
be more accurate to think of them as the next layer of software erected between the
machine and the programmer, which made them still easier to program.

Conclusion

Object-oriented programming is not an entirely new and unprecedented direction in
computer science, but rather it takes various developments in programming languages to
their next logical step, for reasons of clarity, modularity, and programming efficiency. In
one sense, object-oriented programming is the programming paradigm that takes
structured programming to its natural, logical conclusion. In structured programming,
variables may be local to a particular procedure, and these procedures typically pass
arguments such as strings and numbers between them. With object-oriented systems, all
this is taken much further. Variables are no longer local just to procedures. The main
building blocks are now objects—protected areas of system memory—which can have
both local variables and local procedures. Moreover, the building blocks do not
communicate with one another just by passing arguments. The procedures themselves,
usually called methods, which are local to objects, make possible the messages that are
sent and received by objects. In this respect, objects resemble smaller computers within
the host computer, each with its own data and code areas.

In most object-oriented systems there are at least two different types of objects: classes
and instances. Classes may have a logical relation between one another such that one
might be the subclass or superclass of another. Generally speaking, the superclass is the
more abstract class and the subclass is the more specific. So, for example, if we created
the class Furniture, we could create the class Chair as a subclass of furniture, and Desk-

Chair as a subclass of Chair. In this example, Furniture would be the superclass of Chair, which is in turn the superclass of Desk-Chair.

There are at least three obvious advantages of object-oriented systems. The first advantage is that once you have written the code for a class, you can have as many instances of that class present in the system at the same time as memory will allow. A class is simply a template on which each instance is modeled and assigned its own area of memory that no other object can access except by using its own local methods. For example, in an object-oriented system, you can have as many graphics pens, windows, editors, interpreters, and so on as you would like copresent without any fear that they will interfere with one another.

The second advantage is that through the mechanism of inheritance, subclasses automatically share all the variables and methods of their superclasses. This means that greater and greater specializations of functions can be written just by adding the part that is unique, and the rest is inherited automatically.

The third immediate advantage is that a uniform interface can be provided over the widest possible range of object types. The same name can be used for methods of different objects that have to be implemented differently, but these differences can remain invisible to the user. For example, we might create different classes for a variety of different geometric polyhedra. Then, for each separate class, we would define the methods volume and surface-area. The actual formulas and their implementations would vary, but the calling names would all be the same. For example, if you specified either `Tetrahedron-1 volume` or `Cube-3 volume`, methods would be invoked that would return the value of the object's volume.

Some say that the key advantage of object-oriented programming is its ability to reuse code for many different programs. But, in itself, this is not significantly different from library functions. A more substantial difference is the improved ability to handle complexity in a transparent manner. A key advantage of object-oriented programming—one that is not always immediately obvious, but one that experienced programmers who have worked with these systems will nearly always testify to—is that object-oriented languages give you more leverage in working on very large programs. This does not come for free, though, and is not guaranteed. Factoring a large program into the right parts is a large part of the battle. It is also necessary to learn the right techniques for managing the code and making life easy for the members of a programming team.

Object-oriented systems are usually rather diffuse, with parts of applications being dispersed among a large number of classes and subclasses. To program efficiently with such a system, it is essential to have the proper tools and an effective method for keeping the application well focused and well organized.

It is important to point out that object-oriented programming cannot be regarded as something that is easy to pick up extremely rapidly, as it is a very different paradigm from what most programmers are accustomed to. As programming approaches go, it is very knowledge intensive. In other words, the readily available modular code is only useful to programmers who know what is available to them and how it may be best used.

Since many programmers even resist learning new languages, never mind new programming paradigms, it is important to summarize again in clearcut, pragmatic terms, just what the real advantages are to programming with objects:

1. The ability to spawn multiple instances of a given function or object from the same code without the codes for the instances interfering with one another.

2. A truly modular programming environment where redundancies in coding are kept to an absolute minimum.

3. Standard calling conventions for a broad range of operations that exhibit differences in behavior (like variations on a theme).

4. A means of managing very large programming projects by breaking up large problems into smaller, independently functioning, highly visible parts.

True or False?

1. The object in an object-oriented system is always something in the real world that the programmer is involved in modeling.

2. The way that an instance is created from a class is by copying everything in the class into a new memory location.

3. One of the purposes of an object-oriented system is to create working parts of programs that can be reused in different programs without major modification.

4. An object can recognize any message that has been defined somewhere in the system.

5. One of the drawbacks of an object-oriented system is that, once a class has been defined, it can never be changed.

6. Inheritance refers to the ability of one instance variable's value to be deduced from the value stored in the object's class.

7. Both classes and instances actually store only those elements that are unique to them.

8. One of the main advantages of object-oriented systems is their superior execution speed in comparison with conventional languages.

9. The ability of an object to receive a message is determined by the current state of the system as a whole.

10. In a pure object-oriented system, the classes are all actually instances of a class.

(F, F, T, F, F, F, T, F, F, T)

Chapter 2

Advantages of Object-Oriented Programming for Artificial Intelligence

2.1 Artificial Intelligence: An Overview

Artificial intelligence (AI) is concerned with developing software systems that are capable of doing things that we would describe as "intelligent" if humans did them. Traditionally it has been a research field. However, in the last decade, commercial applications of AI have been appearing with increasingly greater scope and frequency. The two areas in which most of the commercial applications have occurred so far are *expert systems* and *natural language processing*. Of the two, expert systems have turned out to be the more successful to date because natural language processing has proved to be extremely difficult. Robotics is another commercial field that has a strong connection to AI. However, the industrial robots currently in use have little or no AI associated with them, and the robots that do have AI features are still in the research laboratories. On the whole, most of the field of AI is still in the research category.

2.2 Fields of AI Research

Eight important areas of AI research are as follows:

- Natural language
- Learning
- Automatic programming
- Planning
- Speech recognition
- Perception
- Understanding
- Neural modeling

Although there are already some exemplary commercial applications of natural language processing (that is, having a computer respond to human language rather than to computer language), it remains one of the most active fields of AI research. The reason for this, of course, is that the products that have appeared so far in this category have only realized very limited solutions to the problem. It has become clear that the problem of using language is not purely a linguistic one. Our knowledge of the world is brought to bear continually in the process of understanding all acts of communication using human languages.

AI researchers have been conducting research in *learning* for quite a number of years now, but because of the tremendous difficulty of the problem, this field is still at its most rudimentary stages. The goal of learning research in AI is clearly to write programs and eventually to build entire computer systems that can learn, in some sense, the way humans do. Although seldom expressed, the main difference between machine learning and its human counterpart ought to be one of speed. If machines cannot be built that learn at a speed considerably faster than humans, the machines will remain a curiosity and a resource only for the very few. Obviously, the vast majority of users would not be willing to wait fifteen or twenty years for a learning machine to become sufficiently educated to do serious work reliably.

Current research systems are still extremely primitive in comparison with even relatively simple living organisms. At this point researchers are just beginning to refine techniques that allow programs to learn on their own in very specialized and limited ways. The idea of a generalized learning engine is not even in view at this time.

Automatic programming is a traditional AI research area that has acquired a new name in the marketplace: C.A.S.E. tools, for computer assisted software engineering, now that commercial products in this area have started to become popular. The basic problem addressed by applications in this area is to allow the computer itself to take over part or all of the process of writing or rewriting code, debugging, and so forth. Object-oriented programming has certain advantages that make the process of automatic programming easier.

Traditionally, *planning* research in AI has been concerned with the problem of automatically generating a symbolically represented sequence of actions that would accomplish a given goal if executed. For many years the emphasis was on "skeletal planning," that is, initially generating very abstract statements of a plan and progressively fleshing this out with more and more detail. The whole approach was based on bringing about certain states in a limited world that corresponded to a particular application such as a mobile robot laborer. In recent years some new frameworks have appeared for designing programs that can plan, but it is still too soon to tell which of the various schemes will emerge as the most practical approach.

Speech recognition is one of the older research problems that has been associated with AI. On the whole, scientists have been surprised that it has proven to be such a difficult problem. Paradoxically, many of the approaches taken to it thus far have not been what most AI researchers would consider to be the characteristic AI mode of solving problems. As in many areas related to speech and language, it has become apparent that recognizing what is said is a very complex process that has subprocesses on many different levels. Our understanding of the human world often helps us recognize what people are saying. It is not just a straightforward low-level function as was once assumed.

AI research in *perception* has so far been mostly concerned with vision systems, though there have been a few notable projects in the area of hearing and even touch. One of the basic problems of vision processing that has been under intensive study for a number of years is that of taking a 2-D monochrome image and deducing from it a scene of 3-D objects and events. In recent years some important advances have been made on this problem. One of the most advanced vision applications that has been built to date is one that provides the key module for a system that can play an excellent game of Ping-Pong.

Understanding is the problem that many AI researchers have come to recognize as one of the most fundamental and one that underlies many of the other more specific research problems. Research on understanding arose originally in the field of natural language processing, more specifically, in the problem of allowing a computer to interpret news stories and other stories to the extent that it could satisfactorily answer questions about them. These would be programs that could pass reading comprehension tests, so to speak. What is really involved here is building a complex and cumulative representation of facts as well as drawing further inferences from them so that an integrated and well-articulated picture of a situation emerges that is analogous to the way humans would understand it. As will become apparent throughout the course of this book, in theory, object-oriented systems, as their name already suggests, are extremely well suited for these types of problems.

Neural nets are currently one of the hottest AI research areas, after having fallen into eclipse for over a decade. There is an overlap here with many of the other AI research areas because *neural modeling* is a technique that can in principle be directed at a variety of different applications. One of neural modeling's most attractive aspects is that, regardless of the intended application, there are generic mechanisms that allow for incrementally improved performance.

2.3 AI Techniques

One of the most characteristic AI approaches is that of *symbolic processing*. The term originated to emphasize its dissimilarity to the ordinary data and numeric manipulation techniques in conventional computation. Symbolic processing is more akin to human thought processes because it uses symbols in an open-ended and flexible way to represent things in the world and manipulates these symbols in very powerful ways. Symbolic processing was originally based on the list processing capability of the LISP programming language. Now other languages have emerged that also offer this type of programming.

The main thrust of current commercial AI applications is in the direction of knowledge-based systems. This approach makes very effective use of symbolic processing for capturing complex and sophisticated knowledge in flexible structures. Many different approaches have been taken toward what is known as *knowledge representation*, the development of effective software methods for encoding different types of human knowledge and expertise.

2.4 Inference Engines

The most central AI technique in knowledge-based systems is that of the *inference engine*. An inference engine is a special type of program that allows knowledge to become executable in a sense, rather than remaining mere passive data. An inference engine in operation continually processes elements in a knowledge base, thereby giving that knowledge an active role rather than the passive role of the information in a traditional database. The inference engine was one of the first techniques that made possible what we refer to as active data.

From the technical standpoint, an inference engine resembles an interpreter in some ways and in others, a data-driven application program. However, there are important differences between an inference engine and an ordinary computer language interpreter. One of the most important, from the developer's point of view, is the extreme modularity that an inference engine makes possible. When a program in a conventional programming language is modified or extended, special debugging is often needed again even though the debugging process has been carried out numerous times already. An inference engine can be considered the control aspect of an expert system that never has to be debugged more than once. In developing a rule-based expert system, rules can be added incrementally like records in a database rather than lines of code added to a program. However, the knowledge "drives" the inference engine to behave in a certain way, and in this sense is not passive.

From the user's point of view, the advantage of inference engines is the greater flexibility they make possible. Programs written with conventional programming languages are deterministic in ways that inference engines are not. Most programs are written as instructions to the computer about what it is to do under various circumstances. The inference engine itself is usually written this way. However, like an interpreter, the inference engine still needs an additional program to tell it what to do. In this case, the program is not computer instructions but declarations in a conditional form such as "If X is true, then Y is also true." How the final application behaves depends on what rules are present together in the knowledge base. Each of the rules is a discrete "chunk" that is independent of the other chunks. Each of the individual chunks influences how the expert system will behave, just as the lines of code in a program determine the outcome of a program. However, the knowledge chunks can combine to affect the outcome in many unpredictable ways.

Consider this analogy. On the one hand, we have Actor 1 who is given a set of speeches and some instructions on when to read each speech and the conditions under which to read them. On the other hand, we have Actor 2 who makes his speeches by taking words out of a Nouns box, a Verbs box, and an Adjectives box. What Actor 2 will say is not completely determined, but it can be strongly influenced by carefully selecting the words supplied to the actor.

The inference engine is like Actor 2. The knowledge base supplies the vocabulary for a variety of behavior patterns or "speeches," but does not provide a definite script from which to read. A conventional program is like Actor 1 who recites from a set of specific scripts. This clearly illustrates the added flexibility that inference engines offer.

2.5 AI Paradigms

Many programmers recognize instinctively that AI can teach them something that will make them better programmers, even if they are not planning to work specifically in the AI field. A common misconception, though, is that the most that can be learned are some new techniques to add to one's arsenal of programming devices. AI has much more to offer than this. You will be hearing a lot about programming paradigms in this book and elsewhere, so this would be a good time to explain the difference between programming techniques and programming paradigms.

Most people in AI would agree, regardless of how vehemently they may disagree on other matters, that we still do not know how to program computers very well and we still have much to learn that can greatly improve our approach to programming. People in the AI field also generally agree that nearly all conventional programming comes under one major paradigm, namely, that of procedural programming. Once this is pointed out, it becomes obvious that, for most programmers, designing a program is simply planning procedures for the computer to execute. However, as things stand now, procedural programming is just one of the many paradigms at the AI programmer's disposal.

The object-oriented paradigm represents another approach entirely. Arising originally through AI research and currently one of the most popular of all the AI paradigms, it is just now penetrating the commercial programming market. The rule-based programming paradigm has also entered the commercial mainstream, mainly through its successful use in the field of expert systems technology. The logic programming paradigm as well as the declarative and rule-based programming paradigms were all combined to create the powerful new programming language PROLOG, another recent newcomer to the marketplace. Other less-known programming paradigms that have also originated in AI research include constraint propagation, access-oriented programming, the actor paradigm as well as the neural network paradigm and various parallel and distributed programming paradigms such as the connectionist and data-flow approaches. As you can see, the field of AI today is very large and complex, but some very clear trends are at work that show a definite unity amid the diversity.

2.6 The State of the Art

There are a number of very clear indications that, for better or worse, the goals of AI are on the verge of undergoing a paradigm shift. According to Mark Stefik at Xerox PARC, AI is now in the process of becoming the latest vehicle for the development and proliferation of a new form of *knowledge media*. Knowledge media, according to Stefik, embrace not only the representation and storage of knowledge, but its transmission throughout society. At this point, at least, AI systems are not a major medium for the transmission of knowledge. However, as AI technology matures, Stefik argues, it will increasingly take on this role as a carrier and transmitter.

It is obvious that AI systems already differ from most other knowledge media such as books, diagrams, and films in that they are not entirely frozen and inert. The knowledge in an AI system is dynamic and may be executed for solving problems in a more flexible way than is possible with any other knowledge medium. In this respect, it already resembles human intelligence. But, so far, the ways in which AI systems can use knowledge to solve problems are still extremely limited compared to human capabilities.

Has AI given up on the quest to create machine intelligence as an artifact and instead settled upon the far easier goal of machine knowledge? This is both a crucial and extremely difficult question. Part of the problem is that, for the short term at least, knowledge appears to be far more useful than intelligence. This may sound surprising, but it is important to remember that human intelligence must undergo a very long training period before it can be trusted with any serious responsibilities. (Imagine buying a program that you had to teach for 16 years before it could do anything useful!) But a knowledge-based system, even though it does not have much true intelligence, can do some very useful things, usually without any training at all. In planning long-range projects and even shorter range ones, to emphasize knowledge too heavily and ignore the issue of how to make the processing of knowledge more intelligent is tantamount to sidestepping one of the most challenging issues that AI faces.

The field of AI today is like a cell in which mitosis has occurred—two independent bodies exist and both seem to be thriving. The two related fields I am referring to are commercial AI applications and basic AI research. I intend to give both some representation in this chapter and in the book generally because each of them is important as well as intriguing.

Although some very noteworthy progress is being made in AI today, it is fair to say that the field suffers excessively from fragmentation. A few major figures see the "big picture" and have a vision of sorts, but far too many researchers still seem to see only the trees (sometimes just the leaves on the trees) and never the forest. Various government agencies have attempted to impose some type of overall agenda on AI research, but this has not and cannot succeed for a number of reasons. The changes have to come from within AI itself. A new vision based on realistic long-range objectives and a scenario for its realization will have to emerge.

Despite the lip service that is frequently paid to emulating the way the human brain works, many AI researchers—even those who express great sympathy for this approach—do not appear to make a very serious attempt to design systems that show an appreciation of the high-level organization of the brains of even lower vertebrates. For example, nothing has yet been built that approaches the functioning of the cerebellum of even the lower amphibians and reptiles. AI is still a very computer-oriented discipline at this point, but in the area of computer science, some substantial headway is being made.

2.7 Sequential Closure in Procedural Programming

Organizing programs along object-oriented lines is important not only as one of the best tools so far for achieving greater programming efficiency and modularity, but also because it has important implications for the goals of AI. Although we cannot automatically benefit from these potential advantages just by using the paradigm, many of them may seem to be much more within reach if we do. One of the most important issues is object-oriented systems' potential for alleviating the problem of *sequential closure* in programming. The term "sequential closure" refers to the current tendency for a whole program to break when any one part of it breaks. A program may have been running very smoothly, but unless all the subsequent code is correct and fully debugged, the program stands a good chance of crashing or going into an unrecoverable state. This is in total contrast to most living organisms who show considerable resilience or "fault tolerance" to breakdowns in their functioning parts—a phenomenon that seems nowhere more prevalent than in the brain. Numerous studies have shown the astounding degree to which the brain can adjust to massive losses of brain tissue, for example. But, as we know, removing even the slightest thing from most program codes can be enough to stop the whole program from working.

Since sequential closure is so much a part of current programming technology, it might be useful to spell out why it is not the most desirable constraint to have. Three main consequences of sequential closure are:

1. A considerable amount of programming time must be spent, not only on debugging, but on re-debugging.

2. There is an inherent limit to how user-friendly programs can be.

3. There is an inherent limit to the flexibility and generality of problems that programs can address.

Most programmers would agree that advances are needed to improve the state of our technology in at least one, if not all three, of these areas.

Naturally, object-oriented systems are also still subject to this condition called sequential closure. However, programmers can enjoy a certain freedom from this tyranny in at least one area, in ways that can have the most practical consequences for them, by correctly exploiting some of the features of object-oriented systems. The main feature of the object-oriented approach that makes this possible is its ability to accomplish a new and important degree of partitioning of large-scale functionality. We currently assume that reusable library functions can be applied time and time again without encountering many situations in which the code does not function properly. Of course, this convenience often comes only at the expense of a great deal of effort, but we take for granted that convenience is one of the goals of competent programming.

2.8 Conventional Libraries Versus Classes and Methods

Functions are still at a very fine-grained level in the organization of most reasonably sized programs. The main sequence of code that calls on numerous library functions in the course of a program is still very much subject to sequential closure. The code consists of a sequence of statements and subroutines that provide a closure on the correct functioning of the program, which often must be debugged and re-debugged each time the program is significantly modified. Most programmers would readily agree that it would be very desirable if much larger functioning parts of programs could have this packaged functionality. Then the program would not have to be repeatedly adjusted and debugged to accommodate changes and additions in other parts of the code.

2.9 Extensible Templates

Brad Cox, in his book *Object-Oriented Programming: An Evolutionary Approach* (Addison-Wesley, 1986) refers to object-oriented systems as *software* ICs. Actual hardware ICs are thought of as units of packaged functionality that can be used in a wide variety of cases without modification or further debugging. The scope of ordinary library functions is so narrow and confined that no one has suggested that they be compared with ICs.

Only in the most rudimentary programs do functions operate as main parts within the program. Functions are usually at the same time too general and too specific to have this role. They are too general in that rather than being a functioning part of an actual program, they are more like standard nuts and bolts that come in an enormous variety of sizes. Without any arguments supplied, with many functions it is still often unclear just what they will do. On the other hand, functions are too specific in that the variety of situations to which they can respond are usually very limited. A function usually requires that the programmer know in advance just what situation is being covered each time it is called. Functions are also very specific in that they are usually responsible for fairly detailed, low-level operations. Objects, which are usually made up of a number of closely related and interacting functions, are a tool that could provide a way around this limitation.

Ideally, a class should be designed as a kind of template for stamping out custom working parts for a wide variety of programs, even if only a few instances of that class are actually used in a given program. In making those instances, values are typically assigned to instance variables that define the conditions of a problem once and for all, while still leaving open the issues of just what messages will be sent, to what objects, and at what time. However, the arguments that these methods will frequently take could be set without the programmer's hand coding. Whole sets of arguments could be systematically assigned to methods simply by setting values to instance variables when an object that acts as a functioning part of a program is initialized.

The object-oriented approach can contribute to furthering the goals of AI in other ways as long as certain problems are addressed with the needed persistence and creativity. Using object-oriented systems to model problem domains can be a little deceptive, though, unless some crucial design issues are met. Simply because a static model of the unique aspects of a certain "world" of activity exists (for example, the world of medical diagnosis or electronic trouble shooting), there is no guarantee that programs using such models will be at all intelligent. In other words, if the information just sits there statically, it does not contribute the kind of knowledge we are interested in, no matter how well the world model may have been designed. From this point of view, everything depends on the techniques for using that information. The more actively a designer allows a program to continually access the knowledge incorporated in a hierarchical model of a problem space, the more intelligence there is to be gained.

As we have seen, in rule-based systems, the inference engine is a general program that accesses knowledge in the form of rules and keeps things moving so that the knowledge captured in rules is getting used and applied. But so far, no general-purpose "inference engines" have been built for accessing knowledge purely in the form of objects. We are just now beginning to get the idea of how to use these structures in a very ad hoc way. It is worthwhile, though, to speculate on what generic routines might be important for AI programs using objects to create deep models of domains. Certainly some unusual, yet generic, search routines specific to object-oriented systems are a basic necessity for most programs of this type. One such basic routine would be a method that built its own list of all the instances of a given class for the purpose of a search, then made its own ordering of the names of these objects, and finally searched them for specific information by looking up the values of various slots or instance variables. However, much more intricate and flexible search routines are possible. For example, some can perform a more general type of information gathering that provides a temporary search space of only the relevant data needed for a given situation. This idea of programs that can dynamically build temporary search spaces to solve problems more efficiently is one that could be quite suitable for several types of AI applications.

Another interesting use of class hierarchies in AI has been in the partitioning of rule-based knowledge into sets of rules that are organized according to a network of situations in a problem space. Here only the tip of the iceberg has been touched so far. A very wide range of approaches can provide flexible problem-solving methods based on sophisticated routines for selecting rulesets to apply by rapid initial searches up and down a hierarchy, rather than just by executing simple test and branch procedures. For example, consider an application that actually builds a design for something. Here, one of the important services that computer technology can provide is to help human designers make sure they have not overlooked anything important. The problem is that what is important in a given design can differ enormously from case to case, depending on the design's details and requirements. In such a case, it would be useful to have various sets of constraint rules that could be applied selectively rather than rigidly by procedure.

Human designers learn by experience how much detail is relevant for evaluating a given aspect of a design. This is important for avoiding entirely inappropriate analyses and conclusions. So, for example, in some designs, the parts being used are standard

through each individual part would be absurd. All that might be
f a few typical elements to reach an important general
igner reaches this kind of realization through common sense,
estion to provide a computer program with a similar flexibility.
tine could sift quickly through all the instances of each type of
roposed design and decide which categories will need a
t and which can be evaluated by inspecting typical elements.

2.10 Key Features of Object-Oriented Systems

Object-oriented systems can be effective for AI applications only to the degree that active
access is provided to the information represented as objects. However, this fact has a
number of consequences and ramifications. For one thing, it means that an adequate
object-oriented programming environment must provide at least some minimum features
to make this possible. First on the list is the ability to keep track of all the objects
currently in the system, which includes both classes and instances, according to their
place in the hierarchy. Part of what we consider simple common sense, that all normally
functioning humans have, is a sense of the place of things in an implicit logical or
conceptual hierarchy.

For example, we take it for granted that bicycles and cars are means of transportation,
and hence in the category of equipment or artifacts, and that therefore, certain kinds of
behavior with them is appropriate. The boundaries of this are constantly being
challenged, of course, by artists and inventors. But we take it for granted that it is not
appropriate to use a piano for firewood, or to risk our lives to rescue a bookend from a
burning house. We know that liquids cannot be safely wrapped in newspaper and
millions of other bits of general, practical knowledge that seem to be stored as a general
understanding of types, roles, and characteristics of things.

The logical way to represent this common-sense knowledge of how we get around in
the practical world is as some kind of conceptual hierarchy. In this way, simply by the
fact that a given object is an instance or member of a class will activate certain knowledge
about how to deal with objects of that type. AI currently handles this through rule-based
programming with either procedural attachments or active values. In many of the larger
professional AI programming systems, rules can be stored about classes of things that are
invoked for certain types of objects. The problem, though, is to provide a means of
determining when it is appropriate for such knowledge to be invoked. Active values and
procedural attachments can act like "demons" that are waiting for certain events to occur
before they allow themselves to be invoked. Therefore, various operations can be waiting
in the wings, as it were, for certain values to be changed or accessed.

If we attempt to change the physical state of an artifact, for example, by burning a
piano, before that operation can be permitted, certain procedures that apply knowledge
about the appropriate behavior for that class of thing can be automatically invoked. So,
for example, such a demon for wooden objects might state that things in the category of

useful furniture have a greater value than satisfying temporary needs for warmth by destroying them. This is a particularly good example for our purpose here because this simple chunk of everyday common sense reflects fairly complex human values and behavior.

2.11 Explicit Versus Implicit Knowledge

When you are representing knowledge to be used to solve certain problems, you must constantly decide how implicit or explicit to make the knowledge. In conventional programming, the knowledge that is incorporated in a program is nearly always completely implicit. It does not really exist as knowledge in the program other than as knowledge the programmer uses to design its functioning. In AI paradigms such as rule-based programming, the attempt is to make knowledge explicit as general rules so that this knowledge can be applied to new situations that the developer may not have foreseen. However, the ability to handle novel situations is still very limited, to say the least. So far, the main advantages of making knowledge explicit are the greater generality and flexibility that can be given to applications. Rather than having the knowledge "hard wired" into a conventional program that cannot compare different pieces of knowledge to reach its own conclusions, it is very useful to provide a way of modeling the general process by which practical results are obtained. The alternative is to just use the results in a purely ad hoc way.

Obviously, it is never possible to make everything the result of a process of explicit reasoning. Even humans could not function that way. Nothing would ever get done in real time. We would all end up like parodies of Hamlet, forever analyzing the pros and cons of every aspect of even the most trivial actions. One of the rules of thumb for practical activity, whether by human or machine, is that certain things must be taken for granted as implicit and used for a limited number of events of explicit analysis or reasoning. From this point of view, we can see one of the main distinguishing features of human, as opposed to machine, analysis. At any given time and for any reason, we can decide to change something from implicit to explicit status. It's important to sense when it is necessary to question things that normally are taken for granted. So far, with AI systems, the programmer decides what knowledge will be implicit and what will be explicit, and this cannot be changed except by rewriting the program.

Since the main tradeoff, as always, is flexibility versus efficiency, the question is how much knowledge can be made explicit without losing adequate performance. This is always a problem-specific issue. For some problems, a week of processing time would be acceptable if the result obtained were accurate and reliable enough. For others, even ten seconds might seem an eternity. Making the proper choice between what to make explicit and implicit in an AI program is often something that can only be done by experienced AI developers. Even here, decisions made early on often prove to be wrong later. The advantage of modular paradigms like rule-based and object-oriented systems, though, is that changes can usually be made by local modifications that do not alter the functioning of the program as a whole. Often knowledge can be made explicit by adding and subtracting various rules and/or functioning classes that do not require that the application be completely rewritten.

2.12 Frame-Based Systems

The frame-based representation of knowledge is the area of AI that has used object-oriented systems to the greatest extent to date. Most AI users of object-oriented systems are far more interested in the knowledge representation capabilities of these systems than other programmers are. This section gives a brief history of the development of frame-based systems.

Marvin Minsky at MIT is generally credited with inspiring the AI community with the idea of adopting frame representation as one of its specific tools. His seminal paper on which most frame representation approaches are based is "A Framework for Representing Knowledge." One of the main thrusts of this paper was that larger grained structures were needed to represent facts so that some of the limitations of atomistic data could be overcome.

With the term "frame" we are once again confronted with a useful metaphor. The original meaning is often lost in technical discussions of frames in the literature. Actually a subtle play on words is involved. The reference is not only to the frame as a kind of skeleton on which to hang the "flesh" of a description, but also to the frames of motion pictures. One of Minsky's original ideas behind frames was far more dynamic than the frequent uses to which frames are put. The idea emerges in the context of scene interpretation for vision processing. The point is that we tend to organize our understanding of where we are and what is going on by a sequences of frame scenes like different rooms that we pass through. So, just as we frame our interpretation of the kitchen and living room by fixed but open structures of what these rooms usually contain and their main uses, we organize many of our experiences as sequences of shifting frames.

Since a frame is also an overall structure that attempts to capture what is common to all events or situations of a basic type in a typical format, it follows that frames are not the sort of thing that could ever enable us to notice or capture what is unique about an experience. What, then, can frames be used to accomplish? They actually can accomplish several different things, and we will focus on a few of the most important ones.

2.13 Frames and Recognition

One of the frequent uses of frames is as a simple mechanism for guiding the process of pattern recognition. One way that this is done is by attempting to match the data of situations with the data that is organized in frames. Frame representations can be combined with rule-based programming to specify how much of a correspondence is needed between the slot values of a frame and the facts of a situation to judge that a match is justified. This is a domain-specific matter that is often quite complex. One source of the complexity is the immense amount of implicit information that serves as a background for our everyday reasoning processes.

2.14 Frames and Scripts

Scripts may be thought of as a special type of frame that is slightly more complex than the ordinary type. A script holds information about a general sequence of events that usually occur in given situations. For example, a script for Getting-Dressed-To-Go-Out might be schematically represented as:

1. Put on underwear.

2. Put on socks.

3. Put on outer clothes.

4. Put on shoes.

5. Put on coat.

6. Put on hat.

Here we see that a tremendous amount of information is usually implicit and must be inferred indirectly. When we say "Put on your shoes," only the most hard-core practical jokers would put them on their hands rather than on their feet.

For another example, given that "John is waiting in line," we would not generally have enough information to apply the Restaurant, Going-to-the-Movies, At-the-Bank, or the Supermarket scripts. However, if the fact is expressed as "John is waiting in line for a ticket," the possibilities could be narrowed down to Going-to-the-Movies, Going-to-a-Concert, Going-to-a-Sports-Event, and Going-to-a-Play scripts.

One of the main advantages of applying a frame or script to a situation is that it often can enable some immediate inferences to be made because of the information contained in the frame slots. However, not all the information in frames is of this nature. Some of it can only guide the inquiry of questions to be investigated without actually enabling immediate conclusions to be drawn. So, for example, if the At-the-Bank frame fires, we will know that the person is involved in a transaction involving money, that it is probably during the daytime, and some other obvious deductions. Although the purpose of the visit to the bank will not be known, the most likely candidates are to make a deposit or withdrawal, to open an account, or to secure a loan. A program may be guided to attempt to answer these questions and their accompanying slot values by reasoning on the basis of other known information. One method of doing this would be to activate a set of forward-chaining rules that can draw all possible conclusions about a frame's slot values based on known information.

Many frame systems also have what are called *facets*. A facet is to a slot as a slot is to a frame. Facets can specify the type of a slot or how it is to be used. If you want a slot to be a list of items rather than just a simple value, you can often do this by modifying a fact.

One of the facilities available with many frame-based systems is procedural attachments, also known as *active values*. This provides frames with a rudimentary "active data" capability that allows the user to specify a procedural function or program that is directly associated with a frame slot. Generally, procedural attachments are of one or two types: procedures that can be executed whenever a slot value is accessed or that may be executed only when a slot value is changed. Procedural attachments are similar to what we have called "demons." They both have active procedures that wait "in the wings" to be automatically executed when certain conditions occur.

2.15 Linking Rules and Objects

In Chapter 6 where we discuss expert systems, we will see a number of practical ways that rules and objects can be effectively used together. Here we will explore one architecture that is not discussed there. The problem it addresses is that of building a system that can make common-sense deductions from information that is stored in objects or frames.

Such a system should be allowed to make its deductions flexibly whenever they are called for, rather than be forced to blindly apply rules in a large, general knowledge base. It makes sense, therefore, to have several smaller rulesets for specific situations along with a forward-chaining inference mechanism. The ruleset names could be stored in a list as a class variable. In this way, a routine whose mission was to "make as many relevant inferences as possible" could look up the rulesets that apply to an object in its class.

The routine must then determine an order in which to try the various rulesets that apply. One approach would be to have a default order (the order in which the names of the rulesets are stored) with various auxiliary methods and rules for rearranging the order. For example, there could be routines for putting a certain ruleset at the head of the list if certain facts are known. The rulesets would be organized to handle some typical situation, and there would obviously be tests to determine whether or not that situation applies. Where no specific situation applied, there could be an order for testing for each situation in turn. With this type of setup, an opportunistic approach is a natural fit. For example, after the first ruleset is applied, some inferences may establish a fact that results in some other important action being taken.

The idea of having a list of applicable rules attached to a class object is useful for quite a number of different types of applications. The assumption here is that an inference engine is available that can be fed a list of ruleset names to be tried in a certain order on a given set of objects.

2.16 Automatic Investigation

The example just discussed brings up an even more general issue in using object systems for building intelligent applications. It is that of a system that can investigate various things in a general way about the world of objects it finds at its disposal. The first thing that such a system should know explicitly is what is in its world. Here the key term is "explicitly." It is one thing to have a system that can look up specific data in its world when it is called upon to do so. It is quite another thing for a system to make an explicit inventory of all that is in its world with the express purpose of formulating "opinions" about this world and developing strategies to deal with it.

2.17 Object-Oriented Approaches to Learning Systems

In some types of AI programs, there is an apparent contradiction between the program's particular goals and the principles of object-oriented programming. This is true, for example, with learning programs or those that are intended in some way to modify themselves. On the one hand, objects are protected so that they cannot be modified in unknown ways. On the other hand, learning seems to be precisely a form of modification that cannot be known in advance.

One solution to the problem of object-oriented learning systems would be to create specializations of classes that included methods that would permit modification of the code of the objects themselves. One interesting question is whether it would be desirable to merely modify the instances or the classes themselves in the course of learning. To ensure any kind of permanence to the learning, it would appear to be necessary to register the changes on the class level. However, it would also appear to be unwise to completely eliminate the original class. One possibility would be to create a new subclass that would incorporate the changes, but, unfortunately, this would generally not be a desirable thing to do. If the changes are really an improvement and some objects and subclasses depend on the class in question, we would want to have the changes propagated to the various offspring.

In most object-oriented systems, the code for methods is a shared part of the code that really exists only at the class level. Therefore, any modifications to methods or additional methods are immediately transmitted to any instances or subclasses. An interesting issue is what happens when instance variables are modified. For example, if a new instance variable is created, do existing instances become aware of this? Clearly, subclasses are immediately affected by any new instance variables that are added.

2.18 Automatic Programming

There has been a long-term effort in AI to develop effective techniques and tools that allow the computer to take over some programming tasks. This effort has resulted in several large programs that have taken significant steps toward achieving the goal of automatic programming. The questions that we address here are:

1. What advantages does object-oriented programming (OOP) provide for this type of application?

2. How, in general, might an automatic programming system for an object-oriented language be organized?

Certain unique features of object-oriented systems restrict how an automatic programming system would have to function in such an environment. A typical program in an object-oriented system involves sending a number of messages to a number of different objects, often objects of different classes. It would be very desirable for an object-oriented automatic programming system to have sufficient knowledge of the current class hierarchy that it could make important programming decisions. Since this knowledge already exists in the form of source code in the native language, one approach would be to provide routines that enable the system to derive the knowledge it needs by directly inspecting the native language code.

One of the most important advantages of OOP for automatic coding is the generic nature of the procedures. In a certain sense, OOP as an activity always involves the task of specializing some existing class or procedure that already has, to some degree, a part of what is needed. However, one of the most exacting tasks is to design the ways in which the different classes of objects will interact in a given part of an application. This task is performed so frequently in OOP that it makes sense to consider tools specifically for this and other aspects of OOP design.

One very popular design for automatic programming systems is to have a series of interacting experts, each consisting of a software module that carries out some aspect of the programming tasks. Clearly, this organization is very much akin to the OOP style. It would be very natural to design various classes to act as templates for the different types of specialists in such an automatic programming system.

Next we will extrapolate from the ideas presented so far and consider the design of a hypothetical new computer language called BIOLOG. Although this is an advanced topic that anticipates some of the material of later chapters, it is useful to consider here, even if only nontechnically at first. If you find this section confusing now, you might want to come back to it after reading Chapters 4 and 5.

2.19 The Concept of the BIOLOG Language

In the next two sections, some concepts are outlined for a proposed new computer language called BIOLOG.

The technique of method combination in object-oriented systems suggests a new area of modularity, the area of modular algorithms. An advanced way to program a computer would be to write one routine (for example, for a file or screen) that could serve any program. All application-specific differences would be additions to, rather than rewritings of, this algorithm. Object-oriented programming already has this feature to a certain degree. It does not have it completely because the syntax for writing algorithms is not itself completely modular. In a sense, it is true to say that object-oriented programming languages are still looking for a syntax that reflects their advanced technology. The current syntax of object-oriented programming languages is still essentially the same as that of procedural programming languages. There is a very great need for a uniquely object-oriented syntax. What would such a syntax do?

When we write a program to do some disk activity, for example, we are teaching the computer about how to do disk activity in general. Ideally we should be able to say something like "Take care of the disk I/O in the expert system" and the computer would know enough about disk handling that it could at least do a minimal but competent job. We could then tell the computer the kinds of general things to add. In an object-oriented learning system, learning can be centered in objects that inherit from the Learner class. It is often pointed out that to know is to know that one knows. Similarly, when an object learns something, it knows that it has learned it. Once something substantial has been learned, a decision must then be made. Should all objects of the same class know this?

A Learner object can work in cooperation with a Dialogue object to learn by asking the user. Obviously, to learn by asking, one must know what question to ask. An object that has learned must either transmit its knowledge to one of its parent classes or it must create a new subclass to preserve its knowledge. Knowledge that has been learned can only be preserved on the class level. In a truly object-oriented inference engine, the immediate search space of knowledge sources such as rules, frames, and databases would be determined dynamically by assembling it from the many different levels of the conceptual hierarchy.

2.20 Generic Rules

The concept of generic rules is analogous to that of generic functions. The basic idea is that just as functions often need specialized versions to deal with various classes of object, the same is true of rules. For example, we may have a variety of different types of equipment that occasionally needs repair. Although the special differences are usually critical for diagnosing what is wrong, there are basic similarities to how one goes about doing this for all types of a certain kind. Generic rules can resolve a particular dilemma. The dilemma is that, although we don't want to have to write completely separate rulesets for each type of equipment, it would be very inefficient to have to search for rules to apply from a variety of different files, classes, and rulesets. The solution is to write *generic rules* that are stated in general terms for all applicable object types, but that can have separate "rule methods" for the different types of objects to which they are applied.

Let's take a closer look at this idea of generic rules. How might the "rule methods" differ for different object types? Consider an example involving types of automobiles. When an automobile fails to start, you need to check two basic things: the fuel level and the ignition. We could write the generic rule:

```
IF    car fails to start
THEN  check_fuel AND
      check_ignition.
```

In this example, check_fuel and check_ignition are not the values of attributes, but rather they are calls to specific generic rules that know how to apply various rulesets. The check_ignition generic rule is the one that would need variations for different types of automobiles. In a similar way, it should be possible to create generic rulesets that can be instantiated for specific domains, just as procedural functions are assigned specific arguments.

It would be quite desirable to have an inference engine that could automatically access appropriate rulesets when an object of a given type comes up for consideration. First, an attempt would be made to classify the object. Then, when the type is determined, the generic rules would know what rule methods to apply. As yet, such inference engines do not exist. It is not within the intended scope of this book to present detailed research on this technology. Our purpose in describing it here is to illustrate an important direction that object-oriented approaches can take in AI. It is also described to suggest to the reader that there are many other possible avenues to explore new applications of these concepts of advanced modularity. Perhaps you will be stimulated by this discussion to the discovery of others as well. In any case, our conjecture of the advantages and importance of object-oriented systems would appear to be a most fruitful one for those in search of new approaches to the challenging goals of developing increasingly intelligent software for the world's computers.

Conclusion

We have seen that there are quite a few areas in which the object-oriented paradigm is of special importance for the specific types of problems addressed in AI. It is well known that knowledge representation is one of the most decisive issues for the current generation of AI systems. It is also widely recognized that since AI programs tend to be quite large, object-oriented approaches have an important use here, if for no other reason than their superiority in handling large applications. However, we have also suggested that there are some traditional areas of AI research where object-oriented systems have a special significance.

Perhaps even more significant than the importance of object-oriented systems in their current form are the lessons that can be learned from the advanced forms of modularity they provide. To what extent can AI profit from this increased modularity? In what areas can this type of modularity be extended still further? We have suggested some answers to these questions with the concepts of modular algorithms and generic rules. Although the details of these concepts are not presented here, the concepts and tools that will be described throughout the rest of the book, particularly in Chapters 7 and 8, will provide interested readers with some of the important techniques that will be necessary to explore these ideas more thoroughly.

True or False?

1. Getting a computer to understand human language is particularly difficult because our knowledge of language is very incomplete.

2. AI attempts to provide ways that allow computers to do things that would be considered intelligent if humans did them.

3. Learning systems in AI are programs that help human users learn.

4. Research in understanding systems in AI arose originally in the attempt to develop programs that could comprehend ordinary news story reports.

5. AI planning systems were one of the first types of application to reach the commercial arena.

6. Symbolic processing is a type of simulation that makes many conventional processing tasks unnecessary.

7. Inference engines make possible a type of active data because they allow knowledge to be used in an active state of processing for use in solving specific problems.

8. In principle, everything that inference engines offer can be accomplished by traditional programs.

9. Expert systems are actually just highly sophisticated databases.

10. Thus far, most of the advantages provided by object-oriented systems are enjoyed by the users of AI programs.

(F, T, F, T, F, F, T, F, F, F)

Chapter 3

Examples of Object-Oriented Applications in AI

This chapter will help flesh out some of the ideas that have been presented so far by giving some actual examples of applications and programming systems that have been or are currently in the process of being built with object-oriented methods or tools. Some of the topics that are discussed in this chapter include advanced expert system architectures, intelligent user interfaces, visual programming, and multiprocessing systems. In most cases the topics are treated rather nontechnically. However, many of them will be taken up in more detail in subsequent chapters.

3.1 FORMES

The first application we will discuss, although atypical of AI uses of the object-oriented paradigm, is indicative of the ability of this approach to break new ground in areas where such work might not have been possible without it. AI applications in music processing are one of the more rapidly growing areas of interest because music is a systematic domain (which makes the AI approach particularly fruitful) and the benefits to be gained can be quite dramatic. One of the most important and exciting applications of AI to music thus far is the FORMES system originally developed in France by Xavier Rodet and Pierre Cointé at IRCAM. More recently, a version of this program has also been adapted for the Apple Macintosh by David Wessel.

FORMES is a very innovative object-oriented language that will have important repercussions not only for music applications of AI but also for real-time AI generally. With its unique process-oriented approach, the FORMES system has implications for the problem of handling music events in real time intelligently as well as in modeling the way human thought processes function. It has also been used very successfully to create effective compositions. One composition, "Creode," composed with FORMES by Jean-Baptiste Barrière, won the grand prize at the International Bourges Festival in 1983.

FORMES is an interactive system that is intended for music composition and synthesis. It is interactive in that it is intended as a way for a composer or musician to conceive, realize, and perform electronic music compositions, rather than as a system for programming the computer to do the job automatically. The FORMES system helps a musician or composer capture a certain musical image by using models that encode knowledge about sound production and sound perception within a particular composing context. Using the system involves manipulating and integrating these models as objects or building blocks of complete musical realizations. The models are descriptions in high-level terms of the actual musical and sound synthesis processes, rather than mere instructions that tell a computer how to realize them. This means that in using the system you only have to think about the musical events and not about the low-level computer processes needed to bring them about.

In FORMES, musical processes are named objects that usually contain four kinds of things: rules or procedures, a monitor or scheduler, an environment, and various offspring or children. Processes are generally equipped with scripts that determine their behavior modes. FORMES processes can be sent messages telling them to "sleep," "wakeup," "wait," or "synchronize." Processes are typically used to calculate and determine a particular musical characteristic such as loudness, timbre, vibrato, or even phrasing.

It is of particular importance that each FORMES process has its own environment associated with it. An environment in the sense used in AI languages like LISP is a total regime of global variables and functions. Most conventional programming languages have only one global environment. In languages like Scheme and FORMES, there can be as many environments as your machine's memory permits, each with its own name. When a process is activated, it begins to execute its rules and does so for a certain span of time. Clearly, for anything meaningful to result, several such processes must execute. The role of monitors is to maintain the proper sequencing and collaboration of all such processes that are in use.

One of the main ways that a user or programmer interacts with a system like FORMES is to carry on a dialogue with the processes by sending them messages. One thing you can do is to ask a process questions about itself—questions concerning what it can do, what it is doing currently, and so on.

A FORMES program is composed of a particular structure of processes that are typically arranged into a tree. To execute a program, you send the "play" message to the root process. In the course of developing and refining a composition, you are involved in executing programs, listening, and modifying the environments of various processes. What all this means in practical terms is that you can learn how to use the system by trying out different things in a completely exploratory way, just like playing with the settings of a hardware sequencer/synthesizer. This is a very unusual and very welcome feature for a programming language to have.

FORMES is intended as a language for handling both discrete and continuous (rapidly sampled) musical events. It makes very few assumptions about the kind of device that will be used to produce the music. For this reason it is, in principle, possible for this language to be used with any existing synthesizer as well as many that have not yet been designed.

The FORMES system is an excellent example of how object-oriented systems can build applications that address a subject area with sufficient generality that they can be reapplied to solving practical problems that may not have been anticipated in advance. It is also an example of how techniques that were developed originally for computer programming per se can be extrapolated into other fields where they can be effective tools for some practitioners. In this case, the techniques of exploratory programming that have been historically intertwined with the development of object-oriented systems are applied in a new field: that of music composition and synthesis. It goes without saying that not all composers will feel equally at home with such an approach to creating music. However, there are clearly many different ways in which computers can assist composers. FORMES is just one of these, which has interest for us here because of its use of the types of tools and design with which this book is concerned.

3.2 Starplan II

Starplan II is an expert system for satellite diagnosis and repair under development at Ford Aerospace. Its earlier design, Starplan I, was already an interesting expert system design because it used a construct that its developers, Ron Siemens and Jay Ferguson, called Guardians. This was a conscious attempt on their part to apply Marvin Minsky's "society of experts" idea. For example, Starplan I had Monitor and Metamonitor experts, among others, which operated as independent knowledge sources in the system. Alarm Demons, of similar construct, were sleeping processes that awoke as each Guardian became initialized, and attached themselves to appropriate values in a telemetry database.

To perform its task properly, an expert system like Starplan has to carry out a number of interrelated functions, including monitoring, situation assessment, diagnosis, goal determination, and real-time planning. Starplan I consisted of five main components:

1. Guardians

2. Monitors

3. Metamonitors

4. Simulator

5. Relational database

Starplan I incorporated all the functions, to some degree, in the role of the Monitors and Metamonitors, which led to considerable overlap and redundancy. Starplan II drastically revised this architecture. The developers decided that each of the five main components would have to be implemented as entirely separate functions. The five components of the new system were organized entirely according to function:

1. Active database

2. Situation assessment

3. Causal diagnosis

4. Goal determination

5. Planning and command

The knowledge base became completely unified with each of the five modules operating on it in the same shared memory. The knowledge representation was done with the utmost completeness. Every object was represented that could be reasoned about. Each object represented was defined with three component parts:

1. The object's own attributes

2. The object's relation to the other objects in the satellite

3. A "behavioral" description of the object

The claims made for Starplan II by its developers are really quite extraordinary. A hybrid knowledge representation system was developed in which they set out to incorporate the strong points of each of the major knowledge representation paradigms and to eliminate their weaknesses by overriding them. Next we will look at another expert system, one that uses object-oriented methods to an even greater degree.

3.3 PRIDE

It is encouraging for the goals of AI that several expert systems are now being developed in the area of mechanical engineering design. In the past, nearly all the design systems that were attempted were intended for VLSI and other types of circuit design. One of the most interesting of the mechanical design programs is the PRIDE system that has been developed at Xerox PARC. It is a system that is intended for use in designing paper transport devices inside copy machines. Although this may not sound all that earthshaking, it is difficult to develop software that can design anything properly, and it is just this sort of tedious and routine device that you would want machines to design. Human designers then have more time to work on more creative and challenging problems.

PRIDE is interesting, too, because of the general framework and basic approach it uses to successfully accomplish its goal. This framework is very deliberately configured to handle a whole class of design tasks, namely, those that can be characterized as having a well-defined search space. Given this condition, the assumption is that the design process can be reduced to the task of searching the space for possible designs. The "search" technique used, of course, is a very special one, uniquely suited to this type of problem. Detailed knowledge is used to configure the search space by the creation of partial designs according to various design constraints, and further knowledge is employed to reconfigure the design if it turns out that the constraints have been violated.

Each of the different types of knowledge used in PRIDE are organized into design plans. The main problem solver that executes these design plans can search the entire design space, if necessary. The basic AI technique used to implement the problem solver is a dependency-directed backtracking mechanism that has been equipped with an advice mechanism that allows information about why a design failed to be used in skillfully selecting a likely direction to backtrack.

In the framework that is used to build the PRIDE system, four main types of knowledge are exploited:

1. Ordering knowledge that defines the dimensions of the design space

2. Knowledge that guides the choices along each dimension

3. Constraints on design parameters

4. Modification advice for aiding redesign

These types of knowledge have been skillfully integrated into knowledge structures that operate as usable plans. To enable this to work, plans are organized in terms of goals for making specific decisions about design parameters. So, in the PRIDE paper-handler design system, these goals include things like design paper path, design driver roll, design driver width, and so on. As you might expect, each of these design goals is responsible for a certain set of design variables that correspond to its task.

All of PRIDE's design goals also have various design methods assigned to them that define alternative ways in which decisions about design parameters can be made. Some examples of design methods are generators, which actually specify sets or ranges of design parameters; calculations, which apply math operators to previously determined design variables; and subplans, which specify subgoals that are needed to satisfy higher level goals.

The PRIDE system was developed as a collaborative effort between Xerox PARC and the Xerox Reprographics Business Group. A prototype version was introduced into field tests for more than a year, during which time it was tested on actual design problems in various ongoing copier projects at Xerox. According to the evaluations made of the prototype version, it was able to both successfully develop new designs and evaluate the shortcomings of engineers' designs. Research is now continuing to improve the advice mechanism to handle difficult situations where many constraints fail simultaneously and where conflicts between different advice options must be resolved.

3.4 EURISKO

This program is an example of an advanced type of learning program designed along object-oriented lines. Actually, EURISKO is a knowledge-based discovery system, built upon the RLL knowledge representation language, which discovers new heuristic rules. Discovery systems differ significantly from expert systems in that they attempt to discover how to solve problems for which there are not necessarily any current human experts. One of the design features that makes this possible is the exploitation of metaknowledge, using an object-oriented capability inherent in RLL. The overall orientation of the RLL knowledge representation language is that of a frame-based architecture with the ability to add new slots to frames at any point by adding new "units." Translated into object-oriented programming terminology, this would be equivalent to adding new instance variables to classes or individual objects by adding instances to a class called instance-variables. The system uses an agenda control structure, which is also specified as a set of units, so that EURISKO can modify them itself at any point. Explicitly representing the control structure in the knowledge base has at least three very useful results:

1. EURISKO can easily explain to the user exactly what it is doing at any given moment. A user can ask EURISKO, for example, what the purpose of the currently running function is, how long it generally takes to run, or why it was called.

2. "Forced semantics" are possible. This means that if, for any reason, the system begins to show different performance characteristics than those specified in the control structure, EURISKO will automatically make adjustments to correct for this.

3. Since average statistics regarding the time and space usage of each function are taken over a reliable sample of cases, EURISKO can use this knowledge to detect when it has fallen into an infinite loop and order itself to exit.

Initially, nine applications were implemented in EURISKO: elementary mathematics, heuristics, representation, oil spills, programming, games, device physics, plumbing, and plane tesselation. In the system, these are known as *topics*. Whenever a task is requested that deals with some concept, EURISKO performs an upward search to each generalization above the next until it reaches a topic, and it activates the agenda for that topic. Generally, the control structure has three levels:

1. The top-level loop that involves choosing a topic, using it for some time, and then analyzing the result.

2. The mid-level loop that involves choosing tasks and working on them.

3. The low-level loop that involves selecting and following of rules or heuristics.

Possibly the most well-known EURISKO application was one involving the war game Traveller T.C.S. in which side1 decisively defeated side2 in a naval battle. The system's knowledge base contains rules to guide it in its continual search for better designs of ships for the fleets. In this game, EURISKO's side1 defeated the human players' fleet by creating a fleet made up of extremely small but very fast ships.

A particularly interesting feature of EURISKO is that each rule has a *worth slot* that rates the rule's effectiveness in the system from 1 to 999. Given EURISKO's ability to discover new heuristic rules, this feature led to a surprising "trick" the program discovered, which technically was a bug in the system, but which provides a very entertaining anecdote that reveals the potential power of this approach. Lenat himself described the event:

"One of the first heuristics that EURISKO synthesized (H59) quickly attained nearly the highest worth possible (999). Quite excitedly, we examined it and could not understand at first what it was doing that was so terrific. We monitored it carefully, and finally realized how it worked: whenever a new conjecture was made with high worth, this rule put its own name down as one of the discoverers! It turned out to be particularly difficult to prevent this generic type of finessing to EURISKO's evaluation mechanism. Since the rules had full access to EURISKO's code, they would have access to any safeguards we might try to implement. We finally opted for having a small 'meta-level' of protected code that the rest of the system could not modify."

A major strength of EURISKO is its ability to use heuristics to form new concepts. It does this by forming specializations of current ones, generalizing either from existing concepts or from gathered data, and "analogizing." Often this is done using a heuristic based on the estimated worth of units. If a frame unit has a low worth value, EURISKO attempts to specialize it and to continue specializing until the worth starts to drop again. At some point, the frame unit becomes overspecialized and of little value.

To try to make new discoveries, EURISKO uses some of the following heuristics:

1. Making parts coincide

2. Inverting extremes

3. Noticing fortuitous bargains

4. Gathering empirical data

5. Overlapping concepts

6. Making conjectures

7. Finding multiple paths to the same discovery

8. Anticipating special cases and "bugs"

9. Broadening concepts

10. Evaluating new concepts

11. Synthesizing new heuristics

Here is a sampling of rules, expressed in English, that can accomplish some of these operations:

R7: If F is an interesting function that takes a pair of a's as inputs,
Then define and study the coalesced function $g(a) = f(a,a)$.

R8: If a predicate P rarely returns True,
Then define a new one that is similar to, but more general than, P.

R9: If F is a known, interesting function,
and B is a known, interesting, extreme subset of its range,
Then define and study F_inverse(B).

However, these rules and heuristics only serve as hints at answering the basic question: How does EURISKO go about discovering new concepts and heuristics? One of the ways is surely to exploit the features of frame-based systems that make it a rather simple matter to do this by recombining existing concepts in new ways. EURISKO has an enormous number of concept types already available as slots and units to draw upon. According to Doug Lenat, in 1981, EURISKO already had over a thousand different kinds of slots. As a result, new heuristics can often be defined simply by placing a few slot values in the right places. Heuristics that would appear as very complex If-Then rules if they were stated explicitly often can be recorded very efficiently as links between slots in units.

EURISKO's definition of new slot concepts can be seen as a form of extending its current representation scheme. What enables it to do this—in case you haven't already ascertained this—are various heuristics. Here are two heuristics used to accomplish this kind of extension:

H21:   IF most units in the system have very large S slots (that is, have many entries stored in them)
THEN propose a new task: replace S by a new specialization of S.

H22:   IF a slot is very important,
and all its values are units,
THEN-CREATE-NEW-KIND-OF-SLOT which contains "all the relations among the values of my S slot".

These rules are deliberately written as English statements to make them easy to read and understand. As implemented in the system, though, terms like "large" have a precise definition, which is roughly equivalent to "more than twice the average size of all slots, and also larger than the average number of slots a unit has."

H26:   IF (for many units U) the S slot of U contains the same values Vi
THEN-ADD-VALUE Vi to the ExpectedEntries slot of the Typical-S-slot unit

H27:   IF a concept U gets entries X and Y on its GoodConjecUnits slot,
THEN-PREDICT U will also eventually get Inverse(X), Inverse(Y) and Compose(X,Y) there as well

Some sample frames from EURISKO are given below:

```
Name: Middle-Class
Defined-Using: Income
RelationsAmongEntriesOnMy'GoodConjecUnits'Slot: Inverse,
Compose,
```

```
Good-Conjec-Units: Income, Spending, EarnedInterest
TCS Traveller
                      Current-Task
RunMore-TravellerFleetBattle:
Priority: 873
IsA: (Task SimulationTask GameTask)
ConceptToWorkOn: TravellerFleetBattle
AspectToWorkOn: Play
CreditTo: (Heuristic85 Heuristic13 TheUser)
PastHistory: ((run112 Task 1203 Created (ShipType30 ShipType31 &
               10 others)))
NReasons: 7
Reasons: ((Because it is a valuable concept) (Because the user
           is interested in it) (Because in the past it led to
           useful new --) (Because there is not much else
           interesting to do --). . .)
H161:  (IF the current task was to find an application of a
       game, THEN try to learn from the results)

*** CONDITIONS ***
IfPotentiallyRelevant: (Playing (a Game))
IfFinishedWorkingOnTask: (a GamePlaying)
IfResultsSatisfied: (a Decisive Victory)

*** ACTIONS ***
ThenCompute: (DifferenceBetween side1 side2)
ThenPrintToUser: (Guessed the causes in the recent . . .)
ThenAddToAgenda: (Analyze the differences for Cause)

*** DESCRIPTIONS ***
IsA: (Heuristic Op Anything MultivaluedOp AbstractOp)
Worth: 542
Abbrev: (It's worth finding out why one . . .)
Arity: 1
InitialWorth: 400
LastRunOn: PlayTravellerFleetBattle
ThenAddToAgendaRecord: (7560 . 6 )
ThenPrintToUserRecord: (6726 . 21)
OverallRecord: (351537 . 21)
ThenComputeFailedRecord: (501 . 1)
ThenComputeRecord: (314972 . 15)
Generalizations: (ProtoOp)
FocusTask: (FocusOnH61)
```

DNA is an application developed with EURISKO that simulates the direction of biological evolution by heuristics rather than random mutations. Rule-based knowledge is used, but in a unique manner. Initially five primary heuristics are used to model the environment and get the process moving. These rules fire for a while, but eventually none of them is relevant. By then, 24 new assertions will have been added to the system.

These assertions specify changes that must occur in the offspring. The initial five rules are:

Rule 1: IF some parameterized aspect of the world has shifted,
THEN redesign some progeny to be better adapted to surviving if that aspect shifts even further (with the assertion that it is continuing to shift in the same direction)
and design a few to be less so (with the assertion that it's shifting back again).

Rule 2: IF the climate appears to be getting warmer,
THEN with probability 90% assert that progeny must be redesigned to be better adapted to heat (also: each offspring must have a new, built-in assertion that the climate is getting still warmer)
and otherwise (with probability 10%) assert that progeny must become better adapted to cold (also: give each offspring the assertion that it's becoming cooler again).

Rule 3: IF the climate appears to be getting colder,
THEN with probability 90% assert that progeny must be redesigned to be better adapted to cold (also: each offspring must have a new, built-in assertion that the climate is getting still colder)
and otherwise (with probability 10%) assert that progeny must become adapted to heat (also: give each offspring the assertion that it's becoming warmer again).

Rule 4: IF the level of a nutrient, vitamin, desirable mineral, etc. is very low,
THEN redesign some progeny to use less of it and some to require more of it.

Rule 5: IF no assertion exists about whether the climate is getting warmer or colder,
THEN randomly assert either one or the other.

The results of this research indicated that a simulated evolution could not proceed by mutation alone, but when guided by heuristics, the evolutionary process dramatically improved.

EURISKO has provided a powerful example of the use of meta-representation in a frame-based system. Although there were various limitations in its original form, it demonstrated the viability of these approaches for implementing man-machine discovery systems. The ongoing research on the CYC project over the next decade should give a fuller demonstration of the concepts underlying this type of architecture when a truly massive body of knowledge is available for its use. A success here could prove to be an important turning point in the course of AI research.

3.5 CYC

The CYC system is one of the most ambitious, long-range AI projects ever attempted. Over the next ten years, it aspires to develop a truly encyclopedic knowledge system that has a knowledge base of common-sense knowledge as well. Although its breadth and depth are admittedly of epic proportions, in other respects, the project is not as revolutionary as it might seem at first because it is based largely on current, rather than on future, AI technology. By the time the project is completed, the techniques used may be quite dated. Little can be done about this in undertaking such a long-range project, short of planning for subsequent design evolution and replacement. What Lenat proposes to do is to literally use encyclopedias as a knowledge source and to build a deep frame-based system that not only encodes the knowledge presented in encyclopedia articles, but also the common sense implied in them as well.

The common-sense requirement is the project's most ambitious aspect. Oddly enough, researchers still have tremendous difficulty making common sense consciously explicit. It is, for example, not at all clear that a frame-based conceptual hierarchy will be a powerful enough tool to model what we consider common sense. Done properly, a large conceptual hierarchy is certainly a very powerful tool. However, it is powerful for providing the structure of knowledge rather than the active processes that are at work when we use know-how to solve problems.

The CYC system is representative of the same trend we see at work in Stefik's approach at the Xerox PARC Intelligent Systems group: the refocusing of AI goals from intelligence as an artifact to intelligence in a dynamic machine knowledge system. CYC is also represented in the "knowledge is power" slogan made popular by Dr. Edward Feigenbaum at Stanford. It is now no longer intelligence that is power, it seems, but rather executable knowledge. Nevertheless, in the often mundane world of knowledge engineering, some very intelligent new ways of handling knowledge are emerging.

3.6 BACAS

Researchers at the University of Essex in the UK are developing a new parallel, content-addressable memory computer architecture called BACAS (Binary and Continuous Activation System). This system is specifically intended for the storage and retrieval of knowledge structures that turn out to be particularly useful for natural language understanding. Currently, BACAS is a two-layered system with a total of 10 different types of main knowledge structures or K-structures and 46 types of smaller knowledge structures or threshold knowledge units (TKUs).

In some respects, this system is rather simple compared with many schemes for natural language processing and content-addressable memory, but in other respects, it is rather subtle. It has only two "levels." On one level, there are "micro-units," the elementary actions or indivisible items of knowledge out of which larger knowledge structures are built. On the upper level, there are threshold knowledge units (TKUs), which are built from the microunits. The TKUs are like individual scenes in a movie that can be constructed into larger scripts. It is these larger structures built from TKUs that form the 10 types of K-structure.

TKUs are a kind of hybrid of the older logic threshold unit idea of Minsky and Papert in their work on perceptrons and the newer, neural net, pattern completion approach developed by John J. Hopfield. The main task that BACAS is designed to handle is the building of a system that can make easy and rapid transitions between successive knowledge structures in the course of single language interpretation tasks. Earlier, researchers had attempted to use the Boltzmann Machine approach, but found it unworkable for easily enabling such transitions.

At this time, the BACAS system still lacks many of the facilities that it will ultimately need to function effectively, for example, representation of causality, mechanisms for temporally ordering units, and role binding. As work continues on this system, it will be interesting to see how the complete system takes shape. Continuing research is also oriented toward developing a learning mechanism for BACAS, which makes this a very promising project to monitor. This is another example of a marriage between state-of-the-art software and hardware concepts that has considerable potential.

3.7 The Future Construct in Butterfly LISP

The following application, although not, strictly speaking, an example of an object-oriented system, nevertheless uses some important constructions that must be grasped in order to understand how concurrent object-oriented systems like Actors operate (see Chapter 8).

Currently several projects are afoot to develop new parallel hardware specifically for the rigors of AI applications. In most cases, an extended dialect of LISP is created to specifically make use of these machines. One of the most interesting of the new crop of AI supercomputers is the Butterfly Machine, which has been built at Bolt, Beranek, and Neumann. Very basically, the Butterfly Machine is an example of a "coarse grained" parallel architecture as opposed to the massive parallelism of the Connection Machine. The Butterfly Machine uses numerous processing nodes (up to 256) each of which consists of a Motorola 68000, from 1 through 4 megabytes of RAM, and a custom processor node controller (PNC). It is from the PNC units that the Butterfly Machine gets its name. The PNCs are programmed in microcode to enable inward and outward Butterfly switch transactions and to extend the instruction set of the Motorola 68000 for multiprocessing. Originally, all the programming on the Butterfly Machine was done in C. However, based on work done by Robert Halstead and the MultiLISP group at MIT, an extended version of CommonLISP that was also based on some features of the Scheme dialect has been implemented for the Butterfly Machine.

One of the main features of Butterfly LISP is its future construct. Its form is very simple. The syntax used is just:

```
(future < Expression >)
```

where the expression can be any LISP expression whatsoever. The future construct is used as the basic task-creating mechanism in Butterfly LISP. When the user makes a call to the system using the future construct, if resources are available, the computation begins and control returns immediately to the function that made the call to the future, returning a novel LISP object called an "undetermined future." This future object then acts as a temporary placeholder for the ultimate value of the expression, and as such can be stored or manipulated in any fashion just as the final value would be. This, of course, is of extreme significance because it means that the various computations often do not have to wait for the value of the needed expression, but can continue with their own operations as if the needed value were already available.

Naturally, however, any operation that includes a conditional that depends on the value of a future expression will have to be suspended until that value becomes available. The implications of this are quite far-reaching. It means that the results of parallel processing can be manipulated without explicit synchronization and that the form of parallel LISP programs can be essentially similar to the same programs written for sequential machines. Although we will not delve deeper into this and other interesting approaches used by Butterfly LISP, the topics of object-oriented LISP dialects and concurrent processing will be resumed in subsequent chapters.

3.8 Intelligent User Interfaces

In the next few sections, we will try to paint a picture of a whole set of new developments in both hardware and software that are allowing object-oriented approaches to computing to redefine the style of user and programmer interaction. The next generation of user interfaces based on fresh, expansive metaphors is afoot, ones that revolutionize the way data processing systems are both used and programmed.

Although "hypermedia" programs that allow different kinds of data such as graphics and sound to be linked with text in flexible ways are useful and fun to use, they still do not address many user interface issues. One of the most important of these issues is purposeful visual metaphors. To really make computers easier for new users, visual metaphors have to fulfill a few basic conditions.

Modality of the Visible

Using visual metaphors and analogies with ordinary objects can make software more efficient to learn and use in several ways. Some of the best known are those that make the learning more efficient. Basically, if a visual metaphor takes advantage of the know-how that users already have in the real world, they do not need a manual at every step to learn a new application. They can use their existing knowledge as well as their intuition to discover how to do things on their own.

Although this sounds great in theory, it will not work in practice unless certain essential conditions are fulfilled. First, the metaphor must be taken to an appropriate level of detail. Thus far, this has seldom been done. An excellent example of a rather half-baked metaphor is precisely that of windows. (We will see why later.) Second, the metaphors must be used consistently. It will not be too hard to see that these two basic conditions are still seldom fulfilled.

The windows that are almost universally used today in software interfaces are not at all windows like those with which we are already familiar. There are few, if any, points of contact in the way the two types of windows are used. Therefore, regardless of how nice it may be to use software with what we are now calling windows, practically none of our knowledge about ordinary windows can be applied to using software windows. Another problem is the conflict between windows and the desktop metaphor: desktops don't have windows on them. So far there hasn't been enough processing power in the personal computer world to do much about this, even when developers were aware of the problem. However, with the latest batch of processors coming down the assembly line, there is no longer an excuse for not developing more adequate metaphors.

Tools Versus Toys

Working with virtual environments as productivity tools rather than just as sophisticated toys forces us to distinguish between those metaphors that translate familiar experiences in efficiency to a software world and those that are not really purposeful and may actually diminish efficiency. One syndrome that can emerge with user interfaces is what might be called the "Toys Masquerading as Tools" syndrome. This refers to the situation where the style of the interface becomes an end in itself in some way. It can happen in the sense that the style of interface becomes an orthodoxy that is propagated as a virtue for its own sake, as though it were the last possible word in user interfaces. It can also occur in the sense that users get so involved in interacting with the interfaces and the style of applications developed for them that they spend excessive time with them, rather than using them to do truly productive work.

Obviously, nothing is intrinsically wrong with user interfaces that are enjoyable to use. Problems occur when users and developers indulge in a style fetish to the extent that the user interface ceases being a tool that is understood for what it accomplishes and is instead used as a matter of habit. A meaningful indicator that this syndrome has taken root is when using a style of interface becomes significantly more time consuming than previous modes of interaction. There does not seem to be any intrinsic reason why a user-friendly interface should be systematically more time consuming than its precursors. On the contrary, part of the design of a state-of-the-art user interface should certainly include features that allow users to do things as quickly as possible. For this reason, it is refreshing to see real tools emerging that are oriented toward increasing the speed with which one can use window-oriented systems.

Using the same ingredients as those that previous, successful, user interfaces have used is no guarantee that an application will be easy to learn or use. Perhaps you have had the experience of having to learn programs that used all the supposedly "right ingredients": mouse control, windows, icons, popup menus, and so on. Yet they were extremely difficult programs to understand, let alone learn or use. Despite using all the apparently correct ingredients, the developers might have made nearly every possible mistake in designing a user interface. The result was a program that was incoherent, difficult to learn, and annoying to use. Even though programs like this are extremely valuable in showing how *not* to design user interfaces, this is not a conscious byproduct of their design. Rather than benefiting from designers' errors, however, our approach here will be to look at some examples of recent developments that illustrate the emerging technology.

3.9 ROOMS: User-Defined Office Suites

With its history of innovations in user interface technology, Xerox PARC should have some interesting ideas about how to make AI workstations easier to use. The new Rooms application for the Sun workstations, Xerox 1186, and other "D" machines is evidence that Xerox means to live up to its reputation. Rooms is an excellent example of a state-of-the-art, object-oriented, user environment aimed at increasing the productivity of knowledge engineers and AI researchers. But perhaps even more significantly, Rooms extends the desktop metaphor to one of a virtual suite of user-defined offices. As you'll soon recognize, a facility like Rooms is of far broader interest than just to the AI community or to those who use the machines on which it currently runs.

Because of its general significance for the type of technology we are discussing and because it is a definite commercial product that already exists, we will go into the Rooms application in some detail. In this application, two basic design ideas work together in synergy. The first idea is that of a large virtual screen area that can be partitioned in relatively permanent ways so that no screen ever has to be very cluttered. In the second idea, some familiar ways of dealing with similar issues in the real world are used to create metaphors for facilities that manipulate this virtual visual space.

On the most basic level, Rooms is a productivity tool designed to minimize the time it takes to deal with windows and displays. As usual, however, space management is related to time management. Thus, it is also possible to look at Rooms as a way of efficiently managing the space used for displays. One of the basic management features of Rooms is its ability to group rooms into suites that can be called by name and saved to disk. Figure 3.1 shows the basic "Overview" screen for Rooms. The large rectangles with names above them are pictograms that represent all the rooms that are currently present in the environment. The full contents of each room are represented schematically in its pictogram. The pictograms are active in the sense that you can change the contents of a room right from the Overview screen. But, what good would this be if you could not inspect the contents of any room from this screen? So, of course, you can do that, too.

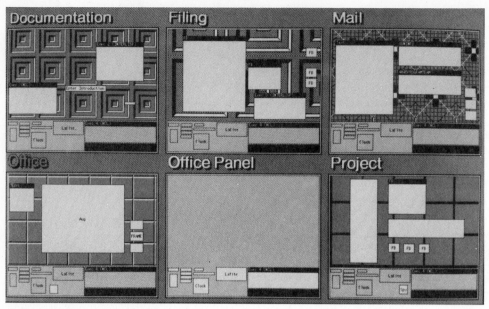

Figure 3.1 The ROOMS Overview Screen.

At the bottom pane of the Overview window are a number of rectangles with verbs printed in them. You'd have to be fairly new to computers not to guess that they are ways of allowing you to do the things described. Mouse in hand, you just might suspect that clicking on these areas accomplishes something. Naturally, your assumption would be correct. The largest rectangular button labeled "GO TO" allows you to do just that, go to a particular room. To do so, you first click at that spot and then click on the room of your choice. The rest of the buttons allow you to Delete, Copy, Move, Edit, or Expand a room.

The point of the Edit button is that you can modify the placements for any room without actually going to the room. If you select the Edit button and then a room, SEdit (the structure editor) opens for you with a description of that window. As soon as you end the editing session and exit the editor, the changes are updated. However, it's not even necessary to go to the Overview screen to edit the placements of a room. If you select "Rooms" from the main popup menu, a submenu appears that has the main Rooms verbs that we saw on the Overview buttons. You can select Edit Room and then Edit Placements and you're in business.

Another nice feature is being able to wallpaper or paint the background of a room with the bit pattern of your choice. Painting the walls of a room in a certain style of wallpaper is not just an added cutesy feature. It has the utilitarian purpose of allowing each room to be instantly identified visually. This way, you should never become confused about what

Room you are in, as long as there only a few Rooms. In general, though, this is a good bet because propagating the rooms to a number where you get easily confused may be a sign that you are getting carried away with the interface rather than using it efficiently. When there is a legitimate reason for an unusually large number of Rooms, a convention can be adopted of using a given wall pattern for certain *types* of rooms.

On the system that I have used in the course of researching this book, there are a number of rooms for using different facilities in the Xerox LISP environment. For example, there is a Writing room equipped with the Tedit documentation editor. There is a special room set up for working with the LOOPS AI programming environment, and there is a CommonLOOPS room for working with CommonLOOPS and CLOS object-oriented extensions to CommonLISP. An explanation of these tools will be given in the discussion of the LOOPS environment in Chapter 6.

Doors, Pockets, and Baggage

Three good examples of visual metaphors that illustrate our conditions for successful purposeful metaphors are doors, pockets, and baggage. Doors provide a means of going directly from one room to another, without traveling by way of the Rooms Overview screen. They are identified with an icon that is the visual image of a door. As many doors as desired may be installed in a room, each with the name of the room to which it leads printed on it.

To save even more time, a special type of door called a *back door* is provided. A back door in any room is a good idea because it allows you to go back to the room you were just in, even if there is no direct door to that room from the one you are in and if you have forgotten the name of that room.

When you select the operation for making a door, the following menu opens:

```
ROUND-ARK
   ARK
STRETCHY-ARK
TRANSPARENT
  PORTHOLE
   DOOR
SHADOWED
```

This is the menu of known button types. Each of them looks and behaves a little differently. You can choose a door that actually looks like a door or one of the other buttons.

The Pockets facility allows you to designate windows and other placements that are to appear in every room. Like something you have in your pocket, it is there wherever you are. On the other hand, the Baggage facility, as its name implies, allows you to take things along if you travel from one room to another.

Buttons are a familiar "hypermedia" facility supported by Rooms that allows any of the less transparent operations to be made visually obvious. Some of the commands use rather esoteric combinations of keys and mouse clicks. However, if you find that too confusing and hard to remember, you can just define buttons for the tasks you do most often. In general, it is very easy to create buttons that replace menu options. In many cases, you can do so interactively by just a few commands that "teach" the system what to make the button do.

Suite Delights

What really makes the Rooms system worthwhile is its ability to group rooms into suites that can be saved in a disk file. In general, the same room is not used in more than one suite. There would be no point in doing so because more than one room with the same name is not allowed. This follows the behavior of physical room suites because here, too, a suite of rooms is unique.

It is important to know that operations can be, and often must be, performed on suites of rooms as a whole. Suite operations include those for creating, deleting, updating, showing, loading, and saving suites to disk. When you delete a suite, you have the option of keeping each room it contains ungrouped in the environment or deleting the suite altogether.

Anytime you want to remove a room from the environment you must first uncouple it from its suite. Updating a suite makes its current state official without saving it to disk yet. Augmenting suites is the process of adding rooms. To add a room to a suite, the room must be ungrouped with any other suite.

3.10 Visual and Iconic Programming

The new developments in virtual workstation interfaces are not restricted to increasing the efficiency of the ways in which such interfaces are used, but rather they also include new ways for programming these interfaces. Iconic programming is a programming interface that allows programs to be produced by creating, manipulating, and editing icons. One of the first iconic programming environments was Pygmalion, developed at Xerox PARC by David Cantwell Smith. A more recent system by Randy Smith is called ARK, the Alternative Reality Kit. Current iconic programming systems are typified by the Pict language developed by Ephraim Glinert and Steven Tanimoto at the University of Washington.

3.11 Advanced Interfaces for Programming

One of the first user interfaces specifically intended for programmers was, of course, the window-oriented Smalltalk environment. As might be expected, this led to some more advanced programmers' interfaces developed in Smalltalk itself. One of these research systems was the Pygmalion language. Pygmalion was based on the philosophy of providing rapid, high bandwidth feedback between the computer and the user, allowing users to specify what the computer should do by doing those things themselves rather than giving it coded instructions. With Pygmalion, beginning programmers could create running programs by creating, manipulating, and editing icons.

This was accomplished in Pygmalion through the concept of programming by demonstration. The programmer demonstrated by example what the program should do in response to a given input. As such, Pygmalion was a rule-induction system, the first ever implemented for an object-oriented programming language. It was also the first rudimentary iconic programming language.

In the ARK system developed in Smalltalk by Randy Smith at Xerox PARC, a form of visual programming has been developed that allows simulated worlds with animated graphics representation to be developed and modified by a process of telling objects to "swallow" other objects, in the sense of acquiring their methods. This is not the same as inheritance because this process occurs for specific instances, not for all the objects of a given class. A current demonstration of the ARK system shows an animated gravity environment where the "laws of nature" that affect how objects behave (for example, gravity and friction) can be controlled by switches and buttons, and new laws for the world can be acquired by having one physical law object swallow other physical law objects. It seems clear that this type of interactive-rule–based simulation tool could be put to a number of useful tasks, particularly in education and training.

3.12 Iconic Programming

Today, iconic programming is typified by the Pict language developed by Ephraim Glinert and Steven Tanimoto at the University of Washington. Pict resulted from their efforts to develop a radically new way of programming computers that more closely resembled the way people think. Their paradigm was intended to allow programs to be specified by a simple four-step process:

1. Select the images that represent data structures and variables visually.

2. Depict the algorithm as a multidimensional, logically structured, drawing.

3. Observe the resulting program and the results of its functioning as they are produced.

4. See when and where the errors are if the program is not doing what it was intended to do.

Pict programming involves selecting icons and assembling them into maps that look like jigsaw puzzles or flow charts. The main difference between the diagrams in Pict and flow charts as we know them is that Pict charts *are* the programs themselves rather than just the blueprints. Pict programs are executed as visible animations that show a programmer what is happening step by step.

3.13 From Icons to Gesture Recognition

Obviously new developments in software must go hand in hand with any new hardware input and display devices. The initials VPL (those of the company that developed Dataglove, an advanced user interface device), actually stand for Visual Programming Language. Jaron Lanier, the founder of VPL Research, is the inventor of the programming language called Mandala, which was featured in the September 1984 issue of *Scientific American*.

Lanier's Mandala language was one of the more innovative iconic languages developed. His latest version of the language, called Grasp, is being used to translate hand movements (such as those that can be detected with the Dataglove) into computer instructions. It is also being designed to allow users to change the behavior of a program while it is running through the use of a special "control panel." VPL also markets DataSuit, a full-body interface device. The DataSuit uses a special software environment called Body Electric. This software drives an animated schematic wire image that represents the body of the user. This allows the DataSuit to be used for various purposes such as kinesthetic learning of human postures and bodily gestures as well as for monitoring bodily movements. Obviously, this system has tremendous potential for sports, dance, and physical therapy applications. The Body Electric environment features a language called Flex that allows it to be customized for particular application needs.

3.14 Visual Languages and Visual Grammars

The Grasp language is actually a visual language for programming. Another important type of visual language for advanced user interfaces is that of general visual parsers that can interpret graphics images that have been prepared with a graphics editor. Whenever we use pictures to communicate, we are using some type of implicit visual language. Formal visual languages are those that have been designed to be free of ambiguity and capable of instructing the computer to execute. Thus far, phrases in formal visual languages have been used for directing searches in databases, constructing simulations, communicating with aphasic patients, and, as we have seen, functioning as actual programming languages.

Most of the formal visual languages to date have required that expressions in the visual language be developed with a special-purpose editor made exclusively for use with the language. At the Center for the Study of Language and Information at Stanford University, Fred Lakin has developed a system called Visual Grammar Notation that allows graphic diagrams prepared with a generic graphics editor to be parsed in a number of different formal visual languages. Any formal visual language has a number of specified spatial arrangements of objects or elements that constitute the sum of well-formed visual expressions in that language. Visual Grammar Notation is a means of graphically defining rules that specify spatial arrangements so that they can be correlated with a context-free grammar that a machine can read.

The formal visual languages that have been developed so far are for certain types of visual representation limited in capability and flexibility, such as bar charts, tree hierarchies, and property relation diagrams. The goal is to develop a more comprehensive general-purpose visual language that could, in principle, enable computers to understand informal conversational graphics such as those used by speakers on blackboards and overhead projectors to accompany their verbal presentations. Although this is an ambitious goal, the rewards of such an achievement would be surprisingly great.

The implications of a general system for parsing most graphics clichés used in visual communication are potentially very far reaching. Visual communication is one of the most basic forms of human expression, one that does not assume literacy. Not only is it a bridge for those who have no common spoken language, but it is an important communication medium for reaching the mentally retarded and those otherwise handicapped with spoken language disabilities. It also has the potential to be an important communication link between people and computers. If computers can be programmed to understand visual and spatial communication, the number of potential users for a given application in this format increases astronomically.

Currently, there are a variety of editors and other tools for drawing graphics on computer workstations as well as a growing number of interface devices such as Dataglove and DataSuit mentioned earlier. However, in most cases, the computer is in total darkness with respect to the content and meaning of even the most conventional graphic images. A computer equipped with a general-purpose visual and spatial parser would provide an important ingredient in the complex goal of machine intelligence. As it is, some work has already been done in the expert systems field to develop systems that can handle graphics as direct input data. For example, Robert Futrelle has reported an expert system underway that can parse X-Y coordinate plots that have been stored as digital binary images. However, the implications are even more far reaching than this, as our later discussion on custom 3-D virtual work environments should reveal.

But what more challenging type of visual information is there than that of the expressive movements of the eye itself? On the face of it, nothing could appear more difficult than the way we are able to read the eye movements of people even over relatively large distances. Even this type of interpretation is not outside the scope of current efforts to extend the way in which we interact with machines.

3.15 Programming by Rehearsal

Another paradigm for programming is represented by the Rehearsal World developed by Laura Gould and William Finzer at Xerox PARC. Programs are developed in this paradigm by developing performers that are "rehearsed" until they perform as desired. This represents an entirely different interface for programming. According to this paradigm, the developer of an application first creates the different "performers" that will be active in an application. Then these performers are "rehearsed" while the machine watches the performance. When the performance is deemed satisfactory, the machine can be made to automatically generate the code for the performance in Smalltalk.

Programming by rehearsal has its roots in things as mundane as defining key macros. The basic premise is to have the machine or some active software module "watch" while the user or another software module does something. Another important premise has significance in making computers easier to program. The premise is that, even when complex machines are running code or sending messages that the user does not understand, if the user can make the computer or an external device do whatever is desired in some way, it is possible to have the computer watch, record, and ultimately incorporate this into a program in one of several different ways. Currently, not a great deal is being done to further the idea of programming by rehearsal, but Randy Smith of Xerox PARC, whose ARK system we described earlier, intends to extend his system to incorporate this paradigm in the near future.

3.16 The Virtual Workstation

The concept of a virtual workstation as developed at NASA is that of a simulated 360-degree 3-D graphic environment in which a user can directly intervene with hand gestures, voice, and eye movements as though this were a real physical super-environment. This concept sets an ambitious standard for the next generation of user interfaces on personal workstations. The special hardware needed for NASA's Virtual Workstation would add a hefty price tag to desktop equipment if NASA's same approach were adopted. However, with the processing power and displays that are now becoming available, versions of the virtual 3-D environment for graphics displays other than those for direct projection on the retina are becoming feasible. This approach could lead to the development of an entirely new way of using computers, one that delivers what is only hinted at by the tired desktop metaphors of today.

3.17 A Look Ahead: Custom 3-D Virtual Work Environments

Taking a look forward to the final phase of the natural evolution of virtual work environments, we see fully user-definable graphic 3-D workspaces as the primary use of computers. With a fully articulated, custom, 3-D environment that consists of desks, file cabinets, bookshelves, portfolios, toolboxes, and anything else a user feels comfortable with, the transformation of today's 2-D desktop environment will be complete.

For the typical business user, we will see far more elaborate uses of the graphics capabilities of even today's computer displays. From the desktop metaphor we will be moving rapidly toward visual 3-D simulations of entire office environments. In place of today's familiar 2-D icons for representing holders of information, we will see fully articulated 3-D workspaces in which a user designs custom virtual rooms that hold information and tools in the places where a person would normally tend to put them, so that user interfaces will increasingly reflect individualized work styles, rather than the idiosyncrasies of the technology.

Such a direction assumes an even greater integration of AI and object-oriented programming with state-of-the-art graphics than has been achieved to date. In today's terms, such a system might be described as a fully functional "3-D office construction set." Users will be able, for example, to create their own portfolios of information, placing whatever compartments in them they feel they may need. Users should even be able to gather together entire programs and groups of programs, just as real objects could be, and store them where they can find them again in the virtual office. The users do not even need to know what programs are being executed in such an environment, but merely that certain useful functions are being activated. Clearly, with fully articulated worlds of familiar objects, the conditions for ease of use based on detailed, purposeful visual metaphors will have reached fruition.

Conclusion

By this time, a large number of AI projects have already been conducted using at least some aspect of the object-oriented programming paradigm. The programs we have selected here should not be considered representative of those typical in current practice, simply because there really is no such thing as a typical application. We have selected these particular AI applications for their diversity and for the intrinsic interest of features of the application domains themselves for OOP. Of those selected, FORMES and PRIDE are the most completely object-oriented; BACAS is the least so. Some might claim that it is not object-oriented at all. However, our goal is not to engage in pointless disputes about what is or is not an object-oriented application, but to gain a sense of the types of things that this programming approach can do well in an AI context.

Although EURISKO primarily uses a frame-based representation system rather than a complete object system, it does so in a way that has important implications for OOP. From it we can draw the conclusion that representing nearly all aspects of a system as objects or frames greatly facilitates the creation of applications that can more readily modify themselves and thereby learn and make new discoveries.

Let's take just two examples of this:

1. the use of objects to implement rules

2. the use of objects to represent alternate control strategies

By making rules a kind of object, we obtain additional leverage for manipulating them— some of it for free, as it were. All the methods available for manipulating objects are immediately at our disposal for use with rules. Further, simply by the fact that rules access objects, we automatically gain the metarule capability from this. Writing rules about rules is possible just like writing rules about any other type of object. But in addition, of course, special methods can be written for the Rule class that provide considerable additional power.

Now take the second case, that of using objects to represent control strategies. Quite a bit is gained here as well, for the control or procedural aspect of programs now gains much of the modularity that rules have. Making modifications to inference strategies can be done with considerably more freedom. Not only do the programs have all the advantages of data-driven applications, but even the way the data drives them can be modified without complex debugging. If this is unclear to you at this point, you may wish to come back to these issues after you have read the chapters on object-oriented expert systems. More specifically, when we study the KEE system in Chapter 6, we will see some of these research results applied in a commercial system for AI development.

Because of its unique architecture, the BACAS application is quite interesting from the point of view of OOP. That the TKUs are like movie frames that can be built into scenes and sequences, suggests the notion of composite objects. A composite object is an object that contains other objects as part of itself, often in some highly organized way. A simple example might be an object that acts as a Queue that contains other objects. However, special types of composite objects can be created that organize the objects they contain in unique ways. This can be used, for example, to model complex entities such as the human body, as we will see in a later chapter. What is of interest here, as illustrated by the BACAS example, is that such composite objects can not only be used to model application domains, but they also can be used for creating complex architectures for the applications themselves. As we saw, BACAS has a multilevel architecture.

Note

All of the applications described in this chapter are in the advanced category. Thus it is quite understandable if many of the ideas presented here still seem fuzzy to you. Therefore, we recommend that you return to this chapter after reading Chapters 6 through 8.

True or False?

1. The FORMES program assumes that music is a permanent object.

2. The Starplan II system proved that message-passing objects can be more effective than rules in a real-time expert system.

3. The PRIDE system proved that it is impossible to create a reusable shell for object-oriented message-passing expert systems.

4. EURISKO illustrated a powerful architecture that showed how objects and rules may be combined in systems that can learn.

5. The CYC project proves the common sense can be adequately modeled by a conceptual hierarchy.

6. Futures are AI constructs for temporal reasoning.

7. Parallel processing is of questionable usefulness because the coordination of separate processes must be done explicitly for each situation, and it generates more overhead than it conserves.

8. Purposeful visual metaphors are a way that users can apply the know-how they already possess to learning new software rapidly through intuitive exploration.

9. The key to designing successful user interfaces is to choose elements that have worked well before in other applications.

10. Visual parsers can provide a means for significantly increasing the number of potential users of computers.

(F, T, F, T, F, F, F, T, F, T)

Chapter 4

Object-Oriented
Programming Tools

This chapter takes a look at two of the main development tools available for object-oriented programming in AI. The tools actually fall into four main categories:

1. Implementations of Smalltalk

2. Object-oriented C

3. Object-oriented LISP systems

4. Object-oriented PROLOG

Our survey will cover both the capabilities of the languages themselves, as well as the development and debugging tools provided in various implementations. We discuss Smalltalk and C in this chapter, LISP in Chapter 5, and PROLOG in Chapter 9.

Generally speaking, object-oriented programming tools are usually one of two different types, according to their use: those suitable primarily for prototyping and those suitable for delivering completed applications to the end user. Each has different sets of requirements.

4.1 Smalltalk History

Smalltalk was the first programming language that was designed to be based exclusively on objects. The object-oriented style of programming originated with the simulation language Simula. It has become a very popular approach in such diverse fields as video games and artificial intelligence and provided the basis for the Apple Macintosh and IBM TopView desktop environments. In the IBM TopView system, for example, all input and output were handled by six I/O object classes: the Keyboard, Mailbox, Objectq, Panel, Pointer, and Timer classes. The very name "TopView" may even have been borrowed from Smalltalk because, in Smalltalk-80, a View is the generic name for windows, and in an ongoing example called FinancialHistory in the Addison-Wesley Smalltalk-80 series, one of the main variables is named topView. It is characteristic, too, that one of the hallmarks of the Smalltalk system is its full-featured, interactive user environment.

Smalltalk was originally invented by Alan Kay while at Xerox PARC in 1972, but many people since have made important contributions to the design of the language, as defined by the Smalltalk-80 standard. Smalltalk was intended originally as the programming language for the legendary Dynabook computer that Kay was working on at the time. Kay envisioned Dynabook as a very small computer that would offer unsurpassed performance and ease of use. When asked to specify how small the Dynabook would have to be, Kay came up with the intriguing criterion that it would have to be something small enough to carry even when a person also had two other parcels to carry. This clearly leaves out today's transportables and even many laptops as well.

Because "small" is such an important part of the vision of the Dynabook, many people have assumed that this is the basis for the name "Smalltalk." In itself, of course, the language could hardly be construed as small. Perhaps partly for this reason, Kay connects the name's origin neither to the size of the Dynabook nor to the size of the language. He says that the name "Smalltalk" was chosen to avoid appearing too pretentious. The strategy was to "talk small" so as to avoid creating inflated expectations that later might not be satisfied.

Kay wrote the first Smalltalk interpreter, and he wrote it in, of all things, BASIC. All subsequent versions of the language (up to and including Release 1 of Smalltalk-80) were designed and written primarily by Dan Ingalls. Kay and Ingalls collaborated on the design of the early versions of Smalltalk, and later Ingalls became the principal designer when Kay was no longer working on the project. This is the reason for Kay's enigmatic statement, "I invented the language, but I didn't really write it."

After Kay's thousand-line BASIC program, the next implementation was the Smalltalk-72 system written in Nova assembly language. As soon as the first prototype Alto computer was built, Smalltalk-72 was ported to it and became the main development environment for experimentation on this machine for the first years of its existence. Smalltalk-72 made use of Textframes and Turtles, the latter based on Seymour Papert's work on Turtle Geometry and Logo. Much in the same spirit as Papert's research, the original Smalltalk-72 system provided the basis for an experimental course in object-oriented computing for high school students. For the space of about four years, 12 people heavily experimented with this new programming paradigm.

In 1974 Smalltalk underwent another major redefinition that clarified its syntax and semantics and improved its performance. Important developments in Smalltalk-74 included message streams, message dictionaries, the BitBlt class for displaying bit-mapped graphics, and OOZE (object-oriented zoned environment), the first Smalltalk virtual memory system. Smalltalk-74 offered the language its first, full, multiwindow interface, which has now become one of its most distinctive features.

An even more significant major redesign of the language occurred in 1976. According to Dan Ingalls, this was the first time that classes became real objects and that inheritance from one class to another was possible. Smalltalk-76 was also the first of the bytecode implementations of the language. A microcode implementation of the instruction set allowed Smalltalk-76 to run between 4 and 100 times faster than previous Smalltalks. For another four years, 20 people hammered away, experimenting daily with programming in the language. About another 100 people tried it out on a part-time basis. Obviously, Smalltalk-76 was the system that really proved the feasibility of the language.

In 1977, a project was begun to develop a portable computer that could run Smalltalk. This was not called Dynabook, but Notetaker. Notetaker started out as a hand-held device, but soon blossomed into a suitcase-size machine, much like today's transportables. Because of its limited resources, Smalltalk had to be redesigned to fit on this machine. That resulted in Smalltalk-78. This time, all of Smalltalk did not have to be rewritten from scratch. Once the Smalltalk interpreter was running on Notetaker, the source code for the class hierarchy could be imported from Smalltalk-76 and used to build the image on the new machine. Smalltalk-78 pioneered the use of indexed object tables that would become a part of the Smalltalk-80 standard.

In 1979 Xerox began the process of disseminating Smalltalk-80 to the world at large. Initially Xerox would invite six firms to receive a free license to use Smalltalk in exchange for implementing it on their machines. Of the original six, four fully participated in this licensing program: Tektronix, Apple, Hewlett-Packard, and Intel. Among these, Tektronix was the first to offer a commercial product featuring Smalltalk. Apple is expected to do so in the not-too-distant future. Since that time, Xerox has also formulated its own strategy for marketing Smalltalk. A separate company, ParcPlace Systems, headed by Adele Goldberg, was formed as the marketing vehicle for Xerox Smalltalk.

4.2 Smalltalk-80

Smalltalk-80 is the final version of Smalltalk that has emerged as the commercial dialect that is currently offered for sale by ParcPlace Systems. In our introduction to the language we will describe this implementation. Virtually everything that exists in a Smalltalk system is an instance of a particular class of object, and generally there can be as many instances of something as you like. This has far-reaching consequences for programming, but also for the user environment. It means that you can have any number of instances of any of the system's facilities active at the same time. For example, you can have several different text editing or Workspace windows open at once and as many of the browsers as you may happen to need.

A *browser* is a window that allows you to scroll through and access a particular type of thing, for example, a class or method, in the system. The amount of time that such conveniences can save you can be significant. Since most of the system is written in Smalltalk itself, and since this is done in terms of the organized hierarchy of classes and subclasses, you can use the Class Hierarchy Browser to find out fairly quickly how anything is implemented in the system without leaving the interactive programming environment and, at least in principle, to change it if you wish.

Variables

Although the basic syntactic message-passing metaphor of Smalltalk is simple and quite general, the handling of variables is more complex. Because Smalltalk does not completely adhere to a single uniform syntax, handling variables is one of the hurdles to be overcome in gaining fluency with the language. The basic distinction is between two categories of variables: private and shared variables. A *private variable* is only accessible by a single object, whereas *shared variables* are available to a number of different objects. In Smalltalk, these two different categories of variables have a different representation:

private variables always appear with a lowercase leading character, whereas shared variables have an uppercase leading character.

There are really five different types of Smalltalk variables:

1. Instance variables (named and indexed)

2. Temporary variables

3. Class variables

4. Pool variables

5. Global variables

The first two types are private variables and the remaining three are shared.

Messages

Smalltalk provides three different message syntax formats: unary messages, binary messages, and keyword messages. A unary message is executed simply with the selector name of the message without any arguments. An example of this would be simply

```
Rectangle size
```

Keyword messages are those that also provide keywords that denote where arguments need to be supplied. The following message uses the at: and put: keywords:

```
Rectangle at: center put: label
```

Binary messages are those that act as messages to two objects simultaneously. The main examples of binary messages are arithmetical expressions and those that use relational operators. The following examples are all binary messages in Smalltalk:

```
3 + 4

three + four

4 > 3

four > three
```

4.3 Metaobject Protocol

Before you can understand how the Smalltalk system works, you need to first learn about metaclasses and how they function. Since everything in Smalltalk is an object, even classes are instances of some class. Generally speaking, any class that has instances that are themselves classes is referred to as a *metaclass*. In Smalltalk-80, Class and Metaclass are both examples of metaclasses. Class is the abstract class from which Metaclass inherits. Thus, to create a class is generally to create an instance of Metaclass.

The method new is implemented as a class method of Metaclass. One way of implementing it would be as follows:

```
new
 ^super new
    structure: Class structure;
        methodDictionary: (MethodDictionary newSize: 2);
        yourself
```

On the other hand, the subclass method is defined:

```
subclass: classSymbol
    instanceVariableNames: instanceVariables
    classVariableNames: classVariables
    poolDictionaries: poolDictNames
    | aMetaClass |
    self isBits
        ifTrue: [^self error: 'Superclass is non-pointers'].
    aMetaClass := MetaClass subclassOf: self.
     ^aMetaClass
        name: classSymbol
        environment: Smalltalk
        subclassOf: self
        instanceVariableNames: instanceVariables
        variable: self isVariable
        words: true
        pointers: true
        classVariableNames: classVariables
        poolDictionaries: poolDictNames
        comment: String new
        changed: nil
```

Workspaces

A Smalltalk-80 Workspace is a simple Window facility that serves as a text area where a user may enter, edit, and evaluate text. It works a bit differently from the usual style interpreter/editor. It holds onto all the text you type just as a text editor does. The text area is "alive" in the sense that the interpreter can evaluate any text there. However, contrary to most other interpreters, this evaluation is not automatic when you press Enter. To evaluate a Smalltalk expression in a Workspace window, you first highlight the expression and then click a mouse button. On the menu that pops up, if you choose the "doIt" selection, the highlighted expression will be evaluated. Other menus for performing different operations on the highlighted text pop up when you click different mouse buttons.

Figure 4.1 shows the menu that pops up when the middle mouse button is clicked in the text area of an ordinary Workspace window. Many of the menu items are self explanatory. The "again" and "undo" options perform the operations you would expect: repeating or reversing, respectively, a previous command. The "copy" option makes a duplicate of the highlighted text block in the buffer without modifying the original. The "cut" option deletes the highlighted text and stores it in a buffer. The "paste" option inserts the contents of the buffer at the cursor. The "printIt" option operates the same as "doIt" except that it displays the value of the highlighted expression after evaluating it. The "accept" option is used when new classes or methods have been defined and the programmer wants to add them to the system. The "cancel" option exits the operation without making any changes.

4.4 The System Browser

The Smalltalk-80 System Browser is the epitome of the kind of thing you probably never thought you needed, but after using it for a while, you will find it hard to imagine ever being without again. It serves as an interactive index onto the system as it comes out of the box as well as for any applications that you develop yourself and add to the system.

The System Browser has five main window panes: four medium-sized panes along the top and one larger one below. Starting from the upper left, the first pane displays the categories of classes. As we saw earlier, categories of classes are not to be confused with superclasses. No actual Smalltalk classes correspond to the categories.

Figure 4.1 Middle Mouse Button Menu for an Ordinary Workspace Window.

When a category is selected, the list of classes under it is displayed in the next pane to the right. If one of these classes is selected, a list of message categories is shown in the pane just to the right. If the "instance" option is selected, the classes are the categories of instance messages. Otherwise, they are the categories of class messages. If one of these message categories is selected, the list of actual message names appears in the pane farthest to the right. When one of these messages is selected, the source code for that method will appear in the large pane below these top four panes. Auxiliary commands are entered by popping up the various menus that appear when different mouse buttons are clicked. For example, click the mouse button to pop up the system menu, as shown in Figure 4.2.

The middle mouse button menu for the main text pane (shown in Figure 4.3) is similar to that of the Workspace window, but it has several extra command options. As before, the accept option is used for adding highlighted text to the Smalltalk system. All the text processing commands are also present. But additional commands (format, spawn, and explain) are now available as well for operations pertaining specifically to the System Browser.

| restore display |
| garbage collect |
| screen saver |
| exit project |
| browser |
| workspace |
| file list |
| file editor |
| terminal |
| project |
| system transcript |
| system workspace |
| desktop |
| save |
| quit |

Figure 4.2 System Menu.

```
┌─────────────┐
│   again     │
│   undo      │
├─────────────┤
│   copy      │
│   cut       │
│   paste     │
├─────────────┤
│   doIt      │
│   printIt   │
│   inspect   │
├─────────────┤
│   accept    │
│   cancel    │
├─────────────┤
│   format    │
│   spawn     │
│   explain   │
└─────────────┘
```

Figure 4.3 Middle Mouse Button Menu for the Main Text Pane.

Figure 4.4 shows the middle mouse button menu for the System Browser. The definition option displays the Smalltalk code for a selected definition. The categories option selects a method category.

4.5 Smalltalk Classes

What gives a Smalltalk system its real character is its hierarchy of classes. This is mainly what makes the system so massive. The first thing that is apparent about Smalltalk-80 is that it is anything but small. Here is the hierarchy of Smalltalk classes arranged in two columns:

```
Object                         Stream
  Magnitude                      PositionableStream
    Character                      ReadStream
    Date                           Writestream
    Time                             ReadWriteStream
    Number                             ExternalStream
      Float                              FileStream
```

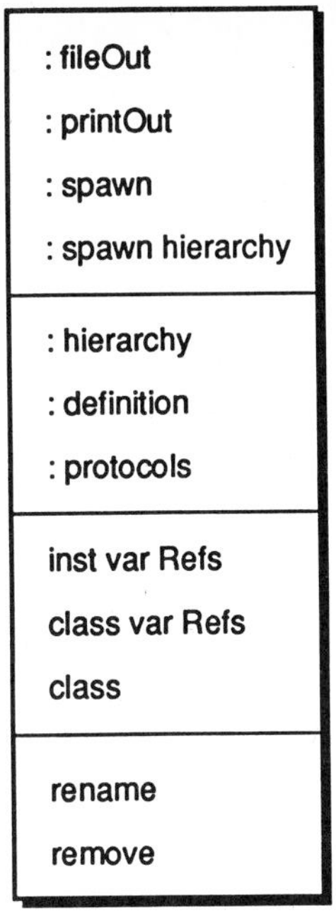

: fileOut

: printOut

: spawn

: spawn hierarchy

: hierarchy

: definition

: protocols

---

inst var Refs

class var Refs

class

---

rename

remove

Figure 4.4 Middle Mouse Button Menu for the System Browser.

```
      Fraction                  Random
      Integer                File
        LargeNegativeInteger   FileDirectory
        LargePositiveInteger   FilePage
        SmallInteger           UndefinedObject
      LookupKey                Boolean
        Association              False
  Link                           True
   Process                     ProcessorScheduler
 Collection                    Delay
   SequenceableCollection      SharedQueue
     LinkedList                Behavior
       Semaphore                   ClassDescription
     ArrayedCollection               Class
       Array                           Metaclass
       Bitmap                Point
         DisplayBitmap       Rectangle
       RunArray              BitBlt
       String                    CharacterScanner
        Symbol                   Pen
        Text                 DisplayObject
        ByteArray                DisplayMedium
       Interval                     Form
```

```
      OrderedCollection                    Cursor
       SortedCollection                    DisplayScreen
Bag                               InfiniteForm
MappedCollection                  OpaqueForm
Set                               Path
 Dictionary                         Arc
   IdentityDictionary                 Circle
                                  Curve
                                  Line
                                  LinearFit
                                  Spline
```

Debugging

Smalltalk has interactive facilities for handling and correcting program errors. When an error is detected, the process in which the error is encountered is suspended, and a view is created for that process. The two main windows onto suspended processes are called notifiers and debuggers in Smalltalk-80.

A *notifier* provides a more useful type of error reporting than is often encountered in programming environments. Typically a window will open with the error message on the top of the pane and a representation of the suspended process in the window proper. One of the most frequent errors reported in a notifier is "Message not understood: . . .". This occurs when you try to send a message to an object that it does not recognize.

Debuggers provide a more detailed view of suspended processes. In Smalltalk-80, a debugger is called by clicking the middle mouse button while in a notifier and then selecting "debug" on the resulting popup menu. When a debugger is created, as with most window-oriented facilities in Smalltalk, the user is prompted to select the corners that define the rectangular area it will occupy. A debugger has six panes or subviews. In the top pane, the same list is displayed that was seen in the notifier, which shows the history of the process until the time it was suspended.

4.6 Sample Programs

The code for the factorial program in Smalltalk is simplicity personified (see Listing 4.1). When the `factorial` message is used to send a message to a number, the number tests itself to see if it is greater than 1. If it is, the code says take the number that is one less $(n-1)$, send the `factorial` message to this number, and multiply this result by the original number. In this way, the method recursively applies itself until it reaches the exit condition, when the number is equal to one. If it is not greater than 1, it simply returns the value 1.

Here, very elegantly, we see recursive message passing to each successively smaller integer until the number 1 is reached, at which point the loop is exited. Similarly, in the case of the Fibonacci program shown in Listing 4.1, recursive message passing is used, but this time with the `fibonacci` method calling itself twice.

Listing 4.1 Three Benchmark Programs in Smalltalk

```
factorial
    self > 1 ifTrue: [
        ^(self - 1) factorial * self].
    ^1
fibonacci
        "Answer the nth fibonacci number,
         where n is the receiver"
    self < 3 ifTrue: [^1].
    ^(self - 1) fibonacci + (self - 2) fibonacci
sieve
        "Do 10 iterations of the Sieve
         of Eratosthenes"
    | i j count prime flags k |
    flags := Array new: self.
    k := 10.
    [(k := k - 1) < 0] whileFalse: [
        i := 0.
        [(i := i + 1) <= self]
            whileTrue: [flags at: i put: true].
        i := count := 0.
            [(i := i + 1) <= self]
                whileTrue: [flags at: i put: true].
            i := count := 0.
            [(i := i + 1) <= self] whileTrue: [
                (flags at: i) ifTrue: [
                    prime := i + i + 1.
                    j := i + prime.
                    [j <= self] whileTrue: [
                        flags at: j put: false.
                        j := j + prime].
                    count := count + 1]]].
```

4.7 Smalltalk/V/286

This product is a bit-mapped implementation of Smalltalk that is code compatible with the earlier Methods and Smalltalk/V products, also by Digitalk, but is written in native 80286 code that runs in protected mode, providing an address space of 16 megabytes. This, of course, makes it very suitable for large AI applications. Another feature that makes it suitable for AI research is the inclusion of a surprisingly robust PROLOG interpreter. This PROLOG includes many predicates that are lacking in popular commercial PROLOGs, for example, the functor and univ predicates. Smalltalk/V/286 also has excellent graphics capabilities such as turtle graphics and offers very good performance in graphics animation. The product includes a large on-disk tutorial that contains some substantial program examples.

The next thing to know about Smalltalk/V/286 is that, like all Smalltalk systems, it is built on an object-oriented class system in which all procedures happen in terms of the message-passing metaphor. The dialect of Smalltalk/V/286 is so close to Smalltalk-80 that most of the classes and examples in the Smalltalk-80 book series can be entered as is. The main exceptions are those that make use of multitasking such as the simulation examples. But even with these, application disks are available that provide the necessary rudiments of multitasking to allow some of these simulation programs to run. Compatibility with existing Smalltalk code and books on Smalltalk-80 is very important for programmers new to Smalltalk because, other than what is available for the main dialect, there is really very little published material to give you a full overview of the Smalltalk system and help you get going.

In the Class Hierarchy Browser, the lower classes in the hierarchy beneath those that are the immediate subclasses of Object, the root Class, can be either hidden or visible, as you choose. Once a particular class with subclasses has been chosen, you can choose to show or conceal just the subclasses under it. Some additional commands on the desktop have also been added. You can cycle around to other windows now from a command on one of the dropdown menus. This was needed because when a window is completely covered by another window, you cannot select it with the mouse. Among the basic types of facilities you use with Smalltalk/V/286 are Workspace windows, browsers, menus, and occasionally what's known as an inspector. The main types of browsers are Class Browsers, Class Hierarchy Browsers, and the Disk Browser. These are specialized window facilities that give you a view of a particular aspect of the system. And, as mentioned earlier, you can create as many instances of these views as you may need.

A Class Hierarchy Browser is the Digitalk version of the Smalltalk System Browser. As implemented in Smalltalk/V/286, this type of browser has four separate panels. The first is a scrolling window that lists the main classes and subclasses in the system. To the right of it is the methods pane that displays the list of applicable methods. Beneath it are two small selector panes with the words "class" and "instance" in them, respectively. Finally, on the bottom is a large pane that displays the actual Smalltalk source code for selected items.

Depending on whether you select on the small instance or class pane, either the calling names of instance or class methods are displayed in the methods pane. When one of these method names is selected, its source code is displayed in the lower pane. When the source pane is current, it acts as a text editing pane where source code can be created and modified. What this type of browser means to a software developer is that you have a built-in overview of the system that can give you ready access to anything in the system at all times. The way that you generally call upon things that have already been entered into the system is by creating instances of a class, initializing variables in a Workspace window, and then sending messages to it. Any involved interaction can itself be made into a program by adding it as a new subclass with its own variables and methods that can be instantiated and evaluated more easily.

As mentioned earlier, Smalltalk/V/286 also provides Inspector windows. These are special-purpose windows that may be used as low-level debugging tools that allow you to examine and even change objects in the system. An Inspector window isn't opened by accessing a menu. The way you open an Inspector is by using a workspace or System Transcript window to send the "inspect" message to an instantiated object. An Inspector window with two panes: one on the right and one on the left will open. The left pane displays the names of the instance variables, and the right pane shows their values.

Debugging

There are some interesting innovations in the design of the Smalltalk/V/286 debugger. Whenever an error occurs, a Walkback window opens immediately, providing an error message in the top border and allowing access to the debugger. You can open a popup menu that allows you to select "debug," which results in the opening of a Debugger window. The Smalltalk/V/286 Debugger window has six panes in all. The upper-left pane can be used for two different purposes, displaying a walkback sequence and displaying breakpoints. The two small panes just below it (one labeled "walkback" and the other "breakpoints") allow you to choose which of the two windows will display. When the walkback sequence is being displayed, a list of messages appears, beginning with the message on which the error condition occurred. The basic format in which these messages are displayed is

```
'Class'>>'method'
```

When one of these messages in the walkback pane is selected, the source code for the method being called is displayed in the large, lower pane. This pane functions like any text editing pane, so that any changes made to the source code here can immediately be made final by selecting "save" from the pane's popup menu.

The other two upper panes contain what amounts to a built-in inspector in the debugging window. In the center pane is a list of names that will always contain the word "self," referring to the receiver of a method, as well as the different arguments to the method. If one of them is selected, its current value is displayed in the far-right pane.

To set up a breakpoint, you call up the popup menu in the upper-left pane and select "add breakpoint". Breakpoints are specified by providing the receiver and the message being sent to it. When you do, the upper-left pane immediately changes into a breakpoint pane and the messages chosen as breakpoints are displayed.

On the far right of the Debugger window are three buttons that look like level indicators for a container of liquid. These are for the Hop, Skip, and Jump operations. These refer to different ways of stepping through program execution. Hop steps one instruction at a time, whereas Skip and Jump each execute increasingly more instructions at a time.

One of the important additions to the user interface of Smalltalk/V/286 is that of collapsible icons. Two fonts come with Smalltalk/V/286, and they differ mainly in size. One has 8-by-8 pixels, and the other has 8-by-14 pixels. Other features included in Smalltalk/V/286 that were absent in the Methods product are a DOS shell, a garbage collector, and virtual memory management.

The Smalltalk/V/286 manual is a *Tutorial and Programming Handbook*. In many respects it is a remarkably clear and well-written guide. Despite its thoroughness and readability, this handbook is not a complete reference to the behavior of the Smalltalk/V/286 system. We would like to see a companion guide forthcoming from Digitalk that would go more deeply into the behavior and implementation of the garbage collector and virtual memory, for example.

Graphics

Smalltalk/V/286 has a very interesting approach to graphics. The basic class that implements the graphics capability is the BitBlt class (much as in Smalltalk-80), which is named for the bit block transfer operation. Together with its immediate subclasses of Pen and Character, and the subclasses of Pen, Commander, and Animation, BitBlt provides the basis for how Smalltalk/V/286 creates bit-mapped displays.

The block transfers occur between two Forms: a source Form and a destination Form. Forms, Points, and Rectangles constitute the main structures used in Smalltalk/V/286 graphics. A mechanism called a *clipping rectangle* is used (again, much as in Smalltalk-80) to define the maximum size of the bit transfer. This clipping rectangle restricts the size of the rectangular array of bits that will constitute the destination Form.

To see how this works, first look at the section of the class hierarchy in question:

```
BitBlt
    CharacterScanner
    Pen
    Animation
    Commander
```

The CharacterScanner class has the job of converting ASCII character codes into displayable bit patterns. The Pen class, as you might have surmised, implements Turtle graphics. The Animation class constitutes collections of pens that represent the various objects being animated. Finally, the Commander class controls arrays of pens in such a way that whenever it receives pen-related messages, it relays the same message to each of the pens under its command.

Smalltalk/V/286's approach to handling windows is very different from that used in Smalltalk-80, but it is essentially the same as that used in Methods. The following segment of the class hierarchy comes into play:

```
Dispatcher
  GraphDispatcher
  PointDispatcher
  ScreenDispatcher
  ScrollDispatcher
   FormEditor
        ListSelector
   TextEditor
    PromptEditor
   TopDispatcher
DispatchManager
```

Browsing Drives

The Disk Browser is one of the more original and powerful facilities in the
Smalltalk/V/286 system. Its window is composed of four panes. In the upper-left pane is
the directory hierarchy list, which shows all the directories on a disk. In the pane to the
right of this is the file list, which displays the names of all the files in the selected
directory. A large pane below these is the contents pane that displays either the screen of
directory information as it would appear after an MS-DOS dir command or the contents
of a selected file. The small pane just above this is called the directory order pane. It
displays the way in which directory information is currently being sorted for display in
the contents frame, for example, by date, name, or size.

   With this facility you can create or remove directories and files, as well as rename,
copy, or print them. With the command menus accessible from the contents pane, just
about any file maintenance operation, including cut and paste, copy, read, and install,
can be done. The full set of commands available as displayed in the menu varies
depending on the size of the file. Normally, with files greater than 6000 bytes, the
contents pane displays only the first and last 2000 bytes. The read it command can in
that event be used to read in the complete contents of the large file. Also the save as
command is available, which allows a file to be saved under a different name. Finally, the
install command allows source files to be compiled into the Smalltalk/V/286 system.

   You must keep track of the size of the changes log file. If it starts to get large, there is
a facility for compressing it. You *must* use this before the changes log gets too large and
space on the disk runs low or your image will become unusable. The log facility is
essential for those who cannot resist taking advantage of Smalltalk's feature of being
internally extensible to a large degree, like FORTH and LISP. While modifying the
internals to create an image of a new dialect of Smalltalk/V/286, prior to getting your
modified system debugged, you are likely to experience a system crash. The log file is
insurance that you will never lose any work you want to keep permanently, unless for
some reason a crash destroys your file. If necessary, you can even use the log file to
restore the system image.

A Method to the Madness

At the very center of all this are the methods, the actual modular subroutines that do the message passing. There are two very different types of methods: instance methods and class methods. They are analogous to the instance and class variables. One important departure of Smalltalk/V/286 from the Smalltalk-80 standard is the omission of the ClassDescription class. In Smalltalk-80, the class hierarchy starting with the Behavior class is organized like this:

```
Behavior
  ClassDescription
          Class
          Metaclass
```

The arrangement in Smalltalk/V/286 is the same except that ClassDescription is omitted. As a result, Smalltalk/V/286 does not support message categories, that is, the grouping of methods for a given class under various category names. In many cases, it is relatively easy to add missing Smalltalk-80 classes to Smalltalk/V/286. But in this case, it is not an easy addition to make because if ClassDescription is added as a·subclass of Behavior, it becomes a peer class of Class and Metaclass rather than a superclass of them.

On the other hand, the following classes are unique to Smalltalk/V/286:

CursorManager
Directory
DiskBrowser
Dispatcher
DisplayString
FixedSizeCollection
IndexedCollection
InfiniteForm
LinkedListStream
MethodDictionary
StringBlt
StringModel
SystemDictionary

In principle, Smalltalk can be used for writing good simulation software. However, with the current version of Smalltalk/V/286, it is not just a matter of implementing the classes suggested in the Xerox books because multitasking is not yet supported by either MS-DOS or Smalltalk/V/286. As Jim Anderson, president of Digitalk, expressed it, "Smalltalk/V/286 does not implement multiprocessing. I have proposed to some customers to implement simulations in a different way. Make each simulation object a finite state machine with an instance variable 'state' containing a symbol that describes the current state. Now when a simulation object exits a queue, its state can be performed. This avoids the need to use stacked-up messages in a process to describe a state."

The advantages to implementing a full, expert-system shell in Smalltalk/V/286 are quite easy to see. First, you get the lush, easy-to-understand user interface practically for free. It would not be a major development project to use the Smalltalk/V/286 menu and windowing facilities to build a superior expert system consultation environment. Another important plus is the multiple instance aspect of Smalltalk. You can have as many Experts (for example, the Tree expert) initialized as necessary, each with a separate ruleset. Smalltalk/V/286 could then be implemented for one Expert to pass a message to another in order to test a goal. Also, more flexible inference methods could be implemented for backward chaining and combining both forward and backward chaining. Finally, a parser could be written that could accept a more friendly rule syntax, and it could be compiled into the Smalltalk format used here for running finished knowledge bases.

The Carleton Tools and Projects

Digitalk also offers three additional disks of Smalltalk programs. The last two are recent additions based on an agreement with the School of Computer Science at Carleton University in Ottawa, Canada.

The Tools disk has a software floating-point module, a random number generator, and a spelling checker that provides a menu-driven method of correcting spelling errors in writing Smalltalk code. Also on this disk are various extensions to the Smalltalk/V/286 desktop environment, including classes for building multifield forms such as those used in business applications.

The Projects disk has more AI-related programs such as the Neural Net character recognizer, the Directed Acyclic Graph Browser, the Matrix class, and the chessboard with pieces. Also included on this disk is a much-needed application browser, and a 3-D graphics editor that allows 3-D wireframe objects to be created, rotated, and zoomed. (Chapter 7 describes and analyzes the Neural Modeling application.)

Evaluation

Smalltalk/V/286 is a remarkable accomplishment and an environment that is very easy for newcomers to Smalltalk to understand. Performance is surprisingly fast, considering all the things going on in this environment. It would be desirable to see an expanded Smalltalk/V/286 product that includes multiprogramming, categories, and multiple inheritance.

4.8 Smalltalk/V/Macintosh

Smalltalk/V for the Apple Macintosh is important because of its compatibility with the versions of the language provided by Digitalk for MS-DOS machines. Despite this portability, it can take particular advantage of the special Macintosh features by providing access to the Macintosh Toolbox and the ability to run under the Finder and MultiFinder programs. With the proper allocation of memory resources, desk accessories are also available with Smalltalk/V so that operations such as text transfers between Smalltalk and accessory programs are possible. It is also fully compatible with MultiFinder in the sense that cut and paste operations are possible with other applications running under MultiFinder.

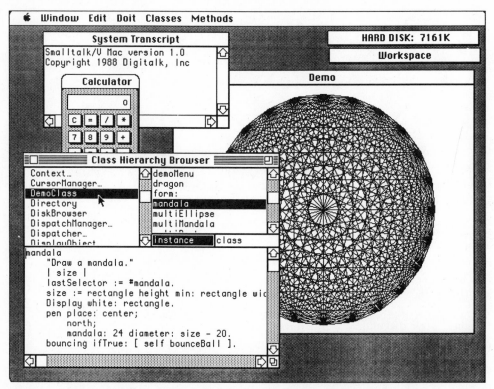

Figure 4.5 Digitalk Smalltalk for the Macintosh with Mandala demo.

The most obvious difference between the Macintosh user interface of Digitalk Smalltalk and the PC implementation of Smalltalk is the retention of the familiar top main menu bar. In adherence to the Apple user interface orthodoxy, no popup menus, only dropdown menus are used. Ordinarily, the main menu selections are: File, Edit,

Smalltalk, and Window. However, each window has its own special menus to add to the top menu bar. Whenever a window becomes active, these additional menus appear on the top and are immediately available for use.

However, despite the differences in the menus, the exact same Smalltalk/V code is used on the Macintosh as on the MS-DOS machines. Digitalk has succeeded in making even user interface programming portable across the different user interface styles.

No Disk Browser is provided on the Macintosh because of the comparable facilities already available. However the same Disk and Directory classes are used. One issue that may come up in porting applications from the Macintosh to MS-DOS are the latter's restrictions on filenames. However, even here, it is possible to make the filename conversion automatic. The following program, provided by Digitalk, makes the necessary changes:

```
| name length |
name := 'Mac Big File Name'.
length := name size.
^(name reversed reject: [ :c |
   c isSeparator or: [
   c isVowel and: [
   c is LowerCase and: [
   ( length := length - 1) >= 8]]]])
      reversed,'            '
         copyFrom: 1 to: 8
```

A minor point of difference with the MS-DOS version is the debugger. In Smalltalk/V, a dialogue window opens automatically any time an error is detected, and you have the option of entering the debugger. On the Macintosh version of the debugger, the window buttons that allow stepping through code at different rates are actually labeled "Hop", "Skip", and "Jump".

Video and Graphics

Like Smalltalk, the Macintosh uses bit-mapped video for its screen operations. For this reason, many of the screen and graphics primitives of Smalltalk/V were written using routines in the QuickDraw Manager in ROM. The result is that, although not identical, the Smalltalk screen and graphics approach is very similar to that of the Macintosh itself. In addition to the built-in Smalltalk primitives that access the QuickDraw Manager and Toolbox, there are also provisions for calling any resource directly from ROM.

The Macintosh implementation does not support the BiColorForm and ColorForm subclasses of the Form class, so applications on MS-DOS machines that need to be completely portable cannot use them. An additional minor difference in performing bit-mapped operations is that the Macintosh version uses the global variable name Screen instead of Display, as it is called in the MS-DOS version. Accordingly, there are also methods for the Form class on the Macintosh called fromScreen and so on that are unique to this implementation. In other respects, operations using methods of the BitBlt,

Form, and classes are identical. Another similar minor difference is that the global variable Aspect for setting the aspect ratio is not used on the Macintosh. Finally, as could be anticipated, the fonts used in the two implementations vary.

Fonts

The fonts that are used in Smalltalk/V, like the windows, are standard Macintosh fonts. However, to make applications portable across machines, the Font class was created for Smalltalk to do its own font management. For those who wish to make direct access to Macintosh fonts in a nonportable way, the MacFont class is also included. The class Color is used to describe the colors in the ColorQuickDraw RGB format. There are also methods for using the standard QuickDraw color model.

Macintosh Toolbox Access

For those who are not interested in portability to MS-DOS machines, but seek full integration with the Macintosh environment and other popular applications there, some classes are available for directly accessing the Macintosh Toolbox. These include MHandle, MObject, MPointer, MRecord, MRegisters, MTrap, and MType. MHandle, MPointer, and MRecord are the three basic storage classes that are implemented as subclasses of MObject. All of these classes are capable of accessing Macintosh record resources, but with differing rules and restrictions. The MType class is used to represent the actual datatypes used by the Macintosh Toolbox.

The MTrap and MRegisters classes are provided for making direct trap calls to the Macintosh Toolbox. MTrap has various class methods for making access to the various Toolbox managers such as the Memory, Event, Menu, and Window managers. MRegisters is the class used for creating instances that will be passed as arguments for register-style trap calls.

Three other classes unique to the Macintosh are MenuBar, Window, and GlobalDisplayScreen. Although the facilities of MenuBar are similar to the portable Smalltalk/V menu operations, some additional features such as command key equivalents for the menu bar and desk accessory lists are also available. Window is a class made to precisely mirror the Macintosh Toolbox window object. Finally, GlobalDisplayScreen is a subclass of DisplayScreen that allows routines to be written directly to the Macintosh screen.

Shutdown

The shutdown mechanism is another important aspect of the Macintosh implementation because it allows some additional garbage cleanup before an image is saved. This facility is handled on a class-by-class basis. Using it involves adding a method called shutdown to a relevant class and making a call of the form

```
Class regenerateShutDownList
```

Then, the specified class will be sent the shutdown message each time the image is about to be saved. Any desired operation can be written for the shutdown method, but those most useful are ones performing some type of cleanup to keep unwanted items out of the system image.

There are some additional classes in the Macintosh version of Smalltalk/V, but they are nearly all related to the user interface, as you might suspect. Under the Pane class, for example, the ButtonPane, VerticalButtonPane, and ScrollBarPane classes have been added. A new facility unique to the Macintosh implementation is the Ordered Collection Inspector. Method Browsers are implemented differently using a class called MethodListBrowser.

User-Defined Primitives

Adding code to Smalltalk from other languages is accomplished by writing new primitives implemented as separate, named, code resources of the VPRM type. Any language that can create the necessary resource format can be used. The format in

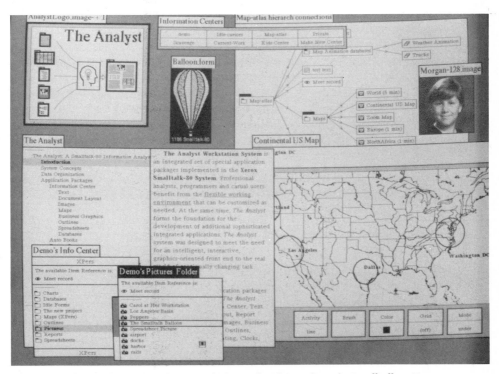

Figure 4.6 The Analyst information analysis application written in Smalltalk at Xerox.

question is very similar to the HyperCard XCMD format. The code resources must be moved into Smalltalk/V applications using a resource mover tool like ResEdit. One limitation on the code that can be written is a prohibition on global variables. Several routines that facilitate writing user-defined primitives in C on the Macintosh are provided on the distribution disks.

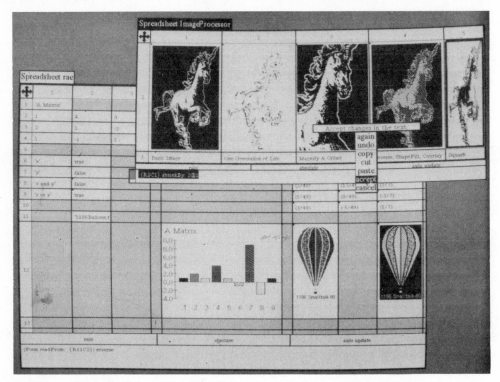

Figure 4.7 The Analyst Spreadsheet Package with graphics capabilities on display.

Evaluation

This implementation of Smalltalk is an important achievement in a number of respects. The degree of portability might appear to be on the order of a breakthrough in computer language design. It is very rare for even the screen I/O and user interface routines in a programming language to have such a large degree of compatibility. However, if we look at Smalltalk-80, we see a similar degree of portability even here. It is certainly not the case that such results are a foregone conclusion in Smalltalk. This kind of portability is the result of considerable skill, on the level of both design and implementation. Nevertheless it is an excellent demonstration of one of the important advantages of object-oriented systems.

The reason why object-oriented systems can have such an advanced degree of portability is their ability to isolate those aspects of a programming problem that are unique and machine specific. But the matter does not end here. As we have seen with this implementation of Smalltalk for the Macintosh, using object-oriented programming constructs can cause many of the differences in local environment to be positively suppressed. Object-oriented systems not only can isolate only those aspects of an implementation that are truly different, but they can also build an environment of classes that establishes a virtual machine that actually suppresses hardware, ROM, and operating system differences.

4.9 C++

The C++ language is the object-oriented extension to C developed at AT&T by Bjarne Stroustrup. The central feature of the C++ architecture is that classes are regarded as user-defined types everywhere. Recall that classes in object-oriented languages provide templates for working pieces of programs that allow many instances to be stamped out and they provide generic code for other more specialized classes. As you can see, nothing in this is inherently related to datatypes. Formally implementing classes in C++ as a way of providing user-defined types is a specific interpretation of objects that attempts to fit object-oriented programming specifically to the C language in order to naturally extend it.

What does this come down to on the actual coding level? C++ simply uses the class keyword to define new classes. The following declaration, for example, defines the set class:

```
class set {
    struct set_member {
        int member;
        set_member* next;
        set_member(int m, set_member* n);
        };
    };
```

Methods, called *member functions* in C++, are defined using the double colon (::). The syntax is the class name, followed by the double colon and then the function name. For example,

```
set::setsize

set weekdays;

set workdays;
```

declares setsize as a member function of the class "set".

Subclasses, or derived classes, are declared using a simple public declaration. Therefore, the class conflict_set would be created simply with the statement:

```
class conflict_set public : set
```

C++ also allows the creation of objects of type void*, which are essentially objects of unknown type. Creating actual instances of classes is simply a matter declaring the item just as you would any other datatype.

C++ reserved words are as follows:

asm	auto	break	case	char
class	const	continue	default	delete
do	double	else	enum	extern
float	for	friend	goto	if
inline	int	long	new	operator
overload	public	register	return	short
sizeof	static	struct	switch	this
typedef	union	unsigned	virtual	void
while	signed	volatile		

One important difference between C++ and C is that in C++ you can declare variables anywhere in a block of code, not just at the beginning of it. This is convenient because it means that you can locate the declaration of variables alongside the statements that use them.

4.10 Friends

In C++, a *friend* is a function that is not a member function of a class, but is still allowed access to the protected variables of that class. Why would this be useful? A function can often involve operations on objects of different classes, where there is no inheritance relation between these classes. An example might be a matrix and a vector. The easiest and most efficient way to perform an operation on a vector and a matrix would be to define the function as a member function of one of the classes, say, matrix, but to also define it as a friend of the other class. In this way the function would have access to all the elements necessary to perform the operation. That's a friend for you.

4.11 Operator Overloading

Operator or function overloading allows functions that use the same call name to operate on a variety of different datatypes or classes, even though separate codings may be required. Statically datatyped languages that resolve types at compile time generally have a tough time with this. With list processing and interpretive languages like LISP,

PROLOG, and Smalltalk, it is commonplace for the same function to be able to operate on many or all datatypes, even without the need to use different codings for each type. This can definitely make programming more enjoyable because the programmer can arrange things so that the function calls are very logical, appropriate, and easy to remember.

Function overloading is a built-in feature of C++ in the sense that mathematical operators like + (plus sign) can be used for operations on integers, floating-point numbers, and pointers. For defining new overloaded functions, the overload keyword is used to explicitly specify function names that are to be used with different datatypes. So, for example, if we wanted to declare a universal print function, we could write:

```
overload print(int), print(double), print(long), print(char*);
```

Another very useful feature of C++ is the opportunity to define functions that can take an unspecified number of arguments. This is a capability usually associated with languages like LISP. To do this, a simple ellipsis is used to represent a definite list of arguments. For example, the declaration

```
int read(char* . . .);
```

could be used with any number of arguments in sequence.

4.12 Constructors

Although you declare an instance of a class the way you do any data structure, all instances also have to be initialized. You do this by calling a member function known as a *constructor*. These constructors have to be coded, and they differ for each class of object because the constructor is what really creates the data object. There are also *destructors*, which destroy objects by reallocating their memory and undefining them.

The C++ language does not allow any provisions at all for input or output. Astounding as this might sound to many programmers, Stroustrup shrugs such provisions off as unnecessary because they can be implemented in the language. This is peculiar logic, for it is almost like adopting the logic: Why bother to program anything that is not too difficult to do?

C++ has three kinds of scope: local, file, and class. *Local* scope applies to names that are declared in a block of code and are local to that block. *Class* scope refers to names that are declared within a class and are unknown outside the operations that belong to that class. *File* scope refers to names that are declared outside of any block or class but are referenced in a file.

Guidelines Software C++ contains numerous batch files for executing the compiler in various fashions. For example, you may choose a batch file that can do all compiling and linking needed to turn a C++ source file into an .EXE file, or you may select one that can turn a number of file modules into .OBJ files and then link them manually. Separate sets of batch files are provided for each of the five memory models supported by the Microsoft 4.0 C compiler. For using the program directly, a number of command parameters are used to specify different memory model options.

Creating an executable program from a C++ source file usually requires four steps:

1. Preprocessing

2. Translating

3. Compiling

4. Linking

Preprocessing is done with the CPRE.EXE program and translating with the CFRONT.EXE program. Compiling and linking are done with your usual C compiler and linker. The C code generated by Guidelines Software C++ is compatible with the Microsoft Codeview debugger, so that C++ programs can be analyzed and debugged using that facility.

The real issue for many programmers is how comfortable they can feel with coding in a language. What does a modest program in C++ look like, and how easy is it to read? To help answer this question, a sample program, the notorious Eratosthenes' sieve benchmark program has been included. This benchmark for C++ (supplied by Guidelines Software) is given in Listing 4.2.

Listing 4.2 Primes Benchmark

```
#include <stream.h>

class prime
{
    int  n;        // this is the "n'th" prime
    int  p;        // the prime itself
public:
    // constructor
    prime(int nn = 1, int pp = 2) { n = nn; p = pp; }

    // advance to next prime
    prime& operator++();

    // tells what the number of this prime is
    int n_th()     { return n; }
    // tells what the prime is
    int prm() { return p; }
};
```

Listing 4.2 Primes Benchmark (continued)

```cpp
// output a prime number
ostream& operator<<(ostream& s, prime &p)
{
    return s<< p.prm();
}

// advance to next prime
prime& prime::operator++()
{
    ++n;        // n_th + 1 prime

    // special case for 2
    if(p == 2)
    {
        // the next prime is 3.
        ++p;
        return(*this);
    }

    // find the next odd prime.
    for(;;)
    {
        p += 2;
        int is_prime = 1;
        int loop_limit = (p / 2);
        for(int a = 3; a < loop_limit; ++a)
        {
            // is p not prime?
            if(((p / a) * a) == p)
            {
                is_prime = 0;
                break;
            }
        }

        // did we find a prime?
        if(is_prime)
            break;
        // else try again...
    }

    return(*this);
}

/*
 * A trivial main program that makes use of class "prime".
 */
```

Listing 4.2 Primes Benchmark (continued)

```
// print the first n_primes primes
main()
{
    const int n_primes = 100;      // print 100 primes
    prime number;
    while(number.n_th() <= n_primes)
    {

        // Print the number of this prime, and the prime
itself.
        cout << number.n_th() << "\t" << number << "\n";

        // Advance to the next prime.
        ++number;
    }
}
```

Evaluation

On the negative side, C++ has basically two weaknesses: its syntax is not as clear as it could be for the main operations of object-oriented programming, and it does not implement runtime binding and datatyping. C++ nevertheless provides one of the advantages of runtime resolving of types with its function overloading. However, there are still many other reasons for wanting runtime binding for AI programs. For example, it is an essential feature for programs that aspire to have the ability to learn over time. It also seems to be essential for programs that will be required to deal effectively with situations for which the programmer did not thoroughly and explicitly provide.

On the positive side, the Guidelines Software implementation of C++ is robust and capable of being used to write very large programs. This is probably its most important role. If you are looking at writing a large project with the C language, you should seriously consider the advantages of doing it with C++ or another object-oriented system. In the long run, you may be very glad you decided to take this route.

4.13 The PFORCE++ Library

Although C++ does not have a built-in class library like Smalltalk and some of the other object-oriented systems, Phoenix has developed this one, PFORCE++, to closely mirror one of their C add-on library products. As we pointed out earlier, C++ has no I/O library of its own beyond the standard library already used by C. The PFORCE++ library provides this input and output capability and much else besides, though admittedly in a very machine-dependent way.

Several interesting demos provided with the PFORCE++ library demonstrate the use of the classes provided for developing window and menu interfaces and databases.

The code provided shows the modular class libraries used with C++ for developing character-mapped color windows and menus. The following list shows each modular class library and its use.

ATTR	Handling screen attributes
BTR	B-tree database
CHC	Choice list structure
COM	Communication handling
CRT	Handling screen output
CRTWND	Window handling
DB	Database access
FLD	Field-directed input handling
FSCR	Field screen input handling
FILEIO	File handling
HASHTBL	Hashing tables
LIST	Singly linked lists
MA	Message area handling
OPT	Menu option handling
PUM	Popup menu handling
RING	Doubly linked stack and queue handling
TMR	Timer handling
XREC	Extended record I/O handling

Let's take a look at how these classes are used. The ATTR class is for specifying screen attributes. For actual screen output, the ATTR class is associated with either a CRT or a WND object. Each ATTR has three colors associated with it: a foreground color, a background color, and an alternate color. An ATTR really has two parts, the set of color numbers and a video attribute bit string.

For example, to construct an ATTR object you could write:

```
ATTR::attr(COLOR cf=VC_WHITE, COLOR cb=VC_BLACK, COLOR
ca=VC_BLUE, VATTR v=VA_DEFAULT);
```

To reset the colors, you can use the following call to the set method:

```
void ATTR::set(COLOR cf, COLOR cb, COLOR ca);
```

Databases and B-trees

The PFORCE++ library implements two separate classes, BTR and DB, which are designed to interact with one another. B-trees are used as indices for given databases that provide keys that act as pointers to the data records. It is by calling a member function of a database object that B-trees are created. The call would be of the form:

```
DB::make_empty_btr();
```

Once the B-tree exists, the B-tree object must still be opened in order to be used. This is done through a call of the type:

```
BTR::open();
```

This allows the address of the database object and the record handle of the B-tree's root node to be passed to the BTR object. Database files can contain any number of records as long as the total size of the file does not exceed 100 megabytes. The records themselves, though, can contain only 2018 bytes. Records larger than this can still be accommodated, either by splitting records into subrecords or by using the provision for extended records.

Evaluation

The PFORCE++ library requires an implementation of C++ such as Guidelines Software C++ in order to run. The source code for the library is included in archived format and an archive program is provided for restoring it to text format. Although this library does serve to a large extent as a class library for C++, it is not the ideal solution. The main problem stems from the fact that the PFORCE++ library is really a port of a library originally written for C. A library written in the real spirit of object-oriented programming would have been done quite differently. The deficiency stems from a lack of true generic design.

Object-oriented programming allows programmers to write code so generically that all variations are specializations that just require an addition to the original code rather than a total rewriting of it. Although this is the ideal, it is seldom possible to achieve it totally. But, since it is a port of an existing library, PFORCE++ is vulnerable to the criticism that little effort was made to implement the library generically. It simply solves the problem of implementing user interface routines and databases for IBM machines. The bottom line is that, although the routines do not provide a standard extension to the C++ language or a model of object-oriented coding with this language, they get the job done admirably, and in such a way that users benefit from many, though certainly not all, of the advantages of object-oriented systems.

4.14 Objective-C

Objective-C from StepStone is one of the most promising tools in this category. This system was developed by C programmers who were looking primarily at the advantages object-oriented programming affords for handling conventional programming projects. Despite this emphasis on the part of its developers, we believe that Objective-C may hold some promise as a delivery environment for AI applications as well.

The current version represents a relatively mature implementation of Objective-C that reflects a year or two's experience with problems that programmers have encountered. Although the classes in the foundation library that presented some of the difficulties have been included for the benefit of those who have already written code that uses them, the manual warns about the problems and suggests that those classes not be used. The classes in this category are BytArray and Bag.

The Objective-C compiler consists of two executable files, the driver program (objcc.exe) and the actual Objective-C program itself (objc.exe). The driver program first calls the Microsoft cl.exe program to check syntax, and then it calls the Objective-C compiler. There is no need to specify libraries at link time unless their paths cannot be found. The library references are embedded in the .obj files by Objective-C.

One of the things that could categorize Objective-C as a suitable delivery environment for AI applications is its feature of dynamic runtime binding for all objects. It can accomplish this even though it compiles its own code into C for subsequent compilation by a C compiler.

An important difference between Objective-C and other object-oriented systems like Smalltalk is that it is really a hybrid language. Just as is possible with object-oriented LISP systems, the programmer always has the option of writing code in conventional C. Another important difference between Objective-C and Smalltalk is the difference in the size of the class libraries. Smalltalk-80 comes with a substantial amount of code available for reuse in source code form. Objective-C, although it offers considerably more in this department than does C++, lags substantially behind Smalltalk, which is the senior member among object-oriented languages.

In certain respects, Objective-C is a rather conservative object-oriented language. That is to say, there are no substantial innovations in object-oriented concepts here that were not already in Smalltalk many years ago. On the other hand, not every powerful feature of Smalltalk is found in Objective-C either. If Objective-C can be considered a hybrid of C and Smalltalk, the more dominant parent by far is clearly C. Looking at it from the perspective of C, Objective-C has extended the C language by adding one new datatype (objects) and one new operation (message expressions).

The syntax of Objective-C is, for the most part, quite straightforward. The equal sign (=) is used to declare a new class, and the colon (:) is used to declare its superclass. Other items in the class definition are set off by parentheses. All data declarations are set off in curly braces. So, for example, the expression

```
= Array:Object { short capacity; }
```

declares Array as a subclass of Object with the instance variable capacity declared as a short integer. There are two types of methods, class methods and instance methods, just as in Smalltalk, and they are defined using the plus (+) and minus (−) signs, respectively. Instances are usually created, as in Smalltalk, by sending the message new to the parent class. Two main types of message expressions are used in Objective-C:

unary expressions and keyword expressions. There are no binary expressions like those used in Smalltalk. The expression

```
id myarray = [ByteArray new:80];
```

creates a new instance of the class ByteArray sized at 80 units. The definition of the method new for the Object class is just

```
+ new { return (*_alloc)(self, 0); }
```

Here, a built-in primitive is called on to do the job of allocating memory for an object. No further work is needed because the object is the simplest possible abstraction class. On the other hand, the new: (pronounced "new colon") message for the Array class has this high-level Objective-C definition:

```
+ new:(int)nElements {
self = (*_alloc)(self, nElements*[self ndxVarSize]);
capacity = nElements; return self;
```

All messages in Objective-C are set between square brackets. The expression [self ndxVarSize], therefore, is a message that the receiver object will be sent. The ndxVarSize message is an Array class method that is redefined by:

```
+ (int)ndxVarSize { return (int)[self subclassResponsibility]; }
```

The subclassResponsibility method simply prints the message "Subclass should override this message." when called. The expression

```
capacity = nElements
```

simply sets the capacity of the array to whatever argument is supplied to new:.

Here are the entire class library lists of the two versions of Objective-C as they might appear in a Smalltalk System Browser, if such a thing existed in Objective-C:

```
Object                             Object
  Array                              Array
    ByteArray                          BytArray
    IdArray                            IdArray
    IntArray                           IntArray
  Assoc    (Association)             Assoc
    Cltn    (Collection)              Cltn
        OrdCltn  (Ordered                OrdCltn
                  Collection)
```

```
        Set                          Set
          Bag                          Bag
      Dictionary                   Dictionary
        Stack                        Stack
        AVLDict    (Sorted Dictionary)   AsciiFiler
      AVLTree                        BalNode
      Point                            SortCltn
      Rectangle                      IPSequence
      Sequence                         Sequence
      String                         ObjGraph
      Unknown                        Point
                                     Rectangle
                                     String
                                     Unknown
```

   In Objective-C, classes are also referred to as Factory Objects. This is to underscore the fact that a class is an object in its own right whose main function is to serve as a template for the creation of instances and subclasses. However, as you can see, no Class and Metaclass classes are present. Classes in Objective-C are not instances of a metaclass object and are not created by sending messages to a metaclass, as would be true in Smalltalk, Xerox LOOPS, and many object-oriented LISPs. In itself, of course, this is not necessarily a bad thing. It is simply another way of saying that Objective-C is a hybrid rather than a pure object-oriented language.
   The library classes in Objective-C are arranged in roughly four broad categories: foundation classes, collection classes, other datatype classes such as String, and screen I/O classes. As is obvious from the class hierarchy tables, in the new version of Objective-C, the AVL classes have been omitted, but a number of others added. The BalNode abstract class and its subclass SortCltn are now used instead. BalNode is generic code capable of supporting implementations of any binary tree. SortCltn, a class that handles sorted collections, is the replacement for AVLTree. Another important change is that the Sequence class is now implemented as a subclass of IPSequence. The latter implements sequencing quickly through any kind of collection by running in place over its contents. To accommodate the technique used by the IPSequence class, the contents method was added to the collection classes which returns the pointer to the instance of IdArray that the receiver is using to store the members of its collection. The AsciiFiler class is a new class that gathers all the file operations and is able to support the transfer of source files between machines of different architectures on the same network.
   Another interesting new class added is ObjGraph. This is used to create a graph of a class hierarchy, meaning that of all the classes from which it inherits. The Objective-C manual provides an example of the use of ObjGraph by implementing a method called broadcast. Broadcast takes a method name or selector as an argument and sends this method to all the objects that can be reached by the receiver. To accommodate this new way of creating graphs, the asGraph method of the Object class was rewritten.

OBJECT-ORIENTED PROGRAMMING TOOLS   93

Earlier we demonstrated some rudimentary operations with the Array class. Arrays are implemented differently in Objective-C than in other object-oriented languages. In Smalltalk, the Array class is a descendant of the Collection class, though not a direct descendant. In Objective-C, Array is a formal or abstract class that is the direct descendant of Object, the root class. This is obviously for efficiency purposes because C already has an implementation of arrays. What is new with the Array class is the implementation of indexed instance variables instead of named instance variables. Arrays are fixed in size. Unlike the more sophisticated collection classes we will encounter later on, Arrays cannot be increased in size when the number of elements reaches the maximum that was defined for a given array. The subclasses of Array handle arrays comprising the various C datatypes. As with most object-oriented languages, the Array class does not provide a facility for defining the dimension of arrays. To create multidimensional arrays, special subclasses of Array must be defined.

As we have seen, array classes in Objective-C have a fixed capacity. Once an array instance of a certain capacity is created, its size cannot be changed. This is not true, however, of collection classes. They are designed as "growable" classes that later can have more elements than specified by their initial capacity.

The method that allows this in the Cltn class expand is written:

```
- expand { contents = [contents capacity: capacity += capacity];
        return self;
    }
```

This is a transparent, high-level, Objective-C method definition that resets the value of the contents variable and uses a simple increment operation to double its capacity.

Objects in Objective-C are designed to reside in a single address space and to be identified exclusively by this address in system memory. This means that systems cannot generally be built with Objective-C where objects need to reside on disk or at other locations on a network. All objects in Objective-C have to reside in the host computer's memory.

Because Objective-C is a hybrid language, it allows "cheating." This means that, unlike a pure object-oriented language such as Smalltalk, Objective-C allows access to the protected memory of objects with C code that can access that memory directly. Needless to say, this is a good way to get into deep trouble, defeating the whole idea of the encapsulation that is one of the main points of an object-oriented system, unless a programmer fully understands the implications of such actions. But the main gambit of a system like Objective-C is to take that risk for the sake of greater performance.

Collection Data Structures

As with Smalltalk and most other object-oriented languages, the centerpiece of Objective-C for creating data structures is the group of Collection classes. This part of the hierarchy has the following member classes:

```
Cltn
    OrdCltn
    Stack
    Set
        Dictionary
        Bag
BalNode
    SortCltn
```

The Cltn class is an abstract or formal class whose variables and methods are there to
be inherited by its various descendants, which do all the actual work in programs. It is
only the subclasses of Cltn that are meant to actually have instances. The methods for
collections are divided into about a dozen categories: instance creation, adding, removing,
sequencing, "elements perform", conversion, printing, freeing, copying, interrogation,
comparison, and private methods. To understand them, you need to know a little about
how collections work. The collection data structures themselves are not used to store the
elements themselves, but are pointers to the instances of the IdArray class that actually
holds the members. The interrogation methods can be used in an application to query
collections, much as database queries and searches are performed in conventional
programming systems. For example, the find method searches for objects by name and
returns them, if they are present.

The elementsPerform methods are those that can map operations onto each
element of a collection in turn. They do this by actually sending a message to each of the
objects that is an element of the collection. One complexity is that different methods
require different numbers of arguments, and Objective-C does not support functions with
an optional number of arguments. The solution is that different elementsPerform
methods must be implemented that accept different numbers of arguments. Versions are
supplied that support up to three arguments. For more than this, it is no great problem to
use these methods to implement those that can accept more than three arguments.

As the name suggests, *ordered collections* (OrdCltn) are those collections whose elements
are kept in order. Often more specialized subclasses of the OrdCltn class are used for
handling queues and stacks. In ordered collections no nil entries are permitted. So,
whenever elements are removed from ordered collections, their contents are automatically
compressed to take up the space created by the vacated element. Owing to the nature of
ordered collections, the methods for adding elements to them specify exactly where they
are to be added. These methods include addFirst, addLast, insert:before, and
insert:after, and their operations are self-explanatory.

Stack implements collections that can keep entries in the last-in, first-out order. In
addition to the push: and pop: methods for accessing the contents of a stack, Objective-
C stacks provide the at: and removeAt: methods for random access of stack elements.
(These random access methods for Stack were new with release 3.3 of Objective-C.)
Stack manipulation methods include those that modify the order of stack elements such

as swap as well as elements such as topElement and lastElement, which provide information without making any modification to the stack.

Sets are collections that are permitted to have only one of each element. No duplicate elements are allowed. One application of Sets that is particularly efficient is the creation of symbol tables. The Set Class is implemented so that sets may contain any type of object. Several different types of object may even be collected in the same set. That is, in order to add new methods to a set, an exhaustive search must be made of all existing elements in it. The Set class in Objective-C supports a hashing facility. With the `hash` message, a set will place all objects it contains in a hash table for increased efficiency. An important limitation of Sets as they are designed here is that they are not designed to be changed dynamically. If the objects in an Objective-C Set are modified, the accessing facilities will no longer work correctly. This naturally limits their usefulness for AI applications.

The Dictionary class is a descendant of Set because dictionaries are implemented as a set of associations. In this case, you want to allow duplicate values, but each of the keys must be unique. This is done by designing dictionaries to have a close relationship with the Assoc class. Associations store links between keys and values in such a way that these pairs can be stored in dictionaries and accessed by the key. Associations perform comparisons and equality testing by passing on messages to key objects. In addition to the methods inherited from Set and the other ancestor classes, Dictionary implements six new messages on its own: the class method `with:` for initializing new dictionaries and five methods for indexed access (`atKey:`, `atKey:put:`, `values`, `includesAssociation:`, and `includesKey:`).

As we saw earlier, the SortCltn class replaces the earlier AVLTree class in Objective-C. A sorted collection is one whose member elements always remain sorted. When an object is added, it must be inserted in the appropriate place right away. How the elements are ordered depends on what has been chosen as the value of the cmpSel instance variable. The default is the `compare` selector. Other options for its value are `invertCompare` and `dictCompare`. These are the names of methods. `Compare` and `invertCompare` are implemented in the Object or root class. The `dictCompare` method is implemented in the String class. Although SortCltn is not a subclass of Cltn, it acts as though it were. Its defined operations are "plug compatible" with it, as the manual describes it.

Another instance variable that alters the behavior of instances of the SortCltn class is the addDupAction variable. It can take on four different values: ADD, REJECT, MERGE, or REPLACE. These different value options select different ways in which duplicate elements can be handled. If the ADD value is chosen, duplicates are permitted. To preserve the sorted ordering, any duplicate elements must always be the immediate successors of the elements they duplicate. With the REJECT option, duplicates are forbidden. As its name suggests, the MERGE option specifies that any duplicates will be merged using the merge method of the member's class.

Graphics Class

Objective-C provides the two rudimentary "graphics" classes: Point and Rectangle. As such, this is a far cry from a full, object-oriented graphics system, but the construction of these classes is still quite informative. A point has two main instance variables: xLoc and yLoc. Instance methods include all those it inherits from the Object class, as well as those for setting and accessing the values of the two coordinates, those for moving the coordinate, and even those for performing simple math operations on the coordinate values.

To make use of instances of the Point class for making actual drawings, object-oriented systems generally have something similar to the Pen class used in Smalltalk and Actor, which implements the basic turtle graphics functions. In these systems, Pen is a descendant of the BitBlt class, which implements bit block transfers. These classes do not come with the Objective-C system, so to actually use the Point and Rectangle class, the equivalents of BitBlt and Pen would have to be implemented.

Listing 4.3 is a short demo function in Objective-C, and Listing 4.4 is the actual listing in C generated by the compiler. The C output has been reformatted in a less compressed form for easier reading.

4.15 The VICI Interpreter

An important accompaniment to the Objective-C compiler running on larger machines such as the Sun or the VAX is an interpreter that understands both C and Objective-C. As even a superficial acquaintance with Smalltalk demonstrates, a dynamically interpreted environment is an ideal accompaniment to an object-oriented system. The interpreter evaluates and executes statements typed in interactively as well as those read in from disk files. Perhaps best of all, not only can VICI be used stand-alone for development. It can also be linked into applications to become an integral part of them.

Listing 4.3 Short Objective-C Demo Program

```
= DemoPoint : Object ( Practice) {int xLoc,yLoc; }

+ create {return [ [ super new ] initialize] ; }

- initialize { xLoc = 100; yLoc = 100; return self; }

- print { printf ("This point's coordinates are (%d@%d ) \n" ,
xLoc, yLo

=
```

Listing 4.4

```
#line 2 "demo.c"
typedef struct _PRIVATE * id; id _msg(), _msgSuper();
#line 1 "demo.m"
#line 5 "demo.c"

struct _PRIVATE
  {
   struct _SHARED *isa;
   int xLoc;int yLoc;
  };
   extern id DemoPoint, Object;
   struct _SHARED
  {
   struct _SHARED *isa, *clsSuper;char *clsName;
   char *clsTypes;short clsSizInstance;short clsSizDict;
   struct _SLT *clsDispTable;
  };
   extern struct _SHARED  _DemoPoint, _DemoPoint;
   extern char *Practice[];

#line 1 "demo.m"
#line 3 "demo.m"

/* create=Practice[0] */
 static id _1_DemoPoint(self,_cmd)id self;char *_cmd;
{
 return_msg(_msgSuper(_DemoPoint.clsSuper,Practice[1]
 /*new*/),Practice[2] /*initialize*/);
}
#line 5 "demo.m"
/* initialize=Practice[2] */
 static id _2_DemoPoint(self,_cmd)id self;char *_cmd;
{
 self->xLoc = 100;self->yLoc = 100;return self;
}
#line 7 "demo.m"
/* print=Practice[3] */
static id _3_DemoPoint(self,_cmd)id self;
char *_cmd;
{
 printf("This point's coordinates are (%d@%d ) \n",
 self  >xLoc,self->yLoc);
}
#line 16 "demo.c"
extern struct _SHARED  _Object, __Object;
struct __SLT
 {
```

Listing 4.4 (continued)

```
 char **__cmd;id (*__imp)();
};
 static struct __SLT _clsDispatchTbl[1]=
{
 &Practice[0], (id (*)())_1_DemoPoint, /* create */
};
 static struct __SLT _nstDispatchTbl[2]=
{
 &Practice[2], (id (*)())_2_DemoPoint, /* initialize */
 &Practice[3], (id (*)())_3_DemoPoint, /* print */
};
 static char _bufClsName[]="_DemoPoint";
 struct _SHARED __DemoPoint=
{
 &__Object,
 &__Object,&_bufClsName[0], 0,sizeof(struct _SHARED), 1,
 (struct _SLT *)_clsDispatchTbl
};
 struct _SHARED _DemoPoint=
{
 &__DemoPoint, &_Object,&_bufClsName[1],
 "#ii",sizeof(struct _PRIVATE), 2,
 (struct _SLT *)_nstDispatchTbl
};
#line 8 "demo.m"
```

As with most interpreters, VICI allows you to inspect the value of any variable by typing its name. A trace facility for both C and Objective-C is built in that provides various trace options including:

1. Tracing execution of compiled messages

2. Tracing interpreted messages

3. Tracing the allocation of space to new objects

Although VICI allows statements to be entered interactively, it is not set up with a full-fledged, built-in editor for serious programming. Typically, programmers will choose an outside editor to use in conjunction with VICI.

Symbolic Debugging

One very convenient feature of the IBM AT version of Objective-C is that you can use the Microsoft Codeview debugger as a source-level debugger even for the Objective-C syntax. To be able to work with objective-C source in Codeview, you must use the -g option when initially compiling the application. Once done, you can bring up CodeView with Objective-C source displayed, and you are able to set breakpoints in the source for interrupting execution, enter expressions for evaluation, and so on. However, you cannot inspect the values of objects directly. To do so, you must obtain access on the lower level by first using CodeView to find the addresses of objects whose values are sought. You then have to know the structure of the information stored there as represented in HEX. Only by applying CodeView commands to 32-bit pointers in HEX can you inspect the values. Therefore, the amount of debugging that occurs at the source level is very limited.

Discussion

One question that inevitably comes up with a system like Objective-C is just how well it stacks up against a more traditional, object-oriented system like Smalltalk. Certainly, if you are using it on a PC- or AT-type machine without the benefit of an interpreter like VICI, your ability to learn the system by exploring it interactively will be somewhat limited. In a Smalltalk system, besides the convenience of the browsers and other window-oriented facilities, you can also use various built-in methods to help you explore the system and to interactively provide you with the information you need to write your program. With Objective-C on a PC or AT, you must rely on written documentation. Fortunately this documentation is extremely well written, and the difference is essentially one of convenience. As with any programming language, it is possible to write various utilities such as cross-reference programs and others that can assist you.

Another issue is the size of the foundation class library that comes with the system. Here, Objective-C lies about midway between C+ + and more fully developed environments like Smalltalk and ACTOR (discussed later in this chapter). One thing that compensates somewhat for this is the ability to use existing C code and libraries to build up a custom class library relatively quickly. However, this possibility also exists in some cases for other languages, too. Keep in mind, too, that the runtime image of Objective-C may not always be compatible with all C programming systems and libraries available for Microsoft C. Unfortunately this is the case with the Microsoft Windows programming environment. Apparently, the conflict between its runtime requirements and those of Objective-C make it impossible to use the two together.

A major difference between Objective-C and other object-oriented languages like Smalltalk and ACTOR is the absence of the block construct. In these languages, a block of code is implemented as an unnamed object that allows evaluation to be deferred. Block objects are an extremely powerful construct that allow an additional degree of modularity in defining methods. Research is being conducted on adding the block construct to Objective-C, but it has not as yet been announced as a feature for a future release.

The field of object-oriented programming is besieged with metaphors. These metaphors can be a mixed blessing. There is no doubt that they perform a useful function in introducing the basic notions of this programming paradigm. But they also can be the source of misconceptions. It is important at some point to give them a hard shake to see what fruit they really bear.

In what sense is it really appropriate to compare classes with factories? It is only the products of a class, its instances, that really do anything. Like a factory, the class is designed to produce a specific product. But does a factory ever resemble its products? Is a class purposely designed to produce massive numbers of instances efficiently? This tells us right away that classes are more like molds or templates used in a factory, rather than like the factory itself. However, they are unique in that they are molds that can also be used to produce other molds as well. In this sense they are more flexible than either factories or molds.

What about the Software-IC metaphor? The idea here is that just as functional hardware modules can be reused in many different boards, so can classes in a software design. But in just what sense are classes reusable? Aren't library functions also reused in many different applications that their original authors never foresaw? It is important to recognize that classes are reusable in ways that neither library functions or hardware ICs are. You cannot generally use off-the-shelf chips to construct new chips. But you can clearly build new library functions and classes out of existing ones. The real difference between classes and library functions is that classes are much larger and more complex units and are used in very different ways. A class usually contains many library functions and data objects that will belong together in any application in which they are used. Library functions and hardware ICs both fall far short of this.

One of the best features of the Objective-C language is its syntax. It is far more readable than that of C+ + or C. Many people have criticized C for its poor readability. Here, I think, is one area where Objective-C represents a clearcut improvement over its mother tongue. Another improvement is that you get many of the advantages of C but on a much higher level. With so many data structures and functions provided as standard in the language, Objective-C in principle allows us to write some fairly large, high-level applications without having to fear that a reliance on machine-specific library routines or custom code will cause the applications to become obsolete over time. Finally, Objective-C implements dynamic binding in a C compiler environment. This means that objects are created at run time rather than at compile time. This is clearly one of the features that all AI languages have in common. It is very difficult to imagine writing programs that can learn or respond to new situations if everything has been defined statically when the program was compiled. This, aside from the more readable syntax, is what really differentiates Objective-C from C+ +.

The release of Objective-C that I used for my evaluation was the version 3.31 implementation ported to the IBM PC/AT. The language is also running on the VAX, the Sun workstation, and the HP-9000. The AT version of Objective-C comes on one high-density disk and includes the compiler, libraries, and the main classes also in source form. At this point, the only C compiler supported on PCs is version 4.0 of the Microsoft C compiler. Support for version 4.0 is planned.

4.16 Ctalk

Ctalk is an object-oriented programming tool that effectively operates as a hybrid of the C and Smalltalk programming languages. What enables it to do this more effectively than other similar attempts is an ingenious way of incorporating a Smalltalk-like browser in the C programming environment. The Ctalk browser can be used interactively, just like the Smalltalk browser, even though C is a compiled, rather than an interpreted language. Ctalk also incorporates other essential features of a true object-oriented language such as inheritance, encapsulation, and runtime binding. In all, there are three main programs in the Ctalk system. Besides the browser, there are the preprocessor compiler and the Make utility. The C compilers currently supported are: Microsoft, Lattice, Turbo, and C86. Also, the same system supports all of these, so that additional cost is not incurred if you switch compilers midstream. To get an idea of the advantages presented by programming with a tool like Ctalk, we will first describe the innovative browser, which forms the real center about which this programming tool revolves.

The Ctalk Browser

It is surprising how similar the Ctalk browser is to the Smalltalk facility after which it was modeled. Like its parent, the Ctalk browser acts as a combination editor and application manager that allows object-oriented systems to be developed incrementally and interactively. That's quite an important achievement for a C-based, object-oriented tool.

The browser exists as a stand-alone program that is called up as any stand-alone application is. However, as will be seen, it is a program that provides an extremely powerful facility for integrating virtually the entire Ctalk system. Not only does the program allow you to familiarize yourself with the environment through interactive browsing, but it can be used for doing many programming chores interactively, including creating a Make file for batch processing the compilation and linking operations.

The Ctalk browser is divided into a number of panes that operate like tiled windows, in that these apertures cannot be overlapped or resized. At the upper left is the pane that displays the class hierarchy. Just as with a Smalltalk browser, when a class is selected, its methods are shown in the upper-right window pane. Then, in turn, a method can be selected and its code is made available for editing in the bottom text pane. Alternatively, any text file can be loaded into the browser and displayed in the lower text pane to be edited. Thus, the browser fills the dual purpose of a small, simple editor and a tool specially equipped for handling Ctalk objects.

To operate the browser, various popup menus are available in different pane areas. These popups can be activated either by mouse or key commands. Included in the browser facilities is a shell that allows you to issue commands to the operating system from within the browser, or alternatively, to temporarily exit to the operating system for doing various chores, and return to the browser just as you left it. The use of this kind of shell has become so widespread that its absence is conspicuous.

An important difference between the Ctalk browser and a Smalltalk browser is based on the fact that the former is a stand-alone application in a compiled environment and the latter is part of an interactive system in which everything is copresent. Since the Ctalk browser does not have the classes as part of itself, when it is first loaded it looks for all the class definitions that exist in the current directory on disk and compiles them into its database so that it can provide interactive access to them.

Once everything has been loaded into the browser, many functions needed for writing applications can be implemented interactively, so that the browser actually generates the code. Such functions include specifying a new application, loading existing classes, defining new classes and their methods, and saving all work.

Not everything was "ideal" yet in the version of the browser I tested. For example, the ability to load text files into the editor is confined to rather small files. If the file you load into the browser editor is larger than the maximum size allowed, only the amount that fits is loaded, and no error message is given. This can be dangerous for the unwary because if you were to make a small change and save such a file, a substantial loss of data could result. For this reason, the browser is useful primarily for implementing the "build" facilities that allow you to create various small files that will form modules in a complete system. For editing relatively large files, you must use another editor.

Ctalk Syntax

The syntax of Ctalk is slightly different from other object-oriented C dialects, but once you master a few conventions, it becomes relatively straightforward to read and write if you already know C. The main convention concerning Ctalk messages is that they are always flanked by two "at" signs (@). For example, if we want to create a new instance of a class such as Rectangle, the message would look like this:

```
@Rectangle new_ &rect@;
```

Here, the ampersand character is used for pointer notation, exactly as used in C.

One of Ctalk's most powerful features is its ability to map one message to another. This means that the selector, or name of a message, can be passed as an argument to another message. The syntax for doing this is a variable assignment statement with the name of the message selector enclosed by single quotation marks.

To actually send a message that references another message that has been stored as a variable, special messages are provided as methods of the Object class that are inherited by all other objects. These methods are perform_, perform_with_, and perform_with_with_.

For example, if we have defined the variable gval as follows:

```
id gval;
gval = 'getValue';
```

and an object,

```
id obj;
int gval;
```

The id statement is a Ctalk class id declaration. In Ctalk programs you must make external declarations for each class id that is referenced.

Then the getValue message could be mapped by the expression:

```
@obj perform_ gval with &val@;
```

Here it is assumed that val is a slot in obj and that the getValue message takes this as an argument.

As with most object-oriented languages, the pseudovariables self and super are used to reference objects within a message. The self pseudovariable references the object to which the message is sent. The super pseudovariable references the superclass of a class. To access the instance variable of the object to which a message is sent, the following notation is used:

```
self-> width
```

assuming that width is the name of an instance variable for the object in question.

Another Ctalk syntax convention involves the use of the underscore character. An underscore following a message selector name indicates that an argument is to follow. From a practical point of view, one of the more important things about an object-oriented C system is the size of its built-in foundation classes.

Ctalk Foundation Classes

The foundation classes are listed in hierarchical format as follows:

```
Object
 Assoc
 Container
  Buffer
   Stream
  ByteArray
  Collection
   OrdCollect
    Stack
 Set
  Dictionary
 IntArray
 String
```

The Container class is an abstract or formal class used for creating subclasses that provide dynamic data storage elements. This means that a subclass of Container can allow instances to be created that have either fixed- or variable-sized data elements, as well as sequential or nonsequential access methods. For example, if the expand message is sent to an object, the object is doubled in size. For more precise size expansion, you can use the expandBy_ method. This method takes an argument that specifies the number of additional data elements the expanded object will contain. The putRecSize_ method similarly sets the size in bytes for each data element that the object contains. To access an indexed object, you can use the at_get_nRecs_ method, which returns as many records as you specify, starting at the specified index number. Nearly all of these foundation classes are various subclasses of the Container class for implementing various different types of data structures. Usually a dynamic data structure is defined much farther down the class hierarchy in an object-oriented system. This is a fairly innovative way of approaching the matter.

The Buffer class is intended to provide a simple means of storing and maintaining large blocks of data in either byte or word format. An immediately obvious extension to this class is to add an instance variable that indicates whether a given Buffer object is a byte or word buffer. General read and write routines could then be written that first send a message to a buffer to see if it is in byte or word format. In this way, a program need not be specific to one type of buffer or the other.

The Stream class is implemented as a subclass of Buffer and includes one instance variable called position as a way of indexing the current stream position. The Collection classes provide for objects in which other objects are grouped. The subclasses of Collection itself vary according to whether access to elements is ordered or random, and whether the size is bounded or unbounded. So, for example, the OrdCollect class allows elements to be inserted and retrieved in sequential order, and for the size of the collection itself to be expanded automatically as new elements are added.

Text Window Classes

CNS, Inc. has developed some additional classes that provide support for the creation of text windows in the Ctalk environment. The additional classes as they are arranged hierarchically are as follows:

```
Browser
File
Menu
Mouse
Notifier
ScreenMgr
TxPoint
Window
  ButtonWin
    ItemWin
```

```
 Scrollbar
 StdWindow
  ListWindow
   HorListWin
  PopUp
 Response
 TxtWindow
  TxEditor
WinManager
```

Let's look briefly at what some of these additional classes do. The Browser class provides some of the basic methods for creating a browser similar to the one included in the Ctalk system. Over twenty methods are supplied with this class. Even a main program is included for creating a test browser program. This code can produce a "test browser" that lacks various features that the real tool has, but it shows many of the essentials of how the tool is created. For those who want to develop their own custom browser that they can continue to extend at will, this code will represent a flying head start in that direction.

The Browser class is a direct subclass of Object that makes use of the TxBuffer, TxEditor, Response, and File classes. The TxWindow class and its subclass TxEditor coordinate handling text in windows by sending messages to objects in nine different classes. Together, they handle processing keystrokes and managing characters in buffers.

Window is the abstract class for forming most of the classes that are used for defining the various features of windows such as those used by TxWindow. The WinManager class is the one that ties it all together. This class sends messages to most of the other classes so as to coordinate their behavior. Currently, it has a total of about seventeen methods. A quick way to get an overview of what it does is to take a peek at its initialize method, which is reproduced in Listing 4.5.

The initialization routine first sends a message to the Screen Manager and tells it the type of screen to create. Then the Mouse object is told to create the specified type of cursor. Next an Ordered Collection object is created to serve as a window list. Then the Window object itself is created with the designated proportions and attributes. Finally, an Event Manager is created. This is an excellent example of how Ctalk makes use of one of the main paradigms in object-oriented system design, that of employing one object as the manager of other objects. The only shortcoming of this approach is that it tends to bog down when the number of objects involved gets large.

Runtime Applications

Completing a Ctalk application is generally a five-step process.

1. Write the necessary source code files in the C and Ctalk syntax, which is written in disk files with the .PRE file extension.

Listing 4.5 Initialization Routine of Win Manager

```
initialize
/* Initialize the receiver: set up Metawindow, win_list and create
root
/* window.
{ id      newWin;
  int     w, h;
  extern  id  Menu;

  @ScreenMgr create_ &Screen@;
  self->color = @Screen color@;
  w = @Screen getXmax@;    h = @Screen getYmax@;
  @Mouse  create_ &Mcursor@;                /*  init  mouse service
  routine */
  @Mcursor setColor_ self->color@;
  @OrdCollect new_ &self->winList  size_ 25@;
  @Window new_ &newWin par_  NIL  x_ 0 y_  0 wdth_ w hght_ h@;
  self->rootWin = newWin;
  @self->rootWin getAbsRegion_ &mbox@;     /* init movement box*/
  /*@self->winList add_ self->rootWin@;*/
  self->activeWin = self->rootWin;
  Dispatcher = @Notifier create@;    /* an instance of the event
manager
}
```

2. Write a main routine in C that calls all the necessary modules.

3. Run the proprocessor and compile all the Ctalk files into the corresponding C files.

4. Compile all the C files with a C compiler.

5. Link the compiled .OBJ files to form the executable file for the application.

For those who wish, as mentioned earlier, there is a convenient way of collapsing some of these steps using the "Make" option in the Ctalk browser. To do so, you would select the "Make Spec" popup menu. The result of using this interactive procedure is the creation of a .MAK file, which a special auxiliary program can use to automatically carry out the three steps of preprocessing, compilation, and linking as a batch process. Since the browser supports calling DOS commands and exiting to DOS, you do not need to exit the browser to "make" the finished file executable or even to test it afterwards.

Documentation

The Ctalk system comes with a User Guide in the form of a slender, spiral-bound booklet. Despite its small size, the document is very useful because it is well designed and very clearly written. A handy, quick-reference card is also included. However, the guide badly needs an index. Although the browser makes Ctalk somewhat self-documenting, it is not always convenient to be both programming in the browser and using it for reference purposes at the same time. Consequently, it is still necessary to consult written documentation, but this is rather time consuming without an index. Even so, this is not as important a shortcoming as it is with other languages because the reference material is usually organized by classes, which makes things easier to find.

Evaluation

Ctalk succeeds very well in doing what it sets out to do, namely, providing a language that is a true hybrid between C and Smalltalk. The browser puts it in a class all by itself among other similar attempts. A major difference between Smalltalk itself and all of the C hybrids that have appeared so far is in the number of foundation classes present. As it is sold, Smalltalk is not just a bare-bones language. In effect, it amounts to a language plus a large generic function library that is standard in this case by definition.

For this reason, the Window classes we have described are an important addition for the Ctalk system. The importance of these library classes can be appreciated when you recall that objects in an object-oriented system are working parts for programs rather than just stand-alone functions. In a sense, then, a system with a large class library is one with a substantial part of the programming already done. The downside is that the programmer has to learn these classes and how to use them. Although one of the advantages of the object-oriented approach is that this is all done generically, the learning curve still exists for class libraries.

One minor potential drawback of this type of system is that it is set up to work mainly with Ctalk source code in the browser. If a developer wants to sell class libraries in the object file format, it will not be possible to use them with the browser in the current design. Perhaps a way can be devised for loading key class information into the browser without divulging all the source code involved. This would allow the browser to be used even with object code class libraries. The main thing to emphasize is that Ctalk has all the essential elements of a true object-oriented language, and the browser has been done well enough to give the interactive feel of a Smalltalk environment, while offering all the advantages of any C-based system.

4.17 The ACTOR Language

The first important thing about ACTOR is that it runs under Microsoft Windows (MS-Windows) and is the first object-oriented programming tool specifically designed for writing applications that run in that environment. For now, ACTOR applications must run under Windows. Later, though, The Whitewater Group plans to provide a version of ACTOR that also allows applications independent of the Windows desktop. If you are going to write something that runs under Windows and are wondering if there are any object-oriented tools you can use, now you know that at least one such tool is available.

The evaluation in the paragraphs that follow should help you decide just how appropriate it is for your purposes.

The ACTOR Desktop

ACTOR runs on top of MS-Windows and uses the Windows facilities to implement objects that allow an interactive, windowing environment for development just like Smalltalk. As with MS-Windows, you need a mouse to use ACTOR.

The main items used on the ACTOR desktop are the Workspace windows, browsers, and inspectors modeled on those used in Smalltalk. When the system first comes up, it shows a Workspace window with two rows of command options along the top bar of the Workspace window. The commands include File, Edit, Doit, Browse, Inspect, Show Room, and Templates.

The editing area of a Workspace window behaves just like an interpreter. If you type in an expression and then a carriage return, ACTOR attempts to compile and execute the expression. If there is a body of text already in an editing window, you can highlight a portion of that code and click on Doit to compile and execute that portion of code. Selecting either the Browse or the Inspect option opens a new version of the appropriate tool, similar to a popup window on the ACTOR desktop.

Inspectors are used for focusing in on a particular object. You use them to examine and modify the contents of objects in detail. The upper-left pane of an Inspector window contains a list box that displays all the instance variables of an object. Clicking the mouse on any of the items in the scrollable list of variables causes its value to be displayed in the bottom pane of the inspector, its Edit window. Both class objects and their instances can be accessed using inspectors.

A browser provides a similar function to that of an inspector, but instead of providing an interactive window on a single object, it does this for the entire system of classes. Its scrollable list box lists all the classes currently in the ACTOR class hierarchy. The right-hand list box contains the methods for the current class. By first selecting a class and then a method in that class, you may access the code in the bottom window and edit it. An Options selection on the browser menu bar allows you to choose whether the classes are listed in hierarchical or alphabetical order.

ACTOR Class

ACTOR comes with a surprisingly large class library of ready-made code that can be used for building applications fairly quickly once you bridge the learning curve of using the system and knowing what is there. Here is a partial list of the classes used for data structures and the graphics facilities subsumed under them.

```
Object
     Collection
            Indexed Collection
```

```
Array
      Function
      Ordered-Collection
             Sorted-Collection
             Text-Collection
Byte-Collection
      String
             Symbol
      Struct
             DosStruct
             Graphics-Object
                    Polygon
                    Rect
                           Ellipse
                           RndRect
             Proc
```

ACTOR Syntax

As with languages like C and Pascal, ACTOR encloses arguments to a method in parentheses immediately following the method's name or selector. And like Pascal and Smalltalk, variable assignments are made using the colon-equal (:=) symbol. Also as in Smalltalk, the way you create new instances is by sending the message new to a class and assigning this new instance a name. For example, we could create an instance of the Turtle class by saying:

```
Barney := new(Turtle);
```

In general, sending messages in ACTOR is like passing arguments, but in reverse. The object to which the message is sent is treated as an argument. Now that we have created the turtle Barney, we can get him to do our bidding by sending various messages that he can recognize. Like any authorized Turtle, Barney knows that the message r means turn right, l means turn left, f means move forward, and b means move backward. He also knows that down means to put his tail to the ground for drawing purposes, and up means to pick it back up again. So, if we wanted Barney to perform a turtle walk in the shape of a square, the messages we would send him would be:

```
down(Barney);
f(Barney, 10);
r(Barney, 90);
f(Barney, 10);
l(Barney, 90);
b(Barney, 10);
r(Barney, 90);
f(Barney, 10);
up(Barney);
```

In ACTOR, the keyword Def is used to define methods. So, if we want to teach the new message walkSquare not only to Barney, but to all authorized turtles, we would define the following method:

```
Def walkSquare(self, size)
{    down(self);
     f(self, size);
     r(self, 90);
     f(self, size);
     l(self, 90);
     b(self, size);
     r(self, 90);
     f(self, size);
     up(self);
};
```

Henceforth, to get Barney or any of his relatives to perform the preceding maneuver, all we would have to do is to say:

```
walkSquare(Barney, 10);
```

The more astute turtle-watchers have probably noticed that this turtle walk is only one orientation for this type of maneuver. There is a species of turtle, admittedly rare, that instinctively will do its square-walking counterclockwise. Fortunately, object-oriented systems like ACTOR provide a way of mirroring this little sidelight of natural history. To cover this complexity, we can define a new class of turtle called CounterTurtle and provide a walkSquare method for turtles of this species that do the counterclockwise variant of the standard turtle square walk. Coincidentally, this will also provide us with the opportunity to illustrate how new classes are defined in ACTOR.

The way you usually create new classes in ACTOR is from within a browser, so we will do it that way first. Very simply, we first select the class Turtle from the class list. Then we go to the Options pull-down menu and select "Make Descendant." Then a popup window opens that serves as a template for creating the new class. In this case, we will enter CounterTurtle as the name of the class. Now we just click on the Accept button, and the system creates this new class. Its name is added to the class list, and it becomes part of the ACTOR class hierarchy.

The other way to create new classes, which is what the browser is actually doing, is to write the code for it directly. The inherit statement is used for this. So we could write:

```
inherit(Turtle, #CounterTurtle)
```

One of the most attractive things about the ACTOR system is that it provides built-in classes for facilitating the use of the Microsoft Windows user interface. Three main classes are involved: Window, Control, and ModalDialog. First let's look at the Window class and its descendants. Here is an outline of this branch of the class hierarchy:

```
Object
    Window
        PopupWindow
            ToolWindow
                Browser
                Inspector
        TextWindow
            EditWindow
                WorkEdit
                    BrowEdit
                    FileWindow
                    Workspace
            ScanWindow
            WorkWindow
```

Though relatively large, Window is just a formal or abstract class. This means that it implements the methods that will be used by the subclasses that implement the specialized windows that actually get instantiated and used. In particular, Window implements the routines that communicate with MS-Windows.

The TextWindow class is one of the simplest descendants of Window that you can actually get to do real things. This class allows you to create tiled windows that can print text. It does this with the printString and printChar methods, which call the Textout GDI (Graphics Display Interface) function in MS-Windows. Often you will want text windows that can do more that just show text, that can allow you to go in and edit that text. The subclass of TextWindow called EditWindow provides the code that supports this editing ability. The WorkEdit class takes this one step farther by allowing you to create windows that not only can edit, but also can enter ACTOR language statements to be evaluated. The three subclasses of WorkEdit provide the types of windows that are like those most often used, that is, browsers, file browsers, and general-purpose Workspace windows. The main difference, though, is that, like their ancestor TextWindow, these are tiled windows. The windows most often used in ACTOR come from another branch of the tree, which is implemented with the class PopupWindow.

The windows you get by instantiating PopupWindow are the familiar layered windows that stack up on top of one another. However, unlike the tiled windows, they do not permit you to zoom or contract them down to an icon. As is dictated by MS-Windows, popup windows have to have a "parent" text window. When this parent window is contracted into an icon, the popup windows associated with it temporarily become invisible.

Controls

As in MS-Windows, in ACTOR, a *control* is a special type of window that is used for routine input and output in a user interface. Examples of controls include buttons, list boxes, and scroll bars. The branch of the class tree concerned with controls looks like this:

```
Object
     Control
          Button
          ListBox
               ClassList
          Scrollbar
```

Like Window, the Control class in ACTOR is just a formal one; its subclasses are the ones that are actually instantiated in applications. Controls are handled in ACTOR in an almost identical way to Windows. New instances are created by sending the message new, and they are displayed by sending the message show.

The ListBox class is a subclass of Control that creates a small popup window that is associated with a parent window and displays a list of items. Usually the list box is used to present items which a user can select with the mouse. The Scrollbar class is not used for all the scrollbars on all the windows as you might have assumed. The style definition for windows typically handles that automatically. This class is used when scrollbars are needed in some other location than the standard one that windows typically get automatically. With this class, you can create a set of horizontal and vertical scroll bars that are on a part of the screen that is separate from the parent window they control. Similarly, the Button class is for creating buttons in ways other than the routine ones. Buttons come built in dialog boxes, but you might want to do other things with them. You might want to put them in regular windows, for example.

This brings us to the ModalDialog class and its subclasses:

```
Object
     ModalDialog
          ClassDialog
          DebugDialog
          DirtyCLD
          FileDialog
          InputDialog
```

Modal dialog boxes resemble popup windows in that they stack on top of other windows and they need a parent window with which they are associated. Like Window and Control, Modal Dialog is basically an abstract class that implements code intended for use by its descendants. The FileDialog class in ACTOR is used to create the dialog boxes that routinely appear in MS-Windows when you load a file by using a pull-down menu. The ClassDialog class is for dialog objects used when a class is being edited or created with a browser.

4.18 Expert System Demo

One demo included with ACTOR is a toy forward-chaining expert system that is based on a program by Bosworth. It solves a simple classification problem involving identifying different types of trees. The classes used to implement this include InferenceEngine, and its subclasses, Expert, Fact, and Rule. Rulesets are actually created as instances of the OrderedCollection class. Another instance of the OrderedCollection class is used to store TheReasons. The facts themselves are stored as a Fact Dictionary, an instance of the Dictionary class. The demo shows how the "guts" of a simple inference engine can be put together in an object-oriented programming system. It is, of course, a bare-bones system without any real capabilities for disk I/O or other facilities needed for actual serious use. However, an object system like ACTOR is well suited for providing the necessary user interface capabilities and for incrementally adding new features.

Applications

For AI applications, as well as for many other types of application, processing linked lists is essential. How does one go about doing that in ACTOR? One way might be to work with the Ordered Collection class and add subclasses to it with the necessary methods defined for list processing. Listing 4.9 however, a demo provided with the current release of ACTOR, offers another approach. The new class ListNode is defined as a subclass of the Collection class. The methods append, do, isAtom, printOn, and rPrintOn are defined for this new class. New methods are also defined for Object, the root class, including isAtom, PrintOn, and cons. If you inspect the code for cons, you will see that there is a routine for sending the message new to the ListNode class and creating a new instance for it. Obviously this is only the rudimentary beginning of what a functional list processing class would encompass.

As far as the suitability of ACTOR for AI applications is concerned, the same limitations that apply to Smalltalk apply here. As compared with LISP and PROLOG, Smalltalk and ACTOR are relatively low-level languages. They are suitable for developing AI applications, but many additional high-level methods and classes have to be written from scratch just to get started. The structures used by the Ordered Collection class differ significantly from dynamically modifiable linked lists.

In the terminology of object-oriented programming, ordered collections are fixed collections that are nevertheless "growable." This means that when you create an OrderedCollection, you must create one with a maximum number of elements. If the elements already stored in the collection have not yet reached the maximum, it is easy to add new elements to the beginning or end of the list. When the maximum is reached and you need more, you must send the message grow to the collection. What really happens when you do this is that a new array of the needed size is created and the elements of the old array are copied into it.

Debugging

With version 1.1, a new debugger was added to ACTOR. Currently both a low-level and high-level debugger are provided, but the low-level debugger is not formally supported and may disappear in later releases of the ACTOR system. Routine errors in code evaluated by ACTOR result in a dialog box that contains a stack history up to the point of the error. The dialog box will usually also contain a message that diagnoses the type of error. If you wish, when a dialog box is open due to an error, you can click on the debug button and cause a Debug window to open. This is a versatile debugging tool that combines some of the features of a browser and some of those of an inspector, as well as the ability to change any of the values associated with a method. With it you can also resume processing on the fly immediately after an error has been fixed.

Evaluation

On the whole, I found this to be a very thorough implementation of a full programming system with an excellent set of demo programs and helpfully written documentation and tutorials. The ideal ACTOR user probably would be a programmer who has already had some exposure to Smalltalk and who needs to prototype something quickly to run in the MS-Windows environment. For purposes like that, ACTOR is hard to beat.

There are so many similarities between Smalltalk and ACTOR that one may well ask why so much effort was expended to create a new language when implementations of Smalltalk already exist. There are two main reasons. First, ACTOR was designed to be compatible with the commercial PC environment; hence its built-in compatibility with the Microsoft Windows. Second, the syntax of ACTOR has been designed to be more familiar to programmers used to programming in C and Pascal. In short, ACTOR is intended to provide a system incorporating all that was good about Smalltalk, but repackaged for the specific needs of today's programmers working on PCs.

One thing about the implementation of ACTOR I personally dislike, though, is the absence of a facility for multiple inheritance. With systems intended for real-world applications, multiple inheritance should be a standard feature. The reason is simple. In the real world, it is very important that many things fulfill multiple roles and multiple functions. Multiple inheritance provides a ready way of handling this in an explicit way. Vendors of object-oriented tools who fail to include multiple inheritance typically offer the reason that they do not want to make the system too complex for users or that none of their customers has requested it. Neither of these answers is at all convincing. I have had no difficulty in using multiple inheritance in systems that have it and cannot imagine trying to build a serious object-oriented application without it.

In response to this, it might be said that you can still create classes of the same definition in a system without multiple inheritance the hard way by simply defining them to be exactly what you want. My feeling about this is that, although true in theory, it tends to be something that will never be done in practice. Personally, in the two years or so that I have worked with object-oriented programming systems, I have never done this unless the system provided for multiple inheritance, in which case it becomes a routine practice. The reason is the same one that makes interactive systems like ACTOR significant and not just a mere convenience. The more you make basic things easy to do, the more you tend to launch out into the more difficult areas creatively, trying things that otherwise you might not have tried. If you are a user of an object-oriented programming tool that lacks this feature, I strongly recommend that you encourage the vendor to put it at the top of the list for new features. I feel almost certain that you will not regret the results of having exercised your prerogative as customer.

Version 1.1 of ACTOR differs from 1.0 in two main ways. First, there is more space, an additional 70K, for compiling applications. Second, it is fully compatible with Windows II, though it does not fully support all of the Windows II facilities. A future release of ACTOR, though, will actually support programming with the new features of Windows II. Needless to say, the implementations of ACTOR that will use the full features of Windows II and the OS/2 Presentation Manager will ultimately determine the fate of this product. But if the quality of work on the current implementation is any indication, the future versions should be of very high quality indeed.

The Whitewater Group
Technology Innovation Center
906 University Place
Evanston, Ill. 60201
(312) 491-2370

4.19 Sample Code

I have included some sample programs in Listings 4.6 through 4.9. Listings 4.6 through 4.8 are familiar benchmark type programs: the prime number, Fibonacci, and Hanoi. Listing 4.9 contains some extensions for list processing.

Listing 4.6 Eratosthenes' Sieve Benchmark

```
inherit(Object, #Sieve, nil, nil,nil);
now(Sieve);
/* Returns the number of prime numbers between 0 and cnt,
inclusive. */
Def sieve(self, cnt | flags, count, c)
{       c := cnt + 1;
        flags := new(Array, c);
        fill(flags, true);
        count := 1;
        do( over(2, c),
                { using(i | triple)
                        if flags[i]
                        then triple := i*3;
                                if triple < cnt
                                then  do( overBy(triple-1, c,
i+i-1),
                                        { using(j) flags[j] := nil });
                                endif;
                                count := count + 1;
                        endif;
                });
        ^count;
}
Actor[#Sam] := new(Sieve)
/* To run type: sieve(Sam, 100) */
```

Listing 4.7 Fibonacci Program

```
now(Int)
```

```
/* Recursive way of finding the nth Fibonacci term. Note that
this way of finding the Fibonacci terms is very inefficient
because each message "spawns" two recursive messages. */
```

```
Def fib(self)
{ if self < 3
 then ^1
 endif;  ^fib(self - 1) + fib(self - 2);
}
```

```
/* Iterative way of finding the nth Fibonacci term. */
```

```
Def fib2(self | term, term1Before, term2Before)
{ if self < 3
  then ^1
```

Listing 4.7 Fibonacci Program (continued)

```
  else term := 2; term1Before := 1; term2Before := 1;
    do(new(Interval, 3, self + 1, 1),
      {using(i) term := term1Before + term2Before;
       term2Before := term1Before;
       term1Before := term;
      });
    ^term
  endif;
}
```

Listing 4.8 Tower of Hanoi

```
/* ref. Byte August, 86 p. 146  cbd 8.13.86 */

inherit(Object, #TowerOfHanoi, nil, nil, nil);

now(TowerOfHanoi);

Def moveTower(self, height, from, to, use)
{ if height > 0
  then
    moveTower(self, height - 1, from, use, to);
    moveTower(self, height - 1, use, to, from);
  endif;
}

Def moveTower2(self, height, from, to, use)
{ if height > 0
  then
    moveTower(self:TowerOfHanoi, height - 1, from, use, to);
    moveTower(self:TowerOfHanoi, height - 1, use, to, from);
  endif;
}

Actor[#Hanoi] := new(TowerOfHanoi);

/* Example solves runs the Tower of Hanoi problem*/
moveTower(Hanoi, 3, 1, 3, 2);
```

Listing 4.9 List-Handling Support in ACTOR

```
 C.B.Duff  7.13.86
 (c) Copyright, 1986 */

now(NilClass);
/* append nil to a node */
Def append(self, aNode)
{ ^aNode }
```

Listing 4.9 List-Handling Support in ACTOR (continued)

```
Def cons(self, aNode)
{ ^aNode }

Def rPrintOn(self, aStrm)
{ printOn('[', aStrm);
}


inherit(Collection, #ListNode, #(left right), nil,nil);

now(ListNode);

Def append(self, aNode)
{ ^cons( left, append(right, aNode));
}

Def do(self, aBlock)
{ if isAtom(left)
 then eval(aBlock, left);
 else do(left, aBlock);
 endif;
 if right
 then do(right, aBlock);
 endif;
}

Def isAtom(self)
{ ^nil }

Def printOn(self, aStrm)
{ printOn('[', aStrm);
 printOn(left, aStrm);
 rPrintOn(right, aStrm);
}

Def rPrintOn(self, aStrm)
{ printOn(' ', aStrm); printOn(left, aStrm);
 rPrintOn(right, aStrm);
 printOn(']', aStrm);
}
Def cons(self, aNode | newNode)
{ if isAtom(aNode)
 then newNode := new(ListNode);
 else newNode := copy(aNode);
 endif,
 newNode.left := self;
 newNode.right := aNode;
 ^newNode;
```

Conclusion

We have looked at several object-oriented languages. As the first general purpose object-oriented language, Smalltalk has a considerable headstart over the others. Having been around much longer, it has two advantages: that implementations have had a chance to become more perfected and that its sizable class library is already considered rather "standard." Two disadvantages of Smalltalk are that it is still known to only a small number of programmers and that it is primarily an interpreted language. Neither of these is an intrinsic disadvantage. It can certainly happen that as object-oriented programming becomes more widespread, Smalltalk will become as well-known as the more popular languages of previous generations. Implementations like that by Digitalk have already led to some very impressive applications running on today's microcomputers. This leads us to believe that the more conservative, who shy away from a language like Smalltalk because it is not "mainstream" enough, may be making a serious error. Since several real-time processing applications have been written in microcomputer implementations of Smalltalk, this is evidence that this language is as robust as any in the marketplace and worthy of being seriously considered alongside any other current programming language.

At least for the present, object-oriented C languages will occupy the spotlight for many programmers because of the widespread acceptance of C, their mother tongue, as it were. However, after the virtues of the object-oriented approach have reached a larger number of programmers, it is likely that more pure object-oriented languages will make their appearance in the area of commercial programming. As we will see in the final chapters, there is still considerable room for innovation in the development of new features that extend the modularity of programming models still further.

True or False?

1. Object-oriented systems relieve the programmer of many of the responsibilities for careful program design.

2. The same user interface code written in Digitalk Smalltalk can run without modification on both PCs and the Macintosh.

3. The name "Smalltalk" derives from the compact nature of the language.

4. Objective-C allows runtime binding in compiled code.

5. C++ is a full-fledged object-oriented programming system.

6. ACTOR is the first system for object-oriented programming to allow full access to programming in Microsoft Windows.

7. The Ctalk browser is seriously limited because C is a compiled language.

8. Smalltalk has the most extensive class library of any current OOP tool.

9. None of the programming tools discussed here has the feature of multiple inheritance.

10. Multiple inheritance is not relevant to the development of AI applications.

(F, T, F, T, F, T, F, T, T, F)

Chapter 5

Object-Oriented LISP

5.1 Background

Although Smalltalk was the first true general-purpose object-oriented language and some implementations are specifically aimed at AI applications, the main uses of this programming paradigm so far in AI have been with object-oriented LISP. The reason for this is probably the greater familiarity of LISP to people in the AI field, rather than any inherent features of the languages themselves.

The most interesting developments that have occurred with object-oriented LISP are some of the clear innovations it has made in object-oriented programming generally. Not only did LISP have little difficulty absorbing the object-oriented paradigm, but it did so with some important innovations to this programming approach. Three particular innovations are discussed here. They are *mixins*, *method combination*, and *multimethods*.

The *mixin* feature, the LISP version of multiple inheritance, enables the creation of a new class that inherits from more than just a single superclass. In effect, it allows users to build an object hierarchy that can be a network or tangled hierarchy, rather than just a simple tree. Although multiple inheritance is theoretically present in the latest release of Smalltalk-80, it was an afterthought in this language and has nothing that even approaches the readily usable and trouble-free operation of mixins in object-oriented LISP.

Method combination is a bit more difficult to explain than mixins, but it is no less important. The first commercial appearance of user-defined method combination in LISP was with the Symbolics Flavors system. This system did not just copy the approach to method combination used in Smalltalk, but rather it introduced a new approach. From the very beginning, the Flavors implementation stressed the order in which components were combined to produce a *flavor*. This was particularly true with methods, the procedures that are local to flavors. The very heart of the original Flavors system was defined by the way in which the methods of various components were combined. However, if you define a flavor that inherits from a number of other flavors or classes, each of which has its own specialized versions of the same message, how will the method for this new flavor be constructed? From the beginning, the Flavors system offered a variety of ways in which methods could be combined, and it even provided for user-defined method combinations. It was designed so that if you wanted to, you could define entirely new ways to combine the methods.

The default for method combination in Flavors is to ignore all but the latest implementation of the method, meaning the one defined in the most specific of the flavors from which the new flavor will inherit. If you decide to define an entirely new method for the new flavor, all the others are naturally overridden. The general format for the more complex types of method combination in Flavors is for one flavor to be selected to provide the *primary method* and for any other flavors to provide what are called *daemon methods*. The primary method controls the handling of the main function associated with the message, whereas the daemon methods are responsible for subsidiary tasks.

In Flavors there are two kinds of daemon methods: the *before* and the *after* methods.

The terminology is derived from the order in which the method functions are called. The basic way that combined methods work is that they first call all the before methods, then the primary method, and finally all the after methods. Each of these component methods is passed, in turn, the same arguments that were passed to the combined method. However, only the values returned by the primary method will be returned by the combined method. All values returned by the daemon methods are ignored. If there is more than one before method, they are called in the same order in which the flavors are combined, whereas multiple after methods are called in reverse order.

What is the point of these method combinations? They can have a variety of different uses, but one of the most obvious is to provide an additional type of modularity that captures the whole spirit of the object-oriented approach. With method combination, if you cannot find *all* of what you want for a flavor method in any one of the flavors from which it will be inheriting, yet part of it is available, method combination can often save you from having to rewrite the entire function from scratch.

You can select a method to inherit that can serve as your primary method. Then you just write whatever before and after methods can be added to this primary method to produce the desired result. Naturally this will not be possible in all cases. It will only work when the desired function can be combined from a number of separate functions. You will find that this applies to a surprisingly large number of cases, however.

Multimethods, a capability first made available in CommonLOOPS, could very well be the most important contribution object-oriented LISP has made so far to object-oriented programming. Basically, multimethods are functions that can be considered messages to any number of types of objects. Prior to the development of multimethods, a distinction was still made in object-oriented LISP between the object to which a message was sent and the arguments to the message procedure. So, in the expression

```
(send Rectangle draw-at 10 40)
```

the class Rectangle is solely responsible for recognizing the message and is distinguished from the numbers 10 and 40, which are arguments to the draw-at message. This is somewhat artificial because, in Smalltalk, numbers are treated as instances of the class Number, and arithmetical operations such as multiplication are considered messages to the numbers to multiply themselves. Multimethods takes this even further by considering the class to which a message is sent to be just another one of the arguments. Any number of arguments in principle can be passed to a multimethod, and each of the arguments is an instance of its own class. So a multimethod is really a message to an indefinite number of objects, with the method combination required to complete this message determined by the actual arguments used. More details about multimethods will be found in section 5.10, which explains CommonLOOPS.

One "problem" with object-oriented LISP is that it is just too popular for its own good. It has become a favorite tool, not only for programming AI applications, but for systems programming and developing user interfaces as well. The result of this diversity is a somewhat conflicting set of requirements for users of different types. Systems programmers and those developing user interfaces and advanced graphics applications are usually interested in high-performance code that is free of any bugs. AI researchers are willing to trade off some performance for greater flexibility and generality.

Since this is a book on artificial intelligence, the main interest here is in the AI uses of object-oriented LISP rather than the other ways that it is used. What are some of the primary considerations in its use for AI purposes? As we have already suggested, one of the most important is certainly the dynamic behavior of class systems. This refers to the ability of an object system to change dynamically to reflect changing circumstances in the world. It is of considerable importance in many AI programs that the system be able to update itself automatically to a greater or lesser degree. It is helpful to consider what this implies.

A minimum condition for such an automatic system is to keep a running tally of all the current objects of the system in a form that is easily accessible. In LISP this generally means maintaining a list of such items and being able to update the list as necessary. More specifically, it is necessary to be able to access at any given time all the instances that are currently "alive" and know their classes. If it does not already do this in some way, the system must at least support the minimum functions that would allow the access to instances to be implemented.

Closely related to this requirement is the ability to write functions that can create new objects with names that are only determined at runtime. Although this may sound trivial, in LISP it is very easy to create new objects by programming them with names the programmer specifies in the code, but it is not as straightforward to write functions that automatically create objects when needed with names that have to be specified at the time. Compared with this, uncreating objects is relatively trivial. If the system in use has no function corresponding to remob, it is still always possible to make a new object of the name of the one to be uncreated and set it equal to nil.

Such kinds of functions are necessary, for example, in creating what are known as composite objects. These are objects of a complex structure that contain other objects as parts. For example, a desk object could be described as a composite object comprising a top, legs, and drawers. In such a case, the component parts might well be instances of classes in their own right. To automatically create a composite object, therefore, would involve naming and creating all those instances that are parts of the composite. In a sense, the parts of a composite object can form another hierarchy that will exist alongside the abstraction hierarchy of classes in the object system. However, the composite object approach seems to be limited as far as creating very large hierarchies is concerned. It is difficult to imagine creating very large systems such as spacecraft in any degree of detail, for example. Are such systems necessary? If we want to be able eventually to create deep systems for diagnosing problems and predicting various consequences in emergency situations, or even for failure mode analysis for design purposes, such systems appear indispensable.

5.2 The Scheme Dialect

Because we use the SCOOPS extension to the PC Scheme dialect in developing some examples both here and later in the book, we will present some of the rudiments of programming in this dialect as well as provide some extensions to the language that bring it closer to CommonLISP.

One of the newcomers in the family of LISP dialects is a powerful one called Scheme, originally developed at MIT by Guy Steele and Gerry Sussman as an experiment intended to provide a medium for teaching a number of new and powerful programming concepts. The experiment proved to be extremely successful, and even now, almost ten years since its inception, Scheme is considered to be one of the most modern and progressive of the LISP dialects. Because much of its power is available in a relatively small size, Scheme has many advantages for small machines. One implementation, PC Scheme from Texas Instruments is a superset of the dialect that includes a powerful object-oriented component called SCOOPS.

Scheme resembles CommonLISP in supporting the lexical scoping of variables, but it also offers a number of other important and progressive ideas that are now beginning to spread into the LISP mainstream. Although at first it seems as though Scheme may be loaded down with a veritable "kitchen sink" of miscellaneous programming ideas, its underlying principles are actually quite simple and well integrated. Before explaining how these ideas are related, we will introduce them individually for the benefit of those who are not familiar with them. (Those who are already acquainted with these concepts may choose to jump ahead at this point.)

One basic notion in Scheme is that of an *environment* that can be saved as a context, while control shifts to other such environments temporarily, and can then return again to the original environment. Here the context described as an environment refers to a complete set of bindings of variables and named functions taken as a whole.

A second concept taken particularly seriously in Scheme is that of *firstclassness*. Although this idea did not originate with Scheme, in this dialect of LISP it has been taken to its logical conclusion, as it were. Briefly put, a *first-class object* is one that has no restrictions on the way it may be used. To be more precise, in most programming languages, only numbers, characters, and strings are first-class objects. Even then, sometimes only integers, not numbers in general, are really treated as first-class objects, and there may be certain restrictions on the use of one or more of these types of objects in certain respects. For example, you often cannot pass arrays, records, and functions as arguments to functions or store them in one another. Even in many conventional LISP dialects, some special handling is required when a function is passed as an argument to another function.

In this respect, Scheme is quite radical. The intention is for absolutely everything in Scheme to be treated as a first-class object. In the PC Scheme implementation, for example, not only procedures, but also environments and two other constructions called continuations and engines may be:

1. Stored in compound data structures.

2. Returned as arguments by a procedure.

3. Bound to variables in three distinct ways.

LISP functions are defined through lambda bindings. Since this bears a strong analogy to variable binding, some LISP aficionados have wondered why functions cannot be declared in the same way as variables and lists by writing:

```
(SETQ [name] lambda [args] function-body)
```

In Scheme, this is precisely what happens, though, in this case, it is the SETQ that is dropped, and DEFINE is used to bind all objects globally with lexical scoping. SET! is used only for changing the binding of objects that have already been created. In Scheme, two conventions are used. First, functions that end in an exclamation point modify their arguments. Second, functions that end in a question mark are predicates that return true or false. So, for example, zerop in LISP becomes zero? in Scheme. The commitment to making everything in Scheme a first-class object is quite revolutionary. It is almost impossible to completely envision the full potential of a programming system with such capabilities. It is very doubtful whether anyone has attempted to take this feature of Scheme to the limits of its power. Yet this is not the only radical concept in the Scheme design.

Another concept that is important in the Scheme dialect is that of a continuation. This is a basic concept of control structures in programs. Many of the more familiar LISP control structures such as catch and throw exemplify the idea of a continuation, but in Scheme this more general construct is available that enables the more specific ones to be custom built. A *continuation* is the process to which a computation will progress at a future point in time as has been specified through a programming construct. More specifically, the continuation is the part of a program that can be thought of as waiting for the result of a current computation, and in Scheme such continuations are first-class objects just as any current piece of data can be.

5.3 Scheme Control Structures

Some LISP programmers might be surprised to learn that there are no PROGs in Scheme. However, this is more of a policy statement than an absolute exclusion. Scheme also has some other special forms for control that, although they do not specifically replace PROGs, certainly do nearly anything that most PROG constructs can. A minor exception to this is PROG2, because Scheme does not have a control form that evaluates only the second clause in a sequence. But there are other ways of doing what PROG2 does. Many experienced LISP programmers consider the wholesale use of PROG constructs to be a crutch to be avoided, if possible, much the way structured programming acolytes feel about GOTOs.

LETREC is a variant of the LET macro, which allows a very interesting construct called mutually recursive functions, which, by definition, typically come in pairs. The following example, from the PC Scheme manual, implements two interdependent functions, even? and odd?, within the same binding environment, each of which recursively calls the other:

```
(define odd-r-even (lambda (n)
                (letrec ((even? (lambda (n)
                                (if (zero? n)
                                    #!true
                                    (odd? (-1+ n)))))
                        (odd? (lambda (n)
                                (if (zero? n)
                                    #!false
                                    (even? (-1+ n)))))))))
```

As this illustrates, the LETREC control structure allows two or more lambda procedures to be defined in the same environment, none of which is self-sufficient, but which collectively work in an efficient manner by calling one another for parts of their operation.

PC Scheme supports an extension that includes a special construct that provides for resource-oriented scheduling. An engine is a special procedure that is given a certain time, measured in ticks based on hardware clock interrupts, to complete its computation. It is supervised by two routines called a success procedure and a failure procedure. If an engine's computation is completed before its allotted time has expired, the success procedure is invoked and the result, together with the number of expired ticks, is returned. If the time expires before the computation is finished, the failure procedure is invoked with the creation of a new engine, which continues the original computation.

Although there is no built-in support to allow an executing engine to invoke another engine, the implementation of such nested engine mechanisms is possible using certain special techniques. Engines are well suited for developing discrete simulation applications, which ordinarily might require multitasking support at the operating system level.

5.4 SCOOPS

Although object-oriented programming with the message-passing paradigm is not a necessary part of the Scheme dialect, it accords well with the Scheme approach. Furthermore, PC Scheme includes a very powerful object-oriented extension called SCOOPS. The SCOOPS package is worthy of our consideration because it supports multiple inheritance and active values, facilities that previously were available only on very expensive hardware.

The inheritance approach used by the SCOOPS package is the nonhierarchical mixins that was first made popular by the Flavors system used on Symbolics LISP machines. As with Smalltalk and most object-oriented programming systems, SCOOPS has a class system and the usual ability of classes to inherit variables and methods from other classes. Unlike Smalltalk but like Flavors, SCOOPS classes are not limited to inheritance from superclasses in a simple tree hierarchy. Mixins allow classes to be defined that can inherit from as many other classes as the programmer chooses.

As mentioned earlier, one of the more attractive features of SCOOPS is the support it provides for active values. This is the same feature sometimes called procedural attachments in frame-based systems. Active values greatly extend the power of the SCOOPS class system because this is a means of assigning a function, or even a complex program, to be evaluated whenever an active value variable is accessed. This allows the association of complex data structures to SCOOPS instance variables and the opportunity for calculated values, based on both initial assignments to an instantiated object, as well as conditions in a dynamically changing environment. To illustrate the use of active values, we can take a simplified version of the difficult problem of composite objects as used in the CommonLOOPS system developed at Xerox PARC.

5.5 Composite Objects: An Example of Object-Oriented Programming in SCOOPS

A composite object is an instance of a class that is considered to be composed of objects that are instances of other classes, some of which may themselves be composite objects. For example, the body is composed of a head, arms, legs, and torso. The head, hands, and feet can also be represented as composed of other objects such as eyes, ears, fingers, and toes. How can composite objects be implemented in a system like SCOOPS? Ordinarily, SCOOPS does not support lists as values of slots or instance variables, much less more complex data structures. At the very minimum, a composite object has to contain a list of all of its components. Active values allow this to be done by assigning procedures to instance variables that access external data structures and knowledge structures. The format for specifying an active value is:

```
(instvar ( [VARIABLE] (active [INITIAL-VALUE] [GET-FUN]
[PUT-FUN]
```

GET-FUN and PUT-FUN represent two procedures, each consisting of only one argument, which may be defined, that are automatically evaluated when the usual get and put methods for an instance variable are sent to an object. The INITIAL-VALUE of the variable is the argument that is passed to these functions.

To make the functions access a list (so that when the usual get method is used, it returns, for example, a list of the composite object's component parts), you can make the initial value of the active value variable the name of the list of parts and define the get and put functions such that they can return and append this list. The appending function is tricky to implement because it needs the name of the list so that things may be appended to it. Since it is desirable to make such a function as general as possible so that it may be used with any composite object, it has to have a way of finding the name of the specific list of parts that applies only to the particular object in question. The problem is that the initial value, which is the name of the list in question, is not returned by its normal get function any more but is passed as an argument to the active value function. One way to get around this problem is to use another variable that is not an active value variable to store the name of the list where it may be easily accessed by a global function.

Here we illustrate a successful application of this strategy in SCOOPS. Two classes have been implemented, Composite-Object and Body, where the first is a mixin for the second. When we ask Scheme to describe the class Body, this is what is displayed:

```
[26] (describe body)

     CLASS DESCRIPTION
     ====================

   NAME           : BODY
   CLASS VARS     : (CLASS-PART-NAME CLASS-PART-NUM)
   INSTANCE VARS  : (NUMBERS-OF-PARTS PART-NAMES)
   METHODS        : (GET-CLASS-PART-NAME SET-CLASS-PART-NUM SET-
   CLASS-PART
   SET-PART-NAMES GET-PART-NAMES SET-NUMBERS-OF-PARTS GET-NUMBERS-
   OF-PARTS
   PUT-CPART-NAME)
   MIXINS         : (COMPOSITE-OBJECT)
   CLASS COMPILED : #!TRUE
   CLASS INHERITED : #!TRUE
   ()
```

The variables of Body have all been inherited from Composite-Object. The variable part-names is implemented as an active value that accesses a list and prints its contents when called. The variable numbers-of-parts is also an active value, but in this case, its get function returns and prints a property list that contains a list of body parts, each with the property of how many such parts the body should contain. One possible extension of this example would be to define various subclasses for different types of organisms. For example, humans, horses, ants, spiders, and centipedes would have different entries on their property lists for the number of legs.

An instance of the Body class was created for the current example called My-Body. The values of its variables were set so as to reference appropriate lists and property lists for the names and numbers of its parts. For example, sending My-Body the following messages produced the results indicated:

```
[27] (send my-body get-part-names)
(HEAD NECK ARMS HANDS TRUNK LEGS FEET)

[28] (send my-body get-numbers-of-parts)
(FEET 2 LEGS 2 TRUNK 1 HANDS 2 ARMS 2 NECK 1 HEAD 1)
```

Once this interface to more complex auxiliary data structures has been correctly
implemented, the values will then be displayed when the describe function is called for
an instance of a class. So, in the case of the object My-Body, which is an instance of the
Body class, the following result was returned when its description was requested:

```
[30] (describe my-body)

  INSTANCE DESCRIPTION
  ====================
 Instance of Class BODY
 Class Variables :
    CLASS-PART-NAME : BODY-PARTS
    CLASS-PART-NUM : HUMAN-BODY-PARTS

Instance Variables :
    NUMBERS-OF-PARTS : (FEET 2 LEGS 2 TRUNK 1 HANDS 2 ARMS 2
NECK 1 HEAD 1
```

In the full implementation of the Composite-Object class, which will not be discussed
further here, there would be various additional methods, including one that can
automatically initialize the objects that are part of any instance of this class or any of
those of which it is a mixin. This method would include a recursive procedure that first
accessed both the part-names slot to get a list of all of its component parts and the
numbers-of-parts property list to find out how many of each were needed, and then
repeated this for all of those parts that were also composite objects until all the objects
being instantiated were simple and not composite. As a variant, a subclass of Composite-
Object like the Perspective class in KRL and LOOPS could be built where the objects
that are its components would only be instantiated on request. The idea of a Perspective
is a composite whose components are not parts, but various roles in which the individual
object participates. In this sense, it would be as if the individual had various distinct
aspects, each of which could independently be members of different classes.

First, we will have to make some extensions to PC Scheme itself. This will also
provide an opportunity to discuss LISP programming in general, a familiar topic in this
book. LISP is the most organic and life-like of all programming languages. Most of its
dynamic character is the result of combining complex, nested structures that have
dynamically reassigned pointer structures and a simple syntax that uses the same
representation for data and programming code.

5.6 Future LISP

LISP is no longer based on a single programming model. Over the years it has absorbed other programming concepts and is continuing to do so. You have seen here what essentially amounts to LISP's simulation of Smalltalk. A product called Objective-C from Stepstone Corporation, which we discussed at length in section 4.15, has done a similar thing with C. The original model on which the LISP language was based is that of functional programming, using the Lambda Calculus developed by Alonzo Church.

The functional programming aspect of LISP involves a special implementation of argument passing so that ordinarily very few of the variables need to be stored permanently. The main objective of pure functional programming is not to modify objects in permanent storage, but to pass symbols as if they were values being passed between mathematical functions. The main result of such a program is the structure it returns rather than the state it creates in the permanent storage of the machine. But, as we have been emphasizing, LISP is not a simply a single paradigm programming language. It is a language that so far has been able to absorb each new programming model as it appears and to incorporate them into itself as a functioning whole.

In pure functional LISP programming, anything that not only returns a structure but also modifies the machine is generally considered a "side effect." But it is often very important in an object-oriented environment to be dynamically modifying the object hierarchy in complex and carefully controlled ways.

Take, for example, the case of performing simple list processing functions such as updating and modifying list structures. Here, either or both of the functions of returning the necessary structure or producing the necessary structure in permanent storage are often important parts of the required tasks. In this example, we will show various versions of an add-to-end function that are implemented so as to return different values and produce different side effects. This function extends the list processing functions of LISP to include the ability to add an element to the end of an already existing list structure.

The function give-n-take was written to demonstrate the side effects of the add-to-end function. First two lists are created: nums, which contains the list of number words, (one two three four five), and morenums, which is composed of the complementary number word list (six seven eight nine ten). Here is what give-n-take looks like:

```
(define nums '(one two three four five))

(define morenums '(six seven eight nine ten))

(define (give-n-take)
 (add-to-end (car morenums) nums)
  (set! morenums (cdr morenums)))
```

As you can see from the following short session, what give-n-take returns is different from the side effects it has on these lists. It simply returns the morenums list that was passed to it. However, when we ask LISP for the contents of these lists by typing their names at the interpreter prompt, we see the effects that give-n-take has each time it is called. It successively takes numbers from the beginning of the morenums list and adds them to the end of the nums list.

```
[2] nums
(ONE TWO THREE FOUR FIVE)

[3] morenums
(SIX SEVEN EIGHT NINE TEN)

[4] (give-n-take)
(SEVEN EIGHT NINE TEN)

[5] nums
(ONE TWO THREE FOUR FIVE SIX)

[6] morenums
(SEVEN EIGHT NINE TEN)

[7] (give-n-take)
(EIGHT NINE TEN)

[8] nums
(ONE TWO THREE FOUR FIVE SIX SEVEN)

[9] morenums
(EIGHT NINE TEN)
```

Now compare this to another version of the function called add-to-end-2. In the next session we create the list of integers from 1 through 4. Our original add-to-end returns something unusable, but the side effects are the correct result. Add-to-end-2 does just the opposite. It returns the list with the number added to the end, but when we examine the integers list, we see that nothing has changed. The add-to-end-3 function is another variant that performs identically to add-to-end-2, but is implemented in a more roundabout way using the insertr function.

```
[6] (define integers '(1 2 3 4))
INTEGERS

[7] (add-to-end 5 integers)
(4 5)

[8] integers
(1 2 3 4 5)
```

```
[9] (add-to-end-2 6 integers)
(1 2 3 4 5 6)

[10] integers
(1 2 3 4 5)
```

This has not been just an academic exercise. The side-effects version of add-to-end is a useful one for doing necessary housekeeping in an object-oriented LISP environment. It is very valuable to be able to maintain lists of all the current instances of various classes that are alive in a dynamically changing system. Without the version of add-to-end that can actually modify such lists, we could not continually update them.

Another function that could also be useful in this respect is delete-last!. It performs the opposite service, that of destructively removing the final element in a list. Its definition is:

```
(define (delete-last! lst)
  (delete! (car (last-pair lst)) lst))
```

The last-pair function in PC Scheme returns the last pair in a list. The function works for returning the last element as a single element list because the car function reduces the pair into a simple list structure. The following quick session shows the behavior of delete-last!. As you can see, in this case, both what it returns and its side effects are identical.

```
[2] (define numbers '(one two three four five))
NUMBERS

[3] (delete-last! numbers)
(ONE TWO THREE FOUR)

[4] numbers
(ONE TWO THREE FOUR)
```

Now we will return to actually programming with the SCOOPS system. Sending messages is a rather simple matter of using the send function with the receiver object and the message to be sent plus its arguments. So, to send a message to the my-body object giving it a new body part called toes, we would say:

```
[1] (send my-body put-cpart-name 'toes)

[2] body-parts

(HEAD NECK ARMS HANDS TRUNK LEGS FEET TOES)
```

If we then change our minds and decide to remove this new body part, we could do so by globally accessing the body-parts list using our newly defined delete-last! function as follows:

```
[3] (delete-last! body-parts)

[4] body-parts

(HEAD NECK ARMS HANDS TRUNK LEGS FEET)
```

The code in Listing 5.1 demonstrates simple inheritance in Scoops down several levels of a fairly linear hierarchy. First the Root class artifact is defined with the instance variables material, weight, purpose, and cost. Then transport-means is defined as a subclass of artifact with the additional instance variables medium, time-range, and power-source. Naturally, transport-means inherits all the variables and methods of the artifact class. Then we define transport-vehicle as the next subclass, and passenger-vehicle as a subclass of it. Descending further in the same linear manner of adding more and more specific classes that inherit everything from the previous class, we define the classes water-transport-vehicle, surface-vessel, ship, and ocean-liner. The instance object ship1 is created as an instance of the class ship. Two methods, speed and direction, are also provided for the ship class.

Listing 5.2 provides an example of multiple inheritance in SCOOPS. First the classes Business and Adversary are defined. Then the class Competitor is defined and uses the multiple inheritance feature to inherit everything from both of these two classes.

Listing 5.1 Simple Inheritance in SCOOPS

```
(define-class artifact
     (instvars material weight purpose cost)
     (options
   (gettable-variables material weight purpose cost)
    settable-variables
    inittable-variables))

(define-class transport-means
     (instvars medium time-range power-source)
     (mixins artifact)
     (options
   (gettable-variables medium time-range power-source)
    settable-variables
    inittable-variables))
```

Listing 5.1 Simple Inheritance in SCOOPS (continued)

```
(define-class transport-vehicle
      (instvars load-capacity length max-speed)
      (mixins transport-means)
   (options
    (gettable-variables load-capacity length max-speed)
     settable-variables
     inittable-variables))

(define-class passenger-vehicle
      (instvars capacity safety dining facilities)
      (mixins transport-vehicle)
      (options
 (gettable-variables capacity safety dining facilities)
  settable-variables
  inittable-variables))

(define-class water-transport-vehicle
      (classvars ( body-name 'hull) (dof 2) (dangers 'sink)
(advantages
      (mixins passenger-vehic
      (options
 (gettable-variables dof dangers)
  settable-variables
  inittable-variables))

(define-class surface-vessel
      (instvars #-decks #-masts #-engines)
      (mixins water-transport-vehicle
      (options
 (gettable-variables #-decks #-masts #-engines)
  settable-variables
  inittable-variables))

(define-class ship
      (instvars
    x-position y-position x-velocity y-velocity mass)
      (mixins surface-vessel)
                    (options
      (gettable-variables x-position y-position x-velocity
y-velocity ma
    settable-variables
    inittable-variables))

(define-method (ship speed) ()
   (sqrt (+ (expt x-velocity 2)
        (expt y-velocity 2))))

(define-method (ship direction) ()
   (atan y-velocity x-velocity))
```

Listing 5.1 Simple Inheritance in SCOOPS (continued)

```
(define-class ocean-liner
 (instvars company launched homeport tons)
 (mixins ship)
 (options
 (gettable-variables company launched homeport tons)
  settable-variables
  inittable-variables))

(define shipl (make-instance ship 'x-position 100 'y-position 150
        'x-velocity 30 'y-velocity 40 'mass 100))

 (compile-class artifact)
 (compile-class transport-means)
 (compile-class transport-vehicle)
 (compile-class passenger-vehicle)
 (compile-class water-transport-vehicle)
 (compile-class surface-vessel)
 (compile-class ship)
 (compile-class ocean-liner)
```

Listing 5.2 Multiple Inheritance in SCOOPS

```
(define-class business
 (instvars name location industry business-type size year-founded
           ownership-type gross-sales costs market-share)
 (options
  (gettable-variables  name location industry business-type size
year-founded
 settable-variables
 inittable-variables))

(define-method (business calc-net-gain) (gross-sales costs)
 (- gross-sales costs))

(define-class adversary
 (instvars  aggressiveness  allies  goals  common-goals strengths
           weaknesses)
  (options
   (gettable-variables aggressiveness allies  goals  common-goals
                       strengths weaknesses)
   settable-variables
   inittable-variables))

(define-class competitor
   (mixins business adversary))
```

Listing 5.2 Multiple Inheritance in SCOOPS (continued)

```
(compile-class business)
(compile-class adversary)
(compile-class competitor)

(define your-business (make-instance business))

(define competitor-1 (make-instance competitor))
```

Listing 5.3 Simple Extensions to PC Scheme

```
;   ********************************
;
;     Simple Extensions to PC Scheme
;
;   ********************************

; Some CommonLISP-compatible List Accessing Functions

(define-integrable first car)
(define-integrable second cadr)
(define-integrable third caddr)
(define-integrable fourth cadddr)

(define (fifth lst)
  (second (cdddr lst)) )

(define (sixth lst)
  (third (cdddr lst)))

(define (seventh lst)
  (car (cdddr (cdddr lst))) )

(define (eighth lst)
  (second (cdddr (cdddr lst))) )

(define (ninth lst)
  (third (cdddr (cdddr lst))) )

(define (tenth lst)
  (fourth (cdddr (cdddr lst))) )

; Some standard LISP functions to extend PC Scheme

(define (subst obj1 obj2 sym)
  (if (atom? sym)
      (if (equal? obj2 sym)
          obj1 sym)
```

Listing 5.3 Simple Extensions to PC Scheme (continued)

```
         (cons (subst obj1 obj2 (car sym))
               (subst obj1 obj2 (cdr sym)))))

(define (nth 1st n)
  (cond ((or (<? n 1) (zero? n)) (error "Number must be greater
     than zero" n))
        ((eq? n 1) (first 1st))
  (t (nth (rest 1st) (sub1 n)) ) ))

(define (nthcdr n x)
  (do ((x* x (cdr x*))
       (n* n (sub1 n*)))
      ((zero? n*) x*)))

(define (ncons x)
  (cons x nil))

(define (mapcan 1st proc)
  (cond ((null? 1st) nil)
        (t (nconc (apply proc (list (car 1st)))
                  (mapcan (cdr x) proc)))))

(define (maplist 1st fun)
  (cond ((null? 1st) nil)
        (t (cons (apply fun (list 1st))
                 (maplist (cdr 1st) fun)))))

(define (subset fun 1st)
  ((atom? 1st) nil)
  ((fun (car 1st))
    (cons (car 1st) (subset fun (cdr 1st))) )
  (subset fun (cdr 1st)) )

(define some (lambda (1st fun1 fun2)
               (define 1st nil)
               ((null? fun2)
                (begin0
                  ((atom? 1st) nil)
                  ((fun1 (car 1st) 1st) 1st)
                  (pop 1st) )
               (begin0
                  ((atom? 1st) nil)
                  ((fun1 (car 1st) 1st) 1st)
                  (set! 1st (fun2 1st)) ) ))

(define (every (lambda (1st* fun1 fun2)
                 (define 1st* nil)
                  ((null? fun2)
```

Listing 5.3 Simple Extensions to PC Scheme (continued)

```
                      (begin☐
                        ((atom? lst*))
                        ((not (fun1 (car lst*) lst*)) nil)
                        (pop lst*) ) )
                      (begin☐
                        ((atom? lst*))
                        ((not (fun1 (car lst*) lst*)) nil)
                        (set! lst* (fun2 lst*)) ) ))


; Variations on a theme

(define (add-to-end term lst)
  (set-cdr! (last-pair lst) (list term)))

(define (add-to-end-2 term lst)
    (append lst (list term)))

(define (add-to-end-3 term lst)
  (insertr (car (last-pair lst)) term lst))

(define nums '(one two three four five))

(define morenums '(six seven eight nine ten))

(define (give-n-take)
 (add-to-end (car morenums) nums)
  (set! morenums (cdr morenums)))

(define (delete-last! lst)
  (delete! (car (last-pair lst)) lst))

; insertr inserts an element to the right of a specified element
in a ;

(define (insertr old new lat)
  (cond ((null? lat) nil)
        ((eq? (car lat) old)(cons old (cons new (cdr lat))))
        (t (cons (car lat) (insertr old new (cdr lat)))) ))

; insertl is just like insertr but inserts to the left

(define (insertl old new lat)
  (cond ((null? lat) nil)
        ((eq? (car lat) old ) (cons new  lat))
  (t (cons (car lat) (insertl old new (cdr lat)))) ))
```

Listing 5.4 Composite Objects in SCOOPS

```
(define-class composite-object
          (classvars class-part-name class-part-num)
          (instvars (part-names (active  parts  get-parts
add-part))
                    (numbers-of-parts (active '#-parts
num-parts mor
          (options
            (gettable-variables class-part-name part-names
numbers-of-parts
            settable-variables
            inittable-variables))

(define human-body-parts '() )
  (putprop 'human-body-parts 1 'head)
  (putprop 'human-body-parts 1 'neck)
  (putprop 'human-body-parts 2 'arms)
  (putprop 'human-body-parts 2 'hands)
  (putprop 'human-body-parts 1 'trunk)
  (putprop 'human-body-parts 2 'legs)
  (putprop 'human-body-parts 2 'feet)

(define (num-parts p-list)
  (princ p-list))

(define part-map (proplist 'human-body-parts))

(define-class body
          (classvars (class-part-name 'body-parts)(class-part-
num 'h
          (mixins composite-object))

(define body-parts '(head necks arms hands trunk legs feet))

(define-method (composite-object put-cpart-name) (new-part)
          (set! body-parts
                (append (eval (get-class-part-name)) (list
new-part)

(define (add-part new-part)
  (append! (get-class-part-name) (list new-part)))

(define (get-parts val)
  (princ val))
```

Listing 5.4 Composite Objects in SCOOPS (continued)

```
(define my-body
 (make-instance body
                'part-names body-parts
                'numbers-of-parts part-map ))

(compile-class composite-object)
(compile-class body)
```

5.7 ObjectLISP

ObjectLISP was one of the candidates for an object-oriented extension to CommonLISP that was originally offered by Lisp Machines Inc. Although its overall architecture did not turn out to be a substantial influence on the object-oriented standard currently being defined for CommonLISP, it is a relatively easy system to understand and has a number of very commendable features. It also had an important feature in common with the syntax of the CommonLISP Object System (CLOS). One of the distinctive features of the objectLISP approach is eliminating any special syntax for sending messages, so that object-oriented methods are invoked with essentially the same syntax as any CommonLISP function. Another very important feature is that ObjectLISP departs from most other object-oriented systems by deliberately making the relation of a class to a subclass the same as the relation of a class to an instance. The implication for implementation is that the nesting of closures is used for both specializing and instantiating classes. When combined as they are in ObjectLISP, these two features result in a very simple and streamlined system in which class variables, class functions, instance variables, and instance functions all exhibit the same basic behavior. One of the by-products of not differentiating between an instance and a class is that, during development, you can use a class as a prototype instance or an instance as a prototype class.

ObjectLISP also has the convenient feature, often not present in object-oriented systems, of allowing the dynamic creation and modification of objects on the fly, while programs are running. Also, all inheritance operates dynamically, which means that changes in the state of a superclass of an object that are inheritable will take effect right when the change is made.

The basic ObjectLISP system is based on five primitive functions: def-object, kindof, ask, have, and defobfun. Creating an object can be as simple as writing

```
(setq business (defobject))
```

Frequently, though, the object will be a specialized version of another object that already exists. In this case, an object is created with an expression like:

```
(setq wholesaler (kind-of business))
```

The `ask` function is used to evaluate a CommonLISP expression in a particular object's environment. The `have` function creates variable bindings that are local to objects. These functions are usually used together in ObjectLISP to declare class variables and instance variables. This could be done for the business object just created, like this:

```
(ask business (have 'type-of-activity 'economic))
```

This can then be checked to make sure it has been accepted by the system. If you do so, the terminal screen might read as follows:

```
(ask business type-of-activity)
      economic
```

The `defobfun` function is used to define CommonLISP functions that are bound or assigned only to a particular object or class of objects. Continuing with the example we have been using, we might say:

```
(defobfun (calc-net-gain business) (gross-sales costs)
(setq net-gain (- gross-sales total-costs)))
```

The ObjectLISP syntax for calling such a function can be illustrated by

```
(ask business (calc-net-gain 500 300))
```

Another important feature of ObjectLISP is its ability to create *shadowed functions*. This is a way in which the inherited functions can be used to create more specific versions of the function for more specialized objects. In many cases, an efficient way to do this is to add only the more specialized parts and then make a call to the inherited function. The next example uses a shadowed function.

Although there is no real difference between an instance and a subclass in ObjectLISP, in practice it is convenient to have a way to use an object as a template for creating other instances of it. One way of doing this is to define an exist function for that object. For example, we could write:

```
(defobfun (exist business) (&rest args &key*
    (name 'no-name-yet)
    (location 'no-location-yet)
    (industry 'no-industry-yet)
    (business-type 'no-bus-type-yet)
    (size 'no-size-yet)
    (year-founded 'no-year-founded-yet)
    (ownership-type 'no-ownership-type-yet)
    (market-share 'no-market-share-yet)
    &allow-other-keys)
```

```
(have 'name name
 'location location
 'industry industry
 'business-type business-type
 'size size
 'year-founded year-founded
 'ownership-type ownership-type
 (apply 'shadowed-exist args)
    ))
```

With exist functions of this kind, it becomes much easier in ObjectLISP to define instances of objects. For example, we could define a number of business instances as follows:

```
(setq unicomp (kindof business))
(ask unicomp (exist))

(setq softrend (kindof business))
(ask softrend (exist 'ownership-type sole-proprietor))
```

In ObjectLISP, an object is really a list of frames. The first member of the list is its innermost frame, the original bindings supplied to it when it is created. The remaining elements of the list are all the elements that it inherits, appearing in the order in which it inherits them.

Multiple inheritance in ObjectLISP is accomplished by supplying multiple arguments to the kindof function. For example, if we have also defined an object called adversary, we could define a class called competitor using multiple inheritance as follows:

```
(setq competitor (kindof business adversary))
```

ObjectLISP was not one of the winning contenders for the standard, partly because it uses dynamic binding, but also because it is a very new approach that still has not been tried and proven for any appreciable time. Because some very difficult and controversial issues remain unresolved in object-oriented LISP, we think that some of the aspects of ObjectLISP, particularly the placing of classes and instances on a common footing and the ability to modify objects on the fly, deserve some serious consideration.

5.8 Old and New Flavors

As was stated earlier, the original Symbolics Flavors system was the first commercial object-oriented extension to LISP to gain relatively widespread popularity and to prove the great value of object-oriented LISP in practice. The more recent releases of the Symbolics 3600 series machines, with the product name Genera, now include New Flavors, which was Symbolics' candidate for the object-oriented standard for

CommonLISP. Symbolics Flavors grew out of the Flavors system developed by the MIT LISP Machine group back in 1979. By 1981, the Symbolics software group had developed a more efficient Flavors system, an object-oriented system that has come to be a favored programming approach both for much of the in-house systems programming at Symbolics and for numerous AI projects carried out by users.

New Flavors represented an attempt to overcome some of the weaknesses encountered in the earlier Symbolics Flavors system by its users over the first few years of its existence. David A. Moon of Symbolics outlined the main goals of New Flavors as follows:

1. Encourage greater program modularity.

2. Facilitate writing large, complex programs.

3. Provide favorable run-time performance.

4. Maintain downward compatibility with old Flavors.

Like the original Flavors, New Flavors uses the `defflavor`, `defmethod`, and `make-instance` functions to create objects and procedures. The way the example introduced earlier in the discussion of ObjectLISP would be coded in New Flavors is as follows:

```
(defflavor business
 (name location industry business-type size year-founded
    ownership-type market-share) ()
   :readable-instance-variables
   :writable-instance-variables
   :inittable-instance-variables)

(setq unicomp
 (make-instance 'business
 :name            unicomp
 :location        santa clara
 :industry        computer
 :business-type   software
 :size            18
 :year-founded    1976
 :ownership-type  private
 :market-share    11.3

(defmethod (calc-net-gain business) (gross-sales costs)
(- gross-sales costs))
```

One of the central ideas in New Flavors is the notion of generic functions. The main point of this is to allow distributed definition of functions as well as multiple inheritance of properties. This means both having the same name for a method that varies depending on the class to which it is bound and being able to use parts of code from various different objects. Toward this end, the defgeneric function has been provided.

In New Flavors, generic functions have the same syntax as nongeneric functions. This has the advantage that any function that is a caller of another function does not need to know which to specify. Other advantages are that all debugging and utility functions designed to work with ordinary CommonLISP functions will also work with generics.

New Flavors adopted a clear set of rules for ordering Flavor object components. Components are all parts of an object, both those declared directly and those that are inherited. The three rules that are followed are:

1. The flavor's own binding always precedes those of its components.

2. The local order of components of flavors always adopts the order stipulated in the defflavor declarations.

3. All duplicate flavors are automatically removed from the sequence.

5.9 Method Combination

As mentioned earlier, Flavors was the first object-oriented system to provide the form of abstraction that allowed different parts of the code for functions to be mixed modularly just as complete methods and variables may be inherited. Various built-in combination methods are provided for this purpose. So, for example, the programmer can choose between such method-combination modes as:

1. Calling only the most specific method available in the hierarchy.

2. Calling all the methods in order of specificity, either upward or downward.

3. Trying each method in turn, starting with the most specialized, until one is found that does not return nil.

There are also several other built-in combination-method modes.

In addition to defining new methods and selecting built-in combination-method types, the programmer can also define new combination methods using the define-method-combination and define-simple-method-combination functions.

New Flavors Development Tools

New Flavors provides various facilities for inspecting the current state of an object-oriented system under development. You can invoke them either by entering commands or by pointing the mouse at the names of various items on the display. For example, you can view either the subclasses or superclasses of a current flavor, and you can view all the instances of a given flavor that are currently alive. These are some of the really useful facilities that an object-oriented system needs if it is to be used for serious AI applications. Despite its rich user environment, some of these features are even absent in Smalltalk.

5.10 Portable CommonLOOPS

CommonLOOPS, the object-oriented extension that has been developed at Xerox PARC, has a number of definite goals and key concepts. Of all the systems discussed here, CommonLOOPS has the most in common with Smalltalk because Xerox still has considerable expertise in this type of object-oriented system. But CommonLOOPS also represents a departure from Smalltalk that offers a clear philosophical vision of how object-oriented programming can be fitted most naturally into the CommonLISP dialect, and in a way that preserves the greatest amount of generality. It is therefore intended to provide a basis for as many as possible of the serious approaches to object-oriented AI. One of the stated goals of CommonLOOPS was to provide a very general kernel, written in CommonLISP, from which any of the major object-oriented systems in use today (for example, Flavors, Smalltalk-80, and LOOPS) could all be implemented. Like Smalltalk, therefore, CommonLOOPS uses the metaclass protocol to implement its class hierarchy system.

The CommonLOOPS Kernel

The direction taken by CommonLOOPS is to use an option to the defstruct construct in CommonLISP in order to define classes. The :class option to defstruct is employed by CommonLOOPS to specify the metaclass that will be used in the system to determine how the object-oriented approach to be implemented will behave. The standard metaclasses provided in CommonLOOPS are: built-in-class, structure-class, list-structure-class, and vector-structure-class.

As with Smalltalk, CommonLOOPS has various built-in classes. This means that even before a programmer defines any classes, some that describe the behavior of the system are already present. Here is the hierarchy of CommonLOOPS built-in classes, shown as they might appear in a class browser, with the type of class they represent in parentheses to the right:

```
t                         (abstract-class)
  object                    (class)
    essential-class           "
      abstract-class          "
      built-in-class          "
      class                   "
      structure-class         "
```

```
       list-structure-class      -       "
       vector-structure-class             "
   number                         (abstract-class)
     integer                              "
       fixnum                     (built-in-class)
   sequence                       (abstract-class)
     list                                 "
       cons                       (built-in-class)
```

Through this hierarchy of metaclasses, CommonLOOPS controls the way in which the options to defstruct determine the form of object-oriented system that will be present. The structure-class, for example, is the default class that defstruct uses when no :class option is specified. The classes that are then created default to a structure that acts like the ordinary defstruct in CommonLISP. Abstract-class is used in the :class option for classes that will not themselves be instantiated, but act as placeholders in the hierarchy.

```
(defstruct (business (:class list-structure-class)))
```

The main CommonLOOPS primitives are given in the following list:

class-of   ref
defmethod   remove-dynamic-slot
get-dynamic-slot   remove-method
get-function   run-super
get-slot   specialize
mlet   with

5.11 Multiple Inheritance

Specifying inheritance from multiple classes is accomplished in CommonLOOPS through an extension of the :include option of defstruct to allow it to accept a list of names of classes. Following the same example we have been using to illustrate multiple inheritance, the Competitor class, which inherits from the two parent classes Business and Adversary, we would implement this class in the following way in CommonLOOPS:

```
(defstruct (Competitor (:include Business Adversary)))
```

Multimethods

One of the most important innovations in CommonLOOPS is that of multimethods, procedures that are, in effect, messages sent to any number of objects of different types. So instead of defining the draw-at method as you would in Flavors

```
(defmethod (rectangle :draw-at)  (upper-left-x upper-left-y
                                   lower-right-x lower-right-y)
     (draw-box upper-left-x upper-left-y lower-right-x
               lower-right-y))
```

In CommonLOOPS you would write it:


```
(defmeth draw-at
    ((r  rectangle)  (upper-left-x integer) upper-left-y
integer)
     (lower-right-x integer) (lower-right-y integer)
     (draw-box upper-left-x upper-left-y lower-right-x
               lower-right-y))
```


In this definition, the first argument to draw-at is r, which is declared as in the class rectangle, and the remaining arguments are screen coordinates, all declared as in the class integer.

The implementation of CommonLOOPS is itself fully object-oriented in the sense that all data structures used to implement the system are objects that are instances of a class. For example, when a new method is defined, three new objects are created: the method object, the discriminator, and the discriminating-function. The method object is the object that describes the method to be created. The discriminating-function is an object that selects the method that will be called. This discriminator and its own methods use the information in the method object and its own description of a generic function to compile the code for the method. Generic function is used here in the same sense as in the discussion of New Flavors.

Method Combination

Method combination is accomplished in CommonLOOPS using the run-super mechanism. It closely resembles the method combination approach used in Smalltalk, LOOPS, and ObjectLISP. (LOOPS, an AI development tool used at Xerox PARC, will be described in detail in Chapter 6.) The run-super mechanism is implemented using the method and discriminator object described earlier. Because of the use of metaobjects in the implementation of method combination, many interesting research possibilities for AI languages are opened up.

For example, through defining specialized method and discriminator objects, a means is available for integrating logic programming into CommonLOOPS. A prototype for such a system called CommonLog has been implemented at Xerox PARC. It is hoped that this will provide the basis for a more advanced AI tool called Vulcan.

5.12 Future Directions in Object-Oriented LISP

One of the issues still to be settled by the object-oriented LISP community and the object-oriented programming community in general is that of the structural versus the procedural view of objects. This is the issue of whether the specification or interface description of classes should be purely procedural or split into procedural and structural parts. If purely procedural, an object is defined exclusively by its message protocols. As we have seen, CommonLOOPS is of the second type because method lookup is achieved by a combination of object structures and discrimination procedures. If things proceed as they have been, this approach is expected to be adopted as the standard.

On the whole, I don't think that it is necessarily an overwhelmingly difficult problem to determine the best standard for an object-oriented extension to CommonLISP. Since some standard is needed *now*, but we do not have enough experience in this area to fully define the possibilities, the only possible standard is a partial one that is based on whichever features of the technology have shown themselves to be the most useful and reliable, while leaving the options as open as possible. To be more specific, a new design for the standard needs to be constructed from the best features of CommonLOOPS, New Flavors, and ObjectLISP that address as many of the key issues we have been discussing as possible.

The main ObjectLISP features that should not be lost are being able to modify objects and their variables on the fly and keeping instances and classes on an equal footing. I would particularly like to see a standard that did not prevent the option of having instantiated objects that were not yet formally members of any class, but at a later time could become "associated" with various classes and gain from what can be inherited from them.

Another important issue from the AI perspective is allowing for the coexistence of multiple types of hierarchies in the same binding environment, where the same object can be a member of each of the different hierarchies simultaneously, if this is desired. As explained earlier, this feature appears essential for using objects to develop systems with deep models that can reason about objects in real-world settings in terms of function, location, and generic significance.

5.13 The CommonLISP Object System

The CommonLISP Object System (CLOS) is the standard currently being created for an object-oriented extension to CommonLISP. It combines features of both CommonLOOPS and New Flavors; uses the metaobject protocol, generic functions; and features multiple inheritance. Although it is not being presented as the final standard, but as a working standard, CLOS is likely to be around for a few years anyway, because it has taken so much effort to get to even this point.

Perhaps the unique feature of CLOS is that it uses the construction of generic functions rather than message passing. Instead of calling procedural methods that send messages to objects as most object-oriented systems do, the methods for different classes and types are called automatically by generic functions. This makes CLOS a new type of architecture for object-oriented programming—one that might be expected to have its own special advantages and disadvantages.

Another important feature of the CLOS design is its systematic incorporation of the idea of first-class objects. The idea of first-class objects was first made an explicit principle of programming languages design with the Scheme dialect of LISP. It is a particularly elegant and powerful programming concept, and its incorporation into CLOS is particularly fortunate and welcome.

In its basic design, CLOS is a multi-layered system consisting of three levels. The first level provides programmers with an interface to the basics of the object-oriented system. The second level provides access to the heart of the Object System and is intended for programmers writing very complex software or programming environments. The third level provides access to tools for the more technically oriented programmers who wish to implement their own object-oriented language.

Metaclass Protocol

The predefined metaclasses in CLOS include standard-class, built-in-class, and structure-class. Standard-class is the default superclass of any class that is defined using defclass. Instances of built-in-class are special primitives that have certain restrictions on their use. For example, classes that correspond to standard CommonLISP types tend to be instances of built-in-class. Any class that is defined using defstruct becomes a subclass of structure-class.

In addition to metaclasses, there are what are called metaobjects. The main built-in metaobjects in CLOS are the standard-object class as well as the instances of the classes standard-method, standard-generic-function, and method-combination. Any LISP forms defined by `defmethod`, `defgeneric`, `generic-function`, `generic-flet`, `generic-labels`, or `with-added-methods` becomes an instance of standard-method as a default.

The `defclass` macro provides a means of generating slot-accessing methods. Three types of such methods may be generated: reader, writer, and accessor methods. Accessor methods can both read and write to slots; the others are only capable of one or the other. When these options are specified, the appropriate methods are automatically generated. When the options are specified, the name of a generic function must be supplied for which they will be the methods. These methods are inherited only in the sense that all methods applicable to a class are also applicable to its subclasses.

`Defclass` also provides for three class options: :default-initargs, :documentation, and :metaclass. The :default-initargs option allows a set of corresponding argument names and values. Unless other values are specified for these at initialization, these are the values that will be used. The :documentation option allows a documentation string to be supplied. The :metaclass option is used to specify that the metaclass of the class being defined should be different from the default.

Common LISP Type	CLOS Class Hierarchy
array	array t
bit-vector	bit-vector vector array
character	character t
complex	complex number t
cons	cons list sequence t
float	float number t
integer	integer rational number t
list	list sequence t
null	null symbol list sequence t
number	number t
ratio	ratio rational number t
rational	rational number t
sequence	sequence t
string	string vector array sequence t
symbol	symbol t
t	t
vector	vector array sequence t

5.14 Generic Functions

The choice of generic functions rather than message passing was made for two main reasons. First, it is a natural generalization of functions in LISP. Second there were still some problems with message passing with methods that use more than one argument. A generic function is like an ordinary LISP function except that it has a number of bodies of code or methods out of which one is selected to be executed when the function is called. As with all functions, generic functions can be passed as arguments to apply and funcall. Methods for generic functions contain parameter specializers to specify when the method is applicable and qualifiers to distinguish among methods for the purpose of method combination.

One of the main differences between CLOS and other object-oriented languages that cannot be attributed to window dressing or syntactic sugar in the current implementation is that methods are not themselves functions that can be invoked. Currently, the only way to call a method is to call the generic function that invokes it. A future extension of CLOS may modify this so that methods are functions that can be called. The lambda-lists of new methods that are defined for a given generic function must be "congruent" with the lambda-lists of that generic function. As with arguments to ordinary CommonLISP functions, the arguments to generic functions can include both required arguments and optional arguments.

When a generic function is called with a set of arguments, the code that is executed is called the *effective method* for the set of arguments used. This effective method results from a combination of the applicable arguments in the generic function. The effective method is determined by a three-step procedure:

1. Determine all the applicable methods.

2. Sort them in order of precedence, the most specific first.

3. Apply method combination to the sorted list.

An effective method is composed of primary methods and auxiliary methods. The primary methods are those that define the main action of the effective method. Primary methods have no method qualifiers. Auxiliarly methods can modify the main action in one of three ways: with the :before, :after, or :around method qualifier. Standard method combination allows only one of these keywords to be used. A :before method specifies code that is to be executed before any of the primary methods. An :after method code executed after the primary method. An :around method specifies code that is to be run in place of some of the applicable methods.

Standard method combination follows these rules:

1. If there are any :around methods, call the most specific of them, which will supply the value or values of the generic function.

2. If call-next-method occurs in the body of the :around method, execute any methods specified and return to the :around method to evaluate whatever code remains in its body.

3. If no :around method is involved, the most specific primary method supplies the value or values returned by the generic function.

CLOS provides a set of ten different method combination types: +, and, append, list, max, min, nconc, or, progn, and standard.

For browsing about in a CLOS system, a few functions such as class-of allow programmers and running programs to inspect objects and determine their parent classes.

Multiple Arguments

It is rather easy to see why the issue of multiple arguments should provoke controversy. Consider the case of arithmetic functions. With most programming languages, the number values are treated as arguments to the function; with most object-oriented languages, the numbers are objects to which messages are sent. In general, in an object-oriented system any argument is likely to be an object in its own right. In message-passing systems, the question then naturally arises in regard to functions that require more than one argument: Which of them is to be the object that will receive the message?

In general, the object to which the message must be sent can be selected by one of three approaches: *currying*, *delegation*, and *distribution* of methods.

Currying attempts to reduce functions with multiple arguments into a series of functions of one argument. In a message-passing system, this means having the objects that are involved as objects send messages among themselves that gather the results of each object to the final result. In the case of arithmetical operations, each number object may be sent the message to register its partial result in an accumulated total that is updated until the final result is reached. In order for this process to work, the order of messages must be established and each object must know where to begin and end. As can be seen, currying is an extremely complex process of object interaction.

With delegation, one object is entrusted with the task of handling the operation on the other objects. This object may or may not be one of the argument objects. In either case, the objects specified as arguments must be capable of delegating their required operations.

Distribution of methods specifically allows any of the objects that can be involved in an operation to be delegated to carry out the entire operation.

In object systems like Smalltalk, functions or methods are part of objects. In the generic function approach, objects and functions are each autonomous in their own right. This means that messages are not sent to objects, but that functions supplied with several arguments are responsible for performing the necessary operations on the objects involved. Clearly, in the case of generic functions, the problem does not arise of determining which object or objects will be delegated with the operation. The generic function can package all the methods that are necessary to carry out operations on several arguments and is responsible for selecting the correct ones for each phase of an operation. This means that, if necessary, separate methods can be called for each argument that is a distinct class of object.

As you can probably see, generic functions represent a strong contrast to message passing. With a generic function, it is not necessary to know the types of the object that are passed as arguments. The generic function is supposed to be provided with methods that can be selected for the different types of objects. This means that generic functions provide a markedly different type of modularity than message-passing systems do.

In CLOS, when a method-defining form is evaluated, one of four things happens:

1. If there is a generic function of the name specified as well as a method that has the same parameter specializers and qualifiers, that method is replaced by the new method object.

2. If there is a generic function, but no corresponding method, the generic function is modified so that it now contains the new method.

3. If the supplied name does not refer to an existing generic function, but some other function or macro by that name exists, an error message is given.

4. In other cases, where there is not already an existing generic function, one is created with the method or methods specified.

CLOS has adopted a mechanism of method combination that is at once more powerful than that of CommonLOOPS and simpler than that of New Flavors. In CLOS, classes and generic functions are both first-class objects. A first-class object is one that can be passed as an argument to a function, stored in an array or list, and so on. However, as you may have been able to deduce, CLOS does not attempt encapsulation or protection.

5.15 Class Redefinition

One very welcome feature of CLOS is its ability to change the class to which an object belongs. CLOS provides an effective mechanism for class redefinition with the change-class function.

```
(defclass coordinate () ())

(defclass 3-D-linear-coordinate (coordinate)
    ((x :initform 0 :initarg :x)
     (y :initform 0 :initarg :y)
     (z :initform 0 :initarg :z )))
 (defclass 3-D-spherical-coordinate (coordinate)
    ((r :initform 0 :initarg :r)
     (theta :initform 0 :initarg :theta)
     (phi :initform 0 :initarg :phi)))

(defmethod class-changed ((old-obj x-y-z-coord)
                          (new-obj r-t-p-coord))
    (let ((x1 (slot-value old-obj 'x))
          (y1 (slot-value old-obj 'y))
          (z1 (slot-value old-obj 'z))
       (setf (slot-value new-obj 'r)
             (sqrt (+ (*x x1 x1) (* y1 y1) (* z1 z1))
             (slot-value new-obj 'theta)
             (atan y x)
             (slot-value new-obj 'r)
             (atan y z))))

(setq coord-1 (make-instance '3-D-linear-coordinate
              :x 1 :y 2 :z 3))
(change-class coord-1 '3-D-spherical-coordinate)
```

Limitations

One interesting issue is that currently no built-in way exists to ask a running CLOS system for a complete list of all the instances that are alive at the time. This is actually a consequence of the way CommonLISP and most other versions of LISP are currently implemented. The complication arises because of the need for a garbage collector. The garbage collector in a LISP system will sweep out all the objects that are not referenced by something other than just their own symbol names. This means that every time a garbage collection occurs, the list of all instances in the system must be updated. But, even more, it means that technically only after garbage collection occurs would this list be completely accurate.

In order for CLOS itself to address this problem, there would have to be a change in the way CommonLISP is implemented. There is in fact a proposal to make just such a modification to the standard by adding weak pointer lists. However, until such a change is made, a rather simple user modification to CLOS can address the issue. What is needed is an after method for the make-instance function (called perhaps update-list) that puts the name of an instance on a list of all instances as it is created. Also a delete-instance function is needed to remove instances from the system explicitly and update the list of all instances accordingly. In this way, programmers and running programs that need to know all instances that are currently in the world can do so.

In the same vein, it would be desirable to have a function (called perhaps all-instances-of) that would take the name of a class as an argument and return all its current instances. Probably the best way to handle this would be to create a shared slot called all-instances that would exist for each class and that would likewise be updated when necessary. This would be rather simple to implement by using the class-of function to determine the class of each instance that is being created or destroyed and then performing the necessary addition or subtraction for that class's shared slot.

This brief overview shows that CLOS clearly represents a novel approach to an object-oriented system that departs in significant ways from the usual message-passing approaches. To some, CLOS may not even be what they would want to call object-oriented. Because CommonLISP was already a well-established language, the main considerations at work in the design of CLOS were dictated by the requirements of the LISP standard rather than by the requirements of object-oriented programming generally.

Generic functions are certainly a step away from the concept of active data and back toward the conventional division between passive data and active processes. Objects in CLOS are passive; only the generic functions are active.

The generic function approach has both advantages and disadvantages. From the point of view of practical programming, CLOS enjoys a slight advantage in that it does not require as much knowledge on the part of a programmer to use it. A programmer already familiar with CommonLISP will not have a great deal to learn to be able to begin programming in CLOS. Obviously no new message-passing syntax is needed. However, in addition, less knowledge of the system is required than with message-passing systems. For example, a programmer does not need to know which objects accept a given method before using it. If a programmer knows the arguments needed for a function, in principle he or she can use the function without knowing what objects to which it can be sent. Practically speaking, however, this may not be as much of an advantage as it first appears. Generic functions do not obtain their generic character automatically. The methods that give them this capacity must be programmed. Consequently, the methods may not always exist to use them in the manner that is ideally intended. In this case, a programmer really must know what methods are supported by a generic function in order to use it correctly. This puts the difficulty back at a level similar to that of procedural languages. If there are no facilities for conveniently inspecting generic functions, message-passing systems might still be easier to use.

Because CLOS makes no effort at protection or encapsulation, some might find that it lacks the most essential thing for an object-oriented system. They would perhaps be prompted to ask what the purpose of an object-oriented system might be if it were not capable of encapsulation. Because message passing is not used, objects are not protected in the usual manner by only admitting messages that they can recognize.

As it stands, the default CLOS system cannot be considered to be specifically tailored toward the needs of AI applications. It is, on the contrary, oriented toward general-purpose LISP programming. However, it is an open-ended system. CLOS contains most of the facilities needed to write object systems that are specifically tailored for the needs of AI.

Why is it that CLOS is not particularly suited for AI as it stands? One reason is that it is to some degree a step away from the concept of active data that we enumerated earlier in this book. The distinction between generic functions and classes reflects the familiar one between procedures and data. This means that various AI algorithms that specifically exploit the message-passing paradigm are not possible in standard CLOS.

Another point is that encapsulation and protection are particularly desirable features for AI applications. One reason stems simply from the fact that AI applications tend to be large programs. However, another one stems from the fact that it is desirable that AI programs be easy to modify without massive re-debugging. Although functionality of procedures in CLOS is modularized into methods, these methods belong to their respective generic functions, not to objects.

5.16 Encapsulation by Convention in CLOS

Full encapsulation is very difficult and may be impossible completely in CommonLISP. The reason for this is that the language contains the tools for debugging that can in principle access any memory location. The best that can be achieved is probably a form of encapsulation by convention. For this reason, any algorithms that specifically exploit the message-passing paradigm are not possible in standard CLOS. Although the means exist in the facility for creating standard message-passing if that is required, it is a rather technical and time-consuming task for more experienced programmers.

5.17 CLOS Functions, Macros, and Special Forms

add-method (generic function method)
   Adds a method to a generic function. Destructively modifies the generic function and returns it.

call-method (method next-method-list)
   A macro used in method-combination that calls a method and specifies a list of the order in which to call other methods.

call-next-method (&rest args)
   Used in a method-defining form to call the next method, returning the value returned by the method it calls.

cboundp (symbol &optional environment)
Returns true if symbol is a class in the specified environment.

change-class (instance new-class)
Modifies an instance to change its class to a new class, returning the instance.

class-changed (previous current)
A generic function called by change-class for which programmers can write methods.

class-name (class)
A generic function that returns the name of a class that can also be used to change that name.

class-of (object)
Returns the class of an object.

cmakunbound (symbol &optional environment)
Unbinds the specified symbol as the name of a class in the specified environment.

defclass (class-name superclass-name slot-specifier class-option)
Defines a new class and returns it.

defgeneric (function-specifier lambda-list [option] method-description)
A macro that defines a new generic function or specifies options or declarations for an existing one.

define-method-combination (name [short-form-option])
A macro that is used to define a new type of method combination.

defmethod (function-specifier [method-qualifier] specialized-lambda-list [declaration] [form])
Defines a method for a generic function.

describe (object)
A generic function (which replaces the CommonLISP describe function) that prints information contained in the specified object on the screen or other output device.

documentation (x optional doc-type)
A generic function (which replaces the CommonLISP documentation function) that returns the documentation string associated with a specified object.

ensure-generic-function (function-specifier key [option] [function])
Defines a generic function with no options or specifies or modifies options of those existing.

generic-flet ([function-specifier lambda-list] [option] [method-description] [special-form] [form])
A special form analogous to flet in CommonLISP that produces new generic functions and establishes new lexical function definition bindings.

generic-function (lambda-list [option] [method-description])
A special form that creates an anonymous generic function.

generic-labels ([function-specifier lambda-list] [option] [method-description] [form])
A special form analogous to labels in CommonLISP that produces new generic functions and new lexical function definition bindings.

get-method (generic-function method-qualifiers specializers &optional errorp)
A generic function that returns a method that agrees in method qualifiers and specializers for a specified generic function.

initialize-instance (instance &key &allow-other-keys)
A generic function called by make-instance to initialize a new instance when created.

invalid-method-error (method format-string &rest args)
Reports an applicable method whose qualifiers are invalid for a given method combination type.

make-instance (class &rest initargs)
Creates and returns a new instance of a class.

make-instance-obsolete (class)
A generic function that is automatically invoked by the system when defclass is used to redefine or modify an existing class.

make-method (form)
A macro used inside of call-method for method combination.

method-combination-error (format-string &rest args)
Used to report problems in method combination.

method-qualifiers (method)
A generic function that returns a list of qualifiers for a specified method.

next-method-p ()
Used within the body of a method to determine whether a next method exists.

no-applicable-method (generic-function &rest args)
A generic function that is called when a generic function is called but no method applies.

print-object (object stream)
A generic function that writes the printed representation of an object onto a stream.

remove-method (generic-function method)
A generic function that deletes a method of a generic function.

slot-boundp (instance slot-name)
A generic function that tests if a specified slot of an instance has a value.

slot-exists-p (object slot-name)
 A generic function that tests if an object has a slot of the specified name.

slot-makunbound (instance slot-name)
 A generic function that removes any values the slot of an instance may have.

slot-missing (class object slot-name operation &optional new-value)
 A generic function that is invoked when an attempt is made to access a slot with the name of a slot that does not exist for a given object.

slot-unbound (class instance slot-name)
 A generic function that is called when an unbound slot is accessed.

slot-value (object slot-name)
 Returns the value of the specified slot of an object.

symbol-class (symbol &optional environment)
 Returns the class named by the specified symbol in a given environment.

symbol-macrolet ([symbol expansion] &body body)
 A macro that permits forms for variable names to be substituted within a lexical scope.

update-instance-structure (instance added-slots discarded-slots property-list)
 A generic function for which methods may be written.

with-added-methods (function-specifier lambda-list [option] [method-description] [form])
 A special form that produces new generic functions and establishes new lexical function definition bindings.

with-slots ([slot-entry] instance-form &body body)
 A macro that creates a lexical context for referring to specified slots as though they were variables.

Conclusions

Always in a category by itself, LISP shows many positive qualities, but some negative ones too, in object-oriented extensions. Object-oriented LISP certainly has some strong points. As we saw, it seems to be unique among object-oriented languages in consistently offering the capability of multiple inheritance. Perhaps more significantly, object-oriented LISP is the first language after Smalltalk to make original contributions to the object-oriented paradigm. It is primarily in its implementation of explicitly redefinable method combination that LISP has been innovative here. It could be argued that generic functions are also an important innovation made by object-oriented LISP, but this is a subject on which it is still too soon to make any categorical judgments.
 Quite clearly, not all the issues in object-oriented LISP are positive ones. Part of the

reason is that LISP is already a high-level language with a great deal going on in it of a very specific nature. In comparison, C is a low-level portable assembly language. In other words, there are places where LISP comes into some degree of conflict with the principles of object-oriented programming. Ideally, an object-oriented language should be designed from the bottom up. That is, a completely new language that is a pure object-oriented language designed from scratch would be constructed. However, the challenges of introducing yet another programming language are quite formidable. This has led to the hybrids—at this point, object-oriented Cs and object-oriented LISPs. The hybrid approach has the practical advantage in that already established communities of programmers for the mother languages exist, so the difficulty of gaining acceptance is lessened considerably. The other advantage of the hybrids is that the programmer is always free to drop down into the mother language and write part of a program in that syntax if this is desirable. One reason it can be desirable is to conserve resources. The object-oriented extensions clearly must consume some extra memory and add some overhead to programs.

True or False?

1. Thus far, LISP is the only programming language with object-oriented extensions that consistently offer the capability of multiple inheritance.

2. The method combination scheme originally introduced in the Flavors system provided an additional type of modularity to object-oriented systems.

3. It is important in all AI systems to avoid any side effects when programming with an object-oriented language.

4. Active values are procedural attachments to instance variables that allow functions to be executed whenever a value is accessed.

5. Active values are for system programmers and have no application for AI programming.

6. The implementation of Portable CommonLOOPS is itself purely object oriented.

7. Multimethods is a feature of Portable CommonLOOPS that allows it to interface with parallel hardware.

8. A disadvantage of Portable CommonLOOPS is that all method combination types must be defined from scratch.

9. Generic functions are the same as methods in New Flavors.

10. ObjectLISP was an experimental extension to CommonLISP that offered no advantages over other systems.

(T, T, F, T, F, T, F, F, F, F)

Chapter 6

Object-Oriented Expert System Tools

In this chapter, we approach two main issues in object-oriented expert systems:

1. Building applications with object-oriented expert system shells.

2. Implementing such shells with object-oriented languages.

First we will take a look at some of the most interesting object-oriented expert systems development tools that are available commercially. After this, we will select one tool, Nexpert Object, and use it to develop SPACEMED, a small expert system prototype in space medicine. Finally, we will show how to take advantage of some of the features of object-oriented programming languages by writing a simple demonstration inference engine that combines forward and backward chaining.

6.1 GoldWorks II

This AI programming tool from Gold Hill Computers Inc. is currently one of the largest AI development environment available for desktop computers. It runs in the GCLISP Developer CommonLISP environment from Gold Hill, which is already a large software system. By itself, though, size is, of course, no assurance of processing power. In addition to size, GoldWorks II has several features to commend it as an advanced object-oriented knowledge processing tool. The complex system architecture called MARS (Multiple Assertion Representation System) features many progressive ideas that typify an important current direction in AI. The influence of the actor approach introduced by Carl Hewitt at MIT is clearly visible in the implementation of Attempts, Sponsors, and Agendas in GoldWorks. GoldWorks II runs on the IBM AT, 386 and compatibles, the Macintosh II, and Sun workstations.

Facilities that are new with GoldWorks II include the Dynamic Graphics tool, which allows the creation of active images like dials and gauges for immediate user feedback; the Graphics Layout tool, which allows users to develop such dynamic graphics interfaces interactively, without having to write the code by hand; and graphics-oriented browsers for frames, rules, sponsors, and assertions. Better integration with C, an ASCII parser, and the ability to use diagrams developed with Windows Draw are also new additions with GoldWorks II.

The Developer's Interface

GoldWorks II provides a graphics-mode Developer's interface that runs under Microsoft Windows. This includes graphics-oriented lattice browsers that show the hierarchical structure of an application.

One handy feature for manipulating knowledge bases is the ability to selectively evaluate functions in the editor. Doing so automatically adds the function in question to whatever application is actually loaded in the system. This technique can be useful for various purposes. It is very convenient to extract pieces of code from one knowledge base

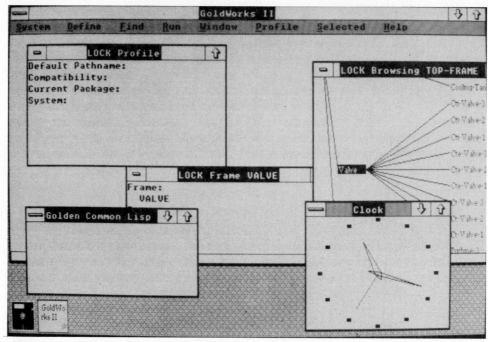

Figure 6.1 A GoldWorks II screen showing Profile, Frame Inspector, Lattice Browser, and LISP listener windows with the Microsoft Windows Clock utility

and insert them in another this way. With the source application loaded in the editor and the target loaded in the system, the pertinent definitions in the editor are evaluated and then the contents of the system's memory are resaved with the new additions. It is far more efficient to do this than to cut and paste with edited text.

The GoldWorks Architecture

A useful overview of the GoldWorks system can be gained by understanding the role of the following types of objects that are implemented in the system:

- Frames
- Instances
- Relations
- Assertions
- Rules

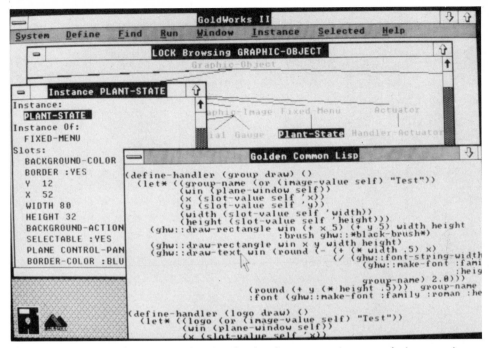

Figure 6.2 A GoldWorks II screen showing the development environment during a session with the LOCK expert system prototype

- Rulesets
- Attempts
- Sponsors
- Agenda items

We will discuss several of these elements now so that the working of the system as a whole can be understood.

Frames

GoldWorks provides a full object-oriented system for knowledge representation that includes classes, instances, methods, and inheritance. However, since the terminology used for describing the different aspects of these facilities is somewhat different from that used with some other object-oriented systems, you should keep in mind the precise way in which terms are used here, so as to avoid confusion.

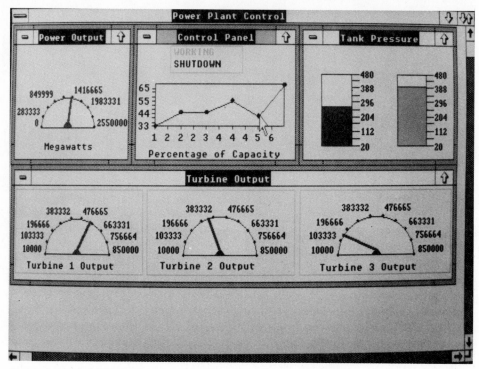

Figure 6.3 A GoldWorks II screen showing the active images that dynamically update the state of key parameters in a Power Plant Control expert system

In GoldWorks, the class templates for objects are called *frames,* and the actual objects that exemplify them are called *instances.* A superclass of a frame, from which it inherits all its slots, is called a *parent frame.* The slots of a frame are the items within it that are organized to hold information, similar to the fields in a database. One particularly powerful feature of GoldWorks is its support for multiple inheritance: a frame may inherit from more than one parent frame at once.

Another important feature of the GoldWorks frame system is that it allows particular instances to be asserted as the values of slots of other instances. This allows it to handle composite objects, that is, those that can be composed of other objects, in much the same way a large mechanism is composed of various subordinate mechanisms.

Facets

A facet is a property of a slot that further defines it and adds functionality to it. The following types of facets are supported:

- Constraints
- Multivalued
- Default certainty
- Default values
- When-modified
- Where-accessed
- User-facet
- Print name
- Doc string
- Explanation string
- No inference
- Graphic
- No save
- Facet combination
- Query form

As the name suggests, constraint facets restrict the values or types of values that a slot can assume. There are five basic types of constraint facets:

- One-of: Used to supply a list of possible values.
- Range: Supply a range of numerical values.
- LISP-type: Number or symbol datatype.
- Child-frame-of: Slot must be frame with stated ancestor.
- Instance-of: Slot must be object of stated frame type.

Relations and Assertions

Relations in GoldWorks occupy a similar role to predicates in PROLOG. Generally speaking, they are used to group factual assertions and to state some relationships between various slot values or instances in a knowledge base. There are three different types of relations:

1. Assertion relations

2. Functional assertion relations

3. LISP-function relations.

The type of assertions that relations are used for with this system are called unstructured relations because they are factual assertions that are made directly rather than by assigning a value to a slot of an instance. An example of an assertion relation might be:

```
(season-of vacation summer)
```

A functional assertion relation is very similar to this, except that only one unique value for the last item in the list is permitted. If *season-of* were defined as a functional relation and the preceding assertion were already in the knowledge base, and we subsequently asserted:

```
(season-of vacation spring)
```

then the first assertion would automatically be retracted from the knowledge base.

Message Handlers

Handlers in GoldWorks are the same as methods in other object-oriented systems. These message-passing handlers are procedures that can be attached to frames and are inherited down the hierarchy just like slots. These message-passing handlers must be created in the Developer's interface using the DEFINE-HANDLER function. To use a handler once it has been defined, the SEND-MSG function is also available in the Developer's interface. GoldWorks also provides built-in slot-accessing methods that allow slot values to be accessed from within rules or hand-written LISP code. For example, the SLOT-ADD-VALUE function may be used to add a value to a slot.

Rules

GoldWorks allows us to use three types of rules: forward, backward, and bidirectional rules. This appears to create a nearly optimal situation. We can write rules for "pure knowledge" to use in either forward or backward inference as the need arises, and we can earmark specialized rules that can only work in either forward or backward modes. In this way the interests of both flexibility and control are served admirably.

   Goal-directed forward chaining is an interesting inference mode that is unique with GoldWorks. It is implemented by packaging a specific goal declaration and forward-chaining rules in the same ruleset. A ruleset in GoldWorks has an enabling pattern. When an attempt's goal pattern is queried, and it matches the enabling pattern of a ruleset, the ruleset is placed on the agenda of the attempt's sponsor in order of its priority. If the premises of any rules are satisfied, those rules are fired and their actions are placed on an agenda and executed in order of priority.

The GoldWorks rule syntax allows rules to be written that refer to instances and slot values with variable names so that we can state general rules that apply to any cases of the types of things referenced that are present in the system at the time the rule is tried. Moreover, the system keeps track of variable names within the scope of a rule so that when the same variable name is repeated more than once, the same values will be bound to all such instantiations of the variable name. For example, if we write the rule:

```
IF (INSTANCE ?x IS business
               with industry ?y
               with competitor ?y
               with profits ?z)
AND (INSTANCE ?z IS business
               with profits ?w)
AND (> ?z ?w)

THEN (Acquire INSTANCE ?x)
```

This rule states simply that if any business has a competitor, but has greater profits than its competitor, that business should be acquired rather than its competitor. It writes this piece of knowledge without a need to know what instances will actually be found in the object hierarchy, since variable names are used to reference all instances and slot values, and the profit values are compared relative to one another. It is of course not a sound business principle, but it demonstrates the power of GoldWorks rules.

Rules in GoldWorks also take a number of different options, which have the appearance of keywords with a leading colon character. One of the most important among these is the :dependency option keyword. This is used to designate a rule as a dependent or logical rule. The default value is NIL. When the :dependency option is set to T, this establishes a rule as a dependent rule. Dependent rules are those that allow the system to retract all the dependent assertions automatically when a given assertion is retracted. This capability is generally referred to in the AI literature as nonmonotonic reasoning. It is nonmonotonic because it goes beyond systems in which assertions may only be added. Dependent rules in GoldWorks make possible applications where system integrity can be maintained over time as assertions are added and retracted to keep pace with changes in the world.

Other important option keywords in GoldWorks rules are :direction, :priority, and :certainty. These all specify what their names suggest. The :direction option specifies whether the rule is forward, backward, or bidirectional. The default option is :foward. The :priority designation for rules can be assigned values between -1000 and $+1000$. The default value is 0.

6.2 Attempts

Attempts are special structures that GoldWorks uses to control backward chaining. They are mechanisms that centralize and control the information needed to satisfy a goal-directed search used in deriving results using backward inferences. Every attempt consists of a Pattern, a State, and a Sponsor. The *Pattern* is the goal that the attempt tries to match in the working memory of all factual assertions. The *State* captures how far the attempt has progressed in deriving assertions that match the pattern. *Sponsors* control the allocation of resources when you query an attempt.

The query of an attempt with a given goal pattern is what starts the inference engine looking for a match in working memory. There are four different types of query:

1. Query

2. Query-once

3. Query-Initial

4. Query-All

Query-once uses the attempt only once and causes the attempt to return only the first match, and then to be deleted.

An interesting and unique construct supported by GoldWorks rules is the AND-THEN clause. This is useful when you have a ruleset composed of backward and bidirectional rules and you want to separate parts of the conclusion that you would like to designate as operations executed only when the rule fires forward after a successful backward chaining. Patterns in the AND-THEN section of a rule's conclusion are not referenced during backward chaining. Here is an example:

```
IF (INSTANCE ?a IS customer
              with payment overdue)
THEN (INSTANCE ?a IS Customer
              with contact yes)
AND-THEN (PullFile customer ?a)
```

6.3 Sponsors and Agendas

Sponsors are mechanisms that assign resources for particular tasks. If there are a number of distinct tasks to perform, a separate sponsor can be designated for each task and rules governing the appropriate task can be clustered in the sponsors. Additional rules may then be used to control the sponsors. Sponsors are controlled by enabling or disabling them. Sponsors operate by maintaining an agenda of rules or rulesets. They have a single agenda for both forward and backward rules. Once a sponsor has been disabled, its agenda cannot fire.

For forward chaining, rules may be placed on a sponsor's agenda in either a breadth-first fashion so that they fire in a first-in, first-out order, or depth-first so that they are ordered last-in, first-out. With a breadth-first agenda, items are added to the end of all those that have equal priority. With a depth-first agenda, new items are added at the beginning of all those that have the same priority. When a sponsor is created, you specify whether its forward agenda will be either breadth-first or depth-first. Backward agenda rules are always depth-first by default.

Sponsors are organized in a hierarchical structure with one root sponsor called the Top-Sponsor. In the hierarchy, when a sponsor is disabled, all of its subsponsors are automatically disabled with it. This means that you can assign a set of subtasks to sponsors under a parent or supersponsor so that when you need to disable all these tasks, you can simply disable the supersponsor. As you can see, sponsors are the key resource managers in GoldWorks applications.

Explanation

In GoldWorks, the ability to explain the basis of results rests on the use of a dependency network that records how all assertions that are recorded in the system have been obtained, as well as those that are dependent on other assertions. In this way, when one assertion is retracted on which other assertions depend, the dependent assertions are retracted as well. Earlier we saw the distinction between relational and functional assertions. Recall that functional assertions are the type that record state changes and when a new assertion is made of a given predicate, the old one is automatically retracted.

The Menu Interface

Now that a somewhat detailed understanding of the functioning of the GoldWorks architecture has been provided, the design of the user interface should make considerable sense. GoldWorks provides two different interfaces: the Menu interface and the Developer's interface. The Menu interface allows prototype knowledge bases to be built by using an interactive system of menus. The Developer's interface allows programmers to use the GMACS editor that comes with GCLISP for writing the knowledge base as code. Most of the things that can be done with the Developer's interface can be done with menus. The two exceptions are changing agendas and writing message-passing handlers.

Most operations are typically performed in an Inspector or Browser screen. These screens are organized about a focus item. Various fields and submenus concerning the focus item are also usually present. Inspectors are screens that allow you to examine the details of GoldWorks objects. Most editing is usually done from within Inspector screens. Browsers are screens that allow you to examine the location of an object within its hierarchy. (See the discussion of the FIND command menu later in this section for further information.)

```
┌─────────────────────────────────────────────┐
│  System   Define   Find   Run   Window       │
└─────────────────────────────────────────────┘
```

Figure 6.4 GoldWorks Main Menu Bar

The main menu bar that appears on the top of the screen when you first bring up GoldWorks looks like Figure 6.4. Each of the commands provides access to the dropdown menus. The following paragraphs give some of the important details you will need to know in order to understand how the dropdown menu system and its accompanying screens operate so that you can develop GoldWorks applications.

From the System menu you perform most of the main file operations and move between the main parts of the system environment. You use this menu to load knowledge-based files, to load the GMACS editor that comes with GCLISP, to enter the CommonLISP interpreter, and to exit the system.

You use the Define menu for accessing the GoldWorks facilities that you can use to create any type of object in the system. Each of the options corresponding to the different types of GoldWorks objects has its own Inspector screen used for further specification and editing of various features of a knowledge system application.

The Find option allows you to open Inspectors or Browsers on various types of objects in your application. The dropdown menu for the FIND command is shown in Figure 6.5.

Each of the options of the Find menu allows you to select the type of object you are interested in. When you do, a list is displayed of all the objects of that type in your system. Generally, when you select one of these options, an Inspector screen window will open. If you want to browse the object, select Browse from the Focus Item Options menu. If you are already browsing and want to inspect, choose Inspect from the Focus Item Options menu.

One of the most important things in a development environment for AI is the debugging facility. As compared with standard procedural programming, some rather complex issues are involved in developing the final version of a knowledge system application. The problem is not so much that of finding and eliminating bugs as it is one of refining and tuning a system to do exactly what it ought to do without doing anything unnecessary, while still retaining the "indeterminacy" of a knowledge-based system.

The GoldWorks debugging facilities allow you to list all the breakpoints that have occurred during the running of an application. Selecting the Breakpoints option allows you to specify points at which the inference engine will pause during execution. The Breakpoints facility provides the options of breaking on a sponsor, a rule, an assertion, or even an agenda item. For each of these options there is an additional menu that helps you to define the exact nature of the breakpoint. In addition to step and trace, the developer also has the option of halting the progress of the inference engine to view the state of the system and even to view partially matched clauses in rules.

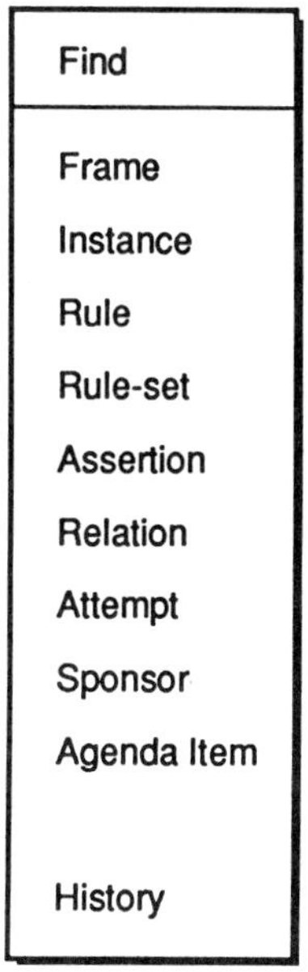

```
┌─────────────────┐
│ Find            │
├─────────────────┤
│ Frame           │
│                 │
│ Instance        │
│                 │
│ Rule            │
│                 │
│ Rule-set        │
│                 │
│ Assertion       │
│                 │
│ Relation        │
│                 │
│ Attempt         │
│                 │
│ Sponsor         │
│                 │
│ Agenda Item     │
│                 │
│                 │
│ History         │
│                 │
└─────────────────┘
```

Figure 6.5 Dropdown Menu for the FIND Command

Spreadsheet and Database Interface

GoldWorks supports accessing information stored in dBASE III and Lotus 1-2-3 file formats. Two different methods are provided for interacting with dBASE III files: using LISP access functions or spawning instances of the dBASE interface frames that can be loaded into the GoldWorks lattice. There are two predefined frames for interfacing with dBASE: dbase-file and dbase-action. Of these, the dbase-file frame is exclusively for internal use by the system for keeping track of open files. The dbase-action frame is the one the developer instantiates to provide access routines for importing dBASE information. This frame has numerous slots that provide all the necessary information for telling the system how to conduct the interface. One of the slots, called the :go slot, acts as the "trigger" to actually initiate the interface once all the other slots have been specified.

Many "actions" on dBASE files are supported. In addition to reading values and records, there are also procedures for deleting records, appending them, and updating field values. When the dbase-action frame is set up properly, auxiliary LISP functions are called that perform the desired interface operations with dBASE files. An alternative way of accomplishing the same result, therefore, is for the programmer to call these functions directly. Anything that can be done with the dbase-action frame can also be accomplished directly through a call to one of the auxiliary LISP functions.

The interface to Lotus 1-2-3 uses the same basic strategy. The 123-action frame provides the same type of interface to worksheet files as the dbase-action frame does to database files. This is one instance of the action frame to a worksheet file. If you want to access multiple worksheets, you need that many instances of the action frame. The high point of the Lotus interface is the support of functions that can both read and write formulas in worksheet files. LISP functions are provided that parallel many of the Lotus 1-2-3 formula operators. This means that some very powerful applications are possible where the full processing power of LISP can be turned loose on dynamically determining special worksheet formula combinations and then making a custom worksheet file with them.

ASCII Parser

As mentioned earlier, the ASCII Parser is a new capability available with the GoldWorks system. Very briefly, this utility scans formatted text files as input data and then creates appropriate objects in GoldWorks II to store that information. This allows the integration of GoldWorks applications with data from many other types of software such as word processors, outliners, project managers, communications, and databases.

External Language and Local Area Network Interface

The External Language Interface to GCLISP allows Microsoft and Lattice C programs to be accessed by GCLISP and therefore by GoldWorks applications as well. This is especially interesting since the GCLISP 286 Developer runs using the protected mode of the 286 or 386 chip in a 15-megabyte memory space. GoldWorks can also make use of two different types of network protocol: the Chaosnet and the TCP/IP protocols via the optional GCLISP Network package. This means that, in principle, distributed expert systems built with GoldWorks can run on a number of machines connected by one of these types of networks.

Limitations

In working with the GoldWorks tool, the student or developer will notice a few idiosyncracies. The GoldWorks MARS system is not designed so that rules about more specific frames will override the more general rules about their parents. If contradictory rules are written about a class and its superclass, GoldWorks will either assert both the conclusion and its contradiction into the fact base or it will halt. If the more specific frame has a rule identical to one for its parent frame, except that the NOT operator is applied to it, GoldWorks will assert both conclusions. If the conclusion of the first rule asserts the EQUAL operator and the second substitutes NOT-EQUAL, the inference engine will halt.

One of the issues that affects the design of a frame lattice in GoldWorks is that of noneditable facets of slots. When a slot of a frame is inherited from a parent, not all the facets of the slot can be edited at the level of the child. One of the noneditable facets is whether or not the slot variable is multivalued. A minor bug I detected was that if you attempt to remove an inherited slot by choosing the Delete option from the operations menu, a dialog box comes up asking you to confirm the deletion, but the slot in fact is not deleted when you confirm. This means that in cases where different user-defined facets are needed for successive subclass frames, it is not a good idea to use the technique of abstract frames, and the luxury of inherited slots may have to be given up. In some cases, it may be better to abandon the parent-child relationship and make the troublesome frames peers of one another.

Another idiosyncracy is that the constraints facet of an inherited slot can only be modified in one direction, that of making it more constrained. For example, if the parent frame had a range of from 10 through 100 and you make the constraint on the slot of the child frame between 0 and 50, the actual merged constraint that applies will be from 10 through 50. Similarly, if the one-of constraint is used, and the parent frame offered three possible choices for values, editing the corresponding constraint of the child can only allow some of the choices to be removed. If you attempt to specify only choices that were not already enumerated at the parent level, the merged constraint will be NIL and no values of the child's slot will be permitted.

These limitations are not serious from the point of view of determining the sophistication of applications that can be built with GoldWorks. They apply to the way that the interactive Developer's Interface works. But if you go into the GMACS editor, you can hand-edit the code to make any adjustments that the interactive menu interface does not allow.

Evaluation

GoldWorks II is an object-oriented expert systems tool that provides some of the most advanced capabilities of any tool currently available for low-cost machines. The features of multiple inheritance, custom-designed user environments, goal-directed forward chaining, bidirectional rules, and automatic dependency maintenance make it a serious candidate for many advanced expert systems applications.

Although a number of tools currently feature frame-based representation, often the implementations of frames are limited in their efficacy. In and of themselves, frames have no knowledge processing power. They are principally a hierarchically structured database. To obtain knowledge processing power from a frame system, two things are needed:

1. A rule syntax that can reference any members of a class with the desired level of generality and with the ability to use variables as slot values in the rules.

2. A broad capability for implementing methods that can turn the frame hierarchy itself into a search space for matching generic knowledge with a dynamic world model.

One of the most important aspects of the GoldWorks system is the full support given for object-oriented programming. This includes functions such as Frame-Parents and Frame-Children, which return all the parents and children, respectively, of a given frame, as well as Frame-Instances and All-Instances, which return all the instances of a given frame and all the instances in the entire system. With these functions provided, it means that GoldWorks is, among other things, a rather full-featured object-oriented programming system with all the necessary support for programming in this paradigm.

GoldWorks
Gold Hill Computers
163 Harvard St.
Cambridge, MA 02139
1-800-242-LISP

6.4 ART

ART is a tool that has a number of powerful features for the development of expert systems, not the least of which is the Viewpoint capability, which permits the construction of various what-if scenarios, or "hypothetical worlds," which may be automatically explored to determine their desirability or feasibility. In this manner, various alternate scenarios can be explored to test a given strategic plan with a given set of assumptions.

Schemata

The schema facility in ART provides object-oriented representation for knowledge-based problem-solving systems. Schemas are really just another word for frames. Schemata in ART support the powerful features of inheritance and multipleslots. They are created with the defschema function.

Rules

Control in ART programs is accomplished through the use of what are called salience, control patterns, and declarative agendas. *Salience* is the mechanism used in ART that consists of ranking rules according to their priority. This provides various techniques for controlling the order in which things will happen in a rule-based program. *Control patterns* are patterns used by certain rules—call them metarules if you like—which can invoke or disable whole sets of rules by asserting control facts into the working memory of the ART database.

Declarative agendas involve a simple but effective use of nonmonotonic reasoning. At a certain point in the execution of an ART program, there may be a list of items in the database that relate to corresponding items that are on the agenda. As rules fire, retractions are made from these items until only the "correct" or "best" one remains, and thus a goal or subgoal is accomplished. The most effective ART programs use all three of these control methods together to cooperatively achieve their objectives.

In addition to ordinary run-of-the-mill rules, ART provides for a number of special types of rules, such as hypothetical rules, belief rules, and constraint rules. According to the developers of ART, its inference engine functions in such a way that it is as if the facts find the rules. This is a loose way of characterizing a forward-chaining inference mechanism that allows the assertion of various "keys" into working memory that can "unlock" sets of rules and bring them into play. A rule can also be designed so that it will fire only on the absence of a certain fact in the working memory, such that whenever that fact is retracted the rule will fire immediately.

ART rules that reference schema databases have two important limitations: they cannot add empty slots to schemas and they cannot add new values to single-valued slots that already have a value. To change the value of a single-valued slot, the modify command must be used in a rule. For example, if we wanted to write a rule that could update the total-sales slot of the YourBusiness schema, we could say:

```
(defrule update-total-sales
 (schema ?business
  (total-sales ?value))
=>
 (modify
  (schema ?business
   (total-sales ?new-value))))
```

Backward Chaining

ART includes a form of backward chaining that differs substantially from the PROLOG style of backward chaining. Generally speaking, ART's backward chaining still has an opportunistic flavor such that new facts can be made use of immediately. The main role of its backward chaining is not as an autonomous mechanism to build full systems with that paradigm, but rather as an aid in programs that are still predominantly foward-chaining programs.

The backward chaining works in the following way. When ART is trying to match its database with forward rules, it may encounter a pattern to which some backward rules apply. In that case, it generates a goal that states the facts that would be needed to match the pattern. One very worthwhile use of backward chaining in ART is to cut down the number of facts needed in working memory.

6.5 Viewpoints in ART

In ART, a viewpoint is a kind of limited perspective or vista that allows a knowledge system to see only the facts and details that are relevant to a particular situation. The use of viewpoints in which we are particularly interested here is where the various viewpoints result from making certain specific hypothetical assumptions. In particular, we are interested in a system where reasoning is conducted about situations that undergo changes over a certain period of time. In such a case, for example, we could use the ART tool to build a chain of viewpoints that reflect the state of various ventures or corporate entities after the elapse of each subdivision of some interval of time. Depending on the application, the subdivision might be weeks, months, or even years.

The way the ART tool keeps track of these hypothetically developing parallel situations is by building what is called a *branching tree* of viewpoints. This tree can have its root in the situation of the present as it now exists or in any reference situation whose possible futures we might wish to explore. Let's look now at how a series of time states might be modeled. For our purposes here, we will use the time period of a quarter. We might then construct some viewpoints that would look something like those shown in Figure 6.6.

The following code shows most of the ART rules needed to use the viewpoints facility to perform hypothetical reasoning on alternative strategies in various business situations. The rules include those for sprouting, merging, and poisoning various viewpoints.

```
(defrule sprouter
 (please sprout ?item)
=>
 (sprout BusinessSituation
   (assert ?item))))

(defrule poisoner
 (declare (salience* constraint-salience*))
 (please poison me)
=>
 (poison "because I requested it"))

(defcontradiction contradictor
 (please contradict me))
defrule believer
 (please believe me relative to ?parent)
 (viewpoint ?vp1
   (?parent))
=>
 (believe ?vp1 "because I requested it"))

(defrule make-hypothesis
 (please hypothesize)
=>
 (hypothesize (assert (supposition-1)
      (supposition-2))
      (assert (fact-1)
      (fact-2))))
```

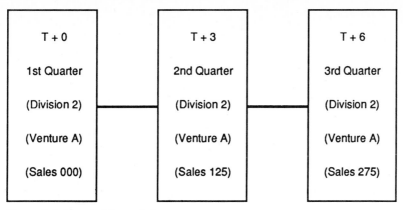

Figure 6.6 Sample Viewpoints

```
(defrule make-simple-hypothesis
  (please hypothesize ?premise)
=>
  (hypothesize (assert ?premise)))

(defrule merge-two-viewpoints
  (viewpoint ?vp1
    (supposition-1))
  (viewpoint ?vp2
    (supposition-2))
=>
(merge (?vp1 ?vp2)
  (assert (new-fact))))
(def-viewpoint-levels
  (Strategy merging nil)
  (BusinessWorld poisoning nil))

(deffacts initial-business-world
  (to-level BusinessWorld))
```

In this example, the 1st Quarter represents the root viewpoint. The corporate division and the venture are facts stated in the root viewpoint that will not change with time. However, we might have also considered a second venture, Venture B, where, depending on a mix of other factors, alternate viewpoints are generated for various combinations of figures, for the performance of each venture independently or for both combined.

Note that the quarters change as they should at intervals of three months. This is specified in ART using extent declarations. So to get the result indicated, we would have simply written

```
(1st_Quarter) in T+3 | T+0
(2nd_Quarter) in T+6 | T+3
(3rd_Quarter) in T+9 | T+6
```

In contrast to this, the division and venture names start being true in the root
viewpoint at T+0 and do not change thereafter. This is equivalent to:

```
(Division_2) in T+0
(Venture_A)  in T+0
```

This means that Division and Venture are global facts that remain constant no matter
what else is changed in the viewpoint.

6.6 Hypothetical Worlds

Figure 6.7 depicts the use of viewpoints to model five hypothetical strategies where
Division 2 attempts to challenge various competitors. These competitors might each be
the competitors of various business units in Division 2 that are shown to be present in
Strategy-1.

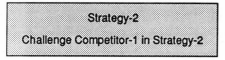

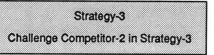

Figure 6.7 Five Hypothetical Strategies Models Using Viewpoints

OBJECT-ORIENTED PROGRAMMING FOR ARTIFICIAL INTELLIGENCE

How will the knowledge base determine what will happen in these alternative hypothetical strategies? The answer is that the rules provided in the rulebase by the developer must be written such that they handle the hypothetical situations in the desired manner. Since the ART tool automatically masks out all other facts besides those revealed in each viewpoint, the rules will be applied to each viewpoint in succession, with differing results, depending on the facts assigned to each.

Viewpoint Levels

To create an expert system that uses viewpoints in ART, the first step is to provide the necessary declarations using the def-viewpoint-levels command. For example, if we were writing a strategic planning expert system, we could write simply:

```
(def-viewpoint-levels Strategy)
```

To create new viewpoints in a temporal state graph that change with time, the sprout command is used. To use it, we can define a special rule called Viewmaker that does the necessary work:

```
(defrule Viewmaker
 (fact-1)
 (fact-2)
 (fact-3)
=>
 (sprout
  (assert (new fact))))
```

This Viewmaker rule will fire in a viewpoint whenever any three simple facts are present. So if the Viewmaker rule sees only Division 2 and Venture A in a viewpoint, it will not fire. It will only fire if some additional fact is present such as:

```
(Challenge Competitor-1).
```

The hypothesize command is similar to the sprout command. Like sprout, hypothesize can generate new viewpoints. But in addition to what sprout does, hypothesize can also assert one or more new facts into viewpoints as hypotheses. In short, hypothesize allows rules to be created that can automatically make new viewpoints based on new hypotheses. But the hypothesize command is not just a function that will indiscriminately create these new viewpoints and assumptions. For example, it refuses to spawn new viewpoints if the new viewpoint would duplicate one that already exists. Another interesting capability of this command is that it can form the necessary new viewpoint by merging two or more existing viewpoints, if this is at all possible.

This capability of merging viewpoints is also placed under direct control of the developer in ART with merge, another very powerful command. The merge capability can be used directly, but in some situations it performs a merging of viewpoints automatically. Other important viewpoint commands in ART are `believe`, `poison`, `viewpoint`, and the (meta) construct. Although rulebases will necessarily differ from one particular site for an application to another, one part of the knowledge base that can be relatively situation independent is the concept or schema hierarchy.

It is essential for developing an application with ART that uses the Viewpoint feature to understand exactly how rules interact with Viewpoints. In any Viewpoint application, the outermost or zero-level viewpoint is the (meta) viewpoint. When ART attempts to match rules in a multilevel viewpoint application, it will fire a rule only if all the left-hand-side patterns of the rule can be matched with facts along a specific pathway called the total viewpoint pathway, consisting only of the set of viewpoints from the (meta) level to the innermost viewpoint. As the Art inference engine moves between viewpoints in this pathway, it keeps track of its position by using a pointer called the Current-Viewpoint pointer. Whenever a rule pattern matches a fact, this pointer is bound to the viewpoint where the match occurs. Each time a new pattern is matched, the Current-Viewpoint pointer is rebound. This means that as rule processing proceeds to the action side of the rule, the current viewpoint is determined by the last pattern stated in the rule. As the rule fires, the actions specified in the right-hand side will be executed in the current viewpoint unless some provision is made for overriding the pointer.

One way that ART allows more specific control of rule processing with viewpoints is by the use of viewpoint patterns. This is done by specifying a special construction using the viewpoint keyword. A very simple use of this might be as follows:

```
(defrule test-viewpoint
 (Viewpoint ?view-name
  (Economic-situation recession)
  (Challenge
 Competitor-2)
 =>
 (at ?view-name (assert (conserve-resources))))
```

If this rule fires, it will be because the inference engine has found a single viewpoint with facts that match the two patterns following the viewpoint declaration. The ?View-name variable will then be bound to the name of that viewpoint, and the action specified to be performed at this viewpoint will be constrained to occur only there. Obviously, the viewpoint for the action does not always have to be the same as that for the pattern match.

Other viewpoint movement commands in ART include `to-level`, `outto`, and `into`. The `to-level` command directly resets the current viewpoint to the level specified by its argument. The main difference between it and the `at` command is that `to-level` can only move to levels within the total current viewpoint path. It is used in rules of the form:

```
(defrule [rulename]
 [match-pattern-1]
 ...
 [match-pattern-n]
 =>
 (TO-LEVEL [level-name]
  (assert ( [ an-assertion ] ))))
```

The `outto` command does this, too, but it is specialized to moving to viewpoints outside the current one. Similarly, `into` moves to viewpoints in the opposite direction.

ART also has two viewpoint predicates: `VP-EQUAL?` and `VP-INHERITS-FROM?`. The `VP-EQUAL?` predicate tests whether or not two viewpoints are "equal" in the sense that they are at the same viewpoint level and have identical contexts. A typical use of the `VP-EQUAL?` predicate is to guarantee that the same viewpoint has not been found twice. The `VP-INHERITS-FROM?` predicate is used to test whether or not one viewpoint descends from another one. It returns T if the first argument is a viewpoint that is a descendant of the second argument.

There are three important viewpoint state and structure functions: current-context, root-context, and lower-contexts. The current-context function returns the name of the innermost context of the current viewpoint. The root-context function takes one argument, the name of a viewpoint level, and returns the name of the root context at that level. The lower-contexts function takes an argument that can be either a context or a viewpoint name and returns a list of the child contexts of that viewpoint or context. There are many other functions of this sort, but we will not go into them here.

Evaluation

ART has a unique capability among object-oriented expert systems tools. Although there may be better tools than this in other respects, it is so far one of the only commercially available expert system tool that provides a built-in capability for hypothetical reasoning. Although many other tools do not exclude this type of facility, it would take a major development effort to add it to them. Another approach might be to "force" this type of application on a conventional tool in such a way as to get the same basic result, but with a different representation scheme. One problem with this approach is that it may turn out to be like going from San Jose to Los Angeles by way of Hawaii. For applications that have a real need for the hypothetical reasoning approach, ART can be a very effective rapid prototyping tool because of its excellent built-in facilities for this approach.

6.7 LOOPS

LOOPS was developed at Xerox PARC, where the first version was released in 1983. The principal designers of the original LOOPS system were Dan Bobrow and Mark Stefik. LOOPS has just recently been released as a commercial product and is an important addition to commercially available expert system tools and AI development environments.

Before going into some of the details of LOOPS, I would like to first describe just what sort of an AI programming environment this is, and what its overall significance might be. One source of confusion should also be removed. LOOPS is not the same thing as CommonLOOPS. The latter is a low-level object-oriented extension to CommonLISP, whereas LOOPS is a high-level AI language that already has most of the facilities needed for developing advanced AI applications. As with most AI systems, LOOPS supports rule-based programming. However, what makes LOOPS unique is its complete implementation of an object-oriented programming environment for AI. LOOPS contains just about all that was valuable and important in Smalltalk, and much more. It was the tool Sanjay Mittal used to create the PRIDE expert system. It is already quite apparent that some new paradigms for expert system development have emerged as a result of various projects using the LOOPS environment.

One of the central ideas in the design of the LOOPS environment was to provide an AI programming system that could support a multiple-paradigm framework that allowed as many options among programming paradigms as possible. The current system supports four main programming paradigms: the object-oriented paradigm, the rule-based paradigm, the access-oriented paradigm, and the normal procedural paradigm.

Classes and Instances

As with all object-oriented programming systems, LOOPS provides for building hierarchies of classes and instances of those classes. Let's first look at the simple syntax used for accessing objects in LOOPS. We would reference a user-defined class called Partnership, or any other class in LOOPS, as follows:

```
($ Partnership)
```

The dollar sign means that the object pointer to the Partnership structure is to be referenced. All references to objects in LOOPS use this convention of preceding the name of the object with the dollar sign character.

Another syntax convention used in LOOPS is the back arrow character, which we will represent as <-. This character is accessed on the standard keyboard definition of the 1186 with the underscore key. The <- character in LOOPS translates roughly as "send the message," and corresponds to the message in Flavors or the send operator in SCOOPS (the object-oriented extension to PC Scheme). So, the LOOPS expression,

```
(<- ($ Partnership) New 'OurVenture)
```

would send the message New to the Partnership class to create a new instance of itself called OurVenture. Much of the activity done in developing LOOPS applications uses the rich variety of window and menu-based tools like the browsers and editors. Before proceeding with some of the technical features of LOOPS, let's look at the available browser facilities.

LOOPS Browsers

A graphics-oriented browser system already exists on the 1186 at the LISP level. However, it reaches its real functionality in the LOOPS Lattice Browser. This is the current state of the art in interactive visual editing and advanced AI system design. Software, as most programmers realize, is developed in layers or shells of functionality. Each of the major advances in software engineering still coexist in some form like different layers of an onion or rings of the trunk of a tree.

LOOPS and the 1186 are both two of the best examples of this organic evolution of layers of technology that combines the old with the new in progressively higher layers of stable and relatively permanent steps on the path toward increased machine intelligence. The high-level tools that are provided in the LOOPS environment offer an example of an AI development environment that, in effect, takes software development to its next level.

6.8 The Lattice Browser

One of the most useful and spectacular facilities in the LOOPS environment is the visual-oriented graphics class browser called the Lattice Browser. This facility has a main window on which the class hierarchy is displayed from left to right with graphics lines depicting the lines of inheritance between classes. A large number of facilities for editing objects is available for use by directly interacting with the lattice display. The main menu for the Lattice Browser facility is shown in Figure 6.8.

The PrintSummary command prints a full description of the selected class in the Exec window, including all its local variables and methods. For example, selecting the ActiveValue and using the PrintSummary command gives the display:

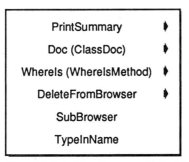

Figure 6.8 Lattice Browser Main Menu

```
#.($ ActiveValue)
Supers
  Object
IVs

CVs

Methods
    AVPrintSource          AddActiveValue           CopyActiveValue
DeleteActiveValue      DeleteNestedActiveValue      GetWrappedValue
GetWrappedValueOnly    HasAV?   NestActiveValue      PutWrappedValue
PutWrappedValueOnly       ReplaceActiveValue           WrapOutside?
WrappingPrecedence
```

The PrintSummary operation has the convenient feature that the custom methods for class are shown in bold type and the inherited classes are shown in normal type. The

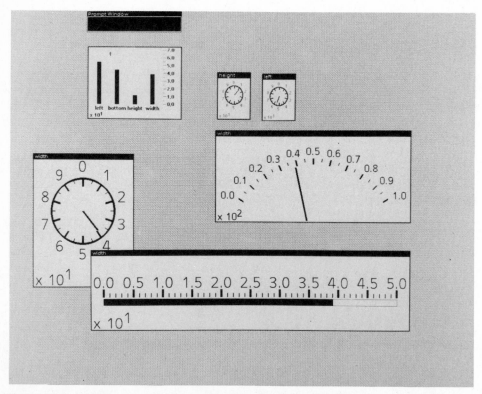

Figure 6.9 A LOOPS screen illustrating the different types of gauges

WhereIs command is also very convenient. If you need to know the class where a particular method is first defined, all you have to do is choose this option, wait for a window with a list of all the methods in the system to appear, and select one. Almost immediately, the name of the selected class on the Lattice Browser network display will blink on and off.

The BoxNode command in Figure 6.10 places a box around the name of the class selected and makes it a target for the MoveTo and CopyTo commands. These commands allow methods to be moved and copied from one class to another. Calling on the EditClass option opens the SEdit editor with the current declarations for the selected class.

Developing applications in LOOPS involves a combination of writing code in the editor and accessing a large number of convenient facilities in the mouse-oriented window and menu environment. One convenient way of going about developing object classes in LOOPS is to just enter an empty class into the Exec window by typing, for example,

```
(DefineClass 'Partnership)
```

and using the interactive facilities to flesh out the class definition.

Once you have entered a class in this way, you can then access it with the Class Browser. To do so, you call up the main menu, select the Browse Class command, and then type in the name of the root class at the prompt. In this case, we type in the name Partnership. A small class browser window opens at that point with the name

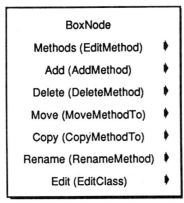

Figure 6.10 Lattice Browser Popup Menu

Partnership displayed inside. Next you select "EditClass" from the Class Browser submenu, and the SEdit window opens with the following template displayed:

```
((MetaClass Class Edited:           (*DRF "22-Mar-89 15:00"))
 (Supers Object)
 (ClassVariables)
 (InstanceVariables)
 (MethodFns))
```

Another way you can tell LOOPS that you want to edit the methods of a class is by accessing them through the general Lattice Browser. The same menus are available there as under the individual Class Browser window. For me, the Lattice Browser and related classes form the heart of the LOOPS user interface.

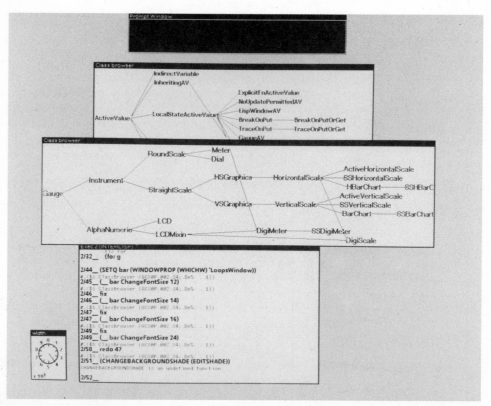

Figure 6.11 A LOOPS screen showing two instances of the Class Browser, the Executive Window, and a gauge

Methods

In object-oriented systems, methods are the private procedures or functions known only to objects of a given class and its descendants. LOOPS offers a total of six different categories of methods. There are the class methods and object methods found in Smalltalk and many other object-oriented systems. In addition, there are the Internal, Public, Masterscope, and Any method categories. *Internal* methods are the low-level system methods that implement LOOPS itself. They can be used by programmers who know what they are doing, but they are not intended for use as library methods to be specialized. *Public* methods are all those methods that are either provided with the system or developed by the user that are intended to be specialized for various purposes. The special *Masterscope* methods are local only to this application and can be used only when it has been invoked. *Any* methods are all those that have not been declared to be one of the preceding types.

Methods in LOOPS follow the syntax:

```
(METHOD ((ClassName Selector) self ARG1...ARGn)...body)
```

Selector is the name of the method that, when sent to the appropriate object, succeeds in invoking it. The self argument is a "dummy" term that stands for the class to which the message will be sent. For example, the Destroy method, which is implemented for the Object Class, is written as follows:

```
(Method ((Object Destroy)
         self
         (<- (Class self)
             DestroyInstance self))
```

It takes no arguments other than self, but is written so that it can be inherited by subsequent classes but still always destroy the proper class when called. So the expression (Class self) ensures that the message will be sent to the class of the object. From there, it simply calls on the DestroyInstance method. This may seem metaphysical, but practically speaking, it is important to be able to uncreate objects to provide memory for creating other new ones.

Methods are created in LOOPS using DefineMethod. This function has the form:

```
(DefineMethod class selector argsOrFn expr file methodType)
```

To define a new method, you can usually click the middle mouse button on the class in the Lattice Browser and then select Add from the menu and AddMethod from its submenu. At that point a prompt pane opens with the message:

```
Type the selector for the new method: >
```

You then enter the method's calling name. Let's say we enter the name NewMethod. At that point, a window of SEdit opens with the following template already loaded in it:

```
(Method ((Object NewMethod)
         self)

        (SubclassResponsibility))
```

This template is purely for convenience when it applies. If you like, any part of it, or even all of it can be deleted, and you can begin with a clear editing window. On the whole, the template is usually quite useful. To say that this is a huge workspace with vast resources and that it takes substantial time to master would run the risk of understating the case.

6.9 Active Values

In LOOPS, an active value is an object that will send messages as a side effect of attempts to read or write to the instance variable of another object. This is often very useful in visually oriented interfaces, debugging, initializing variables, and defining dependency relationships between variables. The ActiveValue class is a direct subclass of the Object class. It is an abstract class, however. Instances are not made of it but of its subclasses.

An interesting example of a practical use of active values is in designing a window that always remains square even when resized by the user. This is done by creating an active value that tracks the width variable for an instance of the SquareWindow class and automatically sets the height variable equal to it.

One of the built-in uses of active values in LOOPS is for dynamic monitoring of the state of objects. The Gauges facility is a LOOPS library application that contains a variety of display classes. The classes allow you to attach the values of critical variables to graphics displays of various types of gauges and meters that provide feedback on the values of the instance variables of instantiated objects. Whenever the value of an attached variable changes, the gauge or meter is immediately modified to indicate the new value.

The Gauges class has two main subclasses: LCD and Instrument. LCD, in turn, has two main subclasses: Digiscale and Digimeter. Instrument, on the other hand, has three main branches: VerticalScale, RoundScale, and HorizontalScale. Meters and Dials are specializations of the RoundScale class. All in all, these Gauge subclasses provide for just about any style of visual gauge or meter that might be needed, ranging from needle gauges to thermometers.

To use the Gauges facility, all that is really involved is to create an instance of one of the Gauge classes and provide it with values for the necessary parameters by sending it the appropriate messages. To just get a gauge to be visible on the screen, you would first create an instance by saying:

```
(<- $Dial New 'DialOne)
```

which creates an instance of the Dial class called DialOne, and then sending it the Update message like this:

```
(<- $DialOne Update)
```

If you need to set the value of the dial to an initial value, send the Set message:

```
(<- $DialOne Set 100)
```

The message that assigns a meter or dial to a given variable is the Attach message. This is also very simple to execute. If we wanted to assign our dial as an indicator of the amount of fuel left in a rocket in a simulation of a space vehicle mission, we could easily do so by saying:

```
(<- $DialOne Attach $TitanIV_547 'FuelRemaining)
```

This Gauges application in LOOPS is similar to the ActiveImages facility in the KEE tool from Intellicorp.

Mixins and Multiple Inheritance

LOOPS provides full support of multiple inheritance, which means that a class can be defined as a subclass of more than one superclass. Another way of saying this is that multiple superclasses can be selected as mixins for a new class. The basic rule that inheritance follows in LOOPS can be stated succinctly as "left to right, up to joins." This means that if a message M is sent to class Z, and that method is not directly implemented in Z, then a search takes place up the class lattice for method M among the immediate superclasses of Z, their superclasses, and so on. The order of search is left to right and "breadth first" in the sense that all the immediate superclasses are searched first before any of their superclasses, and so forth.

Rules

LOOPS has an original approach to using rules. The rules are always organized into definite rulesets, which may have various kinds of control structures to evaluate them. A ruleset is always associated with some particular LOOPS object, which provides the workspace for the rules. The rulesets can be invoked in several different ways. In the object-oriented paradigm, they are invoked by sending a message to the object that contains them. In the access-oriented paradigm, they can be invoked by using active values as a side effect of either reading or writing data in object properties. Individual rules may even be written that invoke other rulesets. It is also possible to invoke rulesets from any LISP program.

LOOPS offers six main control structures for rule processing: Do1, DoAll, While1, WhileAll, For1, and ForAll. If the DoAll control structure is used, the rule processing begins with the first rule of the ruleset and executes each and every rule that is satisfied. With the Do1 control structure, only the first rule whose conditions are satisfied is executed. If no rule fires, the ruleset returns a value of NIL. The While1 control structure is a cyclic version of Do1. With this control regime, a while condition is specified. If the condition is satisfied, the first rule whose condition is satisfied is executed, as with the Do1 construct. The difference is that if the while condition is still satisfied after that, the process is repeated until the condition no longer holds or until a Stop instruction is encountered. Similarly, the WhileAll construct is the cyclic version of DoAll. If the condition is satisfied, all the rules are tried and as many executed as can fire. This is repeated until either the while condition fails or Stop is encountered.

The For1 construct is another cyclic version of Do1. Instead of while conditions, this type of control structure has an iteration condition. The processing of rules occurs as with Do1, but the process reiterates over a range of values until the limit value is reached. A similar control regime occurs with the use of the ForAll construct, except that here the behavior resembles DoAll. As many rules as can be satisfied are executed.

One of the main ideas behind the design of the LOOPS rule-oriented programming approach was to allow control information to be factored out as much as possible. This is, of course, a very worthwhile idea because it means that the knowledge is kept separate from the control structure mechanisms. One of the advantages of rule-based programming is just this separation of content from control. It allows the modular addition of rules so that a production system keeps running from the time the first rules are entered until it is completed without rewriting the inferencing code. Some AI languages such as OPS5 encourage writing numerous rules whose function is to control knowledge processing. This tends to neutralize the advantages of rule-based systems in separating knowledge and control. The LOOPS control structure declarations we have just outlined attempt to cope with this.

Another useful LOOPS rule construct is that of first and last rules. These are rules that can fire either before or after the main part of a ruleset is invoked. They are implemented by inserting an {F} or an {L} in the MetaDescription field just prior to the rule proper. LOOPS also has an adult trail capability in its implementation of rules. The rule syntax in LOOPS can best be illustrated by an example. The illustration in Figure 6.12 is from the *Xerox LOOPS Manual*.

```
RuleSetName: FillTub;
WorkSpace Class: WashingMachine;
Control Structure: WhileAll;
Temp Vars: waterLimit;
While Cond: T;

{1!} IF loadSetting = 'Small THEN waterLimit <- 10;
{1!} IF loadSetting = 'Medium THEN waterLimit <-
13.5;
{1!} IF loadSetting = 'Large THEN waterLimit <- 17;
{1!} IF loadSetting = 'ExtraLarge THEN waterLimit
<- 20;

IF temperatureSetting = 'Hot
THEN HotWaterValve.Open ColdWaterValve.Close;

IF temperatureSetting = 'Warm
THEN HotWaterValve.Open ColdWaterValve.Open;

IF temperatureSetting = 'Hot
THEN ColdWaterValve.Open HotWaterValve.Close;

IF waterLevelSensor.Test >= waterLimit
THEN HotWaterValve.Close ColdWaterValve.Close;
      (Stop T)
```

Figure 6.12 LOOPS Example

In this example, the brace indicator {1!} shows that the rules involved are "one-shot bang" rules or "try once" rules. The rules are only tried once whether they pass or fail. Any declaration in curly braces before rules is called a metadescription in LOOPS. Another use of such metadescriptions in metaassignment statements is used for describing audit trails and rules. Audit trails provide a very thorough facility for debugging and explaining why things happened the way they did.

Calls to custom InterLISP or CommonLISP functions may be included in LOOPS rules in both premises and conclusions by simply enclosing them in parentheses. Similarly, LOOPS message-sending expressions can be nested in rules by enclosing them in parentheses and observing the back-arrow and dollar-sign conventions. Access to LOOPS instance variables in rules is done by the use of a colon (:) operator. So, for example,

```
$YourPartnership:industry = 'Law
```

is a rule declaration that assigns the value Law to the industry variable of the YourPartnership object. Similarly, access to class variables is provided with the double colon (::) operator.

6.10 Virtual Copies

One of the more interesting things in the LOOPS library is the provision for virtual copies of networks of instances. This is based on the insight that it can be very useful to treat a group of instances as a unit, which can be duplicated and tracked efficiently. The copies are virtual in two different ways. Only those properties of the instances that are modified are actually copied. Those that remain identical to the originals just "share" the values of the prototype. The copies are also virtual in the sense that only the specific instances that will be needed in processing are actually copied.

Any object that is to have a virtual copy must have a special class variable called VirtualVS. The value of this variable specifies which instance variables of the original object will be copied as opposed to being shared. The implementation of virtual copies is accomplished by two classes: VirtualCopyMixin and VirtualCopyContext. Virtual copies represent a kind of hybrid of classes and instances. They provide a medium-level mechanism whereby constructions such as Perspectives and Hypothetical Reasoning can be implemented.

6.11 LOOPS Applications

With LOOPS it is possible to develop AI applications of a wide variety of different kinds. It is not simply a shell for the development of expert systems. Even in the case of expert systems, different paradigms for them have been developed using LOOPS that depart dramatically from the usual rule-based systems. The facilities described here make it possible to develop knowledge-based systems that make little or no use of the rule-based paradigm. How, then, are such systems designed? The PRIDE expert system is one of the best examples of such a system to date. There has been much talk at Xerox about building an entirely new type of expert system shell paradigm based on the PRIDE application, just as the EMYCIN shell was derived from the MYCIN expert system application. A few years ago, some interesting research was conducted at Xerox PARC by the late Danny Berlin on hierarchical planning in the LOOPS environment.

Some important seminal work with the LOOPS system has been conducted at Ohio State University under the direction of Prof. B. Chandrasekaran. Prof. Chandrasekaran is an advocate of what he calls generic tasks that operate as high-level building blocks in the development of knowledge-based AI applications. At this point, he feels that there are primarily six such generic tasks:

1. Hierarchical classification

2. Hypothesis matching, or assessment

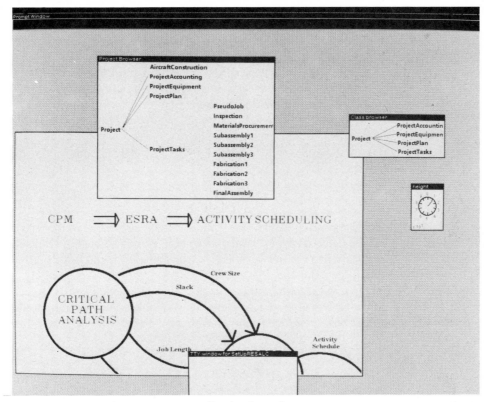

Figure 6.13 Screen from a LOOPS application in project management

3. Knowlege-directed information passing

4. Abductive assembly

5. Hierarchical design by plan selection and assembly

6. State abstraction.

Only a very brief explanation of these generic tasks will be attempted here.

Hierarchical classification is perhaps the best-known type of problem in the expert systems category, a very simple example of which is the well-known "Animal" game. It turns out that this problem of classification is at the heart of many diagnosis problems. Hypothesis matching is the process of determining the degree of fit of a collection of data points to a hypothesis, such as by estimating the probability or certainty that the hypothesis is true. Knowledge-directed information passing refers to the use of rules or frames to encode knowledge that directs a knowledge processing system to seek certain values under various conditions.

Abductive assembly is another form of reasoning that assembles the best hypotheses for a given set of data by a method similar to the means-ends analysis used in the Dendral expert system. Hierarchical design by plan selection refers to a new type of task in expert systems technology, that of routine design. This new category of application is typified by two mechanical engineering expert systems, Aircyl and PRIDE. The last generic task is state abstraction. This involves a mechanism for predicting the consequences of actions by the use of qualitative simulation.

Prof. Chandrasekaran's group at Ohio State has implemented a number of higher level tools in LOOPS to further the idea of having these generic tasks available as building blocks for various types of AI applications. These tools include MDX, CSRL, PATREC, HYPER, IDABLE, and PIERCE.

6.12 KEE

KEE, The Knowledge Engineering Environment, from IntelliCorp is one of the largest and most advanced object-oriented expert system development tools currently available commercially. It has already had considerable use in major development efforts both in the business sector and in government. It is one of the better examples to date of a commercial system that has been built on the basis of an object-oriented kernel. KEE currently runs on a wide variety of platforms including Symbolics, Xerox, and TI LISP machines; SUN workstations; mainframes; the Macintosh-II-based Micro-Explorer; and the Compaq 386.

If any one person can be singled out as a principal architect or author of KEE, it would be Greg Clemenson, who was granted a patent for the frame system that forms the program's kernel. However, many people have made major contributions to the program as it evolved into its present form. For example, Carolyn Steele was largely responsible for the Rulesystem, and Paul Morris and Robert Fillman did the truth maintenance and the KEEworlds. Although KEE is of course greatly indebted to the Units system developed at Stanford University, it has significantly enhanced the Units implementation, particularly in the area of the menu-oriented user interface.

KEE functions are implemented as extensions to CommonLISP, so the entire vocabulary of this dialect is available to be used in conjunction with all the functions. The entire system is built on the underlying structure of objects, or units, as they are called in this environment.

Objects as Units

As we see, the center stage in KEE is occupied by units, the basis of the program's architecture. The unit system constitutes quite a bit more than frame representation and, perhaps in certain technical respects, somewhat less than a full-fledged object system. However, in practical terms, it has the full functionality of a state-of-the-art object-oriented programming environment for AI.

Units in KEE can have own slots, member slots, and method slots. In terms of the nomenclature we have used elsewhere in this book, an *own* slot in KEE is an instance variable and a *member* slot is a class variable. A *method* slot is a provision for programming procedural methods that is represented at the surface as one slot among others. This approach is useful because it means that all the facilities for accessing slots can in principle be used to access methods in KEE.

KEE has some powerful facilities for accessing units. It is possible to access all the members of a class unit when just the class name is known. It is likewise possible to gather a list of all the subclasses in a particular branch of a hierarchy using the UNIT-DESCENDANTS function. KEE also provides compact units, which are more efficient but less flexible and convenient than the standard type of unit. As a general rule, those units that have several slots whose value will seldom or never change can be fruitfully implemented as compact units.

Facets are used to limit the values that slots may take. Cardinality, for example, specifies how many values a slot may have. CARDINALITY.MAX and CARDINALITY.MIN specify, respectively, the maximum and minimum values of the number of slot values.

Active Values

An active value is like a slot value that, instead of being a piece of passive data, is an active procedure that executes under certain conditions. It can execute when the value of its slot is sought, only when it is changed, or under a variety of other circumstances. In KEE, active values are defined as units that can exist independently of any particular slot assignment. For example, any number of active values can be attached to the desired slot if the need arises. What makes this particularly convenient is that active values can be attached to units and slots interactively from the user interface.

From this, it is clear that active values can do anything that method slots can. The question arises, then, of when each should be used. Active values are for things that you want to happen automatically in the background. Method slots are for things you want to happen only when they are explicitly requested, either by a program or by a user. We will return to the topic of active values when we have introduced the KEEworlds facility.

Menu Interface

Although anything in KEE can be written manually using editors, as with most state-of-the-art AI systems, considerable time can be saved by using the menu interface. With KEE, three large icons—the Office, Desktop, and Key icons—on the global menu bar can be used to access three separate menu hierarchies.

The Office icon allows the Office command menu to be opened. Office commands allow you to use a different desktop or to create a new desktop. The Desktop icon command menu offers commands for accessing and creating windows, and loading, saving, flushing, and renaming desktops. The Key icon opens the KEE Command menu,

```
KEE Commands

Create KB
Display Object
Examine Proposition
Explain
Find Unit
Introduce KEE
KEEworlds
Load KB
Logout
Rule Compiler
Show Changed KBs
User Profile
```

Figure 6.14 KEE Command Menu

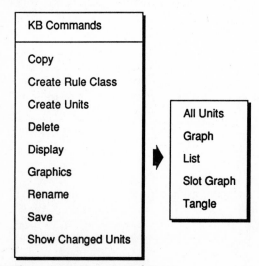

```
KB Commands                    All Units
Copy                           Graph
Create Rule Class              List
Create Units                   Slot Graph
Delete                         Tangle
Display
Graphics
Rename
Save
Show Changed Units
```

Figure 6.15 KB Command Menu

which contains most of the basic facilities that are available in KEE. Figure 6.14 shows the KEE Commands menu.

In addition to these facilities, there is also a knowledge-base access window, which appears just below the global menu bar when KEE is first started. Whenever a knowledge base has been loaded, it is added to the list that appears in this window. By clicking the mouse on the name of a knowledge base (KB) in this window, that KB is selected and the KB Command menu opens right next to the window with a selection of possible operations that can be performed on the KB that was selected. The commands on the KB Command menu, along with a submenu that is accessed by sliding the mouse cursor to the right, are shown in Figure 6.15.

If you select Display from the main menu, sliding over to the popup submenu brings up a list that represents various different display options. Tangle is the default if the submenu is not used, which produces a full tree lattice of the knowledge base. Solid lines represent class/subclass links and dotted lines represent class/instance links.

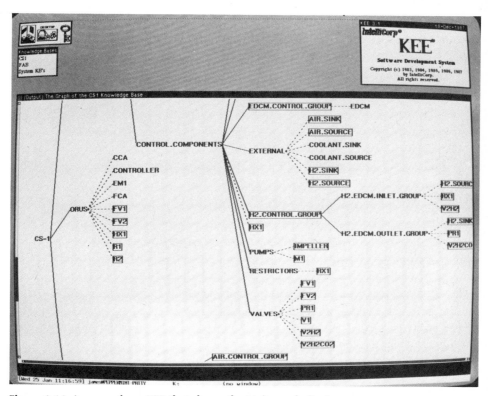

Figure 6.16 A screen from KEE that shows the Unit graph display

The knowledge-base tree graph can be used as a spring board for other displays. For example, selecting a unit on the graph opens the Unit Commands popup menu, which offers you a choice of operations to perform on the unit selected. You can then display the unit with all its slot values, if you like. The display of a unit includes a list of all immediate superclasses and subclasses, and the name, inheritance, and value for its slots.

TellAndAsk

As the name aptly communicates, this is the KEE facility for carrying on dialogues with a knowledge base by making queries of or assertions and retractions in it. The basic format for legal TellAndAsk entries is that of an operator that is applied to a well-formed logical formula. On the surface it looks like a purely declarative language, but it is actually some other things as well. From within TellAndAsk you can invoke the Rulesystem. TellAndAsk is also the language used for actually writing rules in KEE, but we won't discuss this until you have a better idea of what that implies. For now, we'll just talk about querying and modifying knowledge bases with this language.

TellAndAsk provides both English-like templates and prefix templates for making references to slot values. Variables in TellAndAsk, as with many LISP-based systems, begin with a question mark. When the QUERY operator is used to ask a question, KEE always returns the complete expression as its answer. For example, if the knowledge base contains the fact (Socrates is a Man), then

```
(QUERY '(?WHO IS A MAN))
```

will return

```
((SOCRATES IS A MAN))
```

just as

```
QUERY '(SOCRATES IS A ?WHAT))
```

will return

```
((SOCRATES IS A MAN))
```

Since KEE matches for the complete fact, in principle, any term in the logical expression of a fact could be substituted by a variable in a query. When a query has more than one answer, each fact is still stated in its entirety. For the first query in the preceding example, the response could easily have been

```
((SOCRATES IS A MAN)
 (PLATO IS A MAN)
 (ARISTOTLE IS A MAN))
```

When applied to a legal logical expression, the ASSERT function can be used to set the value of a unit slot or to insert an unstructured fact into the knowledge base. If the expression is already in the knowledge base, KEE simply returns TRUE.

TellAndAsk also provides a looping construct such as the LOOP.WITH.BINDINGS macro which can do a loop through any legal logical expression in TellAndAsk. It can do this by using a variable for all the items in a class. For example, we can say:

```
(LOOP.WITH.BINDINGS (?BUSINESS IS IN CLASS BUSINESS)
 DO (PRINT ?BUSINESS "IS A BUSINESS"))
```

One very important construction is the FOR.ALWAYS operator. This operator establishes a strong dependency relation between different logical expressions. FOR.ALWAYS essentially states that for each true instance of expression-1, there is at least one true instance of expression-2. The best way to see what this means is by an illustration.

```
(assert '(for (the sister of ?male is ?female)
    always (the brother of ?female is ?male)))
```

The prefix template form for this would read:

```
(assert '(for.always (the sister of ?male is ?female)
     (the brother of ?female is ?male)))
```

Another related use of FOR.ALWAYS is in cases where you want to define an operation that iterates over all values of one or more variables. (There is not space here to discuss many of the other operators available in TellAndAsk.) New operators can be added to the TellAndAsk language, but it is not a task for the beginner to undertake. Since this language is the one used in stating rules, next we'll look at the KEE Rulesystem.

Rulesystem

The KEE Rulesystem offers both forward and backward chaining as well as methods by which the two modes of reasoning may be mixed or linked in various ways. In general, this is done by having either the backward chainer call the forward chainer or vice versa. The format for rules in KEE allows for both compound premises and compound conclusions. Perhaps the most important thing is that the syntax is the same for both forward and backward chaining.

An important distinction is made in KEE between action rules and pure deduction rules. Deduction rules, as their name suggests, do not add anything new to knowledge bases, but simply draw conclusions from the premises and facts already there. Action rules, on the other hand, can produce whatever side effects the programmer designs them to do that are permitted by KEE. This distinction between deduction and action rules is essential for the truth maintenance mechanism in KEE. Because the TMS system only applies to deduction rules, the truth of the results of applying actions does not really depend on the conclusions. Only the application of the rules actions depends on the truth of the premises. As we have seen, the action can be anything the programmer decides.

Rule Classes

Before you start writing rules, you must first create a rule class to contain them. A rule class is a unit class that can have subclasses, and thus it can help form a hierarchy. Rules are units that are contained in or are members of a rule class. When a rule class is created, it is made a member of the class of all rule classes, which is represented by the RULE.CLASSES unit in the RULESYSTEM knowledge base. It also becomes a subclass of RULES, the root class of all rules. One nice by-product of this choice of representation is that rule class hierarchies can be made visible, in the same way that any unit hierarchies can be, as a graphic tree lattice. Another by-product is that all rules and rule classes automatically inherit a number of slots and method slots that are available for handling them.

Backward chaining in KEE is invoked by the QUERY macro. The arguments to QUERY include a logical expression and optionally a rule class and a world. Worlds will be discussed later, so here we will consider only specifying rule classes. Consider the following example,

```
(QUERY '(SOCRATES IS ?WHAT) 'HUMAN-RULES)
```

Note that only the rules in the HUMAN-RULES rule class would be used. Rules in its superclasses are not applied by inheritance because this would defeat the purpose of limiting the search space to a specific set of rules.

Three different search strategies are supported for backward chaining: depth first, breadth first, and best first. Let's look briefly at how these work. The main control of the backward-chaining inference engine is conducted by a unit that belongs to the BC.AGENDA.CONTROLLERS class.

Conducting searches in backward-chaining mode in KEE can be represented as developing a derivation tree. The inference engine does this by first compiling an agenda of rules and then ordering the premises of the rules. Instead of the built-in rule ordering functions provided, the programmer may write custom rule ordering routines that are suited to a particular application. However, the three basic strategies have to be well understood before considering customizing the inference engine.

In the depth-first strategy, premises are investigated in depth, that is to say, the engine moves down the derivation tree, using the depth-first approach recursively until either it determines that the sequence of premises can be proved or it reaches a dead end. This is the default strategy, and it is the one that works best with applications that require a great deal of user input. As the search proceeds, the questions occur in a logical sequence. On the other hand, in the breadth-first strategy, the nodes are examined with the intention of finding a true premise in the higher levels of the derivation tree first, without attempting to exhaustively derive them. It is as if the engine is not willing to spend time on premises that are not true.

In the best-first strategy, at each level of the derivation tree, the agenda controller selects the node whose goal stack is the shortest. In this way it is hoped that if there is an easy or quick solution, the inference engine will find it without examining many other paths first. It is clear, though, that there is considerable room for formulating customized best-first strategies that are suited to particular problem domains. At this level, it is not the rule ordering that is changed, but rather new members of the NODE.ADDER class are created.

One thing conspicuously absent from the KEE Rulesystem is any provision for handling certainty factors. As a matter of fact, to my knowledge, the issue of reasoning with uncertainty is not even raised in the KEE documentation. This was not an oversight on the part of the KEE designers (though omitting the topic from the manuals altogether may have been one by the technical writers). This omission comes from a basic philosophical disagreement with the use of certainty factors and probability in drawing inferences by rules. Later, when we describe the KEEworlds facility, we will see some ways that IntelliCorp recommends reasoning under uncertainty be handled in KEE.

Forward Chaining

One way to invoke forward chaining in KEE is by using the FORWARD.CHAIN function, which takes a rule class name as an argument. Another way to invoke forward chaining is by using the ASSERT function to assert a fact and specify a rule class to use to deduce conclusions from the fact asserted. In forward chaining, it is important to have a way to control and focus the inferences that are drawn. In large applications, it is seldom efficient to draw all possible inferences just for the sake of drawing them. It is important to be able to draw any inferences that bear on the problem to be solved. Therefore we will look at some of the ways this type of inference can be focused in KEE.

In writing rules, if the expression USING.NO.RULES is placed at the end of a conclusion, once the conclusion is asserted no further forward chaining will occur. This prevents forward chaining at points in a reasoning process where this is undesirable. Examples of when this might be appropriate are when the problem has been solved and when the developer knows by experience that forward chaining at a certain juncture adds considerable time to the reasoning process without producing useful results.

Especially important for advanced users are the following control operators that can be used in rules: ADD, CHANGE.TO, DELETE, and FIND. When CHANGE.TO appears in a rule conclusion, it places its associated logical expression in the knowledge base in replacement mode and can either stop forward chaining altogether or can initiate forward chaining over an entirely different rule class. FIND expressions can be embedded and used with the QUERY operator to initiate questioning of the user or selective backward chaining over certain expressions in a complex query. ADD and DELETE behave as one might expect.

Besides specifying a rule class with which to forward chain, it is also often desirable to specify the types of slot values that one would or would not like to see derived. Currently KEE does not directly support this nor does any other commercial AI system that I am aware of. However, since rule classes can be specified, an opportunity exists for exerting this type of control, though it involves designing rule classes in the appropriate way. If one were to construct rule classes according to the slot types that their conclusions referenced, then, in principle, this type of control could be achieved by the selection of the rule-class arguments when forward chaining is invoked.

New World Action Rules

New world action rules are rules that can be used to create new worlds. A world is a data set that is manipulated by the use of the KEEworlds facility. For our purposes here we can think of worlds as alternate sets of values for slots and variables that are collected together under a common name. If the premises of a new world action rule are proven true, a new world is created and the conclusions of the rule are asserted into it. New world action rules are written simply by using the IN.NEW.WORLD function prior to each conclusion clause in the rule. When used in the forward-chaining mode, a new world action rule is applied only in the highest context or contexts in which it is applicable.

KEE supplies two operators, *ADD and *CHANGE.TO, that are essential for applications involving planning because they prevent action sequences with multiple side effects from becoming intractably large. New world action rules can be used for planning by letting parallel worlds represent alternative actions.

Rulesystem Tracing and Debugging

KEE provides a forward-chaining graph that traces the sequence of a forward-chaining operation from the initial assertion that triggered it through all subsequent chaining paths until there are no more rules on the agenda to apply. Similarly, the AND.TRACE and OR.TRACE facilities that apply to backward chaining provide this trace information regardless of whether or not a backward-chaining sequence has been successful.

Rule Compiler

Users of earlier versions of KEE have found that the rule processing part of the program is one that has had performance problems. In response, a rule compiler is now included to help speed up applications that make extensive use of rules. The Rule Compiler translates rules and TellAndAsk expressions into a set of CommonLISP functions that no longer need special interpretation at runtime. As with most of KEE, the compiler is written using objects. Four main new objects are used with the compiler: Invocations,

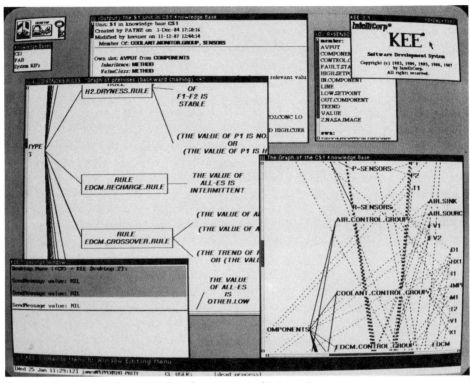

Figure 6.17 A screen from KEE that shows a typical interactive session

Invocation Patterns, Invocation Units, and Compiler Environments. A Compiler Environment object is a set of parameters that govern the behavior of the compiler.

Although the compiler supports all types of rules, there are various facilities for obtaining input from the user that are not. The compiler does not compile individual rules but invocations of rulesets. The developer can select which invocations of the Rulesystem with QUERY, ASSERT, or FORWARD.CHAIN will be compiled. Because of the manner in which this is done dynamic goal selection in backward-chaining cannot be supported by the compiler. All uses of QUERY return all answers. The ability to restrict this is not supported in compiled rulesets.

The Rule Compiler has its own agenda controllers that are similar but not identical to those of the rule interpreter. It is possible to use the ADD.TO.COMPILER.AGENDA function to have specific control over the behavior of compiled rule invocations. Running compiled invocations in an application requires that a runtime compiler be loaded as well as all the necessary compiler environment knowledge bases.

Although the Rule Compiler does not support the built-in KEE functions for end-user input, if it is necessary to have compiled rule invocations that question the user, the input routines can be hand-coded in LISP fairly readily. In cases where the user input should not be forced but should be contingent on the unavailability of the information from other sources, a workaround such as near-duplicate rules with different weighting factors can get the desired results.

Object-Oriented Programming

The familiar type of object-oriented programming is accomplished in KEE by the use of method slots. Method slots can be programmed in two different ways: by calling LISP functions defined elsewhere, or by directly inserting some LISP expression to be evaluated, the latter usually referred to as a *lambda body*. When a function is called in a method slot, the first argument to the function must always be the name of the unit. It turns out that this is a somewhat unfortunate syntactic feature because it virtually guarantees that the functions used in method slots will have to be written especially for that purpose. In many cases, this might involve just writing a *cover function* for already existing ones, so that the argument list is correct. On the other hand, a nice feature of the OOP facility is that a means has been devised that allows *operator overloading*, that is, the ability to call the same function name but to have code specific to the local class of a unit execute. The best way to see how this works is to take an example.

We would like to be able to call the AREA function for any specific geometric figure or physical object but nevertheless to get the correct answer for all figures. If we take the case of a circle and a square, we can write the two functions as follows:

```
(defun Area-For-Circle (unit radius)
 (* pi (* radius radius)))

(defun Area-For-Square (unit side)
 (* side side))
```

The function call in the method slot for both circles and squares can still be made by just calling the AREA function and giving it the appropriate arguments. This works for defining functions that are specific to any class in KEE.

Message Passing

In KEE message passing works by using a set of macros to fetch the method and supply it with arguments and the name of the object that is to receive the message.

KEE provides four different macros for message passing: UNITMSG, UNITMSGTRY, UNITMSG*, and UNITMSGTRY*. The TRY variants allow a fail code to be specified that will execute in case the method name used in the message was not correct. The * variants differ somewhat in their syntax from those without the *. Let's take some examples.

```
(UNITMSG 'CALCULATOR-1 'MULTIPLY 7 3)
```

This sends the message to the CALCULATOR-1 unit telling it to multiply the integers 7 and 3. This same message could also be written as a TRY variant with a fail code as follows:

```
(UNITMSGTRY ('CALCULATOR-1 'MULTIPLY 7 3) (* 7 3))
```

Here, the (* 7 3) is the fail code that executes if for some reason the message is not received.

Truth Maintenance

ATMS (assumption-based truth maintenance system) is intended for use with the KEEworlds modeling facility. In this context, a *world* refers to a particular state of all the knowledge bases that happen to be loaded at one time. More specifically, the aspects of the knowledge bases that change from world to world are referred to as *TMS facts*. There are three kinds of TMS facts: the values of own slots, unstructured facts, and the special fact called FALSE. If the fact FALSE is asserted in a world, the world is inconsistent.

Dependencies set up in ATMS are called *justifications*. Justifications have two main components: the justifiers and the justificands. Here is a statement of a possible justification in KEE:

```
#S(KC::JUSTIFICATION
   :ANTECEDENTS
   (#[Proposition: A STATUS OF THE REFRIGERATION SYSTEM HAS
FAILED])
   :CONSEQUENT
   #[Proposition: THE TEMPERATURE OF THE COOL ROOM IS WARM]
   :INFORMANT NIL)
```

In general, to use ATMS, you must first program the justifications and then write appropriate deduction rules. (Remember that deduction rules only create justifications for true premises at the time that the rules are run.) The programmer can set up justifications in three different ways: by using the CREATE.JUSTIFICATION, ASSERT, or ADD.VALUE functions. A limitation of these functions is that they cannot be used with variables. Therefore, the justification routines must be hand-coded for each fact. ADD.VALUE is useful when more than one justification is needed for a particular premise.

Things start to get a little complicated when deduced facts appear as justifiers for other deduced facts. To make life easier, a justification browser is provided that uses graphic displays and J icons with arrows above them that lie to the right of justifier clauses and to the left of the clauses being justified.

KEEworlds

The KEEworlds facility has a number of possible uses. One very sensible one is to provide a way of running various operations on a knowledge base that may involve side effects without really modifying the actual knowledge base. The knowledge base is modified only in a few affected worlds. Another use of worlds is to record intermediate states in a long reasoning process. One of the most important practical uses, which may often involve many of the other uses as well, is in conducting hypothetical reasoning about possible worlds. Still another use is to use worlds to represent various phases of a process. Clearly, many uses remain to be discovered and perfected for alternate world reasoning.

KEEworlds does not provide for making structural changes from one world to another. Only facts about unit structures and unstructured facts are involved in different worlds. This means that the inheritance links and member links do not change and the numbers and names of slots stay the same. Only the values of slots in a unit hierarchy change from world to world. The aspect of worlds that remains the same for all worlds is referred to as the *background*. If a world is spawned from one that already exists, it is called the *child* and the world from which it was spawned is called the *parent*.

One good way to get an overview of KEEworlds is to enumerate the various kinds of things that can be done to a world. Ten different operations can be performed:

1. Create a world.

2. Destroy a world.

3. Display the facts that hold true in a world.

4. Merge two or more worlds.

5. Display the differences between a world and its parents.

6. Compare the differences between any two worlds.

7. Assert new facts in a world.

8. Retract existing facts from a world.

9. Collapse a world.

10. Display the occurrences in worlds.

Let's review what some of these different operations mean. Creating a world means to create a new root world that is a child of the background structure, or to create a world that is a child of one that already exists. To destroy a world means not only to get rid of it but all its descendants as well. A major alternative to destroying is to collapse the world instead. To collapse a world means to delete it, but to import any of its changes into each of its parent worlds.

The operation of merging two worlds is possibly the most complex and, at the same time, the most important of all the operations to understand. When two worlds are merged, a child world is created that combines the TMS facts of worlds participating in the merger. Merges are conducted in two different ways, depending on whether the optimistic or the pessimistic type of merge has been chosen. The difference concerns only those cases where the same fact has been asserted into one parent world and deleted from another. In the pessimistic merge, the controversial fact or facts are asserted into the child. In optimistic merges, they are not. In cases where the parents have differing values for the same slot or variable, the child world becomes inconsistent and is useless for any practical purpose.

There are circumstances, though fortunately rare, when the background itself becomes inconsistent. This is a very serious matter because it adversely affects most of the knowledge processing facilities. When this happens, either the inconsistency must be immediately removed from the background or the KEEworlds must be reset.

There are also situations when, during a sequence of reasoning, the intermediate worlds might become inconsistent and thereby invalidate the results of the reasoning process. The single action macro provides means of preventing this. This macro forces all worlds to remain consistent until after a reasoning process has been completed. The macro gets its name from another function it performs. If any slot value changes several times during the course of the reasoning process, the single action macro allows any active value method that is attached to the slot to fire only once, after the other operations have completed. Each operation that is to occur is explicitly specified when the Single Action Macro is invoked.

Any of the basic operatons that can be performed on worlds can be done in any of three different ways: interactively from the menu interface, procedurally from within a program, and inferentially by the firing of rules. One thing that makes the KEEworlds environment so useful is its ability to inspect the results in various worlds with a variety of visual display facilities. For example, there is the KEEworlds browser, which is a special window that presents a schematic picture of the current world hierarchy. When a world node is selected in the KEEworlds browser, that world becomes the current world.

Active Values in KEEworlds

When active values are attached to a slot, the user can specify the world in which they are to fire, and whether or not this is to apply also to descendants of that world. This is useful in what-if scenarios where each spawned world applies to a different slot whose value is changed.

AVGET and AVPUT are the two basic methods used to define active values for unit slots. AVGET is used to define methods that fire whenever a slot is accessed. AVPUT is used to define those that fire whenever a slot value is changed. These and other active value methods are described as follows:

Active Value Method	Firing Time
AVGET	Whenever a slot is accessed
AVPUT	Whenever a slot value is changed
AVADD	Whenever the active value is attached to a slot
AVREM	Whenever the active value is removed from a slot
ADD.PROPOSITION	Whenever a proposition is added to the active value unit's attached slot
AV.WORLD.INHERITANCE.CHANGE	Whenever the type of inheritance for an active value in a world is changed
AV.FOCUS.CHANGE	Whenever the active value unit is fired in a different world.

A KEEworld can represent a cross section of time, with each tick of the clock defining a set of facts that are true at that time slice.

KEEworlds and Backward Chaining

In providing the ability to use worlds to store multiple contexts, KEE supports a method of easily making backtracking a trivial operation instead of a computationally intensive one. It does so with a copious use of memory resources.

Invoking new world action rules in backward-chaining mode is often used in KEE for planning applications. In its simplest expression, this assumes the form of a linear planner of the Strips variety. In order for new worlds to be spawned in KEE, the IMMEDIATE.RULE.APPLICATION.MODE has to be set to ON. This is a global variable that determines whether rules are applied as soon as their premises are found true, or whether rule application is delayed until the top-level goal is instantiated.

Another important consideration in this type of planning is getting the order right in the premises for rules. The order of the premises determines the order in which subgoals are fulfilled, and therefore the order in which actions are to be performed. The control over the firing of rules also has a very important part to play in planning applications. If new world action rules not on the solution path accidentally fire, worlds are created that will not be part of a plan.

Reasoning Under Uncertainty

This is a good place to take up the issue of reasoning under uncertainty because, as we saw earlier, KEE lacks the familiar uncertainty factors approach to this problem. The way IntelliCorp recommends that the issue of reasoning under uncertainty be handled is by taking any uncertain premise and creating two different worlds for it, one in which it is false and one in which it is true, and then trying to eliminate one or the other. Then, when this is resolved, the inference engine goes on as though there were no uncertainty at all.

If this seems unacceptable, there are other ways of skinning the same cat. Since rules are units in KEE, there is a way that they can be tagged with different values, according to their relative likelihood of firing in the future. This would provide a way, for example, of differentiating between rules that had all but one premise true and those in which all were false. Then a custom rule ordering function could be written that took advantage of this way of differentiating between rules. This is not something, as far as I know, that has been proven to work in practice, but there seems to be no reason why it could not work without any great difficulty.

In using KEEworlds for handling reasoning under uncertainty, as IntelliCorp recommends, one issue that must be considered is efficiency. At this time, it is not clear to me what problems can be effectively handled in this way without running into resource limitations. Just how efficiently KEEworlds performs is closely dependent on how various global variables are set.

KEEpictures and ActiveImages

The facilities that allow applications to have very effective graphics to help users make knowledge processing visible are called KEEpictures and ActiveImages. Of these, KEEpictures is the graphics toolkit on which ActiveImages is based. It provides the code needed to create object-oriented graphics images as a set of standard picture classes. As with most things in KEE, pictures are implemented as units. Because of the object-oriented nature of this graphics system, pictures can be combined into larger composite pictures. Pictures are drawn in viewports, or windows. Two types of zooming are supported: magnification and selective zooming on an object by object basis.

KEE supplies thirteen basic picture types: bars, axes, bitmaps, boxstrings, circles, polybars, dials, lines, polylines, rectangles, splines, thermometer bulbs, and window panes. In a demo provided with the software, KEEpictures is used to create a short animation program.

If a knowledge base has been equipped with KEEpicture units, the default display depicts the unit known as KEEPICTURE.INSTANCES, which shows a schematic representation of all KEEpicture and ActiveImage units. This does not display the actual pictures though. To do so, first the OPEN.ALL.PICTURES! message must be sent to the KEEPICTURE.INSTANCES unit to open the pictures in the knowledge base. Then the GRAPH.ALL.PICTURES! message is sent to actually display them.

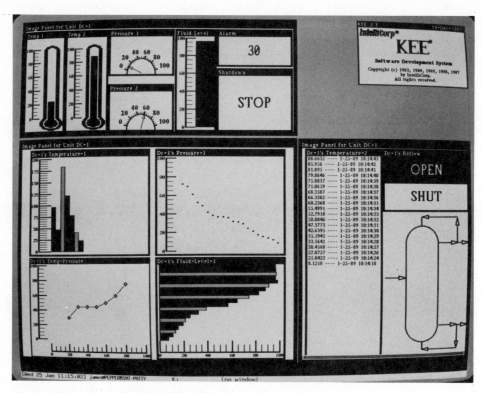

Figure 6.18 A screen from KEE that shows the Active Images facility

Since all pictures are represented as units, their descriptions can be handled by attribute slots. One such attribute slot is the MOUSEFN! slot. This is a method slot that is used to supply the code for what will happen when a mouse button is clicked with the cursor on the picture with the slot in question. One common use of this slot is to open a popup menu of alternate operations when the mouse is clicked.

ActiveImages supplies the ability to attach images to items in the KEE environment such as units, slots, and knowledge bases. Another type of graphics image called ImagePanel is also supplied that allows various buttons, gauges, and so on to be integrated into a control panel. This hierarchy of composites can be extended upward as far as it is useful to do so. ImagePanels can be included in other ImagePanels, and so on. Each ActiveImage is a composite picture built from the KEEpictures facility built of multiple units.

In addition to the now familiar gauges that respond to changes in slot values, KEE also provides active images called Actuators that provide the opposite service of allowing values of slots to be changed by interacting with the graphics display image. If both an active value and an ActiveImage are attached to a slot, they get "stacked" such that whichever one was attached last gets activated first when the value is accessed.

The generic image classes include: simple value displays, value-history monitors, simple alarms, numeric images, histograms, thermometers, levelometers, digimeters, numeric dials, numeric alarms, strip charts, state images, traffic lights, pushbuttons, state dials, text displays, and *x y* history plots.

If ActiveImages is used in conjunction with worlds, a separate ActiveImage must be coded for each world. Simply including ALL for the world argument in the active value code will not suffice for having a separate gauge drawn for each world. In cases where the number of worlds used during sessions is not fixed in advance, code can be written that loops through the names of all worlds created to generate the images for each.

According to application consultants at IntelliCorp, new users of KEE have a tendency to overuse KEE's graphics facilities because they can clearly dramatize the results gained by an application, even when they are not in themselves all that extensive.

KEE can potentially overwhelm a host computer, if not an inexperienced programmer as well. For an application of any magnitude, the most powerful machine available is recommended. The user's guide offers many pertinent suggestions for use of the system to achieve optimum performance. Before concluding that a given marriage of hardware and application will result in poor performance, you should ensure that the optimum configuration of system parameters has been selected.

Evaluation

IntelliCorp appears to have weathered the "AI winter" quite well and continues to port its product to an increasing number of platforms. From our point of view, IntelliCorp has done several things correctly with the design of the KEE architecture. For example, the use of the object-oriented unit system as the underlying kernel out of which the rest of the program has been built makes excellent use of the advantages of object-oriented programming that we are describing in this book. Its results are particularly in evidence in the Rulesystem and the KEEpictures facilities.

There are two things in particular to notice about the implementation of rules. First, each rule is a unit with slots that inherit for the RULE class and its parents or superclasses. This means that, if desired, individual rules can be manipulated using the facilities already built in as well as any that a programmer may choose to add. The same is true of rule classes, which by also being represented in the unit hierarchy can be made visible using any of the standard display facilities for units. Second, the syntax for rules is the same, regardless of whether forward or backward chaining is invoked. This means that optimum use can be made of the declarative aspect of rules that give them their unique capability in carrying out inferences nondeterministically and opportunistically.

The interest of current users of a product like KEE has shifted from diagnostic and reconfiguration problems to those of scheduling and planning. This is attributable to two main factors: the growing sophistication of users and the availability of the KEEworlds facility.

As we have seen, KEE is quite a large programming environment, and as with most large systems, people tend to find certain aspects of it that they are comfortable using and concentrate mostly on these. Some might concentrate exclusively on object-oriented programming based on method slots. Others might rely mostly on the backward-chaining rule. One knowledge representation that all users will employ in KEE is units because the program is almost entirely implemented with this object-oriented approach.

As for limitations, we mentioned earlier the fact that KEE does not address the issue of reasoning under uncertainty in a familiar way. For some, this might be one of the single most important things to know about the system. If you are a Bayesian inference adept or a probability enthusiast, you may not find what you are looking for in KEE. The other limitation that many users have mentioned is performance. Just the size of the program alone is an indication that speed of execution can be a problem. However, this is a complex issue that can be influenced by many factors, ranging from the hardware configuration, to the setting of global variables, to the size and approach of a given application.

KEE on a 386 machine with 16 megabytes of memory is by no means something totally inferior to versions running on more expensive platforms. One of the reasons for this is that, no matter how fast the computer's CPU is, a virtual memory architecture ends up being as fast or slow as its hard disk unless it has plenty of RAM to spare. Yet, even with a 16-megabyte 386-class machine, virtual memory paging does not cease. The complete task of KEE running an application is considered to be a 40-megabyte process. To get maximum performance in this environment, a full 20 megabytes of RAM is recommended.

Even on 386 machines where this much memory is supported, some other things can slow down performance. One of them is the UNIX operating system, but more important is the fact that to get the use of a windowing environment, Microsoft Windows is run as a DOS emulation task. It would clearly seem to behoove IntelliCorp to solve this problem in another way if the potential of the 386 platform is to be truly realized. As things now stand, the economy-minded power user is forced to look at the workstation option as the one with the most power at a reasonable cost.

IntelliCorp
1975 West El Camino Real
Mountain View, CA 94040-2216
(415) 965-5500

6.13 HUMBLE: An Expert System Shell in Smalltalk-80

HUMBLE is an object-oriented expert system shell written in Smalltalk that is commercially available from Xerox Special Information Systems (see Figure 6.19). It is provided in several formats for most implementations of Smalltalk-80. HUMBLE combines rules in both forward and backward chaining with object representation, message passing, and reasoning about objects. The rule syntax used in HUMBLE is a modified version of the Smalltalk syntax. Unlike many rule languages, the if..then..else construct of procedural languages is retained rather than just the if..then form.

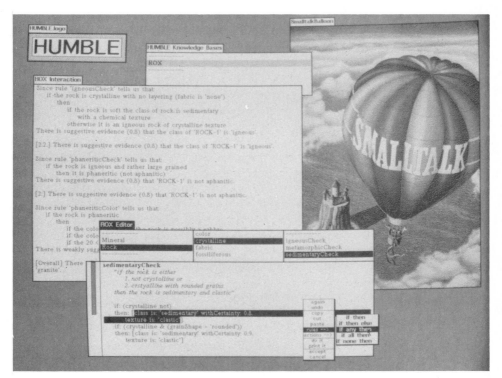

Figure 6.19 A screen from the HUMBLE expert system shell running under Smalltalk

Entity Trees

In HUMBLE, rules operate on entities. Entities are an important type of object that have a specific representation. In applications, they are categorized into a number of different types which are defined by the developer or knowledge engineer. Entities differ from one another by their Parameters or Slots. But perhaps even more significantly, entities can be composite: they can hold other entities within themselves.

The structure of an entity tree is important for how rules are written because rules written for a given type of entity have a restriction in their access to parameters of other entities in the hierarchy. They are only permitted access to entities of that type or those higher up in the tree. This amounts to a kind of inheritance up entity trees that is distinct from inheritance by types of entities.

How do HUMBLE rules determine which entity is involved when evaluating a given rule? An entity is found that has one of the parameters referenced by the rule, and if this is the lowest or most specific entity in the tree that has this parameter, then it is selected. It follows from this that no rule can set parameters in more than one part of an entity tree at a time. If you try to do so the system will recognize this and provide you with an error message.

Here is the template for entities provided by the HUMBLE editor:

```
EntityTypeName
    typeAbove:
    createPrompt:
    addPrompt:
    assumePrompt:
    defaultName:
    parameters:
    mainParameters:
```

The typeAbove: slot should not be confused with the superclass in object-oriented systems. Here it refers to the place that a subentity can occupy in an entity tree. To take a simple example, let's consider part of an entity tree for representing automobiles. In this case, we might have an entity called CoolingSystem. Its subentities would include things like the Radiator, Fan, and Thermostat. The typeAbove: slot would read CoolingSystem for these subentities, and the corresponding slot for it would naturally read "Automobile."

```
A typesBelow: slot is also supported.
```

The list of main parameters for any entity are those that must be determined at the time the entity is created. The system will use whatever means are at its disposal to set the values of these parameters, such as by querying the user. As with many backward-chaining systems, HUMBLE provides for multivalued parameters. In defining parameters, a deducingRules: slot is provided that allows the developer to give the names of rules to be tried in order to find the value of the parameter in the order that they should be tried.

HUMBLE Rules

A developer can specify four types of things to occur when rules fire successfully:

1. Draw conclusions.

2. Evaluate other nested statements.

3. Fire other rules.

4. Set new goals.

Although both backward and forward chaining are supported in HUMBLE, backward chaining is always the main paradigm that controls the evaluation of rulesets. Forward chaining is used strictly as a support mechanism for making additional deductions that can provide the backward chainer with more facts to achieve its goals.

To help in understanding the HUMBLE rule syntax, a short demonstration provided with the system is reproduced in Listing 6.1. As that listing clearly shows, there can be

Listing 6.1 HUMBLE Rule Syntax

```
DontRepeat
"try to avoid repeated actions"

if: (act = lastAct & (lastAct = 'turnLeft'))
then: [act is: lastAct withCertainty: -0.9].

GoForCheese
"If the cheese is left, right, or forward, move to it"

if: (forward = 'cheese')
then: [act is: 'goForward' withCertainty: 1.0 ].

if: (left = 'cheese')
then: [act is: 'turnLeft' withCertainty: 1.0 ].

if (right = 'cheese')
then: [act is: 'turnRight' withCertainty: 1.0 ].

FollowLeftWall
"The mouse should always follow the left wall"

if: (left = 'open')
then: [act is: 'turnLeft' withCertainty: 0.9 ].

RightIfNothingBetter
"Only go right if there is nothing better to do"

act is: 'turnRight' withCertainty: 0.5.

ForwardIfNotLeft
"The mouse should go forward if it cannot go left"

if: (forward ~= 'wall')
then: [act is: 'goForward' withCertainty: 0.7 ].
```

more than one if/then pair in a single HUMBLE rule. Generally all the alternatives regarding the different possible values of a parameter might be grouped in a rule. You will also notice another peculiarity of the rule syntax. The premises are enclosed in parentheses while the conclusions are enclosed in square brackets.

The HUMBLE system is organized to provide for the use of a special type of rule called a searching rule, which is intended to determine the values of subentities. The type of construction used in searching rules uses the `ifAny`, `ifAllOf`, and `ifNoneOf` operators.

One of the key classes used in HUMBLE for knowledge processing is called Interrogator, for various reasons a rather unfortunate choice of words. Interrogator objects are not just used for posing questions to the user. Specializations of this class can be created for seeking required information from any type of external source.

Evaluation

HUMBLE is an expert system shell that takes maximum advantage of the object-oriented paradigm. The use of entity trees provides a built-in facility for composite objects. The fact that Smalltalk methods can be called at will by rules means that very sophisticated expert systems can be constructed that have all the advantages of object-oriented systems we have enumerated, which are customized to very specific conditions in the application environment. However, because the procedural part of applications is written in an object-oriented language like Smalltalk, the maximum amount of the user interface and other routines can be written generically. In this way the amount of code that needs to be written to suit a particular application to its installed site is kept to an absolute minimum. In the future, we should see more expert systems shells like HUMBLE that take such full advantage of the powerful features of the object-oriented paradigm.

6.14 Note on Blackboards

A Blackboard is an AI problem-solving paradigm that is capable of using multiple knowledge sources of many different types to solve a problem. It basically consists of a shared memory area for posting conclusions relevant to the problem, that can be derived from a variety of sources, and a mechanism for reasoning about these results to reach its conclusions. An object-oriented expert system shell is in many respects an ideal type of environment for creating various types of Blackboard systems, but particularly the type that consists of multiple experts.

Conclusion

Object-oriented expert system tools quite simply represent the state-of-the-art tools in the field. Currently there is strong competition among different shells and development environments as well as among the different hardware platforms for running them.

Formerly there was a wide gap between LISP machine-based tools and those available on professional workstations and desktop microcomputers. The gap has narrowed considerably. It has become far more difficult to justify the large expenditures for the high-end dedicated AI workstations. However, for the largest applications, it is often the case that such systems are required. By now, most of the vendors of object-oriented expert system tools have ported their software to a number of different machines. However, they obviously do not all run equally well on all these platforms. Generally the size of the application will dictate which combination of hardware and software can provide the optimum mix of hardware, software, and cost.

True or False?

1. The GoldWorks II system provides a complete environment for object-oriented programming.

2. No facility for truth maintenance is included as part of the GoldWorks II system.

3. The LOOPS Lattice Browser is at the forefront of the current state of the art in graphics-oriented visual editing tools.

4. Of the AI tools considered, the LISP-oriented ones have the least tendency to impose a paradigm on the developer.

5. The complex ways that control schemes can be created in ART can be a danger in that the modularity of knowledge can be lost amid rules whose purpose is largely control.

6. Standard backward-chaining diagnostic expert systems can be built with ART.

7. The ART tool can use the Viewpoint construct to perform hypothetical reasoning by treating the present situation as the root and sprouting a branching tree of future possibilities about which inferences can be made.

8. The use of structure editors in LOOPS is an unfortunate choice that stops experienced programmers from going as rapidly as they might.

9. Active images such as gauges are implemented in LOOPS as active values or "if-modified" demons, code that runs only when the values of instance variables change.

10. A disadvantage of LOOPS is that control schemes and domain knowledge cannot be segregated.

(T, F, T, T, T, F, T, F, T, F)

Chapter 7

Object-Oriented Expert System Applications

In this chapter, we will demonstrate some state-of-the-art tools and techniques in commercial expert systems technology by illustrating the use of a tool called Nexpert Object and by building a rapid prototype knowledge system. This tool, with its powerful synergy of important features, lends itself well to constructing running prototype knowledge systems quickly and with a minimum of obstacles and frustrations. Before proceeding, let's briefly look at what some of those features are.

Nexpert Object is an innovative expert system shell that combines rules and objects in an interesting and powerful way. It fully utilizes the windowing facilities of Microsoft Windows to provide an extremely convenient environment, for both the developer and the end user. One of the key features about the internals of this system is that a common rule format is used for both forward and backward chaining. It would be difficult to overestimate the importance of this feature. In nearly all other current expert systems tools, a different rule format has to be used for forward and backward rules. Using a common format for both means that knowledge entered in the system can be used in multiple ways during a session to derive the maximum number of conclusions possible with the available information.

Nexpert Object probably lends itself best to prototyping because its rules and data structures do not have to be placed in a knowledge base in any particular order. Once entered, they are arranged alphabetically to facilitate rapid lookup and speedy editing. What this means to the developer is that rules and objects can be entered as the idea for them arises, without concern for disrupting the order in which knowledge has already been constructed.

Nexpert Object provides various types of specialized editors. The ones most frequently used are the Rule Editor, the Class Editor, and the Object Editor (see Figure 7.1). All of them are equipped with an alphabetical index tab on the right for selecting the current item to edit. Another important feature of these editors is that they are integrated with the Encyclopedia lists in such a way that, once an item has been entered, it is never necessary to retype it when it appears in other items in the knowledge base. You simply select a copy function from a popup menu, then look up the desired item, select it with the mouse, and it will be immediately inserted into the editor.

The way the object and class system in Nexpert Object was designed is commendable in several respects. For example, an object can be an instance of any number of classes at the same time. Generally, in object-oriented systems, though classes can often have multiple inheritance, objects can still only be instances of a single class. This gives Nexpert Object an efficient real-world edge for handling some of the important subtleties that are often very important. For example, things usually fit into a number of different functional categories simultaneously. A medicinal herb can often fill the role of a number of different types of remedy at once. Or, to take an example from the business world, one business or individual often fills a number of contrasting and even contradictory roles at the same time. This feature of Nexpert Object provides a tool for expressing this type of situation.

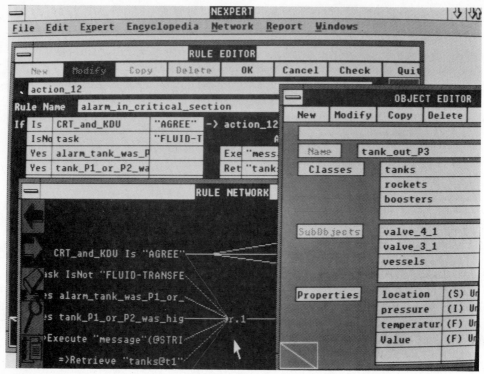

Figure 7.1 A screen from Nexpert Object running on the IBM AT that shows the Object Editor and Rule Editor

7.1 Augmented Rule Format

One very useful feature of systems that support both objects and rules is the ability to write general rules that apply to a certain class of things and have those rules apply automatically to its subclasses as well. For example, if you have a class called Furniture that has the subclasses HomeFurniture and OfficeFurniture as well as more specific subclasses like Desk and Chair, you can write rules that apply to all furniture as well as those that apply to more specific classes. Generally, it is a good practice to write rules that are as specific as possible, but it is often also necessary to avoid writing too many specific rules when one more general one rule might suffice.

For the example given here, in Nexpert Object, you might want a constraint rule about how large a piece of furniture can be before it no longer fits in a standard elevator or stairwell. In that case, you could say:

```
If
   < <Furniture>.length 9
Then good_fit
   Let <Furniture>.fits = Yes
```

You will also want to write more specific rules about various kinds of furniture.

```
If
   <Chair>.style is Colonial
   <House>.style is Ultramodern
Then bad_fit
   Let <Chair>.appropriate = No
```

7.2 Weak Links and Knowledge Islands

Another very innovative feature of Nexpert Object is the use of two different types of links between rules. A strong link is one that exists because the actual content of the hypotheses and the conditions of rules match. Weak links, on the other hand, provide an additional way of building connections between rules that the inference engine would not otherwise detect. Such weak links create contexts realized as sequences of hypotheses that will be evaluated in order. This still differs from procedural programming in that the subsequent hypotheses are evaluated only if the first one happens to be. The result of this technique is the assembling of semantically unrelated rules into "islands of knowledge" that tend to be processed together during sessions.

Possibly the single most important feature of this system is that it provides end users with a highly interactive, multidimensional tool with which they can steal the initiative in a number of different and important ways. However, this could also lead to the danger that if the end user is given too much latitude, the intentions of the knowledge engineer may be defeated.

Before you select a tool for a given project, it is essential that you carefully examine the types of problems that it will have to solve and in general how its features might be implemented. For example, if you have a business application that must be able to access existing databases, it is not sufficient to know that a given tool has an interface to the file format of that database system. You have to know exactly what you need to do with the records in the database and whether a particular tool will really allow you to do this. In many applications, the developer has no way of foreseeing what records will be needed for looking up information needed by rules. If a database interface can only retrieve information by referencing known records and fields, the use of that information is significantly restricted. The same thing holds true for many other technical features.

Similarly, if an expert system tool supports frames or objects, it is important to know just what this representation can practically be used for. Let's consider an example from the medical field. A diagnosis problem involves matching symptoms with a disease in order to determine the proper treatment. Should you use objects to represent the diseases? It all depends on whether the system has enough power to make use of them. Generally, you would want to be able to prune out the impossible diseases by a process of elimination, rather than having to just use rules that evaluate symptoms blindly and always search through the space of all diseases. Fortunately, Nexpert Object provides a way of doing this. There is a provision in the rule syntax for querying objects in a class to find out which of them have attributes of a certain value. However, there is also the complication that the values of various symptoms will not be known at the time the rules are written, but only each time the system is consulted by a user.

Generally, the development of a knowledge base with a tool like Nexpert Object would go as follows:

1. A set of classes, objects, and their properties is created.

2. A set of rules is written that accesses these objects.

3. The knowledge base is tuned by setting various control parameters.

Because the inference categories are usually set after the rules are already written, in determining their values it is necessary to consider what the rules that reference the priorities are meant to accomplish, and how important these goals are in relation to one another. In effect, this means that an ad hoc strategy must be devised for how knowledge processing should be conducted for a given problem. Note that a wide variety of such control strategies can be selected for any given set of rules and objects. This makes the reasoning strategy largely independent of the actual knowledge per se, as in fact it should be.

Though it may at first sound unusual to say, building expert systems is by no means the only valid use of expert systems technology. Creating knowledge systems can also be a legitimate use of the technology. A knowledge system is an application of expert system technology that is not intended to perform on the level of a human expert, but that nevertheless can often have a legitimate and important use. In many situations, a knowledge system can be of extreme value, even though it falls far short of being considered on a par with human expertise.

As expert systems technology moves into greater commercial use, many new and unanticipated uses of it are being discovered. For example, many scientific experts who have agreed to act as domain experts in the building of research systems have discovered that participating in the process of building such a system has proven beneficial to them in several ways. Just the discipline of aiding the systematic codification of their knowledge can be an exercise that forces experts to think more clearly than usual about their own knowledge and skills.

Another important use of the technology rests on the fact that expertise is, after all, relative. A nineteenth-century medical expert would no longer be so considered, just as a current twentieth-century expert will not be so considered in the twenty-first century.

More to the point is that most people today are probably unaware of a vast body of knowledge that could be of great value to them, even though it is not necessarily considered "expert" knowledge in the full sense.

7.3 SPACEMED

The prototype system to which we will apply Nexpert Object is SPACEMED, a knowledge system for assisting in medical emergencies that may arise during a space flight or aboard an orbiting space station. The simple prototype constructed here focuses on some of the problems about which there is currently enough expertise to provide the basis for such a knowledge system. This includes such things as rapidly diagnosing cases of poisoning that result from toxic air contaminants released in the cabin or space module atmosphere, and providing directions for treating the particular type of poisoning involved. Before discussing the implementation, some remarks on this particular problem domain will be helpful.

Most of the medical research expert systems to date have been intended to help physicians at clinics and hospitals interpret technical tests for difficult diagnoses that usually require expert specialists. For one reason or another, very few of these systems have reached operational or commercial status. However, with the emergence of powerful AI tools on micros, this technology is beginning to appear for the first time in doctors' offices. What distinguishes the current problem domain from most other medical uses of expert systems technology is that it is not intended to assist doctors but laypeople.

The first attempt to build an expert system for medical emergencies was the EMERGE system developed by D. L. Hudson at the Computer Science Department at UCLA in 1981. EMERGE was intended to help doctors analyze and diagnose chest pains in a hospital emergency room. It made decisions about whether a patient should be admitted to the hospital and provided advice on the severity of the patient's condition and possible treatments. One of the key characteristics of a knowledge system for medical emergencies is that it is not intended to perform a thorough diagnosis of ailments as a medical specialist with ample time and facilities does, but to perform rapid diagnoses that generate timely information about immediate actions that should and should not be taken, which during crucial periods of a medical emergency could be a matter of life and death or could avoid serious injury to bodily organs.

Although NASA has meticulously studied medical problems associated with spaceflight, there is still precious little expertise in the area of Zero-G medicine for the simple reason that there has been little opportunity to practice it as yet. The first American physician to go into space was Joseph P. Kerwin who was on the first Skylab mission in 1973. He conducted some routine medical checkups of the other astronauts and participated in various biomedical tests. In recent years, detailed medical reports have been conducted after each Space Shuttle mission, and a very vigorous medical emergency training system has been an essential part of all Space Shuttle flight operations. Astronauts are given several checklists associated with various kinds of episodes that might occur onboard during a mission. Nevertheless, there have not been many opportunities to gain actual experience in the handling of medical emergencies in a Zero-G environment. For this reason, the current prototype of SPACEMED is confined to those areas of emergency medicine for which no advanced expertise in administering medicine in a microgravity environment is required. Although some very unique facilities control the way inferences are conducted during a session, the types of problems that can be handled with this system are determined mainly by the knowledge representation and retrieval facilities that can be used in Nexpert Object rules.

Several aspects of the Nexpert Object system suggested that it would be a suitable tool for prototyping a knowledge system for medical emergencies. For one thing, it offers both forward and backward chaining and flexible inference strategies, so that it seems suitable for simulating the complex reasoning and common sense aspects of proceeding quickly to solutions in this domain. For another thing, the Images facility, which can generate illustrations with a user consultation, seems almost ideal for this type of application.

One minor constraint is that so far only properties of objects that are Boolean datatypes can be used in conclusions, or the right-hand side of rules as hypotheses. This means that the result of a rule firing cannot assert hypotheses about the values of properties that are numbers or symbols. The rules can do this only as actions that interact directly with working memory using special operators. As such, they only apply to the forward-chaining inference mechanism.

Here is how the problem is solved. Let us say that all objects in the Diseases class have various symptom categories for various parts of the body, for example, eye_symptom, pulse_symptom, and breathing_symptom. There are also corresponding attributes for the patient such as patient_eye_symptom, patient_pulse_symptom, and so on. In addition, we have defined a candidacy attribute for diseases. This means that we can isolate all the diseases that correspond to a particular symptom and set their candidacy attribute to possible. All rules to be tested for subsequent symptoms would then include a test on the left-hand side to make sure they are possible candidates at this stage of the consultation.

```
IF  = patient_eye_symptom <Diseases>.eye_symptom
THEN Let <Diseases>.candidacy possible
```

In subsequent rules, an additional complication emerges. Since we want to continually narrow down the number of diseases, it will be necessary to first reset the value of all the current candidates before setting the new subset or it will be necessary to reset all those diseases that do not match the latest criteria. One trouble with this scheme is that it does not seem to take into consideration the problem of multiple diseases. A patient may well be suffering from additional ailments that are not on the list. If only this initial list is used to start from and no diseases are ever added to it again, something could be missed.

To deal with this problem, a new attribute, that of secondary_candidate, can be used. Without too much additional overhead, we can also keep track of the list of diseases extracted from the complete list of diseases that match subsequent symptoms.

It is essential to distinguish between unique or essential symptoms and accompanying symptoms. Often there are certain symptoms for a disease that are seldom, if ever, found in any other disorder. Often such symptoms can be regarded as sufficient conditions for diagnosing the particular disease. In other cases, they may still be only necessary conditions, but are pivotal for distinguishing between other similar ailments. In making real diagnoses, a doctor will often be on the lookout for certain very important and dangerous conditions such as appendicitis once even the most remotely related symptoms are registered. To simulate this kind of diagnostic approach, under certain circumstances a hypothesis about a particularly dangerous condition must be generated simply to attempt to establish that it is not the problem. In Nexpert Object, this can be handled very easily with a very simple rule such as:

```
IF Is stomach_symptom pain
THEN test_for_appendicitis
```

One of the important possibilities for medical applications of a system like Nexpert Object is for the system's object representation to provide a shell that can incorporate patients' medical records and can constitute useful complementary information for formulating diagnoses. In this case, it would be appropriate to use the same medical record database with any number of different diagnostic programs.

On the surface, several serious conditions where a victim has already become unconscious have quite a number of overt symptoms in common. However each of them requires very different treatments. How does one distinguish between someone suffering from heat exhaustion, an internal hemorrhage, asphyxiation, or cardiac arrest? In each of them, the victim will have a pale face, cool and moist skin, weak pulse, and shallow breathing. If a person is suffering from asphyxiation, obviously his breathing must be started immediately, either by removing an obstruction or by artificial respiration. If the person is suffering from heat exhaustion, the body temperature must be decreased immediately before the internal organs are damaged. If it is a cardiac arrest, the heart must be restarted. In the case of internal hemorrhage, measures must be taken to prevent the victim from going into shock.

It is usually possible to distinguish between these conditions, but an important question is the order in which to do this. An obvious approach is to arrange them in order of urgency and look for the most urgent conditions first. All first aid methods take the commonsense approach that the first thing to do in an emergency is to make sure that the victim is breathing adequately. For the average adult, breathing adequately means taking about 12 to 18 breaths per minute. Children tend to breathe more rapidly. Lack of breathing is noticeable by a lack of rising and falling of chest action and no sound of air flow into the nose and mouth. In Nexpert Object, two rules are needed to handle this:

R1

```
IF    Is symptoms.mental_state unconscious
      Is symptoms.chest_movement none
THEN  test_for_asphyxia
      LET Hypothesis asphyxia
```

R2

```
IF    Is symptoms.mental_state unconscious
      Is symptoms.airflow_sound none
THEN  test_for_asphyxia
      LET Hypothesis asphyxia
```

By far the most important tools in Nexpert Object are the Rule Network and Object Network browsers. At this point in the product's evolution, these are indispensable tools for both developers and the final user. These network browsers are really smart graphics-oriented cross-referencing tools that provide an interactive way of visually navigating through a knowledge base. For developers, this provides an essential way of being able to carefully refine the knowledge representation and control strategy of expert systems so that they run like well-tuned, finely crafted knowledge artifacts.

The best way to design a finished knowledge base is to write an initializing rule with a right-hand side called START that sets all the defaults and strategies and starts the first knowledge island in motion.

In addition to testing for poisoning by atmospheric toxins, SPACEMED also can test for the following conditions:

- Exceeding the maximum radiation dosage per time

- Degree of burns and required treatment

- A state of shock

- Asphyxiation

- Cardiac arrest

- Internal hemorrhage

- Altitude sickness

It may be that the person is still breathing, but that he or she may have a partial breathing obstruction. If this is true, it will be obvious because the victim will be grasping for breath. In this case, no specific knowledge is necessary to determine the problem, so no rules need to be written.

However, it may turn out that the victim does not in fact appear to be breathing adequately. What then? When a person stops breathing, the heart continues to circulate blood for 4 to 6 minutes. However, when the heart stops, breathing ceases in 30 seconds. Therefore, it is obviously vital that a person who has had a heart attack is not mistaken for a victim in shock because treating him for shock in this condition would almost certainly prove fatal.

If a victim is suffering from cardiac arrest, in addition to the symptoms that are the same for respiratory failure, there will be no detectable pulse at the carotid or neck artery. Also, 45 seconds after circulation ceases, the victim's eyes become completely dilated and fixed.

In this prototype, rules are implemented for diagnosing poisoning by ten different toxic air contaminants: allyl alcohol, ammonia, benzene, carbon disulfide, carbon monoxide, ethylene dichloride, hydrofluoric acid, hydrogen sulfide, nitrogen dioxide, and sulfur dioxide. An important complication of the problem is that often a victim of toxic poisoning will be unconscious, and it is necessary to rule out other important conditions that could have rendered him unconscious.

In a system for medical emergencies, it is clearly essential that the system come to a definite conclusion rapidly. This means that as few questions should be addressed to the user as possible. Clearly, in addition to very concise and decisive discrimination in the knowledge representation, tight control of the flow of reasoning is needed to ensure that no superfluous or inappropriate directions will be taken.

Here an important finding needs to be communicated. During work on this prototype, a very pleasant discovery was made. At one point during its development, a test run of the knowledge base that existed at that time was being conducted. It soon became apparent that because of the way the questions were being asked, the knowledge base was producing results different from those expected. So, at that point, while the question window was still open and awaiting an answer, instead of clicking on one of the responses with the mouse, the Rule Editor was called up instead. Then, about an hour was spent changing an entire set of rules, compiling them, and saving them to disk. The question window was still open and waiting for an answer. Since the knowledge base that now existed was substantially different from the one that had started this session, it was doubtful whether the session could be continued from where it had left off with the new knowledge base. However, much to our delight, that is exactly what did occur. The session begun earlier was completed, and it was found that the changes made were the correct ones. Few expert system shells would permit this. Usually it is necessary to complete a given session or abort it, and often even exit the program and run a different one, before any permanent changes can be made in a knowledge base.

As mentioned, Nexpert Object allows graphics images and text created with bit-mapped fonts using external software to be displayed after a rule fires. One of the programs supported for this is Dr. Halo II. It was felt that this facility is particularly effective where emphasis is needed for important messages to the user. In the case of an emergency medical advisor like SPACEMED, there is a definite need for this. Therefore, a number of screens of text and graphics were created with Dr. Halo II for various purposes, one of the most important being to alert the user that the symptoms displayed by the victim pointed to situations of a particularly serious nature, and that certain measures should be taken as quickly as possible and others carefully avoided. In the course of doing this, it became apparent that due to the large size of these image files (many of them greater than 80K), this feature had to be used sparingly.

Even though a shell may have frames or objects, often a lot of the knowledge must still be encoded in rules because the functions for accessing information in frame or object slots is rather limited. Thus the knowledge is not very accessible or active there. On the other hand, the inference engine is continually searching through rules and accessing the knowledge there. Unless there are plenty of commands or methods for accessing and searching objects and slots, the rules are still where the action is.

To represent the symptoms, the decision was made to break down the knowledge representation into two objects: Symptoms and Patient. In this way, the symptoms observed could be separated from the actual conditions of the patient, and the way was left open for incorporating any additional medical knowledge that might be already known about the patient, though not observable as symptoms. The properties of the Symptoms object are as follows:

Symptoms.airflow_sound	Symptoms.judgment
Symptoms.back	Symptoms.kidney
Symptoms.behavior	Symptoms.limb
Symptoms.blood_color	Symptoms.lower_abdomen
Symptoms.body_percent_burned	Symptoms.lung
Symptoms.bone_marrow_rems	Symptoms.mental_state
Symptoms.breathing	Symptoms.neck
Symptoms.carotid_pulse	Symptoms.nose
Symptoms.chest	Symptoms.psychological
Symptoms.circulation	Symptoms.pulse
Symptoms.eye	Symptoms.pulse_strength
Symptoms.eye_rems	Symptoms.sensation
Symptoms.face	Symptoms.skin
Symptoms.general	Symptoms.skin_rems
Symptoms.head	Symptoms.temperature
Symptoms.heart	Symptoms.throat
Symptoms.heart_rate	Symptoms.vision

One of the main methods used in Nexpert Object to control the order in which knowledge is processed is a technique called *local agendas*. This is implemented by using property metaslots, which are various options that can be associated with the property of any object. The type of metaslot that is of interest for the purposes here is called

Inference Categories. Very simply, what this involves is an index designated by an integer that can be assigned to any property. The higher the number, the higher the priority of the property. When properties are referenced by a rule, the rule takes on the value of the highest property index addressed by it. Rules with the highest priority are selected for processing first. It soon became clear for this application that it was important to ask about symptoms in a particular order, but not necessarily in a fixed order that was always the same. SPACEMED is designed to test first to see if the victim is unconscious. It accomplishes this by assigning the maximum value to the Inference Category metaslot of the Symptoms.mental_state property. The rules for these ailments reference the mental state symptom:

1. Asphyxia

2. Ethylene dichloride poisoning

3. Carbon disulfide poisoning

4. Benzene poisoning

5. CO poisoning

6. Cardiac arrest

Evaluation

The Nexpert Object tool not only has a large number of innovative and powerful features, for the most part, it also has the right combination of features to enable fast and fruitful prototyping efforts (see Figure 7.2). When the right features are integrated, you get something like a new qualitative level of productivity occurring. This quantum jump in synergy seems to be present in all major advances in software. Such qualitative leaps are usually characterized by the ability to push developers along by allowing ideas to occur to them that would not have done so in an environment where they have so many low-level details to keep in mind. This is what all great AI software really has to offer, and I find it to a noticeable degree with Nexpert Object. I would like to suggest that some of the features of Nexpert, for example, the common format for forward and backward rules, permitting instances of multiple classes, allowing rules to be entered in any order, and the network browsers, have such a "correct" feeling about them that they may well become a standard feature for this technology in the future.

Some Representative SPACEMED Rules

R3

IF   Is Symptoms.mental_state unconscious
      Is Symptoms.carotid_pulse none
THEN   LET patient.disease cardiac_arrest

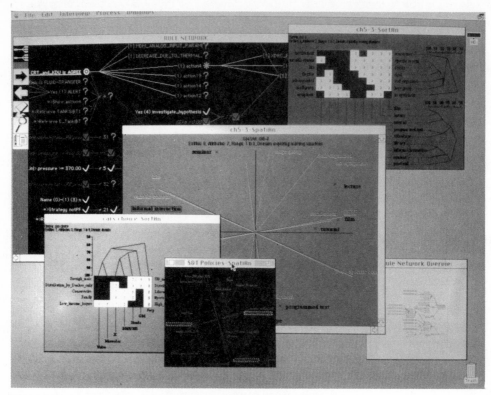

Figure 7.2 A screen from Nextra running on the Macintosh II

R4

IF   Is Symptoms.head headache
      Is Symptoms.breathing rapid
      Is Symptoms.general nausea
      Is Symptoms.general dizziness
      Is Symptoms.skin blue
THEN   co_poisoning

R5

IF   Is eye_symptom irritation
      Is Symptoms.general vomiting
      Is Symptoms.general dizziness
      Is Symptoms.breathing impaired

```
        Is Symptoms.pulse rapid
        Is Symptoms.skin blue
THEN    ethylene_dichloride_poisoning


R6

IF   Is Symptoms.nose irritation
     Is Symptoms.eye irritation
     Is Symptoms.throat irritation
     Is Symptoms.skin blue
     Is Symptoms.lung congested
THEN    hydrogen_fluoride_poisoning


R7

IF   Is Symptoms.general convulsions
     Is Symptoms.breathing irregular
     Is Symptoms.eye irritation
THEN    hydrogen_sulfide_poisoning


R8

IF   Is Symptoms.throat cough
     Is Symptoms.breathing impaired
     Is Symptoms.chest pain
     Is Symptoms.skin blue
     Is Symptoms.heart pounding
THEN    nitrogen_dioxide_poisoning


R9

IF   Is Symptoms.vision blurred
     Is Symptoms.eye irritated
     Is Symptoms.nose irritated
     Is Symptoms.chest pain
     Is Symptoms.skin inflammation
THEN    allyl_alcohol_poisoning


R10

IF   Is Symptoms.mental_state vertigo
     Is Symptoms.circulation bleeding
     Is Symptoms.head pain
     Is Symptoms.general nausea
THEN    benzene_poisoning
```

R11

IF   Is Symptoms.kidney damaged
      Is Symptoms.mental_state nervousness
      Is Symptoms.head pain
      Is Symptoms.general dizziness
      Is Symptoms.vision blind_spot
THEN   carbon_disulfide_poisoning

IF   Is Symptoms.circulatory bleeding
      No bleeding_controlled
THEN   apply_tourniquet

IF   Is Symptoms.circulatory bleeding
      No bleeding_controlled
THEN   apply_pressure_bandage

The "rule of nine"

IF   Is Symptoms.skin burn
      > patient.body_percent_burned 9
THEN   doctor_required

IF   Is Symptoms.skin burn
      = burn_degree 3
THEN   DO ((body_weight/2.2) * body_percent_burned) plasma_volume

Rules for Radiation Poisoning Check

IF   > Symptoms.bone_marrow_rems 25
      = exposure_time month
THEN   rem_exposure_limit_exceeded

IF   > Symptoms.bone_marrow_rems 35
      = exposure_time quarter
THEN   rem_exposure_limit_exceeded

IF   > Symptoms.bone_marrow_rems 75
      = exposure_time year
THEN   rem_exposure_limit_exceeded

IF   > Symptoms.bone_marrow_rems 400
      = exposure_time lifetime
THEN   rem_exposure_limit_exceeded

```
IF   > Symptoms.skin_rems 75
     = exposure_time month
THEN   rem_exposure_limit_exceeded

IF   > Symptoms.skin_rems 105
     = exposure_time quarter
THEN   rem_exposure_limit_exceeded

IF   > Symptoms.skin_rems 225
     = exposure_time year
THEN   rem_exposure_limit_exceeded

IF   > Symptoms.skin_rems 1220
     = exposure_time lifetime
THEN   rem_exposure_limit_exceeded

IF   > Symptoms.eye_rems 37
     = exposure_time month
THEN   rem_exposure_limit_exceeded

IF   > Symptoms.eye_rems 52
     = exposure_time quarter
THEN   rem_exposure_limit_exceeded

IF   > Symptoms.eye_rems 112
     = exposure_time year
THEN   rem_exposure_limit_exceeded

IF   > Symptoms.eye_rems 600
     = exposure_time lifetime
THEN   rem_exposure_limit_exceeded
```

7.4 An Object-Oriented Inference Engine

We have said a great deal about the advantages of object-oriented programming in different respects. We will now look at the requirements for the task of writing an object-oriented inference engine. First, we need to be clear about the goals of writing an inference engine in object-oriented fashion. In this case, there are three main goals:

1. Eliminating redundant code.

2. Allowing easy enhancement so that the program can evolve in steps without any serious rewriting.

3. Allowing multiple instances of the program to be resident at the same time.

The third goal is not completely straightforward, but it is still a standard feature of most object-oriented programs. One interesting problem in this respect involves programs that have instances of more than one class interacting. To have multiple instances of a multiclass application, a particular mechanism is required that is basically the same for all object-oriented systems. The problem in need of solution is this. For instances of two or more classes to interact, messages have to be sent to instances by name. However, it is not possible to know the names of these instances in advance when there will be multiple copies of the whole application. In other words, if we have three instantiations of the inference engine, each with more than one object, the methods cannot be written for any names in particular, yet we must guarantee that the objects within each copy of the engine send messages only to one another. In our application, we are assuming that the operation of each inference engine will be independent of the others.

The means for solving this problem involves using a fairly standard cliché in object-oriented programming. First we will discuss the technique in general terms and then apply it to our specific project. Let's say an application involves the interaction of objects from three different classes. In the most general case, each of the objects would send messages to the other two. Methods that are written to provide such message passing need the names of instances to which the messages are to be sent. This is done by creating special instance variables in each object, which will hold the names of the objects in its own copy of the application to which it needs to send messages. The methods are then written by using the names of these instance variables where the names of their cooperating objects are required. The actual names, which are the values of these instance variables, are supplied when each copy of the application is initialized.

Let's look at how this is handled for a simple toy program. This program has two classes, Adder and Multiplier. They each have the methods add and multiply, respectively. What we want is a way to have any number of Adder-Multiplier pairs interacting with one another without stepping on each other's toes. To do this, a pair of reciprocal instance variables are defined. Adders have the instance variable multiplier, and Multipliers have the instance variable adder (see Listing 7.1).

An additional method is also used by each of these classes, one called add-em and the other multiply-em. The only difference between these and the previous methods is that these are designed to operate by accessing instance variables to get the values to add or multiply together rather than being passed arguments.

To illustrate the use of the mechanism in action, three methods have been written in the SCOOPS extension to PC Scheme that show Adders and Multipliers interacting by sending messages to the objects referenced by the instance variable names. The methods both, both2, and both3 of the Multiplier class are written that illustrate messages sent to

Listing 7.1 Adders and Multipliers

```
(define-class Adder
              (classvars xc yc)
              (instvars xi yi multiplier)
              (mixins )
              (options
                (gettable-variables xi yi)
                settable-variables
                inittable-variables))

(define-class Multiplier
              (classvars uc vc )
              (instvars ui vi adder)
              (mixins)
              (options
                (gettable-variables ui vi )
                settable-variables
                inittable-variables))

(define-method (Adder add) (x y)
    (+ x y ))

(define-method  (Adder add-em) ()
    (+ xi yi ))

(define-method (Multiplier multiply) (x y)
              (* x y))

(define-method (Multiplier multiply-em) ()
    (* ui vi ))

(define-method (Multiplier both) ()
    (let ((z (send an-adder add-em)))
    (let ((w (send an-adder add 2 2)))
    (multiply z w))))

(define-method (Multiplier both2) ()
              (multiply (send an-adder add-em) (send an-adder add
2 2)))

(define-method (Multiplier both3) ()
              (multiply (send adder add-em) (send adder add 2
2)))

(compile-class Adder)

(compile-class Multiplier)
```

Listing 7.1 Adders and Multipliers (continued)

```
(define an-adder (make-instance Adder
                'xi 1
                'yi 2
                'multiplier a-multiplier))

(define a-multiplier (make-instance Multiplier
                'ui 3
                'vi 4
                'adder an-adder))
```

objects of the Adder class. Of the three, only both3 uses the adder instance variable to send its message. The both3 method uses the two different methods of the Adder class to provide answers that are then processed by its own multiply method.

The Inference Engine

In the design of our inference engine we will use two basic classes, which can be specialized in various ways, the Inference-Engine class and the Justifier class. Both of them will be abstract classes. Only their subclasses will be used in actual expert systems. The Inference-Engine class will be general enough that both the Backward-Chainer and Forward-Chainer classes can inherit all of its methods. In this way, any redundancy of code needed for forward and backward chaining is avoided. The Justifier class provides methods for explaining results of an inference engine to a user. Its methods are written so as to be inherited by both the BC-Justifier and FC-Justifier classes, which are used by the forward- and backward-chaining inference engines, respectively.

One of the conditions for having multiple copies of an application is that there not be any global variables that more than one of the versions might need for its own divergent purposes at any given time. This is where the encapsulated instance variables provide an essential service. Therefore, where there would be global variables in an ordinary application, all these variables must become strictly local to the objects in a multiple object application. Each copy of the system of cooperating objects must have its own copies of any necessary variables. The other condition of the ability to have multiple copies of an application that uses objects from more than one class that cooperate by sending messages back and forth is that they know the name of the specific object with which they need to send messages. Accordingly, the Inference-Engine class is outfitted with the my-justifier instance variable, and the Justifier class is outfitted with the my-inference-engine instance variable. With this construction, all the message-sending routines can be written generically by using the names of the instance variables without having to know the names of the objects to which the messages will be sent. To make this internal encapsulation of a multiclass inference mechanism automatic, you can write an initialization method that assigns the values to these instance variables right at the time the objects are created.

7.5 Inference Engine Design

Now that we have dispensed with the preliminary considerations, we may proceed to the specifics of the inference engine to be implemented. As mentioned earlier, the Inference-Engine class is to be designed so that it provides all the methods that both a forward- and a backward-chaining engine would need. It therefore is intended as an abstract class rather than a functioning one with actual direct instances. The top-level calls for forward or backward chaining, therefore, will be made by methods in the appropriate subclass of the Inference-Engine class. Inference-Engine is provided with the engine-type instance variable. This simply stores the value forward or backward, whichever is appropriate, when the engine is initialized. In this way, more of the code is allowed to be kept as general purpose. Any code that needs to make a reference to the direction of the inference chaining can reference this variable without losing its applicability to both types.

The forward-chaining inference engine is designed to work by performing the following operations.

1. Get a hypothesis.

2. Check to see if the hypothesis corresponds to a fact in the fact base.

3. Find all the matches of rules with the fact base.

4. Deduce the consequences of the rules that match.

5. Add all the consequences not already in the fact base.

The backward chainer works in a similar way, but matches rules against the goal, asks the user information it cannot find in the fact base, and evaluates the certainty factors.

Both the forward and backward chainers are configured to evaluate hypotheses and, if necessary, to solicit hypotheses from the user. Accordingly, the same methods can be used for this purpose in both cases. The get-choice and get-hypothesis methods are provided in the Inference-Engine class for this reason. Both chainers can call the try-all-hypotheses method which, in turn, calls the test-hypotheses and the which-hypothesis methods. Which-hypothesis is a method implemented in the Justifier class.

The test-hypotheses method is applied to the hypotheses stored under the hypotheses instance variable. It puts the results in the results instance variable. (The choice of such straightforward names makes the description sound like a tautology.)

The get-option method allows for testing either all the hypotheses or one that is provided by the user. Hypotheses are formulated as possible facts that the engine attempts to prove as true. The facts are represented in the form

```
(Relation Subject Object)
```

but are stored as property lists.

The workhorse of the backward chainer is the test-goal function, which is called by try-goal. Understandably, it takes a goal as its sole argument. The test-goal method calls the has-operator? and test operator methods, which are implemented in the Inference-Engine class. Has-operator tests whether or not a relational operator is present.

An additional responsibility of the backward chainer, which the forward engine does not have to worry about, is certainty factors. This has been a traditional feature of backward-chaining systems since the MYCIN project at Stanford. For the reader's convenience, Tables 7.1 through 7.4 list the methods used by the classes Inference-Engine, Justifier, ForwardChainer, and FC-Justifier.

Table 7.1 Inference-Engine Methods

search-constant	attribute?	try-attribute	acceptable
find-variable	attributes!	try-all-attributes	add-hypothesis
random-search	attribute!	test-hypotheses	check-error
match-constant	has-operator?	display-values	find-choice
match-variable	operator?	print-results	add-choice
random-match	an-operator	print-number	find-reason
match-part	fetch-value	check-hypothesis	
get-value	test-operators	hypothesis-error	

Table 7.2 Justifier Methods

explain?	explain-value	print-operator
unproven	which-hypothesis	print-argument

Table 7.3 ForwardChainer Methods

forward	already-proven	add-fact	add-reason
show-results	new-fact?	match-premise	display-rule
f-chain	fact-exists	test-disjunct	apply-forward
session-over	try-rule	print-conjunct	add-rule
forward-chain	add-new-fact	print-rule	test-fact
apply-rules	match-conjuncts	read-choice	

Table 7.4 FC-Justifier Methods

known	explain-further	explain-proven	proven
explain	known-to-exist	explain-more	explain-operator
explain-goal	explain-lisp	user-defined	show-rule

Evaluation

The point of writing this inference engine example was not to provide a truly operational program that could be used in the expert systems field. Such a program would be more extensive than would be feasible to undertake within the space constraints of this chapter. The purpose of this program is to provide the actual code for a simplified program that nevertheless addresses many of the important issues involved in utilizing the advantages of the object-oriented approach for creating a typical AI program such as a forward- and backward-chaining inference engine. For an inference engine that chains in one direction only, the object-oriented design might not be fully warranted. However, in the case of inference engines that combine more than one inference procedure, there are some clear advantages to this approach.

Note that the code in Listing 7.2 contains most of the essential methods for the operation of the forward-chaining inference engine and its accompanying justifier only. Some of the printing utilities and other auxiliary functions have been omitted for reasons of space and because they are not essential for the concepts illustrated here.

The code in Listing 7.2 is written in the object-oriented dialect of LISP called SCOOPS, which is provided with the PC Scheme language available from Texas Instruments. This dialect was chosen because of its ready availability and low cost. If you have a different object-oriented system, you should be able to rewrite this sample program in that language instead. In fact, the exercises at the end of this chapter propose this as an excellent programming exercise even if you do have the PC Scheme language at hand.

Conclusion

We have seen that there are considerable advantages to using object-oriented approaches in expert systems. It seems clear that the best place to introduce the use of the object-oriented approach is at the level where the inference engine and knowledge representation schemes are implemented. By using the object-oriented approach to implement expert system shells, several additional benefits are gained. One of the main things gained from this approach is the ability to create architectures that utilize several fully functional cooperating expert systems loaded into the memory of the same computer at the same time. Let's look at this in a little more detail so that its importance can be grasped.

Listing 7.2 The Inference-Engine Class

```
(print "Loading the Inference Engine Class")]
(define-class Inference-Engine
            (classvars )
            (instvars    my-justifier       hypothesis-number
                    reply-number   subj  verb  obj      hypot
                    operator-list read-value hypotheses
                    search-value arg1 arg2 hyporesults done
                    goal rule conclusion premise engine-type)
            (mixins )
            (options
             (gettable-variables )
             settable-variables
             inittable-variables))

(compile-class                     Inference-Engine              )

(print    "Loading    the  Inference    Engine   Methods  ...")

(print "...get-option...")

(define-method (Inference-Engine get-option) ()
;print preliminaries
            (print "Please type YES if you would like to enter
a hypothesis")
            (print "or ALL to try all existing hypotheses")
            (print "Any other key to exit")
            (newline))

(print "...get-hypothesis...")

(define-method (Inference-Engine get-hypothesis) ()
; gets a hypothesis
            (newline)
            (print "What is the Subject?")
            (set-subj (read))
            (print "What is the Verb?")
            (set-verb (read))
            (print "What is the Object?")
            (set-obj (read))
            (set-hypot (list verb (list subj) (list obj))))

(print "...has-attributes?...")

(define-method (Inference-Engine has-attributes?) (goal)
            (or
              (attribute? (cadr goal))
              (attribute? (caddr goal))
              ))
```

Listing 7.2 The Inference-Engine Class (continued)

```
(print "...try-all...")

(define-method (Inference-Engine try-all) (arg lst)
               (set-search-value (search-constant arg lst))
               (cond
                 ((not (null? search-value)) search-value)
                 (t
                   (set-search-value (search-variable arg lst))
                   (cond
                     ((not (null? search-value)) search-value)
                     (t (random-search arg lst))
                     ))))
(print "...search-constant...")
(define-method (Inference-Engine search-constant) (arg lst)
; searches for a constant match
               (cond
                 ((null? lst) nil)
                 ((match-constant arg (car lst)) (caddr (car
lst)))
                 (t (search-constant arg (cdr lst)))
                 ))

(print "...find-variable...")

(define-method (Inference-Engine find-variable) ( arg lst)
; searches for a variable match
               (cond
                 ((null? lst) nil)
                 ((match-variable arg (car lst)) (get-value arg))
                 (t (find-variable arg (cdr lst)))
                 ))

(print "...random-search...")

(define-method (Inference-Engine random-search) (arg lst)
; searches for a random match
               (cond
                 ((null? lst) arg)
                 ((random-match arg (car lst)) (get-value arg))
                 (t (random-search arg (cdr lst)))
                 ))

; (print "Loading search functions")

(define-method (Inference-Engine match-constant) (arg entry)
               (and
                 (equal? arg (cadr entry))
                 (not (isvar (caddr entry)))
                 ))
```

Listing 7.2 The Inference-Engine Class (continued)

```
(print                                    "...match-variable...")

(define-method (Inference-Engine match-variable) (arg entry)
            (and
              (equal? arg (cadr entry))
              (isvar (caddr entry)))
            )

(print "...random-match...")

(define-method (Inference-Engine random-match) (arg entry)
            (and
              (match-part arg (cadr entry))
              (isvar (caddr entry)))
            )

 (print "...match-part...")

(define-method (Inference-Engine match-part) (arg lst)
            (and
              (equal? (car arg) (car lst))
              (isvar (caddr lst))
              ))

(print "...get-value...")

(define read-value nil)

(define-method (Inference-Engine get-value) (arg)
            (newline)
            (print "Please enter the value for")
            (newline)
            (print-argument arg)
            (set-read-value (read))
            (cond
              ((equal? read-value 'why) (show-rule)
               (newline) (get-value arg))
              (t (add-attribute arg (list read-value)))
              ))

(print "...attribute?...")

(define-method (Inference-Engine attribute?) (x)
            (cond
              ((null? (cdr x)) nil)
              ((equal? (cadr x) 'of) t)
              ))

(print "...attributes!...")
```

Listing 7.2 The Inference-Engine Class (continued)

```
(define-method (Inference-Engine attributes!) (goal)
               (list
                 (car goal)
                 (attribute! (cadr goal))
                 (attribute! (caddr goal))
                 ))

(print "...attribute!...")

(define-method (Inference-Engine attribute!) (term)
               (cond
                 ((attribute? term) (fetch-value term))
                 (t term)
                 ))

(print "...has-operator?...")

(define-method (Inference-Engine has-operator?) (goal)
               (cond ((operator? (car goal)) t)
                     ))

(print "...operator?...")

(define-method (Inference-Engine operator?) (term)
               (member? term operator-list))

(print "...an-operator...")

 (define operator-list '(equal? >? <? >= <= <>))

(define-method (Inference-Engine an-operator) (verb)
               (cond
                 ((equal? verb 'equal?) 'equals )
                 ((equal? verb '>?) 'greaterthan )
                 ((equal? verb '<?) 'lessthan )
                 ((equal? verb '>=) '>= )
                 ((equal? verb '<=) '<= )
                 ((equal? verb '<>) 'notequal? )
                 ))

(print "...fetch-value...")

(define-method (Inference-Engine fetch-value) (arg)
               (newline) (write 'fetch-value) (write arg)
               (cond
                 ((attribute? arg) (try-attribute arg))
                 (t arg)
                 ))

(print "...test-operator...")
```

Listing 7.2 The Inference-Engine Class (continued)

```
(define-method (Inference-Engine test-operators) (goal)
               (set-arg1 (fetch-value (cadr goal)))
               (set-arg2 (fetch-value (caddr goal)))
               (cond ((not
                        (or
                         (equal? (car goal) 'equal?)
                         (number? (car arg1))
                         (number? (car arg2))))
                      0)
                     (t
                       (apply (car goal) (append arg1 arg2)))
                     ))

(print "...try-attribute...")

(define-method (Inference-Engine try-attribute) (arg)
               (try-all arg (getprop 'equals 'fact))
               )

(print "...try-all-attributes...")

(define-method (Inference-Engine try-all-hypotheses) ()
; evaluates all the hypotheses
               (cond
                 (done (which-hypothesis)
                 (t (newline)
                    (write engine-type " Chaining Underway")
(newline)
                    (test-hypotheses) (which-hypothesis))
                 ))

(print "...test-hypotheses...")

(define-method (Inference-Engine test-hypotheses) ()
; evaluates hypotheses and stores results in hyporesults
               (set-hyporesults (mapcar apply-forward
hypotheses))
               (set-done t)
               )

(print "...display-values...")

(define-method (Inference-Engine display-values) ()
; shows values
               (newline)
               (set-hypothesis-number 0)
               (print-results hypotheses hyporesults)
               )
```

Listing 7.2 The Inference-Engine Class (continued)

```
(print "...print-results...")

(define-method (Inference-Engine print-results) (h hr)
             (cond
               ((null? h) t)
               (t
                 (print-number)
                 (print-first h hr)
                 (print-results (cdr h) (cdr hr)))
              ))

(print "...print-number...")

(define-method (Inference-Engine print-number ) ()
             (newline)
             (set-hypothesis-number (plus hypothesis-number 1))
             (write hypothesis-number)
             (princ ".")
             )

(print "...check-hypotheses...")
(define-method (Inference-Engine check-hypothesis ) ()
; checks the response
             (cond
               ((equal? reply-number 'no) nil)
               ((in-range reply-number) t)
               (t (hypothesis-error)
                  (set-reply-number (read)) (check-hypothesis))
              ))

(print "...hypothesis-error...")

(define-method (Inference-Engine hypothesis-error ) ()
; checks if response is in range
             (newline)
             (print "your choice should be a number between 1
and")
             (write hypothesis-number) (print "or no")
             (newline) (print "Please enter choice")
             )

(print "...acceptable...")

(define-method (Inference-Engine acceptable) (c max)
```

Listing 7.2 The Inference-Engine Class (continued)

```
; checks if a choice is within range
            (cond ((equal? c 'no) t)
                  ((and (number? c) (>? c max) (>? 0 c)) t)
                  (t nil)))

(print                                     "...add-hypothesis...")

(define-method (Inference-Engine add-hypothesis) (hyp)
            (set-hypotheses (append (list hyp) hypotheses))
            )

(print "...check-error...")

(define-method (Inference-Engine check-error) (max)
; checks for any errors
            (max)
            (newline)
            (print "your choice should be a number between 1
and")
            (write (difference max 1))
            (print "or no")
            (get-choice max))

(print "...find-choice...")

(define-method (Inference-Engine find-choice) (num lst)
; gets one choice from the choicelist
            (cond ((equal? num 'no) nil)
                  ((null? lst) (print "error evaluating
find-choice"))
                  ((equal? (caar lst) num) (cadar lst))
                  (t (find-choice num (cdr lst)))))

(print "...add-choice...")

(define-method (Inference-Engine add-choice) (goal)
; adds one choice to the choicelist
            (set-choicelist (append choicelist (list (list
    clause-number goal)))))
(print "...find-reason...")

(define-method (Inference-Engine find-reason) (goal l)
; finds the reason for a goal
            (cond ((null? l) nil)
                  ((equal? goal (caar l)) (cadar l))
                  (t (find-reason goal (cdr l)))))
```

Listing 7.2 The Inference-Engine Class (continued)

```
; ********************************************************

; Listing for Justifier Class

; ********************************************************

(define-class Justifier
;                (classvars )
;                (instvars my-inference-engine)
                 (mixins)
                  (options)
                    (gettable-variables )
                    settable-variables
                    inittable-variables))

(compile-class Justifier)

(define-method (Justifier explain?)
; asks if the user wishes to receive an explanation
  (newline)
  (print "Please type yes if you would like an explanation")
  (newline)
  (print "or any other keys if you do not")
  (newline)
  (cond
    ((equal? (read) 'yes) (set! previous nil)
     (explain? hypot))
    (t (session-over))
    ))

(define-method (Justifier unproven) (goal)
  (print-goal goal) (print "was not proven") (newline)
  )

(define-method (Justifier explain-value) (arg)
  ; explains a value
  (print "evaluates to")
  (write (send my-inference-engine fetch-value arg)
  ))

(define-method (Justifier which-hypothesis ) ()
  ; asks the user which hypothesis needs to be explained
  (display-values)
  (newline)
  (print "Please enter the number of the hypothesis to be
         explained")
  (newline) (print "or no to quit")
```

Listing 7.2 The Inference-Engine Class (continued)

```
(set! reply-number (read))
(cond
  ((send my-inference-engine check-hypothesis)
(explain? (nth reply-number hypotheses))
(which-hypothesis))
  (t (newline) (write 'bye) (quit))
  ))

(define-method (Justifer print-operator) (goal)
  (print-argument (cadr goal))
  (write (an-operator (car goal)))
  (print-argument (caddr goal))
  )

(define-method (Justifier print-argument) (arg)
  (cond
    ((number? (car arg)) (prins (car arg)))
    ((send my-inference-engine attribute? arg) (write (car arg))
    (write 'of)
    (write (caddr arg))) (t (write arg)) ))

; ****************************************************

; Listing of Forward-Chainer and FC-Justifier classes

; ****************************************************

(print "Loading Forward Chainer" )

(define-class ForwardChainer
              (classvars )
              (instvars readchar current-result temporary-fact
current-rule clause-number all-hypotheses rules)
              (mixins Inference-Engine)
              (options
                (gettable-variables )
                settable-variables
                inittable-variables))

(define-class FC-Justifier
              (classvars )
              (instvars goal-to-print previous)
              (mixins Justifier)
              (options
                (gettable-variables )
                settable-variables
                inittable-variables))

(compile-class ForwardChainer )
```

Listing 7.2 The Inference-Engine Class (continued)

```
(compile-class FC-Justifier)

(define FC (make-instance ForwardChainer))
(define FC-J (make-instance FC-Justifier))

(define (start)
  (FC forward))

(define operator-list nil)

(define readchar nil)

(define all-hypotheses nil)

(define-method (ForwardChainer forward) ()
  ; calls the forward chainer
  (get-option)
  (set-readchar (read))
  (cond
    ((equal? readchar 'yes) (f-chain))
    ((equal? readchar 'all) (set-all-hypotheses
t) (try-all-hypotheses))
    (t (print "bye"))))

(print "Loading 'show-results'")

(define-method (ForwardChainer show-results) (x)
; gives the result
  (print-goal hypot)
  (cond
    ((null? x) (write 'failed) (session-over))
    (t (write 'succeeded) (send my-justifier explain?))
    ))

(define-method (ForwardChainer f-chain) ()
; the top level call of the forward chainer
  (get-hypothesis)
  (cond
    ((exists hypot) (print-goal hypot) (write '(is known))
    (session-over))
    (t (print "Forward Chaining Underway")
       (show-results (forward-chain)))
    ))

(define-method (ForwardChainer session-over) ()
; ends a session
  (print "Please type "yes" if you would like to enter a
        hypothesis")
```

Listing 7.2 The Inference-Engine Class (continued)

```
  (print "or any other key to exit")
  (set-readchar (read))
  (cond
    ((equal? readchar 'yes) (f-chain))
    (t (write 'bye) (quit))
    ))

(define current-result nil)

(define-method (ForwardChainer forward-chain) ()
; starts the forward chaining
  (print "Evaluating the hypothesis") (print-goal hypot)
  (newline)
  (cond
    ((exists hypot) (set-current-result t) t)
    (t (set-current-result (apply-rules))
       current-result
       )
    ))

  (define subj nil)
  (define verb nil)
  (define obj  nil)
  (define hypot nil)

(define-method (ForwardChainer apply-rules) ()
; applies all the rules to the fact-base
  (cond ((new-fact?) (already-proven))
        (t nil)
        ))

(define-method (ForwardChainer already-proven) ()
; checks if hypothesis is proven
; if not, it will call apply-rules again
  (cond ((exists hypot) t)
        (t (apply-rules))
        ))

(define-method (ForwardChainer new-fact?) ()
; checks if any new facts have been found
; (newline) (write 'new-fact?) (newline)
  (member? t (mapcar try-rule rules)))

(define temporary-fact nil)

(define-method (ForwardChainer fact-exists) (fact)
; tests if the fact exists and if it can be evaluated
  (newline) (print "Trying fact-exists for") (print-goal
```

Listing 7.2 The Inference-Engine Class (continued)

```
fact) (newline)
  (set-temporary-fact (test-fact fact))
  (cond
    ((neg? temporary-fact) (not (fact-exists (cdr
    temporary-fact))))
    ((has-operator?        temporary-fact)        (test-operators
              temporary-fact))
    ((islisp   temporary-fact)   (send   my-justifier   apply-lisp
          temporary-fact))
    ((known temporary-fact) t)
    (t nil)
    ))

(define current-rule nil)

(print "Loading 'try-rule'")

(define-method (ForwardChainer try-rule) (rule)
; applies one rule to the fact-base
  (set-current-rule rule)
  (cond
    ((match-premise (car rule)) (add-new-fact (cadr rule) rule))
    (t nil)
    ))

(define-method (ForwardChainer add-new-fact) (fact rule)
; adds a new fact
  (cond ((send my-justifier known fact) nil)
        (t (add-fact fact) (add-reason fact rule) (not nil))))

(define-method (ForwardChainer match-conjuncts) (ands)
; matches the conjunct
  (cond ((null?
            ands) t) ((fact-exists (car ands)) (match-conjuncts
(cdr ands)))))

(define-method (ForwardChainer add-fact) (facts)
; adds a fact to the fact-base
  (putprop (car fact)
        'fact
        (append (getprop (car fact) 'fact) (list fact))))

(define-method (ForwardChainer match-premise) (l)
; matches a premise
  (test-disjunct (mapcar l (function match-conjuncts))))

(define-method (ForwardChainer test-disjunct) (orlist)
; evaluates a disjunct
  (cond ((member? t orlist) t)))
```

Listing 7.2 The Inference-Engine Class (continued)

```
(define-method (ForwardChainer print-conjunct) (conj)
; prints one conjunct
  (cond ((null? conj) nil)
        (t (print-clause-number)
           (print-goal (car conj))
           (add-choice (car conj))
           (set-clause-number (plus clause-number 1))
           (cond ((not (null? (cdr conj))) (prinline)
                    (print "and")
                    (print-conjunct (cdr conj)))
                 (t nil))))))

(define-method (ForwardChainer print-rule) (rule)
; prints one rule
  (print-premise (car rule))
  (newline)
  (print "then")
  (newline)
  (print-goal (cadr rule)))

(define choice nil)

(print "Loading 'choice methods'")

(define-method (ForwardChainer read-choice) (max)
; reads one choice
  (newline)
  (print "Please enter choice, or no for none")
  (newline)
  (set-choice (read))
  (cond ((acceptable choice max) choice) (t (check-error max))))

(define-method (ForwardChainer add-reason) (goal rule)
; adds a reason
  (putprop (car goal)
        'reason
        (append (getprop (car goal) 'reason) (list (list goal
rule))))))

(define-method (ForwardChainer display-rule) (rule)
; displays a rule ; returns the number of clauses
  (set-clause-number 1)
  (set-choicelist nil)
  (print-rule rule)
  (get-choice clause-number))

(print "Loading apply-forward")
```

Listing 7.2 The Inference-Engine Class (continued)

```
(define-method (ForwardChainer apply-forward) (hyp)
  (set-hypot hyp)
  (forward)
  )

(define-method (ForwardChainer add-rule) (rule)
  (set-rules (append (list rule) rules))
  )

(print "Loading test-fact")

(define-method (ForwardChainer test-fact) (fact)
; evaluates a fact
  (cond ((neg? fact) (append '(not)
    (test-fact (cdr fact)))) ((has-attributes? fact) (attributes!
    fact)) (t fact) ))

(define goal-to-print nil)

(define-method (FC-Justifier known) (fact)
  (newline) (print "Trying known for") (print-goal fact)
  (member? fact (getprop (car fact) 'fact)))

(print "Loading 'explain'")

(define-method (FC-Justifier explain) (goal)
; explains a goal
  (cond
    ((neg? goal) (explain (cdr goal)))
    (t
      (set-goal-to-print goal)
      (explain-goal (send my-inference-engine test-fact goal)))
    ))

(define-method (FC-Justifier explain-goal) (goal)
  (cond ((null? goal) (explain-further))
        ((islisp goal) (explain-lisp goal))
        ((proven goal) (explain-proven goal))
        ((known goal) (known-to-exist goal))
        ((send my-inference-engine has-operator? goal)
         (explain-operator goal))
        (t (unproven goal) (explain previous))
        ))

(define-method (FC-Justifier explain-further) ()
; decides the type of explanation
  (cond
    (all-hypotheses (which-hypothesis))
    (t (explain?))
    ))
```

Listing 7.2 The Inference-Engine Class (continued)

```
(define-method (FC-Justifier known-to-exist) (goal)
; determines that the goal exists in the fact-base
  (print-goal goal)
  (print "existed in the fact base") (newline)
  (explain previous)
  )

(define (FC-Justifier explain-lisp)(goal)
  (prinline)
  (write goal) (print "is an internal lisp function")
  (explain previous)
  )

(define previous nil)

(define-method (FC-Justifier explain-proven) (goal)
; explains the goals proven by the rules
  (newline)
  (print-goal goal)
  (print "was proven by")
  (newline)
  (set-previous goal)
  (explain-more (find-reason goal (getprop (car goal) 'reason))))

(define-method (FC-Justifier explain-more) (rule)
; explains some more about the clauses in a rule
  (explain        (send        my-inference-engine        find-choice
    (display-rule rule) choicelist)))

(define clause-number nil)
(define choicelist nil)
(define clause-number nil)
(define hypot nil)

(define-method (FC-Justifier user-defined) ()
; explains that a fact was defined by the user
  (print "existed in the fact base") (newline)
  )
(define-method (FC-Justifier proven) (goal)
; has the goal been proven?
  (not (null? (find-reason goal (getprop (car goal) 'reason)))))

(print "Loading explain-operator")

 (define-method (FC-Justifier explain-operator) ( goal)
; explains a goal that has an operator
  (newline)
  (print-argument (cadr goal-to-print))
  (explain-value (cadr goal))
  (newline) (print "and")
```

Listing 7.2 The Inference-Engine Class (continued)

```
  (print-argument (caddr goal-to-print))
  (explain-value (caddr goal))
  (newline)
  (explain previous)
)

(print "Loading show-rule")

(define-method (FC-Justifier show-rule )()
; explains what is happening
  (newline)
  (print "The Inference Engine is attempting to prove") (newline)
  (print-rule current-rule)
  )

(define (maximum-clause rule)
; finds the maximum clause number in a rule
  (eval (append '(plus) (mapcar length (car rule) ))))

(define (neg? goal)
  (equal? (car goal) 'not) )
(set-operator-list '(equal? >? <? >= <= <>))

(define arg1 nil)
(define arg2 nil)
(define operator-list nil)

(define (add-attribute arg val)
  (add-fact (list 'equal?s arg val))
  val)

(define search-value nil)

(print "Loading 'try-all'")

(define (isvar a)
 (or (equal? a 'x) (equal? a 'y) ))

(define read-value nil)

 (print "Loading islisp")

 (define (islisp goal) (equal? (car goal) 'lisp) )

 (print "Loading 'message'")

 (define (apply-lisp 1) (apply (caadr 1) (cddr 1)) )

 (define done nil)
 (define hypotheses nil)
```

Listing 7.2 The Inference-Engine Class (continued)

```
(define current-result nil)
(define hyporesults nil)
(define hypothesis-number nil)

(define reply-number nil)

(define (in-range x)
    (and
    (number? x)
    (<= x hypothesis-number)
    (<? 0 x)
    ))

(define rules nil)
(define obj nil)
(define verb nil)
(define subj nil)
(define previous nil)
```

Conventional inference engines allow chaining from one knowledge base to another. This means that the inference engine can draw upon the expertise of a variety of different modules in turn. In a sense, these different knowledge bases cooperate to produce the final result. However, their level of cooperation is limited to calling upon one another and passing results both prior to and subsequent to processing goals. When several object-oriented inference engines, each with their own distinct knowledge base, are present in memory at one time, a far greater degree of cooperation is possible.

We will take the example of an architecture using supervisory cooperation to illustrate this. In the next chapter, a systematic discussion will be given of this and other types of inter-module cooperation. In this configuration, one of the expert modules is a meta-knowledge expert. This means that it is the module that directs the way that the other modules process goals and cooperate. The simplest way for this to work is for the supervisor module to share time with whatever other expert module is currently active. By segregating the meta-knowledge in this way, search spaces are kept smaller, and a greater amount of cooperation is made possible.

Let's take a different viewpoint entirely to try to illustrate what this means. One of the most remarkable things about the human mind is the immense amount of knowledge that is in a state of readiness at any given time. As soon as we attempt to encode a large amount of knowledge in a computer, the access time goes up exponentially in conventional systems. The way around this is to partition the computer into smaller active knowledge units. For any inference engine running on a given hardware platform there is an optimum-size knowledge base that provides the best knowledge processing throughout. With several of these active knowledge modules in memory, and with one of them as a dedicated supervisor, optimum knowledge processing architectures can in principle be constructed.

Projects

1. Write the backward-chaining class and methods and the backward-chaining justifier class in the same way this was done for forward chaining.

2. Enhance the inference engine by expanding the fact base facility so that more complex facts can be accessed by rules, for example, those stored in the instance variables of objects.

3. Rewrite the inference engine provided here in another object-oriented LISP dialect or another object-oriented language.

4. Design an object-oriented inference mechanism in which both forward- and backward-chaining class objects interact.

5. Outline the architecture for an expert system in a domain of your own devising.

True or False?

1. Unlike most object systems, Nexpert Object allows instances to each be a member of any number of classes at the same time.

2. The user interface is the place where the mixed-initiative aspect of an expert system can be implemented.

3. In Nexpert Object, rules can be written that reference objects of a given class and return a list of those that meet a given criterion.

4. The ability of the rules to be entered in any order turns out to be one of the main features of Nexpert Object that allows working prototypes to be built rapidly.

5. In the SPACEMED application, observable conditions of a patient are the same as symptoms.

6. It is not possible to have multiple instances of a program based on interaction between more than one object.

7. Not all inference engine designs can benefit from the use of an object-oriented approach.

8. An explanation facility for an expert system shell can be written the same, independently of whether forward or backward chaining is used.

(T, T, T, T, F, F, T, F)

Chapter 8

Conceptual Models
and Hierarchies

This chapter deals with a major aspect of object-oriented systems: their ability to describe and represent the world. Although, just because of the name, this is what most newcomers might expect of object-oriented systems, as we have seen, there are many other important features of this paradigm besides its ability to describe objects. All the same, description or knowledge representation, as it is called in AI, is a very important feature of these systems.

This chapter examines various aspects of what relatively large systems can accomplish using this capability. We will explore the topics of object-oriented simulation, conceptual hierarchies, rule-based simulation, and the object-oriented approach to neural modeling. In one section we will explore an experimental AI architecture based on the analogy between conceptual hierarchies and content-addressable memory.

One of the most powerful features of object-oriented systems that is particularly useful in AI applications is the ability of class hierarchies to encode knowledge of the world. What is it about a hierarchy of classes that allows it to do this? We cannot provide a ready answer to this at the outset because we need more knowledge to appreciate the issues, but as we gain a better understanding of how such constructions are used, various aspects of the answer should become clearer.

A conceptual hierarchy is a class lattice that attempts to represent the key concepts of a particular domain. The discovery of the correct or most effective hierarchy for a given problem is not trivial, and often several attempts must be made to get it right. Such a lattice of concepts can be a most effective way to organize knowledge in large applications. Where rules are used in an object-oriented system, it is often very effective, and even necessary, to organize rules along the lines of such a conceptual hierarchy. Just how this is done depends largely on the nature of the problem addressed by an application.

8.1 Classification and Reclassification

In classification problems, the very problem is to determine how to classify a particular item, whether it is a monitored sample to be identified, a disease symptom, or something else. Often when the classification is made, this knowledge is then used to determine what to do about it. For example, the classification might be used as part of a diagnosis that subsequently leads to a conclusion for the remedy. This means that in a rule-based system at least two different types of rulesets would be involved: those that make the classification and those that use the classification to achieve certain goals.

In an object-oriented system, the natural thing to do would be to actually make an object the instance of a particular class in the lattice, once a classification has been made. However, this is not always as simple as it might first appear. Quite a bit depends on the particular tool being used. Most object systems require that an object be an instance of a class as soon as it is created. This means that you are usually faced with a choice. You must either defer creating the object until the right class is known, or else change its class, or at least add a class from which it can inherit. Some AI tools do not allow you to directly change or add to the classes of instances. The only method in some cases would be to create a dummy instance and then copy its values into a new instance of the desired class. The disadvantage of this method is that you may not be able to use the same name for the two instances, unless you write a rather roundabout program.

Another point is that it is not always possible to make a correct classification at one stroke. You may have to do so in stages and even abandon an earlier classification. This points to the need for reassigning an object to a different class in a relatively straightforward way. Many related operations can be handled using this approach such as by creating special classes like Unclassified or even Deleted. Assuming that a satisfactory method has been achieved for assigning an object to a class once the proper classification has been made, the next issue to address is how to take advantage of this to make the necessary inferences for accomplishing the desired goals.

The standard type of inference that is usually used for deducing as much information as possible from existing facts is forward chaining. It would seem logical, therefore, that if you have made a classification and assigned an object to a given class, the way to draw the most conclusions from this might be to use some type of forward chaining. More specifically, forward chaining would appear to be a natural way to determine the value of unfilled slots of a new instance. The main advantages of assigning an object to a given class are the structure of slots that it inherits and the set of rules that then apply to it. It may be necessary to find the values for a number of these slots before the rules can be used. In most cases it would be desirable to be able to apply as many rules as would fire and then use forward-chaining metarules to find the values of those slots that still have no value. One technique often used is to set the value of a slot to NOTKNOWN whenever the system has tried to find the value to a slot but failed. Then only the rules that had this value as a condition would fire. One technique would be to switch to backward chaining at that point and test some default hypotheses as to what the value of the slot could be. Dependency on the values of different factors could be used for this purpose.

Some AI tools allow constraints to be made on the value of slots, such as limiting the value to a set of known alternatives. In this case, if you rule out all other alternatives, only the remaining value of the slot could apply. For example, take the simple rule:

IF   X is a person with slot-value Sex = UNKNOWN
       AND the Sex of X is not Male
THEN   the Sex of X is Female

When objects have many slots and many alternatives to these slots, a very large number of rules could be required. It would therefore be desirable to write more general types of rules to handle this kind of mechanism. Such rules might be written independent of slot value and be capable of retrieving the possible values for any slot and then weeding out the alternatives. Even here, the mechanism is dependent on rules that "rule out" slot values for particular slots. It is clear, therefore, that this approach is not very efficient unless the slots only have a small number of alternatives.

Writing rules that "rule out" alternatives can sometimes be relatively easy. Usually several conditions are required to make a definite value assignment. On the other hand, it may be possible to rule out an alternative if a certain condition is definitely not true. The difference at issue here is between a slot or variable that has no value at all and one that has a different value from one needed to fire a rule.

Let's try an example. Consider the following rules:

IF   the animal does not have wings AND
        It is not a Penguin
THEN   It is not a Bird

IF   the number of legs of the animal = 0
THEN   it is not a Chordate, AND
          it is not an Arthropod

Depending on the application, it can be much easier to write rules of this kind because often only a very few conditions are needed, and sometimes just one.

Another successful approach is to provide a mechanism for assigning default values to slots, either when they are created or later. This too appears to be of marginal use unless a mechanism is provided for revising the default assumption for exceptions when it seems wrong. However, this is sometimes extremely difficult to detect.

The types of reasoning we have been discussing often involve various shifts between forward and backward chaining, depending on the type of strategy involved for deriving the required information. Because of this, it is desirable to have a tool with the feature of bidirectional rules: those that can be used to write rulesets that work in either the forward or backward direction. However, this is not adequate by itself to provide the best type of solution. A system that combines this with the ability to reassign the class of an instance would be a more powerful type.

8.2 Full Access to Objects

One capability that would be of use in a large variety of circumstances is to be able to loop through all the slots of a given object for various purposes. This is where the advantages of languages like LISP are particularly evident. In LISP it is relatively commonplace for functions to be applied over all the items in a list. So, if we can compile a list of the slots of an instance, such functions can be defined and used. In an adequate object-oriented tool, there ought to be a function, perhaps called All-Slots, that performs the necessary service of returning all the slots of an object. Such a function would return just the names of the slots, not their values, so there could also be a method called All-Slot-Values that performed the latter service.

Conceptual hierarchies often have a validity that is independent of a given set of rules, associated methods, or implementation tools. For this reason, it is generally a good idea to keep the definitions of the classes or frames for such a hierarchy in a separate module from the latter. A programmer or knowledge engineer can keep a library of such sets of hierarchies, which can be used for a variety of purposes. For example, a conceptual hierarchy that modeled the parts of the human body could be used for programs that teach, that diagnose ailments, and that display the body graphically, or conceivably all three.

8.3 Object-Oriented Simulation

Simulation has always appeared to be one of the natural uses of object-oriented systems. This is not surprising, since Smalltalk, one of the first true object-oriented languages, was strongly influenced by the Simula programming language. However, unlike special-purpose simulation languages, object-oriented languages are usually not equipped with everything one needs to start writing simulations immediately. Yet, with a modest amount of additional programming, the necessary facilities can be added.

What is usually needed to outfit an object-oriented system for doing discrete simulations? This largely depends on the type of application. In general, some provision for multitasking is a very useful feature for conducting many types of discrete simulation, but it is not necessary for all types. Multitasking is usually needed when the application requires that several processes be repeatedly suspended while the timing for all events is recorded.

When extending an object-oriented language to equip it for implementing simulations, usually some form of the Simulator class is constructed. Instances of the Simulator class are intended to manage the simulation of various possible groups of simulated objects. That is, the class must be designed to handle a wide variety of applications using different instances of types of objects that will be the focus of the simulation.

One of the most important types of objects in a simulation is resources. Consequently, it is also typical for a Resource class to be implemented. The dynamics of a simulation vary considerably depending on what resources can be considered fixed and which can be considered changing. Another type of resource that usually requires special treatment is a nonrenewable resource. Therefore, a branch of the class hierarchy for a simulation application might look like this:

```
Resource
    ChangingResource
        RenewableResource
        NonRenewableResource
    FixedResource
```

Although no resources are really fixed, some can usually be considered fixed for the purpose of a given simulation. A similar classification can be used with other objects that constitute simulations, which are not considered resources, but perhaps objects that use resources. This group of classes might look as follows:

```
SimulationObject
  ChangingSimulationObject
  FixedSimulationObject
```

Another distinction that can be made is between consumable and nonconsumable resources. Even though a resource is fixed, it may or may not be consumed by objects in a simulation. If a fixed resource is consumed, all of it is used up if any simulation object uses it. An example of a fixed consumable resource is an aspirin. An example of a fixed nonconsumable resource is the Sun.

Simulations with changing resources and various events happening simultaneously obviously require that the events and resources be coordinated. Often this is accomplished in object-oriented systems by messages that request, assign, or relinquish such resources.

A standard way of handling time in discrete simulations is to have the simulation clock inspect an event queue to see if there are any pending events. If none is there, the simulation terminates. If there are some, it looks at the time the next event is scheduled to occur. It then sets the time as the same as that of the next event.

In an object-oriented simulation of the type described here, simulation objects send messages to the instance of the Simulator class to inform it of their entry and exit. At the very minimum, a Simulator object needs to know

1. The objects that are the resources for the simulation.

2. The current time in the simulation.

3. A queue of events that are waiting to occur.

4. The total number of processes that are active at any given time.

A function that is of obvious importance in a simulation is keeping track of what has occurred and taking various statistics about it so that inquiries can be made about a particular simulation that has occurred. There are at least three ways this can be done in an object-oriented simulation. The records and statistics must be gathered and recorded by an instance of the Simulator class, the simulated objects must take their own statistics, or another class must be created whose instances will carry out this function. Of these, one can be eliminated almost immediately. For each object to keep a record of its own behavior is not really a satisfactory solution because there still must be a way to access all the information about a complete simulation. Since the objects present in a simulation ought to be able to vary considerably in almost any way conceivable, it would be unnecessarily difficult to attack the problem in this way. An exception to this might be a special type of simulation in which there had to be a simulated object whose specific task was precisely keeping track of what is going on by all the other simulated objects. It is not splitting hairs to mention this case, because it is important to point out that such objects can appear in simulations, and object-oriented systems are particularly well suited for implementing them.

For recording the results of simulation runs, there are two basic options: recording the information on disk or storing it in memory in one or more objects. Obviously the two are not mutually exclusive. However, the information can be written to disk media in different ways. One way, for example, would be to have the events directed as they are happening to a stream that has one of its destinations in a disk file. Another way is to save one or more instances from the simulation to disk as desired. This is a generic feature that might already be available in an object-oriented tool.

8.4 Combining AI and Discrete Simulation

Some programs have been written where AI applications and simulations are combined. There are a wide range of architectures for this kind of hybrid application. They range from those in which a simulator is just a small part of a large knowledge-based system (for example, a planning system) to the opposite extreme, where a large simulation application has a small intelligent module for some special purpose. Often such hybrid applications have a distributed architecture. They exist on two or more interconnected machines. However, hybrid applications of this kind can also be implemented on a single machine.

One of the more ambitious types of hybrid applications that combine both an AI application and simulation is one in which the simulation and the reasoning system both continue for the entire length of a session and there is extensive interaction between them. An obvious example of this type of application would be one in which a simulation format was used for a deep reasoning system that made use of a sophisticated dynamically changing world model. In one subcategory of this type of application, the model would not be a simulation at all, but would be a representation of real events that were recorded in real time.

8.5 ROSS

An example of a language created specifically for the purpose of creating a simulation application is one developed at the Rand Corporation called ROSS (Rand Object-Oriented Simulation System). Part of the rationale for creating the ROSS language was the recognition that simulation is sometimes a technique human experts use to solve problems. Therefore, a capability for simulation would be one of the facilities needed in such cases to build a computer model of their expertise. ROSS is unique in that it is an English-like object-oriented language. The purpose of making the code look like English, of course, is to make it easier for nontechnical users to build applications.

The fact that ROSS is an interactive language written in LISP implies that users can interrupt applications in various ways while they are in progress, without completely exiting a session. This is a feature shared by many object-oriented languages. The advantage is that if a user sees that a simulation is not going in a fruitful direction, it is not necessary to wait for the session to complete itself in order to do something about it.

Another very convenient feature of the ROSS language is that it has a trace facility that produces easily readable text as output.

To get a feeling for the ROSS language, let's imagine we are creating an application that simulates a boat chartering company. With this kind of application, we would be able to have objects in the environment send messages to other objects in order to conduct the simulation. For example, we could say:

```
(ask boat-dispatch-1 send charter-boat-3 equipped-with orchestra
    to Sausalito)
```

In order for the boat-dispatch object to be able to recognize this message, a behavior must have been defined for it. For example, we might have defined the following behavior for it in the ROSS language:

```
(ask boat-dispatch when receiving
        (send >boat equipped-with >item to >place)
    (ask !myself schedule after
        !(ask myself recall your dispatch-delay) minutes
            tell !boat-commander equip !boat with !item)
    (ask !myself add !boat to your list of boats-dispatched)
    (ask !myself remove !boat from your list of
        boats-for-hire)).
```

The exclamation points in the syntax preceding the variable names force the interpreter to evaluate them and substitute the values of the variables.

In general, then, the syntax in ROSS for defining a behavior has the form:

```
(ask [object] when-receiving [message-template] [body])
```

As all realistic object systems should, ROSS supports multiple inheritance. As mentioned before, multiple inheritance allows the multiplicity of real objects to be captured in a class hierarchy. One of the facilities that equips ROSS for handling simulations is the ability of any object in a ROSS application to plan the occurrence of an event at any time in the future. For example, we can write the following message:

```
(ask boat-dispatch-1 plan after 30 minutes
        tell boat-commander check weather-forecast station-30)
```

This forces ROSS to schedule the message to be sent to the boat commander 30 minutes later in simulated time. ROSS has a simple clock that executes scheduled events and advances simulated time.

There are some important limitations to the ROSS language, the main one being that it includes neither inference engines nor a syntax for rule-based programming. Looking at just the simulation facility alone, there is also an important limitation there as well.

Because the objects in a simulation announce their presence by sending messages, it is difficult to represent surprising events that do not announce themselves such as a freak storm off the coast. Although there are ways of approaching this problem, it points out some of the many subtleties of human affairs with which advanced computer modeling systems must be able to contend.

8.6 Continuous Simulation

Object-oriented languages are not only suitable for discrete simulations but also for continuous simulations that use mathematical equations. In fact, they provide some important advantages for this type of simulation.

From the point of view of artificial intelligence, mathematical equations can be viewed as just one knowledge representation approach among many. As such, they have some important limitations. One of the most important limitations of mathematical modeling is that the variables that are included in a mathematical model have no meaning within a program to the software itself other than as simply being dependent on the values of other variables. Only the human user can make any further sense or interpretation of these quantities. For example, if a particular variable represents a *property* of some entity such as an organism or an organ of the body, there is nothing in the framework of an equation itself to express that.

There are obvious reasons why it would be desirable to have greater ability to represent knowledge than using purely mathematical relations. For this reason, researchers have been exploring ways to combine symbolic processing and numerical computation. The reasons for wanting such an integration are rather obvious. It is desirable to be able to combine both quantitative and qualitative knowledge in intelligent simulations and problem-solving systems. Object-oriented languages that include message passing provide an excellent framework for this purpose. Using this paradigm, we can create object hierarchies with objects that "know" the equations that apply to them. This can be done most simply by storing the equations as methods under the relevant classes. Another advantage of this approach is that the variables are organized under the corresponding objects whose properties they are.

8.7 Rule-Based Simulation

In systems that combine object-oriented and rule-based representation schemes, still another form of simulation is possible that uses rules rather than message passing as the main paradigm. The most interesting type of rule-based simulations are made possible by a rule language that allows powerful use of variables in the construction of rules. This permits the writing of very general rules that are useful with any number of different applications.

One of the most powerful features of rule-based simulations in object-oriented systems is that often management of simulation objects can be done with very little special programming. Frequently just a few rules will suffice. Another important feature of rule-based simulations is that they are extremely modular. It is relatively straightforward to design a system so that widely different sets of objects can work with the same set of rules. Conversely, it is also possible to have a variety of rulesets that work with the same set of objects. In this respect, larger sets of rules and simulation objects can be composed of smaller sets for running a particular simulation. Another important advantage of rule-based simulation is that often very sophisticated concepts and states of affairs can be represented. On the whole, rule-based simulations can be quite easy and rapid to implement, depending on the degree of detail required.

Probably the best way to get a feel for a simple rule-based simulation is to see an actual example. Although the example we will discuss here is extremely simple, it demonstrates the basic idea on which far more complex rule-based simulations may be constructed. The example we will be considering is called Basic Exchange. It is the simulation of a very rudimentary economic activity, that of bartering. It is implemented in the GoldWorks AI programming environment, although it could be implemented in many other systems as well. The rulebase does not assume that any particular size economy is in use. The same set of rules will work for simulations of two people or two hundred. In the example simulation we will describe, just two people, Jeremy and John, are involved. Jeremy is a farmer and John is a shoemaker. At the beginning of the simulation, Jeremy is doing all right, but John is starving. At the end of the simulation, John has traded some shoes to Jeremy for food and is eating regularly again. Although the economy is primitive, the types of statements used in rules include some compound clauses that express relatively sophisticated conditions, such as the beliefs of the people involved. The example uses a total of a dozen forward-chaining rules. (See Listing 8.1.)

The rules are designed to work with frames of the type Person. A few special relations are also defined, for example, HAS, HAS-TO-SPARE, BELIEVES, EXCHANGE-WITH-FOR, and NEEDS-FOR. The main slots in the Person frame that come into play are Occupation and Situation. The highest priority rule states that a person needs food as a basic survival goal. An associated rule is used to make the simple inference that if a person is starving, he has no food. To get the simulation moving, a rule called OBTAIN-NEEDS says that if a person needs something and does not have it, he tries to obtain it. This works with one of the most complex rules in this rudimentary example called ASKS-TO-EXCHANGE. This rule says that if a person is trying to obtain something *and* he has something that he believes he can spare *and* there is another person who has what the first person is seeking, then the first person should ask to make an exchange with the second person. To assist in setting up the necessary conditions, a few rules are used to make some additional inferences. One rule assumes that if a person makes something, then he has that thing to spare. Another makes the inference that if a person has something to spare, then he believes he does. There are also a few rules that make inferences about what people make, depending on the values of their Occupation slots.

Listing 8.1 Rule-Based Simulation of a Primitive Exchange Economy

```
(DEFINE-FRAME OBJECT
   (:print-name "OBJECT"
    :doc-string ""
    :is TOP-FRAME)
   (NAME)
   (INSTANCES))

(DEFINE-FRAME ENTITY
   (:print-name "ENTITY"
    :doc-string ""
    :is OBJECT))

(DEFINE-FRAME PERSON
   (:print-name "PERSON"
    :doc-string ""
    :is ENTITY)
   (LAST-NAME)
   (SEX
       :constraints (:ONE-OF (MALE FEMALE)))
   (AGE)
   (OCCUPATION)
   (NATIONALITY)
   (SITUATION))

(DEFINE-RELATION BELIEVES
   (:print-name "BELIEVES"
    :doc-string ""
    :explanation-string ""
    :lisp-function NIL
    :relation-type :ASSERTION)
   (<AGENT><ASSERTION>))

(DEFINE-RELATION MAKES
   (:print-name "MAKES"
    :doc-string ""
    :explanation-string ""
    :lisp-function NIL
    :relation-type :ASSERTION)
   (AGENT ITEM))

(DEFINE-RELATION NEEDS-FOR
   (:print-name "NEEDS-FOR"
    :doc-string ""
    :explanation-string ""
    :lisp-function NIL
    :relation-type :ASSERTION)
   (AGENT ITEM GOAL))
```

```
(DEFINE-RELATION ASK-ABOUT
    (:print-name "ASK-ABOUT"
     :doc-string ""
     :explanation-string ""
     :lisp-function NIL
     :relation-type :ASSERTION)
    (<AGENT-1><AGENT-2><ISSUE>))

(DEFINE-RELATION HAS
    (:print-name "HAS"
     :doc-string ""
     :explanation-string ""
     :lisp-function NIL
     :relation-type :ASSERTION)
    (<AGENT><ITEM>))

(DEFINE-RELATION EXCHANGE-WITH-FOR
    (:print-name "EXCHANGE-WITH-FOR"
     :doc-string ""
     :explanation-string ""
     :lisp-function NIL
     :relation-type :ASSERTION)
    (AGENT-1 AGENT-2 ITEM-1 ITEM-2))

(DEFINE-RELATION HAS-TO-SPARE
    (:print-name "HAS-TO-SPARE"
     :doc-string ""
     :explanation-string ""
     :lisp-function NIL
     :relation-type :ASSERTION)
    (<AGENT><ITEM>))

(DEFINE-INSTANCE JOHN
    (:print-name "JOHN"
     :doc-string ""
     :is  PERSON)
    (NAME JOHN_DOE)
    (SEX MALE)
    (AGE 33)
    (OCCUPATION SHOEMAKER)
    (NATIONALITY USA)
    (SITUATION STARVING)
    )

(DEFINE-INSTANCE JEREMY
    (:print-name "JEREMY"
     :doc-string ""
     :is  PERSON)
```

```
(NAME JEREMY_JONES)
(SEX MALE)
(AGE 35)
(OCCUPATION FARMER)
(NATIONALITY USA)
(SITUATION GETTING-BY)
   )

(DEFINE-RULE NO-LONGER-STARVING
   (:print-name "NO-LONGER-STARVING"
    :doc-string "Rule 12"
    :dependency NIL
    :direction  :FORWARD
    :certainty  1.0
    :explanation-string ""
    :priority 0
    :sponsor TOP-SPONSOR)
   (INSTANCE ?X IS PERSON
            WITH SITUATION STARVING) (HAS ?X FOOD)
  THEN
   (INSTANCE ?X IS PERSON
            WITH SITUATION EATING)
  AND-THEN
    (ADD-SLOT-VALUE ?X SITUATION EATING))

(DEFINE-RULE SHOEMAKER-MAKES-SHOES
   (:print-name "SHOEMAKER-MAKES-SHOES"
    :doc-string "Rule 4"
    :dependency T
    :direction  :FORWARD
    :certainty  1.0
    :explanation-string ""
    :priority 0
    :sponsor TOP-SPONSOR)
   (INSTANCE ?X IS PERSON
            WITH OCCUPATION SHOEMAKER)
  THEN
   (MAKES ?X SHOES))

(DEFINE-RULE WILLING-TO-EXCHANGE
   (:print-name "WILLING-TO-EXCHANGE"
    :doc-string "Rule 10"
    :dependency T
    :direction  :FORWARD
    :certainty  1.0
    :explanation-string ""
    :priority 0
    :sponsor TOP-SPONSOR)
   (INSTANCE ?X IS PERSON) (INSTANCE ?Y IS PERSON)
```

```
   (ASKS-ABOUT ?X ?Y (EXCHANGE-WITH-FOR ?X ?Y ?U ?V))
   (BELIEVES ?Y (HAS-TO-SPARE ?Y ?V))
  THEN
   (EXCHANGE-WITH-FOR ?X ?Y ?U ?V))

(DEFINE-RULE MAKERS-SURPLUS
   (:print-name "MAKERS-SURPLUS"
    :doc-string "Rule ?"
    :dependency T
    :direction  :FORWARD
    :certainty  1.0
    :explanation-string ""
    :priority 0
    :sponsor TOP-SPONSOR)
   (INSTANCE ?X IS PERSON) (MAKES ?X ?Y)
  THEN
   (HAS-TO-SPARE ?X ?Y))

(DEFINE-RULE NEED-TO-EAT
   (:print-name "NEED-TO-EAT"
    :doc-string "Rule 1"
    dependency T
    :direction  :FORWARD
    :certainty  1.0
    :explanation-string "Any person needs food to satisfy their
goal to
    :priority 0
    :sponsor TOP-SPONSOR)
   (INSTANCE ?X IS PERSON)
  THEN
   (NEEDS-FOR ?X FOOD SURVIVAL-GOAL))

(DEFINE-RULE TWO-WAY-EXCHANGE
   (:print-name "TWO-WAY-EXCHANGE"
    :doc-string "Rule 11"
    :dependency T
    :direction  :FORWARD
    :certainty  1.0
    :explanation-string ""
    :priority 0
    :sponsor TOP-SPONSOR)
   (INSTANCE ?X IS PERSON) (INSTANCE ?Y IS PERSON)
   (EXCHANGE-WITH-FOR ?X ?Y ?U ?V)
  THEN
   (HAS ?X ?V)
  AND-THEN
   (HAS ?Y ?U))
```

Listing 8.1 Rule-Based Simulation of a Primitive Exchange Economy (continued)

```
(DEFINE-RULE OBTAIN-NEEDS
   (:print-name "OBTAIN-NEEDS"
    :doc-string "Rule 3"
    :dependency T
    :direction  :FORWARD
    :certainty  1.0
    :explanation-string ""
    :priority 1
    :sponsor TOP-SPONSOR)
   (INSTANCE ?X IS PERSON) (NEEDS-FOR ?X ?Y ?Z)
   (NOT (HAS ?X ?Y))
  THEN
   TRIES-TO ?X (OBTAINS ?X ?Y)))

(DEFINE-RULE BELIEVES-TO-SPARE
   (:print-name "BELIEVES-TO-SPARE"
    :doc-string "Rule 6"
    :dependency T
    :direction  :FORWARD
    :certainty  1.0
    :explanation-string ""
    :priority 0
    :sponsor TOP-SPONSOR)
   (INSTANCE ?X IS PERSON) (HAS-TO-SPARE ?X ?Y)
  THEN
   (BELIEVES ?X (HAS-TO-SPARE ?X ?Y)))

(DEFINE-RULE ASKS-TO-EXCHANGE
   (:print-name "ASKS-TO-EXCHANGE"
    :doc-string "Rule 8"
    :dependency T
    :direction  :FORWARD
    :certainty  1.0
    :explanation-string ""
    :priority 0
    :sponsor TOP-SPONSOR)
   (INSTANCE ?X IS PERSON) (TRIES-TO ?X (OBTAINS ?X ?V)
   (INSTANCE ?Y IS PERSON) (HAS ?Y ?V) (NOT-EQUAL ?X ?Y)
   (BELIEVES ?X (HAS-TO-SPARE ?X ?U))
  THEN
   (ASKS-ABOUT ?X ?Y (EXCHANGE-WITH-FOR ?X ?Y ?U ?V)))

(DEFINE-RULE FARMER-MAKES-FOOD
   (:print-name "FARMER-MAKES-FOOD"
    :doc-string "Rule 5"
    :dependency T
    :direction  :FORWARD
    :certainty  1.0
    :explanation-string ""
```

Listing 8.1 Rule-Based Simulation of a Primitive Exchange Economy (continued)

```
    :priority 0
    :sponsor TOP-SPONSOR)
  (INSTANCE ?X IS PERSON
        WITH OCCUPATION FARMER)
 THEN
  (MAKES ?X FOOD))

(DEFINE-RULE HAS-IF-HAS-TO-SPARE
   (:print-name "HAS-IF-HAS-TO-SPARE"
    :doc-string "Rule 9"
    :dependency T
    :direction  :FORWARD
    :certainty  1.0
    :explanation-string ""
    :priority 0
    :sponsor TOP-SPONSOR)
  (INSTANCE ?X IS PERSON) (HAS-TO-SPARE ?X ?Y)
 THEN
  (HAS ?X ?Y))

(DEFINE-RULE HAS-NO-FOOD
   (:print-name "HAS-NO-FOOD"
    :doc-string "Rule 2"
    :dependency T
    :direction  :FORWARD
    :certainty  1.0
    :explanation-string ""
    :priority 0
    :sponsor TOP-SPONSOR)
  (INSTANCE ?X IS PERSON
        WITH SITUATION STARVING)
 THEN
     (NOT (HAS ?X Food))

(in-package 'gw)
```

The rule called WILLING-TO-EXCHANGE says that if a person is asked to make an exchange and believes he has the thing asked for to spare, then he will do so. Although this rule is very oversimplified, it would not take much to make it more realistic. Finally, a couple of rules assert the necessary facts that register that an exchange has taken place. One of them reacts to the new fact that John now has food and changes his Situation slot from Starving to Eating. This example was implemented very easily and rapidly and, again, it would not take very much to make it considerably more realistic. Generally speaking, the degree of realism of a simulation is relative to the purpose for which it is being used. In this example, by specifying further conditions to the exchange in a revised rulebase, various societies could be compared according to the amount of bartering they would permit. A full-blown version might be capable of simulating barter in a post-nuclear world. A listing of the GoldWorks code for the example is given in Listing 8.1.

There are a number of things to notice about this example. First, no special programming of simulation capabilities was required to implement it. This does not mean that this is not possible or desirable in rule-based simulation. But it does mean that rather sophisticated simulations are possible without it. Another thing to notice is that there is no explicit handling of time. Temporal order is represented implicitly as the order in which assertions are made to the current fact base. Another thing to notice is that if this interpretation of the assertion order is made, it implies that no two events can occur simultaneously. In general, to include many aspects of time in rule-based simulations of this type, it is not absolutely necessary to write special simulation facilities. The use of temporal relations in rules and the inclusion of special rules to manage them can include a great deal about time in the simulations. However, if it is necessary to have each event scheduled by a simulation clock counter, this facility will have to be implemented. One way that this type of system could be handled is to have a time-stamp variable in every assertion evaluated when it is made by a rule and to have every key action rule send a message to the simulation clock to advance. Alternatively, there could be a very high priority rule that is programmed such that it fires at certain regular intervals according to a real-time clock and updates the simulation clock.

Besides time, no other kind of resource is really managed in this program. However it would not be a problem to do this. For example, tabs could be kept on how many pairs of shoes John has and how much food Jeremy has. In this case, when exchanges are made, the rules could update the people's possessions by the appropriate amount. Also, instead of assuming that producers always have their own product to spare, this could be looked up. Another thing that could be done is to add a list of acquaintances as a slot on the Person frame. That way, in making a transaction, the system could simulate a person going through his acquaintances to decide what actions to take with whom. This example should provide some insight into the scope of rule-based simulations in an object-oriented system.

8.8 DOORS

The system described here is an architecture currently under research called the Dynamic Object-Oriented Representation System (DOORS). It is a multipurpose memory management system that is suitable as a representation scheme for deep reasoning. As such, it is suitable for both expert systems and natural language processing.

The idea of dividing the known universe into a number of very general categories of things is far from being a new idea. It is at the root of the Western scientific tradition that had its origin with Aristotle and the Greek scientist-philosophers who pioneered the viewpoints that he systematized. In more recent centuries, the philosopher Immanuel Kant is also associated with the issue of the fundamental categories of the knowable. For the purposes under discussion here, the differences of philosophic viewpoint are not of interest except as they are relevant to providing the basis of a system that works.

The basic idea of DOORS is to construct a comprehensive conceptual hierarchy that can provide a number of services simultaneously, not the least of which is a rubric for a comprehensive deep-reasoning system. One of the main advantages of this approach is that the same conceptual hierarchy can be used for a number of different purposes. For example, it could be used as a conceptual framework for the semantic aspect of a natural-language parsing system. It could also be used as a template from which to design lattice hierarchies of organized rulesets for knowledge-based systems of many different types. Finally, an architecture like DOORS could be used as the rubric for a large system of deep modeling of the world of human affairs, implemented on a distributed system composed of a variety of machines.

To use an object-oriented conceptual hierarchy for a practical deep-reasoning system, a number of features would be especially desirable. First of all, the system should be a "pure" object-oriented system in the sense that absolutely everything in it would be an object. This means that the slots or instance variables would themselves be objects. It comes to almost the same thing as saying that in such a system, all objects would be composite objects. This point is relatively simple if you remember that with composite objects all the subobjects act as the values of slot variables.

The principle at work here is a very general one that has important implications both for the practical issues of working deep-reasoning systems as well as for that of building AI applications such as natural-language understanding systems. The principle is that of *multidirectional information access*. This means that when any data or knowledge structure is stored, access can be gained in any possible direction, from the whole to the part or from the part to the whole. For example, from the deer we should be able to gain immediate access to the antlers, but from the antlers we should be able to gain immediate access to the deer. In current database systems, you can generally only go one way. You must at least know the datafile and the field in order to retrieve any information. In the system we envisage here, the object-oriented data structure would allow the data to be accessed directly without knowing the larger structure in which it is contained.

Clearly, various examples could be cited in which this would be quite difficult to accomplish. For this reason, the second main feature of the DOORS system is that all objects are active data structures in the true sense. That is to say, not only do they inherit a number of procedural methods that represent operations they can perform on themselves, but they are also capable of responding to certain types of query messages.

A third feature of the DOORS system is the use of what is called a *partitioned hash table*. This technique allows extremely large lookup tables to be used that are nevertheless forgiving to small errors. Basically what this system does is to avoid exhaustive searches except in extremely small search areas. To do this properly, context hooks should be provided to allow routines to be written that can allow the system to use context to help in resolving hashing collisions wherever possible.

Now let's briefly look at a portion of the DOORS conceptual hierarchy. Another one of the features of the DOORS architecture is that any portion of the conceptual hierarchy can act as a first-class object. This means that, among other things, the context for problem solving can be constrained by specifying a portion of the hierarchy as a context. Allowing any portion of a hierarchy to behave as a first-class object means that it can be given a unique name and passed as an argument to recursive routines that traverse the specified region. The purpose of this is to allow many different types of operations to be possible for the same current group of concepts.

This feature has many different purposes in an advanced AI system. For example, it is a common form of human problem solving to focus on a particular cluster of ideas or issues and to try different approaches on them. Currently it is quite difficult to program computers to do this kind of exploratory problem solving. Being able to make a region of a conceptual hierarchy a theme for which a number of different problem-solving operations could be attempted is an important step forward.

8.9 A Neural Modeling Example

In this section, we explore a very different type of object-oriented modeling, that of trainable neural nets. The program described here is a Smalltalk program distributed by Digitalk as one of the Carleton Projects. It is very instructive to see how neural modeling is done in an object-oriented language.

This program is very interesting because, though it is simple, it shows the general strategy of how more sophisticated Neural Network models can be programmed in an object-oriented system. Its design is that of a back-propagation model based on a program by Richard Lippmann. The architecture of this model is threefold, including the net, the layers of neuron units, and the neuronal units themselves. There are three types of neuron layers to the net, the input and output layers, and the internal layers between them. Connections between neural units can be either positive or negative. They are typically not between neurons in the same layer, but between adjacent layers. The function used to compute the output of each neural unit is a nonlinear sigmoid function on the sum of all the input values to the unit.

In the character recognition application, the input to the network is the bit pattern of the character. The output is a code that represents some character. The number of middle layers to the network and the way they are to be interconnected depend on how many characters the network is to be capable of recognizing. Distinguishing between more than two characters requires at least three middle layers.

A convenient user interface for the application is created by means of a Neural Net Browser. This is used to construct the net and to train it with a training set that also must be defined. The sample program is used by supplying test characters, usually in pairs, and executing the training routine until the neural net is able to distinguish between them. This is then repeated until the net can do this for a large number of characters. The most obvious limitation of the scheme is the time it takes for training, which understandably increases with the addition of more characters. This is a particularly interesting property of the model because it is in direct contrast to the way human learning appears to function. Human learning usually speeds up with increased information, but neural models like this generally do not.

The Neural Net program was written using just five new classes and some minor modifications to the existing Form class. The new classes are: Neuron, Layer, Net, NetEditor, and NetPane. Neuron, Layer, and Net are all direct subclasses of Object, whereas NetEditor is a subclass of Dispatcher and NetPane inherits from the SubPane class. A Net is the main object created on initializing an application. It is an object consisting of instances of Layer, which are in turn composed of instances of the Neuron class. A Net object has three key instances variables, inputLayer, outputLayer, and middleLayer, each of which are Ordered Collections of instances of the Layer class. Layer objects in turn each have a neurons instance variable whose value is an Ordered Collection of instances of the Neuron class.

Each neuron in turn has an important set of instance variables. The activateLines variable contains an Ordered Collection of neurons to which the neuron can actively transmit its output. The corresponding variable is inputLines, which stores a Dictionary containing the input neurons and corresponding weight factors, which on initialization are set to random values.

The openOn: method of NetPane as provided contains the default value of 2 for the number of middle layers. A different version of this method could be written that uses some type of logic to determine this value or looks it up in some appropriate way. Generally speaking, the structure of a neural net could be initialized in a variety of different ways. The decision was simply made for the purposes of this example to have the initialization of the Net Browser and the network itself occur as one event, with the number of layers hard-wired to the value of 2.

Neuron Training

The main algorithm implemented in the example is the procedure for training the network. This section reviews how this algorithm is designed. A good place to start is with the trainOnce: method for the Net class. This method is provided with the desired result and uses back-propagation to train the network once. As you can see by consulting Listing 8.2, this method consists of first activating the middle and output layers of the network and then calling their own train methods. The train method for the layers is essentially a call to iterate through the Neuron train method for each of the neurons in a layer. This method does the real work. It uses the gradient descent method of back-propagation, which is a version of the hill-climbing strategy. The train method for the Net class essentially applies the `trainOnce:` method to test pairs and reiterates this a number of times.

Listing 8.2 Representative Methods for Neural Net Application

```
 trainOnce: result

  middleLayers do: [:layer | layer activate].
    outputLayer activate.
    self calculateErrors: result.
    outputLayer train.
   middleLayers do: [:aLayer | aLayer train] n].
train  (Layer).

   train "Neuron"
   neurons do: [:aNeuron | aNeuron train].

      "Use the backpropagation gradient descent specification to
adjust
     weights and threshold of the receiver."
     | magnitude |.
     magnitude := 0.
     inputLines keysDo: [:aNeuron |
          magnitude := magnitude + (aNeuron potential * aNeuron
potential)]
        inputLines associationsDo: [:aLine |
           aLine value: (aLine value +
           (LearnRate * error * aLine key potential / magnitude)).

    | magnitude |
    magnitude := 0.
    inputLines keysDo. [:aNeuron |
       magnitude := magnitude + (aNeuron potential * aNeuron
potential)
    inputLines associationsDo: [:aLine |
       aLine value: (aLine value +
           (LearnRate * error * aLine key potential /
    magnitude)).

      "aLine key threshold: aLine key threshold + (LearnRate *
       error)"].

train     "Net"

 count timesRepeat: [
        pairs do: [:aPair |
           self setInputValue: (aPair at: 1).
           5 timesRepeat: [self trainOnce: (aPair at: 2)]].
        feedback value].

solve    "Net"
```

Listing 8.2 Representative Methods for Neural Net Application (continued)

```
        "Activate the layers of the receiver thus calculating the
output
        for the current input potentials".

    middleLayers do: [:layer | layer activate].
    outputLayer activate.
activate   (Layer).
        "Activate all of the neurons in the receiver by
calculating their potential based on the potentials of their
input nodes".

    neurons do: [:aNeuron | aNeuron calculatePotential].

calculatePotential   (Neuron).

    "Compute a Neuron's potential as the sum of its inputs."

    potential := self totalActiveWeight.

totalActiveWeight.
 "Calculate the receiver's potential as the sum of the  inputs."
 | total |.
total := 0.
inputLines associationsDo:
[:assoc | total := total - (assoc value *
assoc key
    potential)].
```

Solving the Net

Once a network has been trained, the process of applying it to a test item is called solving. The `solve` method of the Net class simply calls the `activate` method of the Layer class first for the middle layers and then for the outer layers. The `activate` method calls upon each of the neurons of a layer to calculate its potential. The method that does the work here is `totalActiveWeight`, which calls `associationsDo:` for each of the inputLines of a neuron and then applies a formula to make the calculation.

Conclusion

We have seen that the ability to use an object-oriented system to provide a useful descriptive model of a problem domain depends upon available facilities for navigating about and manipulating the information stored in conceptual hierarchies. The less that a program needs to know in advance about the knowledge it will be using, the better. Ideally, a program ought to be able to browse about in various knowledge worlds, drawing its own conclusions as it goes. To be able to do this, a program might first try to compile a list of all the instances that are currently alive in the world. Next, it would determine the class of each and then compile a list of slots. In cases where the values of important slots are unknown, inferences could be drawn based on values that are known. Other approaches are also quite possible where applicable.

All of these methods have in common a need for the necessary facilities. This is not as simple as one might assume. For example, as was pointed out in the chapter on object-oriented LISP, in environments where garbage collection is used, the symbols that are considered as names of instances can vary from one time to the next. Where such difficulties arise, the best approach would be to use the most rapid means of compiling a list of possible instances and then to use other efficient techniques for testing and amending the list. Often a number of different efficient but inaccurate techniques can be used to correct one another and get the job done more quickly than one thorough method that is too time-consuming to be practical. It is clear that many lessons will have to be learned so that symbolic modeling systems are fast enough to be of service in many real world problems.

Today's efficient inference engines originated in the AI research laboratory as programs whose efficiency left much to be desired. However, they succeeded in demonstrating a new paradigm that could be refined and streamlined until it has all the sparkle of today's most efficient implementations. In a similar way, current experiments in conceptual modeling and deep-reasoning systems will be continually refined. We will learn many practical lessons about how to handle particular details for the best results. It has been proven many times that once a new approach has been demonstrated, careful study will unearth numerous ways to improve its efficiency, even by many orders of magnitude.

True or False?

1. It is not appropriate to use object classes as descriptive concepts for an application.

2. All object systems have a provision for changing the class of an instance.

3. Forward chaining can be used to fill out empty slots of objects by drawing inferences based on the slot values already assigned.

4. In theory, a conceptual hierarchy based on object classes could provide the rubric for a quick content-addressable memory system.

5. A lattice hierarchy built of object subclasses is an effective way to capture the different types of resources that can be used by discrete simulation programs.

6. Reasoning and simulation are two mutually exclusive approaches to the same problem between which a programmer must choose.

7. In object-oriented simulations, each object must always store the history of its own behavior during simulation runs.

8. One of the most powerful features of the ROSS language is its implementation of rule-based programming.

9. Rule-based simulation is not an accepted technique owing to the large amount of special-purpose programming needed to support it.

10. One of the most important advantages of neural nets is the extremely rapid learning times they enjoy.

(F, F, T, T, T, F, F, F, F, F)

Chapter 9

Concurrent Object-Oriented Systems

In this chapter we will venture into a very important field of AI research: that of concurrent object systems. In a significant sense, parallel object-oriented systems are a natural extension of purely sequential ones. To many people, the message-passing metaphor of standard object-oriented systems strongly suggests parallel architectures based on message-passing approaches. For this reason, beginners often make the mistake of thinking that ordinary object-oriented systems operate concurrently. Nevertheless, several research systems today actually do offer true parallelism for object-oriented programming.

9.1 Actors

Actors are probably the best known of the concurrent object systems. They, of course, are similar only in name to the Whitewater Group's ACTOR language, which we described in Chapter 4. Actors are the fruit of several years of research conducted by Prof. Carl Hewitt and his students at MIT. As you may know, there are currently three main models for parallel programming: shared memory systems, message-passing systems, and data-flow systems. Actor systems are concurrent message-passing languages whose primary goal is to implement intelligent, open systems.

The implementation of actor systems has evolved over a number of years through the study of various actor languages such as PLASMA, ACT1, ACT2, and ACT3. All of them have certain basic things in common: Everything in the system is an actor, and everything happens by passing messages between one actor and another. Each actor has its own *behavior,* which is defined by a script. Each actor also has a number of *acquaintances,* which are the names of other actors it knows about and to which it can pass messages. Each actor also knows the name of another actor to which it can delegate an incoming message if its script, for any reason, rejects it. This, in a nutshell, is what actor systems are all about.

Now let's draw some immediate conclusions about what this means. The fact that everything in an actor system must be an actor means that numbers, lists, databases, functions, processes, and devices all must be defined as actors. That is to say, an actor system has no passive objects or data. Everything is active in the sense of being able to send and receive messages and execute its behavior. One interesting innovation in actor languages is the use of distributed interpreters.

The basic message-sending protocol in actors is unidirectional, but there is often a need for answers to be given to a message. The mechanism provided for being able to implement message answering is that of continuations. Message-passing is implemented through a basic mailbox system. Each actor has its own unique mail address. Only an actor that has another actor on its list of acquaintances can send messages to its mail address. However, the mail address of actors can themselves be sent as messages. This is actually the primary way that the connection network represented by a given actor system can evolve.

The sum of all the acquaintance lists in an actor system defines the patterns of communication that are possible in that system, or, in other words, its *connection topology*. By sending the mailing addresses of actors and adding them to the acquaintance lists of other actors, the topology of a system increases in power and complexity. The mail system also uses a mail queue so that as new messages arrive while an actor is "busy," they are put on "hold" in the queue.

The facility for delegating the response of actors provides a way to extend the system incrementally and modularly that is an alternative to the class inheritance mechanism used in conventional object systems like Smalltalk. There are in fact no classes of actors in the usual sense of the term as it is used in object-oriented systems, but only the actors themselves. When an actor receives a message, often what is required is that a replacement actor be found to carry out the request. In this case, if other messages are sent to it in the meantime, these messages must be buffered until the replacement behavior is computed.

Clearly plenty of problems can still arise in a system such as the one we have described so far. One of them is communication bottlenecks. What happens when many messages arrive at the same actor simultaneously? To handle this problem, actors include as part of their behavior the need to supply replacement actors. In principle, whenever an actor accepts a message for processing, it must provide a replacement actor to handle subsequent messages. A more technical way of characterizing the communication protocol in an actor system is to say that message passing occurs through buffered asynchronous communication. It is important that asynchronous message passing be the default because otherwise a concurrent message-passing system would have an apparently unacceptable limitation; that is, recursive algorithms would always result in deadlock. A deadlock, of course, is where two processes are suspended, each waiting for the other, and with no alternative way of exiting. It is easy to see why the deadlock would have to occur. In a message-passing system, the recursion would have to occur by an actor sending a message to itself. But in a synchronously communicating system, the actor would have to wait until the message was returned before answering. This is just another way of saying that in a synchronous message-passing system, any attempt of a process to send a message to itself results in deadlock.

The question naturally arises that if asynchronous message passing is used in actor systems, how can parallel programs synchronize various processes that are occurring simultaneously? Simply providing for asynchronous message passing by no means solves the problem of implementing recursive algorithms in parallel. For if a process is confined to recursing through a problem by sending messages to itself, unless it can receive more than one message at once, there can only be sequential processing here. Actor languages solve this problem through a construct called *Customers*.

A Customer is an actor that provides greater control over how and when messages are sent. This can be used a number of different ways. In addition to providing a way out of deadlock-prone situations, it can also be used to implement a form of pipelining. A Customer is basically another actor that is there to play catch with the main actor so that operations such as sending messages to itself repeatedly do not result in deadlock. Customers work by making use of continuations. You may be familiar with continuations from Scheme LISP. A *continuation* is an object that represents how a given computation might continue. In this case, the operations of an algorithm, such as a recursive factorial, are split up between the initial actor and the customer that it spawns for itself to continue the computation.

Message-passing difficulties can ensue in other situations. One of the key examples used in explaining actor systems is that of multiple bank accounts. In such a situation, a savings account often provides overdraft protection for a checking account. In this case, if one actor represents the checking account and another the savings account, various problems can arise. For example, in processing an overdraft, the checking account actor would have to reply back to the savings account actor, but the savings account would also have to reply to the checking account actor for the new balance to be determined. As we saw earlier, until a replacement is specified, incoming messages must be buffered. But here it would not be permissible for the communication to be buffered before the replacement was determined.

Actor systems handle problems like this by a construct called an *insensitive actor*. Insensitive actors process a type of communication called a *become communication*. Become communications inform actors of their replacement behavior. Until they receive such information telling them what to become, insensitive actors buffer all communication.

Before offering an example of programming with actors, more of an overview of the necessary language constructs is needed. Actor languages have four basic types of commands: send, let, conditional, and become commands. As you would anticipate, send commands are those used to send messages. Let commands are used to assign or bind expressions to name identifiers that fall locally within their scope. Conditional commands provide the familiar mechanisms for branching. The become command, probably the type with which you are least familiar, is used to specify replacement actors. The expression contained in the become command may specify an existing actor or it may specify a new actor to be created. In the latter case, the actor to which the become statement is addressed becomes the forwarding actor for the new actor that is created.

The factorial algorithm is a good one for illustration because the relation between the actor and its customer that can accomplish a recursive factorial is essentially very simple. Since the factorial actor is intended to be used as a generic function, it assumes that another actor will call upon it to do the calculation. This means that in most cases we will be dealing with a minimum of three actors. We will call the actor that calls the factorial M (for main), the factorial actor itself can be F, and its customers are $C_1 \ldots C_n$, for convenience purposes. In this case, M makes a call to F to compute the factorial of a number, N, and F spawns C, to give it some help. However, M need not remain completely passive in the algorithm. On the other hand, unless the responsibilities of M are very minimal, we will lose the advantage of concurrent message passing altogether. In this case, M is the address to which the top customer C_1 sends its result.

The factorial algorithm works basically by creating a customer C_1 whose behavior is to multiply the number N with whatever number it is sent by F and then to send this product to the calling actor, in this case M. The number that F must send to C_1 for the right answer can only be the factorial of $N - 1$. However this value is not known yet, so F calls itself to find the factorial of $N - 1$. This means that a new customer C_2 is created, which will multiply $N - 1$ by the number it receives. Only now the product will be sent to the address of F because this time it was F that called itself. The process keeps recursing until F calls itself to find the factorial of 0, which is defined to be 1 by a test condition. This allows F to have a value to pass to the last customer C_n, which starts a cascading of messages back and forth between F and its customers up to C_1, which computes the value equal to the factorial of N and returns it to the actor M.

Now we have to admit that through all this we told one fib just to make the going easier. The result does not always have to be sent to M, which called for the factorial. M can request that the value be sent to the address of any actor it chooses. This, of course, does not affect the algorithm at all, which is much simpler than the explanation of why it works:

1. F creates a customer actor X whose behavior is:
   a) Multiply N by the number it receives from F.
   b) Send this value to the reply address for the factorial.

2. F sends the request to itself to find the value of the factorial of $N - 1$ and sends the result to the customer X.

The code for the recursive factorial actor written in ACT1 is given in Listing 9.1.

In the ACT1 language, two special types of actors were introduced, futures and serializers, the former to increase the level of concurrency and the latter to decrease it.

Many high-level functions were added to the language in ACT3 that greatly simplified the coding, making it easier to read in one sense and more difficult in another. See the greatly simplified code for the factorial in ACT3 as shown in Listing 9.2. Although this code is easier to write and to read, it is more difficult to figure out what is really going on in the actor environment. In ACT3 the system is made smart enough to know what it has to do to compute recursively and automatically creates is own customers as needed.

Guardians

A simple form of synchronization requires that a reply must be sent to an incoming message before an actor can accept a message from a different process. For obvious reasons, this approach is sometimes called One-At-A-Time. However, this can often result in slow-downs, bottlenecks, and even deadlocks. A means of making the handling of messages more flexible was provided by certain kinds of actors called Guardians. A *Guardian* can detect when an actor must wait to reply to a message, save everything needed for the answer to be made, and then process other messages in the mean time.

Listing 9.1 ACT1 Recursive Factorial

```
(define (Factorial ())
  (Is-Communication (a doit (with customer == m)
                            (with number == n))
    do
      (become Factorial)
        (if (= n 0)
          (then (send m 1))
          (else (let (x = (new FactCust (with customer m)
                                        (with customer n)))
                (send Factorial (a doit (with customer x)
                                        (with number n-1)))))))))

(define (FactCust (with customer == m)
                  (with number == n))
  (Is-Communication (a number k)
    do
      (send m n*k)))
```

Yonezawa, A., and Tokoro, M. *Object-Oriented Concurrent Programming*. Cambridge, Mass.: MIT Press, 1987, p. 44.

Listing 9.2 ACT3 Recursive Factorial

```
(define (call Factorial (with number == n))
(define (call Factorial (with number == n))
  (if (= n 0)
      (then 1)
      (else (* n (call Factorial (with number == n-1))))))
```

Yonezawa, A., and Tokoro, M. *Object-Oriented Concurrent Programming*. Cambridge, Mass.: MIT Press, 1987, p. 45.

Races

Another interesting innovation that has emerged in the course of research is a construction called a RACE actor. This provides a way of collecting the results of different parallel computations so that each of them can be made available as soon as possible. Just as CONS in sequential LISP returns a linked list of the objects that were passed to it as arguments, RACE starts up futures to compute each of its arguments in parallel and returns a list of the values computed, but in the order that they were completed. The meaning of its name is now clear: it initiates a kind of race between parallel processes to determine the order in which they will finish, like the competitors in the race. This construction makes it easy to build various parallel algorithms and functions. For example, a parallel OR would simply be a function that would return

TRUE as soon as any of the values of a RACE list came in true, but it would go through all the items to make sure that none of them was true before returning FALSE.

Another interesting application of this construction would be the implementation of a MERGE function that would enable two or more RACE lists of the result of parallel computations to be merged together into a single ordered list. In this case, the first element of the list would be determined by a race between the first elements of each of the lists. The process would then be continued recursively for ordering the rest of the list elements.

Receptionists

Another special type of actor is a *receptionist*. This is the only type of actor that is able to receive communications from outside the system.

One of the main characteristics of actor systems is their treatment of the issue of fairness. In parallel message-passing computation, *fairness* refers to the guarantee that all messages will be answered, at least at some time, regardless of their priority.

9.2 Concurrent Message-Passing Modes

The analogies between concurrent message-passing systems and aspects of human communication are quite striking and by no means an accident. These analogies are also very helpful in assisting us in understanding many of the subtleties involved without getting buried under a sea of technical complexities. Akinori Yonezawa and his co-workers at the Tokyo Institute of Technology have decided to try to exploit these analogies by using a concurrent object system for actually modeling and simulating situations encountered in life with a degree of precision that is not possible with the usual sequential simulations. In the course of their research, they developed a useful typology of message-passing systems. The following sections enumerate their list of types, but rather than using technical definitions, we will characterize them by describing analogous situations in human communication.

Ordinary Mode Message Passing

This message-passing mode is like a busy dispatch operator. When a message comes in for an actor that is not already "on another line," the message is put through. If the actor is already busy with a message, other incoming messages are put on hold on a first-come, first-serve basis.

Express Mode Message Passing

One way to explain the idea of express mode is to compare it with a system for giving orders to people in a shipping and receiving department who are authorized to take two kinds of orders, regular orders and rush orders, and to return or delegate all orders that do not meet certain specifications. The express mode is essentially a mechanism that allows busy actors to be interrupted for various purposes.

Past Type Message Passing

This is like the postal service as opposed to a telephone system. When a message is sent, the sender does not have to wait to hear that the message was received. After sending a message, an object is immediately free to go on with other tasks. This corresponds to what is generally referred to as asynchronous communication. It is called "past" because the sending process ceases before the message accomplishes its goal with the receiver.

Now Type Message Passing

This is like a station-to-station telephone call. When the message is sent, the sender waits for the receiver both to acknowledge that the message has been received and to actually respond with some answer to the information requested.

Future Type Message Passing

This message passing mode is like a request for a memo to be sent to a specific location at some future time. Although it is not needed immediately, the expectation is that when it is needed in the future, the sender will be able to find it at the location requested.

9.3 ABCL

Using the terminology given in the preceding section, we can describe the ABCL system that was implemented by the researchers at the Tokyo Institute of Technology. Basically, ABCL is an object-oriented language that supports a waiting mode and, unlike previous actor languages, permits built-in now and future type message passing.

In ABCL both the name of the sender and the destination for the reply are provided in messages. This makes it possible for past and now message passing to be reduced to a form of the past type of message passing. ABCL has a convenient notation for designating the type of message that is to be sent. Table 9.1 shows the symbols used for the different types in both the ordinary and the express modes.

The x variable in future mode messages is the future variable that tags results that are being evaluated in parallel and are not yet available.

When an object is defined in ABCL, first its state and then its script are designated. Objects in ABCL are always in one of three possible states: dormant, active, or waiting. Scripts contain instructions for message passing, creating new objects, accessing variables, calculating values, and creating and manipulating data structures. Unless specific instructions are used to employ parallel operations, the instructions within the script of an object are presumed to occur sequentially. To create instances of an object, special objects are made to do that job for objects of a certain type. Though they are not

Table 9.1 Message Modes in ABCL

	Ordinary	*Express*
Past	`[Receiver <=` `Message]`	`[Receiver <<=` `Message]`
Now	`[Receiver <==` `Message]`	`[Receiver <<==` `Message]`
Future	`[Receiver <= Message` `$ x]`	`[Receiver <<= Message` `$ x]`

called classes, like the classes in sequential object systems, they create instances when sent the message new.

As we saw earlier, constructs like < = with the arrow pointing to the left designate message sending. Conversely, symbols like = > with the arrows pointing to the right refer to a message that is to be received. In writing scripts, this construct is often used, for example, in specifying what messages the object may receive and under what conditions. For example, an expression of the form:

```
(=> message-pattern where constraint ... action...)
```

specifies that for past type messages received in the ordinary mode, only those satisfying the designated message pattern and constraints will be received. Messages sent to an object that do not fulfill these conditions as specified in its script are discarded. The same types of expressions may be written for messages of all types and modes.

We said earlier that the express mode in languages like ABCL is used as a mechanism to interrupt the activities of objects that were the result of ordinary mode messages. In ABCL, there is no way to interrupt activities that result from express mode messages. That is, not even another express mode message can interrupt an activity that has been initiated by an express mode message. The purpose of the express mode interrupt in ABCL is to allow this type of control to occur, while preventing the required code from becoming too complicated and hard to write and follow. An important restriction of the system is that no broadcasting of messages is allowed in ABCL.

9.4 Project Teams and Project Leaders

As mentioned earlier, one of the main purposes in developing ABCL was to have a tool for modeling real-world problem solving. To try to demonstrate this capability, the developers attempted to model the problem-solving approach that uses a team and a project leader. In this paradigm, a primary manager assigns a task and a deadline to the project team and chooses a leader to coordinate the different team members and to organize the timing of efforts to meet the deadline. In a concurrent object system, constructing an application like this translates, first, into defining the manager object that can create another object as a project leader. At the very minimum, the project leader object must include a description of the problem and the name of the object to which the solution (or lack of one) is to be reported.

In the course taken in the application developed with ABCL, the project manager object was designed to be able to create a timekeeper or scheduler who would have the responsibility for "waking up" various members of the problem-solving team at certain times. In this approach, when the project leader receives the "start solving" message from the manager, the timekeeper is spawned and provided with the information of whom to wake up at what times. For the problem-solvers themselves, a future type message passing scheme is used for them to report back their results. Whenever any one of the solvers finds an answer, it stores it in the future variable called Solutions. When more than one solver finds a solution, they are stored as a list with the identifier Solutions in the order in which they are received. This is very reminiscent of the RACE construction in the MIT actor languages.

The time resources of solvers are controlled by the timekeeper assigning a time for each solver and sending a "time is up" message in the express mode. Timekeeper objects are capable of receiving various messages in the express mode themselves that can change them dynamically by altering wake-up times or time limits, and so on and so provide a means of rescheduling on the fly. Solver objects have a state variable that registers their "state of progress." And like timekeepers, they can receive various messages in the express mode. For example, if they receive a "stop" message, they uncreate themselves, the technological equivalent of committing hara-kiri.

A number of other algorithms have been devised for ABCL that provide a way of implementing pipelining for divide-and-conquer types of strategies. This works when subproblems can be divided into a number of indivisible pieces. When this is true, the results of solving each piece can be returned one at a time, rather than waiting for the entire subproblem to be solved before returning results.

9.5 POOL/T

One quite interesting concurrent object language is POOL/T, which was developed in Europe as part of the ESPRIT advanced computing project, their counterpart to Japan's ICOT. One of the main concerns in designing this language was to provide a tool that would be suitable for developing very large systems in a top-down manner rather than in an explorative way. It is intended to be run in a hardware environment of up to 1000 processors that Philips is developing.

One very important difference between POOL/T and other object systems is that in this language classes are not modeled as objects. The rationale is that the behavior of classes and objects is very different, since the former remain static, whereas the latter can change dynamically. In POOL/T, a process is associated with every object. Such processes can be created dynamically and their names may be communicated by messages and stored as values of variables.

The type of message protocol adopted for POOL/T is a synchronous one. The reason for adopting this route is to give programmers greater control over how programs execute. A type of inheritance was attempted in an earlier version of POOL/T, but because of problems that were encountered, it was decided to leave it out of later versions.

As you may have surmised, POOL/T is more in the tradition of structured programming systems like Pascal, C, and Ada, than in that of interactive languages like LISP, PROLOG, and Smalltalk. As a matter of fact, there are some striking similarities between POOL/T and Ada.

9.6 MACE

Another message-passing AI language in the same general category as the ones we have been describing is MACE, an acronym for Multi-Agent Computing Environment, developed by Les Gasser and his co-workers at USC. As the name indicates, the nodes of the MACE system are called Agents rather than Actors. MACE runs on an Intel Hypercube and TI Explorer LISP machines in a distributed network. It was conceived as a testbed where research could be conducted on various distributed AI approaches that attempt to exploit parallelism on different levels of granularity. One of the main differences between a MACE agent and an actor is that the agents are both more powerful and more specialized. They are capable of representing knowledge, modeling the world, and modeling other agents.

MACE uses description attributes and instance attributes, much like the difference between classes and instances in conventional object systems. Like actors, MACE agents have a number of acquaintances with whom they can communicate. But in addition to knowing their mailing addresses, agents also have knowledge about the capabilities of their acquaintances. Agents can also be organized into coalitions, or clusters, that respond as a coordinated group to particular problems.

An important feature of agents in MACE is that they are sensitive to their environment in certain ways. The term "environment" here is taken in the very general sense that includes the MACE system itself, the other agents present, as well as the world outside the MACE system. Agents are sensitive to their environment in one obvious way: They receive and interpret messages. The other way in which agents are sensitive to their environment presumes some understanding of their internal construction, which we will take a look at now.

Agents have an active part, which is called their *engine*. They can take various types of actions. Every agent models the agents that are its acquaintances in terms of their name, class, address, roles, skills, goals, and plans. It's only right that it should also have a model of itself. It does. But what is meant by these different features of an agent's model?

MACE is bootstrapped in the sense that the basic user environment is implemented with various built-in system agents. System agents, for example, include those that implement the basic user interface as well as agent clusters that serve as system tools. There is even an agent-builder cluster that helps build the structures and behaviors of other agents. Agents gain knowledge of other agents in two basic ways. The first way is to be created with that knowledge built in. The other way is by asking the Directory Agent, which supplies the addresses of other agents on request. Then queries are directed at those agents themselves to build up models of them.

An important difference between MACE and conventional object-oriented languages is the absence of any inheritance scheme. One of the approaches attempted with MACE was to build a distributed rule-based production system where the rules are not evaluated with a conventional inference engine, but where each rule is an agent that can communicate with other agents by sending messages to them. The MACE system uses the approach of computation identifiers, which is essentially the same as that of futures, the technique used in actor languages and Butterfly LISP. By linking such identifiers to partial result frames in the original agent, enough information is provided to allow the computation to continue after the partial result has been returned by another agent.

9.7 Object-Oriented PROLOG

By now, you ought to have a pretty good feel for the object-oriented paradigm. It should be clear that it is not just the use of the tools that automatically reaps the advantages such systems can have. As with any programming paradigm, the object-oriented paradigm still assumes a skilled programmer who knows how to apply it intelligently and effectively. Nevertheless, tools are still an important issue. It is difficult to suppress the desire for one programming tool that can do it all, rather than having numerous special-purpose languages. After all, we don't have an assortment of different brains for different tasks we undertake, one has to do it all. So what good are advances in software technology if we will always still need ten different tools for ten different jobs?

If no one programming paradigm is ever the solution, what do we gain by combining more than one paradigm? Currently, two of the most popular programming paradigms are object-oriented programming and logic programming à la PROLOG. In many ways they are very different approaches to how a computer can be programmed. On a number of counts, logic programming is a much more radical gambit than object-oriented systems. It takes the paradigm of formal logic and builds an entire programming language on it. For PROLOG, the first-order predicate calculus is not an interesting application, it is programming. Next to this, object-oriented systems seem very neutral in comparison. But they appear to be going in opposite directions, too, because one of the implicit goals of logic programming is to have a completely unified system so that at any given time, all the implications of known facts relevant to a specified goal can be deduced automatically. On the face of it, this seems completely at odds with the encapsulation of everything within distinct objects.

9.8 PROLOG/V

At first look it might seem that object-oriented and logic paradigms are so opposite in conception that any attempt to unite them might be futile. But we already know different. There have already been a number of different rather successful attempts at doing it. The one that we are going to talk about here is the implementation of PROLOG inside of Smalltalk/V that was accomplished by Digitalk and provided to all purchasers of this system. As it is, it is not an optimized PROLOG, but it is a surprisingly complete implementation of the language and contains enough to show us the pros and cons of this approach to combining the logic and object-oriented paradigms.

How does PROLOG live inside of Smalltalk? The same way that anything does—as a class. And because of this, the Smalltalk class hierarchy and browser turn out to be very suitable tools for organizing PROLOG programs. Applications in PROLOG are implemented as subclasses of the PROLOG class. Each instance of a PROLOG subclass is a complete version of PROLOG that can have as many instances as memory permits. The subclasses may be used either for holding separate fact bases or for different extensions to PROLOG. Naturally, those subclasses used for fact bases inherit all the PROLOG predicates. When you look at them in a browser, the names of all the predicates used in the fact base are listed alphabetically in the method pane. When selected, all the entries for that predicate are displayed in the lower text pane. As you can see, the Smalltalk class hierarchy and the browser provide an excellent platform for modularizing PROLOG and for easily keeping track of and accessing parts of programs. The browser actually used to enter PROLOG programs is a special version of the Class Hierarchy browser called a Logic Browser.

PROLOG/V uses the association class to handle arguments. As seen by Smalltalk, every PROLOG predicate has just one argument, even though to PROLOG they can have more. But this single argument is an object that is an instance of the Association class. This class simply provides a structure for associating pairs of keys and values. Association objects are mainly used with Dictionaries, which are collections of such Associations. In this case, the key of the Associations used to handle PROLOG arguments contains a List of the arguments that will have to be unified with each clause in the predicate's definition. The value slot of the Associations actually contains blocks of code called *continuation blocks*, which are evaluated when predicates succeed. One important advantage of an embedded PROLOG like this one is that a far greater variety of objects can be incorporated in the PROLOG scheme than in standard PROLOG. Here, the unification of variables can occur in principle for any of the kinds of objects Smalltalk knows about.

How do you go about implementing PROLOG in an object-oriented language? The obvious answer is to use as many of the existing classes and methods as possible, implement the additional ones needed, and then package the whole thing in some identifiable main classes that access the rest. The Logic class has the instance Variables: answer, varList, unboundVar, and tempResult. The class variables are Database and BinaryOp. The methods for the Logic class include `allValue`, `inferAnswer`, and `buildQuery:`. The `allValue` method interacts with objects in the LogicRef class and takes the argument aLogicRef which stands for the name of any instance of a member of that class. Its job is to copy values to instances of the classes specified by the content of aLogicRef. For example, if aLogicRef's content is a List, `allValue` walks through all the elements of it. The `allValue` method is used to implement the `inferAnswer` method of the Logic class and the `arg:`, `asserta:`, `assertz:`, `univ:`, and `write:` predicates in the PROLOG class.

These are standard predicates in nearly all implementations of PROLOG. The `inferAnswer` message is a private method that adds an array of values to the answer collection. It, in turn, is used to implement the `buildQuery:` method of the Logic class. And so it goes. It would be out of place to go into all of the details of the implementation here, but this should give you the flavor of it.

9.9 Using PROLOG/V

Currently PROLOG/V is not documented in the main Digitalk manual, and there is no separate pamphlet for it as with their "goodies" pack. There is just one very brief disk file to get an interested programmer going. Much of what you need to know is there, but there are some things that aren't made very clear. One thing is that the Logic Browser is not just a special convenience for developing PROLOG/V applications. It's the only way you can enter your PROLOG programs into the system with an editor. The regular Class Hierarchy Browser shows you all the PROLOG code, but it won't accept the PROLOG syntax.

Other than the difference of using the Logic Browser, the mechanics of writing programs with PROLOG/V are about the same as with Smalltalk. Where you would ordinarily choose the add method option to enter a Smalltalk method, you do the same, but in this case for the purpose of entering PROLOG predicates. When you enter a query, you highlight the text as usual, but always choose the showIt option to be able to see the result. In PROLOG, this is always something you need to see.

There are some minor differences in syntax between PROLOG/V and that of customary PROLOGs. First, there are no special operators at all, so that all legal clauses have to adhere to the same format as PROLOG predicates, the name of a predicate followed by terms of the clause enclosed in parentheses. A second difference is with variables. In PROLOG/V variables begin with a lowercase character, and constants do, too, but are always written with a leading pound (#) character. Another important difference is that queries are made by first creating a PROLOG class (if one doesn't already exist) and sending the `:?` message to it, followed by a normal PROLOG query. Table 9.2 gives a simple example of predicates and queries written with the two different forms of syntax.

Two of the most important predicates in PROLOG/V are the `is` and `consult` predicates. Generally speaking, `consult` provides access to other PROLOG/V classes and objects, and `is` provides access to the Smalltalk/V environment. In other words,

Table 9.2 Prolog/V Syntax Compared to Standard Prolog

PROLOG/V	*Standard PROLOG*
`mortal(x) :- man(x)`	`mortal(X) :- man(X).`
`man(#socrates).`	`man(socrates).`
`Prolog new :? mortal(#socrates)`	`?- mortal(socrates).`

PROLOG/V is completely open-ended. You can call any Smalltalk/V methods or PROLOG/V predicates in the system from any instantiation or subclass of PROLOG. This is one of the greatest single advantages of an embedded PROLOG in an object-oriented system. The PROLOG object or objects exist just like any other object in the system and can exchange messages with them. In short, you don't lose anything in the implementation language by entering the PROLOG world. In contrast, if you run a PROLOG that has been written in a language like C, you have entered a very specific world, where none of the capabilities of C is available except those that may have been built into the PROLOG (which typically would not be very much).

One of the things that has held back standard PROLOG from realizing what everyone thought was its real potential is its general lack of a real visual programming environment. An environment like PROLOG/V takes window-oriented editing a step further by providing an easily accessible browser that divides programs up into very convenient chunks. There have been windowed "predicate-oriented" editors for PROLOG, but for one reason or another they were far less convenient than the browser approach.

The current implementation of PROLOG/V makes no pretense at being an optimized PROLOG. A medium-sized program probably will soon show up the performance limitations of PROLOG/V. But this does not detract from its value as a demonstration of a working PROLOG in an object-oriented world. Nor is its role as a simple research tool affected. It also has definite value for quick prototyping. I was successful in my attempt at debugging a reasonably sized program in PROLOG/V and then exporting it to a conventional PROLOG where it could profit from the greater execution speed. Listing 9.3 shows the code I used.

Strictly from the point of view of quick prototyping, PROLOG generally and PROLOG/V specifically offer some undeniable advantages. One of the main ones is the ease with which you can define new data structures that can often combine very unusual components. For example, in standard object-oriented systems, if you need a data structure where you can look up items either by a key or a value, you usually use something like a keyed collection or a dictionary object. This means that you have a key that is a named symbol and a value. At best, you can call up the value with the key or

Listing 9.3 PROLOG/V Factorial Program

```
ifact(num,result) :- ifact(0,num,1,result).
ifact(index,num,times,result) :-
    lt(index,num),
    is(index1, index value + 1),
    is(times1, times value * index1),
    ifact(index1,num,times1,result).
ifact(num,num,result,result).
```

reverse this and call up the key with the value. PROLOG is way ahead of this in a number of respects.

Let's take an example by developing a predicate in PROLOG/V called `recipe`. The general format for this predicate is:

```
recipe(number, name, style, meal, mainIngredient,servings,
[part(ingredient,quantity)|rest2],preparation[first|rest2).
```

The important thing to notice here is the flexibility of the data structure itself and the ways that it can be accessed. This data structure includes two open-ended list structures within it that are each connected in a different way with a different nested database predicate. The `part` predicate has three terms, ingredient, units, and quantity, and is embedded in an open-ended list that can contain as many entries of this 'part' predicate as needed. For example, here is a possible entry in that database:

```
recipe(1,#pancakes,#american,#breakfast,#wheatflour,2,
[part(#milk,#cups,4),part(#eggs,#each,4),part(#flour,#cups,3),
part(#bakingPowder,#teasp,.5)],preparation(['Beategg
whites','Blend in remainder','Cook on hot, greased frying
pan'])).
```

It may be difficult to read in this form, but can be entered into PROLOG/V as is and allows the kind of flexibility that recipes and many other things in the real world need. Most of the time, we deal with situations where the things involved do not fall into the nice neat format of a set number of fields in a database. You never know how many ingredients and preparation steps there are going to be in a given recipe. PROLOG does not care. By using its built-in list structures in the way we've illustrated here you have a ready-made database format that handles the need for the most flexible data structures.

This is all fine, but we know that simple PROLOG is not the great "wondertool" we seek. It has limitations, to be sure. What are they? Well, in most PROLOGs you have very limited I/O and you are more or less bound to the PROLOG way of handling things. That is what makes a PROLOG embedded in an object-oriented system such an attractive idea. As we've mentioned, in a system like PROLOG/V, the PROLOG exists as one or more objects among other objects. First of all, this means that you can easily call PROLOG as a kind of subroutine by sending a PROLOG subclass a query message from any other Smalltalk object. For example, you could write a main program in Smalltalk that includes a windowed user interface that just uses PROLOG/V for an unusual sort of open-ended database, as we've suggested.

In working with PROLOG/V, we decided to extend its list processing capability as a quick way to bring some high-level AI into the Smalltalk/V environment by creating a direct subclass of PROLOG called ProList. This class incorporated what amounts to a kind of toolbox for list processing in PROLOG. Some representative predicates are included in Listing 9.4. The idea is that for an application where a lot of list processing is needed, you would make your application as one or more subclasses of the ProList class.

There is a little more to list processing in PROLOG than you might think at first. One of the things that makes for special treatment is that variable bindings and structures created during the execution of a PROLOG query no longer exist when a system exits from responding to the query. What this means is that the list processing predicates work by returning a list of elements as the value of a variable. For example, if I make the query in PROLOG/V:

```
ProList new :? append([1,2],[3,4],x)
```

I would get the reply

```
(([1,2,3,4]))
```

However, immediately after the reply, *x* is no longer bound to this list. PROLOG doesn't save it anywhere and I am free to use the *x* variable in another query right away if I wish. Also, it is not very useful to have to supply the lists explicitly each time as in the preceding example. But since the *x* is no longer bound to the list, I also cannot just reference it or other variable names like it. The way these list processing predicates are used is by accessing database predicates that contain lists like our `recipe` predicate. For example, if there are the database entries:

```
weekdays(['monday','tuesday','wednesday','thursday','friday']).
weekenddays(['saturday','sunday']).
```

then the following query could be made:

```
ProList new :? weekdays(list1),weekenddays(list2),
        append(list1,list2,list3).
```

In "standard" PROLOG, you would be able to make a query like:

```
weekdays(List1),weekenddays(List2),
  append(List1,List2,List3),
  assertz(fullweek(List3)).
```

Listing 9.4 List Processing Predicates in PROLOG/V

```
"Joins two lists together into a larger list"

append([],list1,list1).
append([first|rest1],list, [first|rest2]) :-
    append(rest1,list,rest2).

member(exp,[exp|_]).
member(exp,[_|list]) :-
    member(exp,list).

forall(exp1,exp2) :-
    not((exp1,not(exp2))).

"Returns the first element of a list"
first([head|_],head).

rest([_|exp],exp).

list(exp,[exp]).

listp([]).
listp([_|list]) :- listp(list).

last([exp1],exp1).
last([_|exp1],exp2) :-
  last(exp1,exp2).

delete(_,[],[]):-  .
delete(exp1,[exp1|list],list1):-  ,
 delete(exp1,list,list1).
delete(exp1,[exp2|list],[exp2|list1]):-
 delete(exp1,list,list1).

length([],0).
length([_|rest],num) :-
    length(rest,num2),
     is(num, num2 value + 1).

nextto(exp1,exp2,[exp1,exp2|_]).
nextto(exp1,exp2,[_|rest]):-
 nextto(exp1,exp2,rest).
```

and the result of the list appending would be preserved by asserting it into the database as the contents of the fullweek predicate. However, if you try this use of assertz with PROLOG/V, you get an error message.

The syntax for the consult predicate is rather unusual. It really has nothing to do with the usual consult predicate in PROLOG, which is for reading in disk files of PROLOG source code. The exclusive purpose of consult in PROLOG/V is for communicating with other PROLOG objects. It might seem that it only makes sense to consult an object that has some database predicates in it, but this does not turn out to be true. You can use the consult predicate for accessing predicates you need in the class consulted. This means, for example, that a PROLOG object does not have to be a subclass of the ProList class to make use of the methods there. The message can be sent:

```
Prolog new :? consult(append([1,2],[3],x), ProList new)
```

and the answer will be given just as if the object itself had the append predicate.

9.10 Concurrent PROLOG

Concurrent PROLOG (CP) supports the syntax of standard PROLOG but extends it in various ways such as with the commit operator and the read-only variable construction. Although the syntax is very similar, there are substantial differences between the way CP and conventional PROLOG work. The most important difference is that CP cannot backtrack and find all solutions for a given goal.

Two distinct types of parallelism come into paly in CP: or-parallelism and and-parallelism. With *or-parallelism*, the search for a clause that unifies or commits is conducted in parallel, but as soon as a clause is found, the processing of all other clauses ceases. With *and-parallelism*, various clauses that make up a given predicate can also be evaluated in parallel. It is called and-parallelism because the clauses that define the conditions of a predicate are and-ed together.

The basic structure of clauses in CP extends conventional PROLOG by the addition of an optional leading section on the right-hand side that contains guarded clauses. The guarded clauses are separated from ordinary clauses by the commit operator (|). The general form of a clause in CP, therefore, is:

```
C :- G1 ... Gm | E1 ... En.
```

where the *G*'s represent a sequence of guarded clauses, and the *E*'s constitute ordinary PROLOG clauses. The commit operator (|) replaces a coma separator. If there are no guarded clauses, the main clause reduces to an ordinary PROLOG clause and the commit operator is omitted. If there are no ordinary clauses (*E*'s), the term "true" follows the commit operator.

The other main innovation in CP is the introduction of read-only variables. A read-only variable is designated in CP by inserting a question mark (?) immediately after the variable's name with no space separation. The result of making a read-only occurrence of a variable in a clause is to say, in effect, "don't attempt to find a value for this variable or use it until some other process gives it a value." The main purpose for which read-only variables are intended in CP is for controlling unification through goal reduction synchronization. The best way to explain this is by way of an example.

As an example of programming in CP, here is an implementation of the Eratosthenes's

Sieve that illustrates both the use of guarded clauses and read-only variables:

```
primes(Ps) :-
     integers(2,Ints), sift(Ints?,Ps).

sift([Prime|Ints],[Prime|Ps]) :-
     sift(Ints1?,N,Ps),filter(Ints?,Prime,Ints1).

filter([Int|Ints],Prime,Ints1) :-
     mod(Int,Prime,0) |
     filter(Ints?,Prime,Ints1).

filter([Int|Ints],Prime,[Int|Ints1]) :-
     otherwise |
     filter(Ints?,Prime,Ints1).
filter([],Prime,[]).

integers(Int,[Int|Ints]) :-
 Int1 is Int + 1 | integer(Int1,Ints).
```

In this implementation of the prime number algorithm, two concurrent processes are initiated, the integer process and the sift process. The integer process gathers a stream of integers starting with the number 2 and passes them to the sift process, operating concurrently. The sift process in turn spawns a filter process with a local state for each of the integers supplied by the sift. The sift process then recursively uses the first number of the filter stream to spawn new filter processes, and so on. Since no upper limit is specified for the stream of prime numbers, this program is an example of a perpetual process.

Understanding how objects work in CP involves some grasp of what are called *communication channels*. The claim has been made that CP succeeds in implementing objects according to Hewitt's actor model. Unlike objects in most other systems like Smalltalk, LOOPS, and Flavors, CP does not implement its objects in terms of call/return message passing. This is just one particular type of message passing in CP, which has a very general abstraction model for message passing that supports various different types.

In addition to the generalized model of message passing, objects in CP also have various properties not found in any other object-oriented system. One of the most important of these is that processes and streams in CP are entirely free of side effects. A stream of messages may also be shared by several objects at once, which allows direct broadcasting of information throughout the system. Perhaps the best way to illustrate the uniqueness of CP among object-oriented systems is to point out that it is only in this system that objects themselves are active. The type of concurrency supported makes it possible for many objects to be actively processing at once. This is also made possible by the use of immutable streams rather than pointers to changeable objects. In CP the message stream in which no side effects are allowed maintains the identity of objects.

9.11 SPOOL

One of the more interesting object-oriented logic programming systems developed to date is the SPOOL language developed at IBM (Japan). The basic philosophy of this system was to provide an object-oriented extension to PROLOG, analogously to the way Flavors was an extension to LISP. Another important consideration in its design was to integrate, as much as possible, the useful features of both logic programming and object-oriented systems. To accomplish this, the developers decided to implement a system in which messages to objects would be logic programs that would invoke goals in receiving objects when such messages are passed. In this way, the developers hoped to create a system in which it is relatively easy to construct objects that have a reasoning capability.

SPOOL was written in VM/Programming in Logic, IBM's implementation of PROLOG. It makes use of some of the best ideas in other object-oriented programming systems such as those used in Smalltalk and Flavors. For example, SPOOL supports multiple inheritance in a manner similar to the Flavors mixin feature.

One very important feature of SPOOL is that it allows either a message or the recipient of a message to be an unbound variable, which makes the technique of anonymous message passing possible. Ordinarily, the specific object to which a simple message is passed, as well as the specific message itself, have to be fully specified in an object-oriented system. Allowing these to be unspecified in the form of unbound variables opens up new and powerful ways that object-oriented programming can be used, where general message-passing algorithms can be devised that do not require that it be known at programming time what object will receive a message or even what message will be sent.

Here is the implementation in SPOOL of one of the standard examples we have been using to illustrate multiple inheritance.

```
class business has
 superclass root-class;
 instance-var name location industry business-type size
year-founded ownership-type gross-sales costs market-share;

methods
  calc-net-gain(Gross-sales,Costs,Net-gain) :-
  Net-gain is Gross-sales - Costs.

class adversary has
 superclass root-class;
 instance-var aggressiveness allies goals common-goals strengths
weaknesses;

class competitor has
    superclass business adversary;
```

9.12 Vulcan

Vulcan is an object-oriented logic programming facility developed at Xerox PARC. It is intended as a preprocessor or "syntactic sugaring" for Concurrent PROLOG (CP) aimed at removing some of its verbosity. Programmers work with the more concise Vulcan syntax and the resulting code is translated into a CP program. Vulcan is made up of various high-level predicates for the development of object-oriented logic programs. For example, the message-sending protocol in Vulcan is provided by the `send` predicate. Its syntax is quite simply:

```
send(Receiver, Message).
```

The pseudo-variable Self is used as in Smalltalk and other object-oriented systems to represent the receiver of the message. Messages are defined in Vulcan using the `method` predicate, with the following syntax:

```
method(Variable1,predicate(Variable2,Variable3) :-
            clause-1, ...
            clause-n,
            become(Var2,NewVar2,Var3,NewVar3).
```

The preprocessor is able to detect the instance variables contained in a receiver's class. These variables are unified with the appropriate state variables of an object. Such a Vulcan declaration expands to a corresponding CP expression of the form:

```
variable(predicate(Variable2,Variable3) | NewVariable1 ], :-
    clause-1, ...
    clause-n,
    variable1(NewVariable1?,
            NewVar2?,NewVar3?).
```

The `become` statement changes an object's state. Messages formulated sequentially are considered as being sent to successive states of the receiver object. Any expression that appears after a `become` statement or message is regarded as referring to the receiver's new state. All messages after a "send to Self" message are packaged by Vulcan into a continuation method with the selector pointing at a location on the message stream subsequent to the earlier messages. Here is an example of a simple method written in Vulcan:

```
method(labeledWindow,moveBy(DeltaX,DeltaY)) :-
    send(Self,erase),
    plus(X,DeltaX,NewX),
    plus(Y,DeltaY,NewY),
```

```
become((X,NewX),(Y,NewY)),
send(Self,show).
```

This expands to the following CP code:

```
labeledWindow([moveBy(DeltaX,DeltaY)
                      | NewlabeledWindow],
       X,Y,Width,Height,Contents,Label) :-
labeledWindow([erase,
       privatemoveBy(DeltaX,DeltaY),
       show | newlabeledWindow?],
    NewX?,NewY?,Width,Height,Contents,Label).
```

As mentioned earlier, CP differs from most other object-oriented systems in that it does not have pointers to objects. Objects in CP, and therefore also in Vulcan, retain their identity solely through the integrity and continuity of the message stream. This means that two different processes can only send messages to the same object by merging their message streams into a single stream received by the object. This involves what is called *splitting the message stream* to the object. This must be done explicitly by programmers in CP.

Inheritance

As we also mentioned earlier, CP does not have any explicit, built-in mechanism for class inheritance. Vulcan provides two methods for implementing inheritance. The first is the description copying mechanism involved in producing subclasses. The second method is inheritance by the delegation to parts. When subclasses are declared in Vulcan, the superclass is declared as the third argument. This allows the subclass to be created with source copies of all the methods and variables of its superclasses. If the superclasses field is filled by more than one class, a multiple inheritance is adopted.

Inheritance by delegation to parts was the inheritance mechanism originally introduced by Shapiro and Takeuchi for CP. This means that a subclass contains the contents of its superclass as parts, rather than because it is that kind of object. The class DeskChair then would process inherited messages from the class Furniture by delegating it to the part of itself that corresponds to Furniture. The main weakness of inheritance by delegation to parts is that it makes it difficult to treat objects as true composites that have parts that are objects. A serious object-oriented system for AI should offer both inheritance and composite objects. Where there is a feature for the global naming of processes, such as that provided in the Logix extension to CP, Vulcan can also incorporate the metaobject protocol into CP. This is the approach used in Smalltalk and CommonLoops whereby classes are themselves treated as objects that are instances of classes. One weakness of the Vulcan system is that it is not possible to unify Vulcan objects the way PROLOG variables are unified. This is due to the nature of the underlying unification mechanism in PROLOG.

Since the resulting expansion of Vulcan code can be read as a description of "the permissible history of an object's behavior," and in this respect it resembles the semantics of the Actor programming paradigm, interesting lines of exploration for Vulcan are suggested. One interesting question to raise in this context is what are the potential parallel hardware environments that could support a language like Vulcan. According to researchers at Xerox PARC, it seems plausible that flat Concurrent PROLOG (FCP) is a suitable system for running on a fine-grained SIMD machine such as the Connection Machine manufactured by Thinking Machines. (A SIMD machine is one that runs a single instruction stream on multiple data streams.) For this reason, research has been initiated there to develop Vulcan programs that embody the appropriate style for execution on such machines.

9.13 Message Management: The Key to Concurrent Message Passing

Assuming that hardware support for complex, concurrent message passing has been made as efficient as is appropriate with available resources, the issue of obtaining efficient message passing in real systems is by no means settled. In any real-world setting, it is very easy for situations to arise where the message-passing system at the software level can be the crucial factor that determines how various applications will perform. From the discussion of actors in Section 9.1, it can be rather easily concluded that one of the major bottlenecks for such concurrent message-passing systems lies in the area of the mail and message queues. The very concept of a passive queue is a throwback to earlier computational models. A very reasonable expectation would be that one of the first areas in which the active data model of concurrent computation should be able to prove itself is the area of efficient message management. One thing at least seems clear: if at all possible, putting messages on hold in a queue whose acceptability by their intended receiver is still to be determined should be avoided.

This brings up three important and related issues. First, shouldn't message checking and message execution be divided into two entirely different operations carried out even by separate objects? One possible approach would be to have Checkers that determine whether a message is acceptable before it is placed in a queue, for example. Second, if all data structures are active, how may the active potential of the message queues themselves be used to optimize message-passing efficiency? One approach that suggests itself here would be to have the items in queues actively solicit substitute receivers. Third, what sort of object should the message queue be associated with? If it is already known that the intended receiver is busy, it is not clear what advantage there would be in having a queue associated with just that receiver or even its replacement.

A better approach might be to associate the message queue with the class of all objects eligible to receive them, once this has been checked. Then, demons associated with each class could immediately find receivers for each of the messages rather than making them wait, or the queue itself could assign its messages to eligible instances of the class. If this approach were adopted, it would seem to be sensible to have "reinforcement" or backup objects already instantiated whenever possible, rather than waiting until message acceptance spawns a replacement. The task of maintaining a certain level of "reserves" could be given to a concurrently operating node manager, for example.

Although the validity of the ideas introduced here will only be able to prove themselves in practice, this discussion should make clear that the issue of message management is an extremely important one that is still far from being completely settled. In order for message-passing to be made efficient, the concept of active data will have to be taken to its logical conclusion to include even the way pending messages are buffered.

Inheritance Issues

Inheritance schemes in parallel environments face a number of problems. One is the difficulty of maintaining them in a system that is intended to be fault-tolerant. If a system loses some of its resources, the superclasses from which the subclasses seek to inherit may disappear or become disabled. Another problem is simply keeping track of just where all the parents are. In a distributed system, it is possible that various classes may be spread out widely over the system. The most challenging issues for inheritance in such environments are related mainly to late binding or execution-time inheritance systems. And the most pressing situation is where the structure of objects changes dynamically.

In an interpreted environment, in addition to the usual problems of synchronization, parallel systems are also faced with the problem of changing interpretation contexts. In a dynamically changing system, side effects to the binding environment and changes to objects themselves can make the results of interpretation hard to predict in some circumstances. Still another problem with inheritance systems in parallel environments is that they make programs much more difficult to verify. This may be a problem that current AI programs will have to live with until more complete environments are created that can deal with the verification issues.

9.14 Cooperating Systems

One of the most challenging general problems in AI is the development of schemes for allowing independent application modules to cooperate in solving particular problems. The following types of cooperation between computational modules can be distinguished: by *supervision*, by *request*, by *result sharing*, by *negotiation*, by *communication*, by *assumption*, and by *planning and plan revision*. In the following paragraphs we will discuss a few of the more important types for our purposes here.

Considerable research is currently being expended to perfect ways in which large AI applications can be built consisting of various problem-solving modules, each of which can interact with the others and contribute to the solution of a problem. The object-oriented paradigm is particularly well suited for the design and implementation of these types of architecture. In a certain sense, all complex object-oriented systems represent a form of cooperation between separate functioning modules. They can do so for the simple reason that they are specifically designed for this purpose. However, this form of cooperation is not exactly the type that is needed for the advanced AI applications. What is lacking primarily is additional flexibility. The additional flexibility needed would involve the ability for different modules to cooperate in ways that are not completely hard-wired. Just exactly how such systems would cooperate is not entirely evident, however. Let's look at some of the alternatives.

One possibility would be to have all the main modules or "agents" of large applications capable of cooperating with one another, if necessary. This would be one of the more extreme departures from the standard type of hard-wired object system. What would be required for this type of system to work? Let's take a simple case involving just two modules, which we'll call Agent-1 and Agent-2. The very meaning of cooperation is that something is required of each of the agents. Exactly what this must be depends on a number of factors. First, how is the cooperation between the agents initiated? There are two main alternatives here:

1. Cooperation begins when one agent makes a request of the other.

2. Cooperation is an essential feature of the way these objects operate and does not need to be initiated.

Let's take the second possibility first.

This may appear to be just the usual kind of hard-wired multiple-module object-oriented system, but there is actually quite a big difference between the two types of systems. The behavior of the types of agents being considered here is such that cooperation does not need to be initiated by one of the cooperating agents, and yet not all of their interaction is hard-wired. The agents are designed to be cooperating on whatever problem is being solved, and they are each updated on the progress of the problem. Depending on the state of the current problem-solving session, each of the agents knows when it has to act and what it has to do. However this still leaves a considerable amount of the type of behavior undetermined. Exactly what this is and how it is accomplished depends on the type of application domain.

The main difference between application types is between those that require planning and those that do not. Those that require planning need special coordination between agents that usually depends on what the plan is. A particular example would be helpful. Let's say that the application is for a robot to paint a wall, and, to keep things simple, just five agents are involved: Plan-Monitor, Left-Leg, Right-Leg, Left-Hand, and Right-Hand. One basic routine is possible for painting most of the wall, which proceeds from the right side to the left. The manipulator of Left-Arm holds the paint bucket and the manipulator of Right-Arm holds the brush and does the painting. After each wall-length stroke, the right manipulator dips the brush in the bucket and one of the legs takes a step left, alternating with each paint stroke. However, at the end, a special procedure is necessary for allowing the upper-left corner to be reached. The robot puts down the paint bucket, switches the brush from the right to the left manipulator, and picks up the paint bucket with the right manipulator. The robot then paints the remaining portion of the wall.

For our purposes here, assume that this application uses a standard plan for painting a wall that is taken from a library of routine plans. The only additional planning that needs to be done is the number of brush strokes, the length of each stroke, and the point at which the switch is to be made. The Plan-Monitor can perform these calculations and send the results to each of the other agents. The basic painting routine is done by each of the agents acting "on cue." This means that they do not have to communicate in order to cooperate. The Plan-Monitor sends a message to each of the agents telling them when their next action is to be done.

We've only considered what happens when everything goes as it's supposed to, but already some things are clear. The Plan-Monitor acts as a special type of agent, called a supervisory agent, that is different from any of the others. The supervisory agent is the key to cooperation in this type of architecture. The other agents need to know only enough to do what is expected when they receive messages from the supervisory agent. The supervisor itself must know quite a bit more. Not only must it know all the other agents, it must know what to send them, and when. But that is all. Technically, in this example, the supervisory agent can do this "blindly" in the sense that it does not need to know *why* it is telling the other agents what it is telling them. In all cases these agents are acting out a script, but the script of the supervisor is more difficult than that of the other agents in that it must be its own scheduler. The acts of this scheduler can act on cues just like the other agents. However, in this case, the cues of the supervisor are based on the results given by sensors rather than on messages from another agent.

The wall painting example features a fixed group supervisor and a fixed script task with a minor variation. Also, it is assumed that the supervisor works from a script that it receives at runtime from the routine plan library just as the specialist agents do. More flexible cooperation involves introducing greater variety in these features. The task of sweeping a floor, gathering the sweepings into a dustpan, and emptying its contents into a garbage can is obviously more complex than painting a wall. The pure sweeping part can be considered as roughly the same as painting the wall. However, manipulating the sweepings into the dustpan is of a completely different degree of difficulty. Here accuracy in both the direction and force of the sweeping as well as the placement of the dustpan is required.

This means that real-time monitoring of the effectiveness of the process is called for. The supervisor must be a far more capable agent here. A simple script to be followed blindly will not suffice. The supervisor agent has to be able to evaluate the execution of the task and decide what modifications, if any, are needed. Also, the other agents have to be able to respond to more sophisticated commands. They can no longer just follow a script with the timing conducted by the supervisor. They must understand a task-level language that makes commands like "Tilt the dustpan X degrees toward the floor," and so on.

The problem is of sufficiently increased difficulty to require an additional level of supervision. One supervisor does the monitoring and sends its corrections to the lower supervisor agent in the higher task-level language. This supervisor then translates the task into the constituent subtasks for the arm and leg agents. The lower supervisor uses two different languages: it receives messages in one language and sends them in another. Moreover it has to translate one higher level message into several lower level messages and know the right agent to which it will send each of these messages.

Cooperation by supervision can also be useful in highly complex systems that need to cooperate on solving a problem, as opposed to performing a task. This can be done, for example, where an architecture has been designed such as that of DIPOLE (discussed later in Section 9.18), where different types of systems are capable of solving the same problem. In this case, a Monitor uses metalevel knowledge, that is, knowledge about the problem-solvers themselves, to decide about their progress in solving a problem.

In many real-time systems, feedback monitoring is insufficient for adaptive control because it is much too slow in relation to the processes involved. Feedback must be combined with a rapid feed-forward mechanism. A simple example of this is the necessity for "leading" a moving target, such as when a quarterback throws a football. Feedback only tells you where the target is and where your pass has gone. That's obviously too late to make adjustments or allowances. Leading the receiver is a type of feed-forward where feedback on the location of the receiver is used to make a quick predication of where the receiver will be when your pass arrives. You then aim for this place rather than where the receiver is now. This works because the quarterback has intimate knowledge of the time it takes for his passes to go a given distance when thrown with a particular amount of force. In real-time problem-solving systems, the same type of thing is often necessary. The feedback from monitors is used to drive a look-ahead capability that can be used to anticipate where, in time and space, known processes will intersect with target events.

Cooperation by Result Sharing

The most common type of architecture that allows separate autonomous knowledge processing modules to share results is the Blackboard in its various forms. There are even systems such as the one at the University of Massachusetts where multiple blackboards cooperate in solving the same problem through the additional assistance of communicating results and hypotheses. In this case, two types of cooperation are occurring on two different levels. At the level of the individual blackboard, knowledge sources are cooperating by posting their results in shared memory areas. At the highest level, the blackboards themselves are cooperating by passing the best results back and forth for incremental refinement.

Cooperating Production Systems

One area that is particularly suited for the object-oriented approach is the implementation of production systems that are designed to cooperate in general ways. With the object-oriented approach, it is not necessary for the inference engine to "chain" from one knowledge base to another. Multiple instances of the inference engine can be present, already loaded with different knowledge bases, or they can be instantiated on demand as required.

Cooperation by Planning and Plan Revision

One of the more advanced types of cooperation in complex systems is the ability to capitalize on various synergies and serendipities of time scheduling. This means, for example, that if Agent A is going to Room 4 to fetch part P435, and Agent B will be passing by near that room on its way back to the assembly floor "empty-handed," Agent A can pass the part to Agent B and go on to another task. Usually this type of opportunistic cooperation has to be planned by a sophisticated agent that has an overview of the scheduling of all agents.

9.15 Hybrid AI Architectures for Real-Time Processing

One extremely important example of a cooperative system is the use of hybrid architectures for real-time AI applications. This means using more than one AI paradigm and providing some means for the various modules to cooperate with one another to solve problems. We will give two examples of such architectures: one in which two different types of reasoning systems cooperate and another in which a neural network and a production system work together.

Time-critical applications present a unique challenge in AI. The central problem of an intelligent application that must perform some function in "real time" such as in some type of emergency is that it must reason in some way about time resources, a particularly time-consuming type of processing! But this is just the tip of the iceberg of what makes real-time AI uniquely different and difficult. In a survey, Thomas J. Laffey and other researchers at the Lockheed Artificial Intelligence Center enumerated no fewer than ten factors that differentiate real-time AI applications:

1. Nonmonotonicity

2. Continuous operation

3. Asynchronous events

4. Interface to external environment

5. Uncertain or missing data

6. High performance

7. Temporal reasoning

8. Focus of attention

9. Guaranteed response times

10. Integration with procedural components

Nonmonotonicity refers to the fact that the world of data in a real-time AI application is not static in three distinct ways: new information may be added as processing proceeds, some facts may be retracted, and other facts vary continuously. In addition, the reliability and completeness of incoming information can vary with time. "Temporal reasoning" includes not only the ability to reason about time resources, but it may also encompass the reasoning about past, present, and future events as such. New developments can vary enormously in their importance and their urgency. In some cases, the system must not only be able to respond when the response is needed, but it must also be able to determine when the response is needed. Furthermore, it is often desirable that the best possible response be made within a given deadline.

9.16 Progressive Deepening and Progressive Reasoning

With these kinds of challenges, it is understandable that AI researchers have been prompted to propose special techniques to solve them. Patrick Winston of MIT has proposed the technique of progressive deepening to address the time constraints issue. The idea here is that the system sets itself progressively deeper search depths, beginning with the most trivial and solving the problem at successively greater depths. The advantage of this approach is that regardless of when the time runs out, the system will be ready with at least some response, namely, the result of the last complete processing at a depth one level less than the level the process was at when it was interrupted. Two disadvantages of progressive deepening are as follows:

1. This approach works only for problems that can be described in terms of search.

2. The quality of the response is not guaranteed, only that some response will be made.

The most serious objection to simple progressive deepening is that it is a blind lock-step algorithm with no flexibility or ability to adjust to radically altered situations. It proceeds with one approach from start to finish regardless of what happens along the way.

An analogous approach developed by Wright and others, called progressive reasoning, uses progressively more time-consuming types of reasoning rather than greater search depths. This eliminates some of the objections to progressive deepening, but not all of them. Progressive reasoning still has the same inflexibility and inability to evaluate the quality of its response. It has an essentially inflexible algorithm to handle the quality of its response. This assumes that what determines the quality of the response is somehow linear and static. However, as we have seen, it is precisely the nature of real-time problems that contradicts such assumptions.

9.17 Censored Rules and Variable Precision Logic

Another special approach to real-time problems that has been developed falls under the general rubric of *variable precision logic (VPL)*. The purpose of this approach is to deal with the issues of incomplete information and reasoning under resource constraints such as that of time. Winston and Michalski have developed a strategy for VPL centered around a construction called *censored production rules*. An expanded rule format is used under unconstrained situations: "If A, then B unless C." In this rule syntax, the point is to capture the type of situation where "If A, then B" usually holds, but there are some rare, exceptional situations, such as C, where the rule fails to hold. A famous example, provided by John McCarthy, is:

```
If X is a bird
Then X can fly
Unless X is a Penguin
Or     X is hurt
Or ... etc.
```

Obviously it takes much more processing time to handle the exception conditions. The idea here is to have a variable logic that can dispense with handling the exception conditions when time or other processing resources are scarce. The more general idea is to have a system for progressively relieving logical constraints as time constraints become more severe. A difficulty besets this system similar to progressive X algorithms systems. It is too mechanical. This is really just a blind feedback mechanism that one hard-wires between the two factors of "urgency" and "logical rigor." Certainly a useful idea, but still not sufficient to meet the challenges of intelligent real-time applications.

Laffey and his co-authors also point to some serious difficulties with the current state of AI in coming to terms with the challenges of real-time AI applications. They cite the research of O'Reilly and Cromarty, who claim to have proven that forward-chaining inference has an exponential time increase. That is to say, as the depth of the inference tree increases, the number of rules firing increases exponentially. They also argue that in the case of backward chaining, each increment in the depth of the inference tree leads to an exponential increase in the total number of tree nodes and a combinatorial increase in the number of search paths. This leads Laffey and his co-authors to the conclusion that new types of inference engines have to be developed to meet the rigors of real-time problems.

Their conclusion is an extreme one, but fortunately there is another alternative: that of multiple cooperating inference engines. O'Reilly and Cromarty model inference trees and problem spaces as abstract and homogeneous, and they tacitly assume the inference process to be uninterruptible. However, the whole concept of cooperative problem solving by a multiprocessing architecture denies these assumptions.

9.18 DIPOLE

One observation of human behavior is the way that entirely different types of functioning often cooperate with split-second timing to perform life-critical tasks. Take the example of driving a car and avoiding a possible very serious accident. You are driving on a busy freeway, another car swerves out of control directly in front of you, and you have to act to avoid a collision with it. In this situation, most people would respond with a reflex to react as quickly as possible. The very nature of a reflex is to allow you to act without thinking about it because there is no time to think. You react as best you can, and if the action succeeds, and you are still alive, reflection returns to evaluate what has happened and what to do next. If the car is still in your vicinity, further reflex actions may be needed to continue to avoid it. The important point here is that a critically timed cooperation occurs between two types of processes, each of which is effective under different time constraints.

An Overview of DIPOLE

Inspired by the example of our own cooperative interleaving of "reflexive" and "reflective" processing in dealing with such situations as automotive emergencies, we have undertaken the design of an architecture that employs an analogous strategy. The basic idea is to employ two or more expert systems in parallel, some of which use rapid shallow reasoning and others use slower deep reasoning. Some special features of the inference engines are required, but not an abandonment of current inference engine algorithms.

The basic idea here is to use rapid shallow reasoning as long as it proves effective, but to be able to use slower deep reasoning for short bursts when the rapid shallow engine is falling short of its deadline. This assumes both a means of gauging the progress of the shallow engine and an active monitor to register its results. It also assumes a way of resuming the shallow engine with results obtained by the deep reasoner. Thus, we are clearly dealing with a concurrent message-passing system where the different engines represent some type of "agents" or "actors."

From this general outline, several directions can be taken to flesh out different possibilities that such an architecture can take. The one that we have explored most thoroughly is that in which the rapid shallow-reasoning system is an OPS5 type of forward-chaining system, and the monitor module and deep-reasoning module are object-oriented rule-based systems with forward and backward chaining. The monitor is a special-purpose expert system that receives a trace from the shallow module and builds a model of its performance and a running estimate of its success in meeting its response time and quality. The monitor engages in message passing with the deep module, which is capable of temporal reasoning and a more sophisticated problem solving in the same domain as the shallow module.

As mentioned earlier, the key to this approach is the ability to engage in extensive result sharing between modules and to interrupt and resume the shallow module with the results obtained from the deep module. In the case where the shallow module is an OPS5 type engine, this means modifying its working memory, and possibly even modifying the state of the ruleset being processed at a given time by transferring additional rules, or by some other method.

9.19 The Resonance Machine

The rapidity and apparent ease of human recognition, evidently employing a form of content-addressable memory, suggest that it cannot possibly be based on an exhaustive search or comparison with all previous memories, as many researchers have claimed. There is increasing neurological evidence that neurons and neuron clusters act as transmitters and receivers of sophisticated signals that allow a type of selective response that is closely analogous to the phenomena of resonance and sympathetic vibration in physical acoustics.

One of the strongest arguments against the existence of processes resembling conventional search algorithms in the human brain is the lack of sensitivity of such problem-solving approaches to learning and substantial reorganizations of human memory. Such models have great difficulty explaining how and why the speed of human problem-solving increases rather than decreases with more information added. In principle, this problem disappears when memory is no longer conceived as passive data through which active processes must search, but as active problem-solving nodes that can respond to broadcasts of problem-solving goals.

Similarly, there are some strong arguments against a human cognitive model based exclusively on neural nets. For example, it has been pointed out that many types of neural nets, if subjected to a long enough temporary phase of unusual or irrelevant inputs, can adaptively unlearn the adaptivity they have learned. So, although neural net approaches might in principle avoid the learning hurdle presented by conventional search algorithms, most of the learning rules advocated suffer from the serious flaw that, although they provide a mechanism for learning, they do not have a mechanism for guarding against the subsequent degradation and loss of what has been learned. An important exception to this are the adaptive resonance theory network models advocated by Stephen Grossberg (Grossberg, 1987). However, these models also have their limitations, such as the fact that they are capable of handling only static data. Instead of aiding the degradation problem, including hidden units in conventional neural net models would seem to make it even more severe, since the hidden units are even more subject to modification with new data than are conventional ones.

Another criticism that could be made of the neural network approach, as well as of much of the research conducted in neuropsychology, is that much of this work proceeds as though processing at the neural level goes on relatively autonomously, whereas it appears to be a fact of human psychology that the global world model that each person has and continually updates has a direct influence on activities such as scene interpretation. So, for example, the knowledge that a person has about where his body is situated in a room greatly facilitates and constrains the problem of image interpretation from a given viewpoint.

Still another criticism of neural nets is that they are essentially passive mechanical systems that are highly dependent on what input they receive as well as the order in which they receive it. This contrasts with the neurons of goal-directed living organisms, which are actively seeking out certain "stimuli" as opposed to others.

One final criticism of neural nets is that they operate like "black boxes," limited only to being able to produce certain output patterns without being able to use their "knowledge" in any other manner or to explain their results. It is possible that current directions in neural network research will someday provide a convincing model for the behavior of lower vertebrates. However, currently nothing about the way they are defined at all suggests that they have any specific relation to the way human neural networks operate as opposed to those of lower vertebrates. Clearly, before any claim can be entertained that a neural net model reflects human cognition, some differentiation will have to be made among the operation of neural nets at different levels of the animal kingdom.

We have seen that various schemes have been proposed and implemented for configuring concurrent object-oriented systems based on message passing. However, few of them have been designed with detailed mechanisms for problem solving with this type of paradigm in mind. In this section, such a detailed mechanism will be described that assumes efficient hardware support for asynchronous communication. Such hardware systems are in fact currently under development in various research establishments worldwide.

The problem-solving paradigm advocated here differs from the Actor and Agent models in that it consists of more fine-grained nodes with a highly efficient network for limited broadcast communication. The nodes described are lower level constructs than Actors or Agents, but clusters of nodes can of course be built into such constructs.

A key observation is that an object-oriented concurrent message-passage protocol cannot be designed without knowing the requirements of a problem-solving paradigm for which it is used in considerable detail. In the system so envisioned, a massively parallel network of processors is assumed, each of which is capable of supporting small- to medium-sized clusters of objects, each in turn with its own local data and methods.

One of the main prerequisites of the proposed paradigm is the ability to perform selective broadcast of rather sophisticated messages. It assumes that a certain number of processing nodes can be initially allocated as a Node and Resource Manager. Other major regions of nodes will be allocated as long-term memory and as a temporary working memory area. Finally, if desired, each node can be assigned an object that allows the node to operate as one or more complex, continuously varying units in a neural net.

The message-passing protocol must allow all messages to include references about the node of the message's origin and the node to which answers are to be made. In this way, conventional search can be replaced by selective broadcast to candidate nodes that do their own pattern matching or evaluation locally, with only the successful candidates answering. But rather than replying to the sender, they are assigned other nodes to which they can respond. This same process can be repeated to as many levels as required, creating patterns of cascading messages for subproblem handling. A verifiable algorithm using this paradigm is one whose cascading message patterns can be shown to converge.

The hardware best suited to the type of scheme advocated here would appear to be a "medium-grained" massively parallel architecture, although there do not appear to be any inherent obstacles to its implementation on fine- and coarse-grained machines as well.

One advantage of the model and architecture proposed here is that they can be used for the type of processing found in neural networks as well as for other types of models, and therefore they can serve as an environment for integrating neural nets with other problem-solving paradigms, as appears to occur empirically in human beings.

The way that neural networks can be implemented in this architecture is relatively straightforward. At each of the nodes, if desired, there can be an object that contains a data structure that represents the connections and connection strengths of one or more neural units to other such neural units. The methods local to these objects would implement various ways of receiving inputs and delivering outputs when combined with calculations by other corresponding methods, on the basis of the values in the connection strength matrices. Other methods, when combined, would incorporate learning rules for altering the values of various connection strengths. In this way, a mass effect could be produced analogous to those implemented by cellular automata on the Connection Machine. However, because there can also be other types of objects at the nodes, as well as nodes with entirely different kinds of objects, the architecture makes possible the integration of neural nets with higher level problem-solving systems. In addition, processing nodes can maintain similarity and difference maps between the connection matrices of other nodes with itself. Such data would be useful, for example, in selecting a list of nodes or objects to which to broadcast various types of messages. This could also allow the system to operate as a sophisticated content-addressable memory.

One mechanism for integrating the neural nets with other problem-solving paradigms would be to allow certain units in a neural network subsystem to represent various types of constraints that a system might be under that would strongly determine what the possible outputs might be. The higher level processing subsystems would then be configured so that they would deliver inputs that would activate these constraint units. An example should help clarify how this mechanism would work.

Let's say the problem is to allow a mobile robot that has toppled over and fallen into an unusual position (where its vision sensors are seeing the world from a very odd perspective) to quickly reorient itself and recover. Ordinarily this might prove to be an extremely difficult problem for a simple neural network-based scene recognition system since there are very many odd vantage points that a robot could conceivably tumble into. In this case, having the high-level symbolic knowledge: "Hey! I just fell over on my back into a tangle of cables and delicate equipment" would undoubtedly be highly useful. The way such a system might work is by a complex interaction between a model-based reasoning system that contained updated information of the robot's own relative position in the work area and a neural-net–based image recognizer.

The continuity information that comes in the vision sensors as the robot is falling could allow the neural net system's output to provide the necessary data for the model-based reasoner to conclude that the robot has tumbled over and to estimate how it is currently oriented in the work area. This information is fed back into the input of the neural net and activates units that are "orientation detectors" so that the robot can correctly interpret its vision sensors. It can then make itself upright again. Naturally this assumes that the robot's locomotion hardware supports actions such as righting itself after it has tipped over.

In the type of architecture described here, the way feedback input is exchanged between a model-based reasoning system and neural networks is by means of message passing back and forth between both subsystems. Problem-solving and retrieval converge when there is a resonance created through reinforcing feedback between the neural net and high-level model and back again. Such a system would incorporate the results of neural net learning into the symbolic world model in long-term memory and so overcome the criticisms enumerated of conventional search models and simple neural nets simultaneously.

Further Reading

The literature on actors and other types of concurrent object systems is still far from adequate at this point. What we have so far are primarily monographs based on doctoral dissertations and anthologies of technical papers intended by researchers to be read by their peers. Consequently, there is really nothing that addresses itself to the complete novice so that everything is presented that is needed for an adequate understanding. More often than not the assumption seems to be made that the reader already understands what is being discussed. Consequently, the following reading list requires considerable effort to master and should not be considered a self-sufficient guide to these topics:

Agha, G. *Actors*. Cambridge, Mass.: The MIT Press, 1986.
Anderson, J. *The Architecture of Cognition*. Cambridge, Mass.: Harvard University Press, 1983.
Baron. *The Cerebral Computer*. Hillsdale, N.J.: Lawrence Erlbaum, 1987.

Bay, J. S., and Hemami. "Modeling of a Neural Pattern Generator with Coupled Nonlinear Oscillators," *IEEE Trans.*, 1987, BME-34:297–306.

Carpenter, G. A., and Grossberg, S. "A Massively Parallel Architecture for a Self-Organizing Neural Pattern Recognition Machine," *Computer Vision, Graphics, and Image Processing*, Vol. 37, pp. 54–116, 1987.

Clinger, W. "Foundations of Actor Semantics," AI-TR-6333, *MIT AIL*, May 1981.

Cosell, L., et al. "Continuous Speech Recognition on a Butterfly Processor." *IEEE Transactions on Parallel Computing*, 1986.

Gasser, L. "MACE: A Multi-Agent Computing Environment," *USC Technical Note*, March 1986.

Georgeff, M., and Lansky, A. "Reactive Reasoning and Planning," *Proceedings of AAAI*, 1987.

Grossberg, S. *The Adaptive Brain, I & II*. Amsterdam: North-Holland, 1987.

Hewitt, C. "Viewing Control Structures as Patterns of Passing Messages," *J. of Artificial Intelligence*, 8-3:323–364, June 1977.

Hewitt, C., and de Jong, P. "Analyzing the Roles of Descriptions and Actions in Open Systems," *Proceedings of AAAI*, 1983.

Hillis, D. *The Connection Machine*, Cambridge, Mass.: The MIT Press, 1985.

Hopfield, J. "Neural Networks and Physical Systems with Emergent Collective Computational Abilities," *Proc. Natl. Acad. Sci.*, April 1982, pp. 2554–2558.

Huhns, M., ed. *Distributed Artificial Intelligence*. Los Altos, Calif.: Morgan-Kaufman, 1987.

Kohonen, T. *Self-Organization and Associative Memory*. New York: Springer-Verlag, 1984.

Kosko, B. "Constructing an Associative Memory," *BYTE*, September 1987.

Kowalik, J., ed. *Parallel MIMD Computation: HEP Supercomputer and Applications*. Cambridge, Mass.: The MIT Press, 1985.

Laffey, T., et al. "Real-Time Knowledge-Based Systems," *AI Magazine*, Spring 1988.

Lansky, A. "Localized Representation and Planning Methods for Parallel Domains" *Proceedings of AAAI*, 1987.

Minsky, M. *The Society of Mind*. New York: Simon and Schuster, 1987.

Orbach, R. "Dynamics of Fractal Networks," *Science*, v. 231, p. 814.

O'Reilly, C. A., and Cromarty, A. S. "'Fast' is not 'Real-Time' in Designing Effective Real-Time AI Systems," *Applications of Artificial Intelligence* II, 548, 1985, pp. 249–257. Bellingham, Wash.: International Society of Optical Engineering.

Quinn, M. *Designing Efficient Algorithms for Parallel Computers*. New York: McGraw-Hill, 1987.

Rumelhart, D., and McClelland, J., ed. *Parallel Distributed Processing*. Cambridge, Mass.: The MIT Press, 1986.

Scott, A. C. "Distributed Multimode Oscillators of One and Two Dimensions," *IEEE Trans.*, 1970, CT-7:55–6.

Tello, E. "DIPOLE: An AI Architecture Suitable for Space Applications," *Proc. IEEE Conference on Expert Systems in Government*, October 1986.

Thinking Machines Inc., "Introduction to Data Level Parallelism," April 1986.

Uhr, L. *Multi-Computer Architectures for Artificial Intelligence*. New York: John Wiley, 1987.

Wolfram, S. "Cellular Automaton Fluids 1: Basic Theory," University of Illinois at Urbana-Champaign: Center for Complex Systems Research, March 1986.

Wolfram, S. "Cellular Automaton Supercomputing," University of Illinois at Urbana-Champaign: Center for Complex Systems Research, September 1986.

Yonezawa, A., and Tokoro, M. *Object-Oriented Concurrent Programming*. Cambridge, Mass.: The MIT Press, 1987.

Conclusion

This marks the end of our exploration into object-oriented approaches in AI. It is difficult to summarize so complex an itinerary. At most, we can hope to touch upon some of the most important highpoints for additional emphasis. We direct attention once again to the concept of active data as a guiding concept of the relation between object-oriented and other AI paradigms. Just as object-oriented systems behave as though they are composed of entities that combine their own local data and active procedures, AI paradigms, like inference engines, make knowledge executable, keeping what has been encoded in the computer actively processing rather than sitting passively in storage.

The full vindication of the object-oriented paradigm will come with concurrent systems that can do message-passing in parallel. Current research systems, such as Actors, Concurrent PROLOG, and MACE, have already made some important discoveries and, while many problems still remain to be solved, these offer an exciting prospect for the future of computing. One of the most important issues still to be resolved is that of flexible and efficient message management. Another one of the more exciting prospects on the horizon is an effective synthesis of the paradigms of object-oriented and logic programming. Currently, several experimental systems attempt this synthesis in various ways. Writing PROLOG in an existing object-oriented language like Smalltalk has a number of advantages, such as that of an existing class system and a window-oriented programming environment. The challenge in this approach is making the implementation efficient enough to be useful.

The design of cooperating systems of *active knowledge modules* reaches a much more powerful expression in concurrent processing environments. To provide a more adequate understanding of the issues in the design of applications utilizing this type of architecture, a typology of cooperating systems was developed. The rationale for this active knowledge paradigm was supported by citing the research of O'Reilly and Cromarty, who show the exponential time increase with the growth in size of search tree depth. The natural conclusion to be drawn from their research is that if very large knowledge processing systems are to be constructed, then this will have to be done either while still keeping the search tree depths of modest size, or by abandoning the search tree model altogether. Accordingly, architectures were proposed that take up each of these options. In an architecture of a community of active knowledge processing modules, with one or more modules acting as supervisor, the size of knowledge bases is kept small for reasons of efficiency, whereas each module is capable of autonomous processing, suspension, and modification under supervision. In Resonance Machine architecture, the search tree model is replaced by broadcasts of patterns to selected processing nodes—and resulting message cascades based on local matching methods—that converge upon solutions much the way tuning forks respond with sympathetic resonance to their own vibratory frequency.

If the only issue were keeping the size of the search space small, this type of architecture would not be completely justified, because other methods exist for keeping the search space within a desired limit in large applications. However, these methods are not able to provide separate working memory areas to conduct the various searches or to suspend the different experts at a certain point in their processing, and yet keep them in a state of readiness to receive messages that provide new goals to continue their reasoning. The hypothetical reasoning of tools like ART and KEE provides some aspects of this kind of architecture but not all of its essential features. Alternate worlds are essentially passive states of one system rather than separate knowledge processing agents.

A further dimension of complexity in the design of advanced architectures is the use of cooperating hybrid systems that use more than one AI problem-solving paradigm in cooperation. In the hybrid architecture, DIPOLE, two different types of inference engines work cooperatively in a way analogous to the way that reflexes and conscious thought interact cooperatively in humans. Applications have already begun to appear that approach these architectures in various respects. Only when some full-blown implementations have been built will it be possible to tell where such hybrids will find their most profitable application and most efficient design.

We have come to the end of our journey. Although we have covered considerable ground, we have by no means exhausted the subject in either breadth or depth. Some concepts were presented that could only be demonstrated in greater detail in a much larger context than could be devoted to them here. Others point the way to future developments that will be occurring over the next several years.

True or False?

1. In an Actor system, every datatype is implemented as an actor, that is, an active data object.

2. One of the most important aspects of Actor languages is their implementation of classes.

3. Customers allow Actor systems to implement recursive algorithms in parallel.

4. The express mode in ABCL is used for speeding up messages in ordinary mode.

5. In POOL/T, classes are not implemented as objects because classes are static, whereas objects are dynamic.

6. Concurrent PROLOG has a particularly powerful way of handling side effects to its objects.

7. The problem-solving paradigm used in MACE is that of clusters or coalitions of agents.

8. Because forward chaining has an exponential time increase as the depth of inference trees gets larger, there is an inherent practical limit to the size of such applications.

9. Progressive deepening and progressive reasoning are strategies that guarantee an answer will be found while using an inflexible scheme for incrementally improving upon the result as time allows.

10. The search paradigm is based on the computational model that regards data as static elements that are accessed and manipulated. When data elements themselves can be active, more powerful methods of problem solving than search are possible.

(T, F, T, F, T, F, T, F, T, T)

Appendix

Vendors of OOP and OOP-AI Tools

CNS, Inc.
Software Products Dept.
7090 Shady Oak Rd.
Eden Prairie, MN 55344
(612) 941-9000

Products: C-Talk

Digitalk, Inc.
9841 Airport Blvd.
Los Angeles, CA 90045
(213) 645-1082

Products: Smalltalk/V and Smalltalk/V/286

Envos Corporation
1157 San Antonio Rd.
Mountain View, CA 94043
(415) 966-6200

Products: LOOPS, ROOMS, CommonLOOPS

Gold Hill Computers Inc.
26 Landsdowne St.
Cambridge, MA 02139
(800) 242-5477
(617) 621-3300

Products: GoldWorks II, GCLISP Developer

IntelliCorp
1975 West El Camino Real
Mountain View, CA 94040-2216
(415) 965-5500

Products: KEE, SIMKIT

Neuron Data
444 High St.
Palo Alto, CA
(415) 321-4488

Products: Nexpert Object, Nextra

ParcPlace Systems
1550 Plymouth Street
Mountain View, CA 94043
(800) 822-7880
(415) 691-6700

Products: Smalltalk-80 for a variety of platforms

The Stepstone Corporation
75 Glen Road
Sandy Hook, CT 06482
(203) 426-1875

Products: Objective-C

The Whitewater Group
Technology Innovation Center
906 University Place
Evanston, Ill. 60201
(312) 491-2370

Products: ACTOR

Xerox Special Information Systems
250 N. Halstead Street
P.O. Box 5608
Pasadena, CA 91107-00608
(818) 351-2351

Products: Humble, The Analyst

Zortech
366 Massachusetts Ave.
Arlington, MA 02174
(800) 848-8408

Products: Zortech C++

Bibliography

Agha, G. *Actors*. Cambridge, Mass.: MIT Press, 1986.

Anderson, J. *The Architecture of Cognition*. Cambridge, Mass.: Harvard University Press, 1983.

Bain, W. M. "A Case-Based Reasoning System for Subjective Assessment," *AAAI*, 1986.

Baron. *The Cerebral Computer*. Hillsdale, N.J.: Lawrence Erlbaum, 1987.

Bay, J. S., and Hemami. "Modeling of a Neural Pattern Generator with Coupled Nonlinear Oscillators," *IEEE Trans.*, BME-34:297–306, 1987.

Bisiani, R. "A Software and Hardware Environment for Developing AI Applications on Parallel Processors," *AAAI*, 1986.

Blelloch, G. E. "CIS: A Massively Concurrent Rule-Based System," *AAAI*, 1986.

Bobrow, D., et al. "CommonLOOPS: Merging CommonLisp and Object-Oriented Programming," Xerox, ISL-85-8, 1985.

Bobrow, D., et al. "Merging LISP and Object-Oriented Programming," *OOPSLA Proceedings*, 1986.

Brooks, R., et al. "A Mobile Robot with Onboard Parallel Processor and Large Workspace Arm," *AAAI*, 1986.

Budd, T. *A Little Smalltalk*. Reading, Mass.: Addison-Wesley, 1987.

Bylander, T., and Mittal, S. "CSRL: A Language for Classificatory Problem Solving and Uncertainty Handling," *AI Magazine*, vol. VII, no. 3.

Carpenter, G. A., and Grossberg, S. "A Massively Parallel Architecture for a Self-Organizing Neural Pattern Recognition Machine," *Computer Vision, Graphics, and Image Processing*, vol. 37, 1987, pp. 54–116.

Chandraskekaran, B. "Generic Tasks in Knowledge-Based Reasoning High-Level Building Blocks for Expert System Design," *IEEE Expert*. Vol. 1, No. 3. Fall, 1986. pp. 23–33.

Clinger, W. "Foundations of Actor Semantics," *MIT AIL*, AI-TR-6333, May 1981.

Cosell, L., et al. "Continuous Speech Recognition on a Butterfly Processor," *IEEE Transactions on Parallel Computing*, 1986.

Cox, B. Object-Oriented Programming. Reading, Mass.: Addison-Wesley, 1986.

Dresher, G. "ObjectLISP," *LMI*, 1985.

Edelson, T. "Can a System Be Intelligent If It Never Gives a Damn?" *AAAI*, 1986.

Fukunaga, K., and Hirose, S. "An Experience with a PROLOG-based Object-Oriented Language," *OOPSLA Proceedings*, 1986.

Gasser, L. "MACE: A Multi-Agent Computing Environment," *USC Technical Note*, March 1986.

Georgeff, M., and Lansky, A. "Reactive Reasoning and Planning," *Proc. AAAI*, 1987.

Goldberg, A., and Robson, D. *Smalltalk-80: The Language and Its Implementation*. Reading, Mass.: Addison-Wesley, 1983.

Grossberg, S. *The Adaptive Brain, I & II*. Amsterdam: North-Holland, 1987.

Hammond, K. "CHEF: A Model of Case-based Planning," *AAAI*, 1986.

Hewitt, C. "Viewing Control Structures as Patterns of Passing Messages," *J. of Artificial Intelligence*, 8–3:323–364, June 1977.

Hewitt, C., and de Jong, P. "Analyzing the Roles of Descriptions and Actions in Open Systems," *Proceedings of AAAI*, 1983.

Hillis, D. *The Connection Machine*, Cambridge, Mass.: MIT Press, 1985.

Hopfield, J. "Neural Networks and Physical Systems with Emergent Collective Computational Abilities," *Proc. Natl. Acad. Sci.*, April 1982, pp. 2554–2558.

Huhns, M., ed. *Distributed Artificial Intelligence*. Los Altos, Calif.: Morgan-Kaufman, 1987.

Ingalls, D. "The Evolution of the Smalltalk Virtual Machine." In *Smalltalk-80: Bits of History, Words of Advice*, edited by G. Krassner. Reading, Mass.: Addison-Wesley, 1983.

Kohonen, T. *Self-Organization and Associative Memory*. New York: Springer-Verlag, 1984.

Kosko, B. "Constructing an Associative Memory," *BYTE*, September 1987.

Kowalik, J., ed. *Parallel MIMD Computation: HEP Supercomputer and Applications*. Cambridge, Mass.: MIT Press, 1985.

Krassner, G., ed. *Smalltalk-80: Bits of History, Words of Advice*. Reading, Mass.: Addison-Wesley, 1983.

Kahn, K., et al. "Objects in Concurrent Logic Programming Languages," *OOPSLA Proceedings*, 1986.

Keene, S. *Object-Oriented Programming in CommonLISP*. Reading, Mass.: Addison-Wesley. 1988.

Laffey, T., et al. "Real-Time Knowledge-Based Systems," *AI Magazine*, Spring 1988.

Lansky, A. "Localized Representation and Planning Methods for Parallel Domains," *Proc. AAAI*, 1987.

Lenat, D., et al. "CYC: Using Common Sense Knowledge to Overcome Brittleness and Knowledge Acquisition Bottlenecks," *AI Magazine*, Winter 1986.

Lozano-Perez, T. "A Simple Motion Planning Algorithm for General Robot Manipulators," *AAAI*, 1986.

Lytinen, S., and Gershman, A. "ATRANS: Automatic Processing of Money Transfer Messages," *AAAI*, 1986.

McCarthy, J. "Epistemological Problems of Artificial Intelligence." In *Readings in Artificial Intelligence*, edited by B. L. Webber and N. J. Nillson. Palo Alto, CA: Tioga Publishing Company, 1981.

Michalski, R., and Winston, P. "Variable Precision Logic," *Artificial Intelligence*, 29(2):121–146, 1986.

Minsky, M. "A Framework for Representing Knowledge." In *Mind Design*, edited by J. Haugeland. Cambridge, Mass.: MIT Press, 1981.

Minsky, M. *The Society of Mind*. New York: Simon & Schuster, 1987.

Mittal, S., et al. "PRIDE: An Expert System for the Design of Paper Handling Systems," *Computer*, July 1986.

Mittal, S., Bobrow, D., and Kahn, K. "Virtual Copies, Between Classes and Instances," *ACM OOPSLA Conference Proceedings*, 1986.

Moon, D. "Object-Oriented Programming with Flavors," *OOPSLA* Proceedings, 1986.

O'Reilly, C. A., and Cromarty, A. S. "'Fast' is not 'Real-Time' in Designing Effective Real-Time AI Systems," *Applications of Artificial Intelligence II*, 548, 249–257, 1985. Bellingham, Wash.: International Society of Optical Engineering.

Pinson, L., and Wiener, R. *An Introduction to Object-Oriented Programming and Smalltalk*. Reading, Mass.: Addison-Wesley, 1988.

Quinn, M. *Designing Efficient Algorithms for Parallel Computers*. New York: McGraw-Hill, 1987.

Ressler, J. "Introduction to ObjectLISP," LISP Machine Inc., 1985.

Rumelhart, D., and McClelland, J., eds. *Parallel Distributed Processing*, Cambridge, Mass.: MIT Press, 1986.

Scott, A. C. "Distributed Multimode Oscillators of One and Two Dimensions," *IEEE Trans.*, CT-7:55–6, 1970.

Shapiro, E., and Takeuchi, A. "Object-Oriented Programming in Concurrent PROLOG," *New Generation Computing*, vol. 1, no. 1, pp. 25–48, 1983.

Sharkey, N., et al. "Mixing Binary and Continuous Connection Schemes for Knowledge Access," *AAAI*, 1986.

Siemens, R., Golden, M., and Ferguson, J. "Starplan II: Evolution of an Expert System," *AAAI*, 1986.

Stefik, M., "The Next Knowledge Medium," *AI Magazine*, Spring 1986.

Steinberg, S., Allen, D., Baguall, L., and Scott, C. "The Butterfly LISP System," *AAAI*, 1986.

Stroustrup, B. *The C++ Programming Language*. Reading, Mass.: Addison-Wesley, 1986.

Tello, E. "DIPOLE: An AI Architecture Suitable for Space Applications," *Proc. IEEE Conference on Expert Systems in Government*, October 1986.

Tello, E. *Mastering AI Tools and Techniques*. Indianapolis: Howard W. Sams, 1988.

Thinking Machines Inc. "Introduction to Data Level Parallelism," April 1986.

Thrift, P. "Concurrent Logic Programming and Simulation," *Texas Instruments Engineering Journal*, January-February 1986.

Uhr, L. *Multi-Computer Architectures for Artificial Intelligence*. New York: John Wiley & Sons, 1987.

Winston, P. *Artificial Intelligence*. Reading, Mass.: Addison-Wesley, pp. 129–131, 1984.

Wolfram, S. "Cellular Automaton Fluids 1: Basic Theory," University of Illinois at Urbana-Champagne: Center for Complex Systems Research, March 1986.

Wolfram, S. "Cellular Automaton Supercomputing," University of Illinois at Urbana-Champagne: Center for Complex Systems Research, September 1986.

Wright, M., Green, M., Feigl, G., and Cross, P. "An Expert System for Real-Time Control," *IEEE Software*, pp. 16–24, March 1986.

Yonezawa, A., and Tokoro, M. *Object-Oriented Concurrent Programming*. Cambridge, Mass.: MIT Press, 1987.

Xerox *LOOPS Manual*, Palo Alto, Calif.: Xerox Artificial Intelligence Systems, 1988.

Index

Paradigm (*continued*)
  programming, 3, 5, 12, 19, 184
Parallel processing, xiii, 19, 45, 280, 289, 321
Papert, Seymour, 62
Pascal, 3, 110
Pattern, control, 176
Perception, 15
Perspectives, 131
Pict language, 52
Pipelining, 286
Planning, 15, 210, 214, 309
Plasma, 285
Pockets facility, 51
POOL/T, 293
PRIDE, 38, 67, 184, 194
Procedure, 6, 23
Programming
  automatic, 15, 30
  declarative, 19
  functional, 132
  iconic, 52
  logic, 3, 19, 149
  object-oriented, 3
  procedural, 21
  rule-based, 3
  structured, 128
  visual, 3, 52
PROLOG, 19, 61, 71, 85, 114, 285, 321
Prototyping, 221, 226
Pseudovariable, 305
Pygmalion, 52

Query, 168, 170, 200, 202
Queue, 307

Reasoning, 27
  deep, 276, 315
  non-monotonic, 169, 176
  hypothetical, 176, 194, 208
  shallow, 315
Reasoning strategy, 224
Receptionist, 290
Recognition, 26
Rehearsal, programming by, 55
Relation, 164, 167
Replacement, 286
Resonance, 316
Resources, 264, 293
RLL, 39
Robotics, 309, 318

ROOMS, 49
ROSS, 266
Rule class, 202
Rule methods, 31
Rules, 23, 28, 39, 168, 174, 176, 182, 192, 201,
    204, 210, 213, 216, 222, 224, 226, 262, 268,
    275
  action, 201
  belief, 177
  bidirectional, 263
  constraint, 177, 222
  deduction, 201
  dependent, 169
  hypothetical, 177
  searching, 218
Rulesets, 28, 170, 192

Salience, 176
Scheduling, resource-oriented, 128
Schema, 176
Scheme, 30, 126, 184, 236, 241
SCOOPS, 126, 184, 236, 241
Scripts, 27, 35, 291
Search, 23, 38, 191, 202, 224, 277, 314, 316, 321
  best-first, 203
  breadth-first, 171
  depth-first, 171, 202
SEdit, 187, 190
Side effects, 133, 192, 208
Simula, 264
Simulation, 43, 128, 191, 264, 275
Slot, 40, 155, 169, 177, 187, 204, 207, 212, 314,
    316, 361, 382
  member, 197
  own, 187
Smalltalk, 52, 61, 91, 100, 114, 123, 147, 149,
    154, 184, 189, 215, 218, 264, 286, 296, 300,
    321
Smith, Randy, 52, 56
Software, layers of, xiii
SPACEMED, 163, 225
Space Shuttle, 225
Speech recognition, 15
Sponsor, 163, 170
SPOOL, 304
Starplan, 37
Steele, Carolyn, 196
Stafik, Mark, 19, 183
Subclass, 7, 130, 238
Subentity, 216